Targeting Regional Economic Development

T0304242

Targeting regional economic development (TRED) has a long and rich tradition among academic economists and in the world of economic development practitioners. This book builds on a series of workshops and papers organized by The Northeast Regional Center for Rural Development (NERCRD) at the Pennsylvania State University and the Rural Policy Research Centre (RUPRI) at the University of Missouri. Through the coordinated efforts of NERCRD and RUPRI, a network of university-based researchers and Extension education specialists was developed and provides the foundation of this new edited volume.

For the first time in a single book, Goetz, Deller and Harris present an innovative approach through a collection of chapters discussing industry targeting and the relevance of TRED as an important analytical tool for practical targeting purposes. The papers present issues surrounding community economic development, clusters in industry and rural communities and the role of agglomeration economies. The book provides the reader with insights into not only the theoretical foundations of targeting as well as empirical methods, but also approaches for using the community-level analysis to affect policy directions.

This book will be of particular interest to researchers and community development educators and economic development practitioners. It is also useful to students of economics, agricultural economics, business economics, development economics, regional science and urban and regional planning.

Stephan J. Goetz is Director of The Northeast Regional Center for Rural Development and Professor of Agricultural and Regional Economics at Pennsylvania State University, USA.

Steven C. Deller is Professor of Agricultural and Applied Economics at the University of Wisconsin, USA.

Thomas R. Harris is Director of the University Center for Economic Development at the University of Nevada, USA.

Routledge Studies in Global Competition

Edited by John Cantwell, Rutgers, the State University of New Jersey, USA
and David Mowery, University of California, Berkeley, USA

Targeting Regional Economic Development

Edited by Stephan J. Goetz,
Steven C. Deller and
Thomas R. Harris

Routledge
Taylor & Francis Group

LONDON AND NEW YORK

First published 2009 by Routledge
2 Park Square, Milton Park, Abingdon, Oxon OX14 4RN

Simultaneously published in the USA and Canada
by Routledge
711 Third Avenue, New York, NY 10017

*Routledge is an imprint of the Taylor & Francis Group,
an informa business*

© 2009 selection and editorial matter, Stephan J. Goetz, Steven C.
Deller, Thomas R. Harris; individual chapters, the contributors

Reprinted 2009

Typeset in Times New Roman by
RefineCatch Limited, Bungay, Suffolk

First issued in paperback in 2013

British Library Cataloguing in Publication Data
A catalogue record for this book is available from the British Library

Library of Congress Cataloging in Publication Data
A catalog record for this book has been requested

ISBN13: 978–0–415–74354–9 (pbk)
ISBN13: 978–0–415–77591–5 (hbk)
ISBN13: 978–0–203–88349–5 (ebk)

Contents

Figures and tables

Figures

Contributors

Jonathan Alevy is an Assistant Professor in the Department of Resource Economics at the University of Nevada, Reno. His primary areas of research are in experimental and developmental economics as well as in behavioural finance. Dr Alevy's research has appeared in the book series *New Horizons in Environmental Economics* and in *The Journal of Finance*. He has also worked for international organizations on community development in Asia and Eastern Europe.

Barbara Andreozzi is a Community Development Extension Agent and Adjunct Faculty for the Montana State University. She is currently working with USAID on a community development pilot in Armenia. Barbara has served on the Community Business Matching national team since its formation in 2003.

David Barkley is a Professor of Applied Economics and Statistics and Co-director of the EDA University Center for Economic Development at Clemson University. His primary teaching and research interests are regional economics and rural development policy. His research has appeared in *The Journal of Regional Science* and the *Review of Regional Studies*. His extension programmes include industry and occupational targeting studies for South Carolina counties and metropolitan areas.

George Borden is an Associate Professor of Community Economic Development in Cooperative Extension at the University of Nevada, Reno. His primary area of research and teaching is regional and community economic analysis and planning. Borden's research/extension has appeared in the *Journal of Extension* and the *Journal of Travel Research*.

Hanas A. Cader is an Assistant Professor in the Department of Accounting, Agribusiness and Economics at South Carolina State University. His primary areas of expertise are regional economic development, agribusiness management, and entrepreneurship.

Linda J. Cox is a Community Economic Development Specialist and professor in the Department of Natural Resources and Environmental

Management at the University of Hawaii at Manoa. She has authored or co-authored, produced, and edited more than 200 journal articles, books, book chapters, workbooks, fact sheets and other publications, as well as videos, on a variety of topics including sustainable community development, entrepreneurship, and resource management. She has organized, co-organized, or spoken at more than 180 conferences, short courses, workshops, meetings, and seminars across Hawaii. She has also won state and university awards for her community work and for mentoring students.

John M. Crespi is an Associate Professor in the Department of Agricultural Economics at Kansas State University. Dr Crespi's research is broadly in the area of industrial organization, including product differentiation and marketing. Dr Crespi teaches courses in agribusiness marketing, economic research methods, and quantitative methods for economists.

Alison Davis is an Extension Professor in the Department of Agricultural Economics at the University of Kentucky. Her primary area of research is local economic development and rural health care. Davis's research has appeared in the *Journal of Regional Analysis and Policy*. Her extension work has been funded by the USDA and the State Office of Rural Health to promote new economic development strategies in rural Kentucky.

Steven Deller is a Professor and Extension Specialist in the Department of Agricultural and Applied Economics at the University of Wisconsin, Madison. His primary area of research and extension programming is in better understanding regional economic change and policies that can be used at the local level. Deller's work has appeared in the *American Journal of Agricultural Economics*, the *Review of Economics and Statistics, Regional Science and Urban Economics, Land Economics*, the *Economic Development Quarterly, Rural Sociology* and *The Journal of the Community Development Society*, among others. He currently serves as co-editor of the *Journal of Regional Analysis and Policy*.

Gerald Doeksen is a Regents Professor and Extension Economist with Oklahoma State University. His primary area of research and extension has dealt with infrastructure issues and most recently health sector impacts on local economies. Doeksen has made over 350 regional, national, and international presentations and his research has appeared extensively in health journals and other publications. He is the Director of the National Center for Rural Health Works.

Mary Emery is the Associate Director of the North Central Regional Center for Rural Development and a professor of Sociology at Iowa State University. Her primary area of research and teaching is rural and community economic development. Emery's research and extension has appeared in the *Journal of the Community Development Society*.

Edward Feser is a Professor of Urban and Regional Planning at the University of Illinois at Urbana-Champaign where he teaches courses in state and local economic development policy and strategy, regional development theory, and methods of urban and regional analysis. He is a specialist in state and local technology policy, industry clusters and industry cluster policy, regional modeling, and analytical methods for economic development planning. He has served in the government as the Assistant Secretary for Policy, Research and Strategic Planning in the North Carolina Department of Commerce, and he continues to work regularly with state and local agencies, corporations, non-profit development organizations, and planning firms on economic development policy issues, strategy design, and economic analysis.

Todd Gabe is an Associate Professor in the School of Economics at the University of Maine. His primary area of research is regional economic development. Gabe's research has appeared in the *Journal of Regional Science, Land Economics*, the *Journal of Regional Analysis and Policy*, and *The Review of Regional Studies*. In his home state of Maine, Gabe has worked on cluster-enhanced projects related to the biotechnology industry and the environmental and energy technology industry.

Stephan Goetz is a Professor of Agricultural and Regional Economics and the Director of The Northeast Regional Center for Rural Development at Penn State University. His research focuses on entrepreneurship, employment and land use issues. Goetz's research has appeared in *Social Science Quarterly*, the *Journal of Regional Analysis and Policy*, the *Review of Regional Studies*, the *Journal of the Community Development Society*, and *Papers in Regional Science*.

Paulo Guimarães is a Clinical Associate Professor in the Department of Economics at the University of South Carolina. Dr Guimarães' primary research interests are in industrial economics, regional economics, and applied econometrics. Some of his recent publications include articles in the *Econometrics Journal, Economics Letters*, the *Journal of Regional Science*, the *Journal of Urban Economics*, and the *Review of Economics and Statistics*.

Thomas R. Harris is a Professor and State Extension Specialists in the Department of Resource Economics and the Director of the University Center for Economic Development at the University of Nevada, Reno. His primary areas of research and extension programming are economic and fiscal impact modeling and rural economic development. Harris' work has appeared in the *American Journal of Agricultural Economics*, the *Journal of Agricultural and Resource Economics*, the *Journal of Regional Analysis*, the *Journal of Regional Analysis and Policy*, the *Review of Regional Studies, Growth and Change*, and the *Journal of the Community Development Society*. He currently serves on the editorial board of the *Journal of Regional Analysis and Policy*.

Mark Henry is a Professor of Applied Economics in the Department of Applied Economics and Statistics at Clemson University. His primary area of research and teaching is regional economics. Henry's research and extension has appeared in the *Journal of Regional Science* and *Regional Science and Urban Economics*.

La Dee Homm is a former graduate student at Oklahoma State University. She received her M.S. in Agricultural Economics in 2001. Her research focused on target industry analysis and included several applications to rural regions of Oklahoma.

David Hughes is a Professor of Applied Economics and Statistics at the Clemson Institute for Economic and Community Development at Clemson University. His primary area of research, teaching, and outreach is rural development economics. Dr Hughes' research has appeared in the *Review of Regional Studies* and the *Journal of Agricultural and Applied Economics*, among others. Current work includes linking industry targeting to local workforce attributes and training.

Thomas G. Johnson is the Frank Miller Professor of Agricultural Economics in the Harry S Truman School of Public Affairs at the University of Missouri. His primary area of research and teaching is rural economic development. Johnson's research has appeared in agricultural economics, regional science and other social science journals. Johnson directs the Rural Policy Research Institute's Analytic and Academic Programmes.

Terry Kastens is a Professor of Agricultural Economics at Kansas State University. As an extension agricultural economist, Kastens' goal is to increase the profitability and community viability of those involved in agriculture. His main areas of emphasis are land ownership and leasing, machinery management, and technology adoption. Kastens' research interests center on unconventional statistical predictive modeling techniques, for example, neural networks, fuzzy logic, genetic algorithms, and entropy.

Jun Koo is an Assistant Professor in the Department of Public Administration at Korea University. His research focuses on technology-based regional development and industry clusters. His recent work has appeared in *Regional Studies, Urban Studies, Annals of Regional Science*, and the *International Regional Science Review*.

John Leatherman is a Professor in the Department of Agricultural Economics at Kansas State University and a University Extension Specialist with K-State Research and Extension. He first began working with the Cooperative Extension Service in 1984 and has held rural development positions in both Wisconsin and Kansas. His areas of research and teaching interest are community and regional economic development, local and state public finance, and natural resource management. Leatherman's work has appeared in a variety of agricultural economics and regional science journals

James R. Nelson served as a Professor in the Department of Agricultural Economics at the University of Idaho from 1989 to 2006, and as Department Head from 1990 to 1999. Dr Nelson passed away on December 8, 2006. His work in rural economic development and business development was highly regarded and he was an accomplished teacher, researcher, and extension specialist.

Henry Renski is an Assistant Professor in the Department of Landscape Architecture and Regional Planning at the University of Massachusetts Amherst. Dr Renski's research interests include regional influences on entrepreneurship; empirical tests of agglomeration theory; industrial cluster analysis and cluster-based development strategies; and the application of spatial-analytical techniques to local economic policy decision-making. His work has appeared in the *Journal of Regional Science* and *Growth and Change* and has received funding from the National Science Foundation and the Kauffman Foundation.

Martin Shields is an Associate Professor in the Department of Economics at Colorado State University. His primary area of research is on regional economic growth and competitiveness, and he teaches classes in regional economics and labor economics. Shields is also the research economist for the Northern Colorado Economic Development Corporation, and he has worked extensively in developing strategies to grow the region's targeted economic clusters.

Qiuyan Wang is a Senior Research Analyst in Informatics at Independence Blue Cross. Her research focuses on the development of statistical methods for health services and outcome research including profiling of health care providers, modeling of health care costs and evaluation of programme effect on health care interventions. She is responsible for formulating research studies, conducting data analyses, writing research manuscripts, and presenting results to internal and external clients. Prior to joining Independence Blue Cross, she was a postdoctoral researcher at the Northeast Regional Center for Rural Development where she participated in a number of research projects on regional economics, demographic economics and economic development.

Michael D. Woods is a Professor and Head of the Department of Agricultural Economics at Oklahoma State University. His primary areas of work include rural economic development and economic impact analysis. He holds a joint appointment that includes teaching, research, and extension responsibilities. Woods' research and extension efforts have appeared in agricultural economics journals, the *Journal of Extension*, and the *Journal of the Community Development Society*.

Doug Woodward is Professor of Economics and Director of the Division of Research in the Moore School of Business. His primary areas of research and teaching are regional economics, international economics, and economic development. His publications include books on foreign direct investment in the United States and papers on industry location and agglomeration economies that have appeared in the *Journal of Urban Economics, The Journal of Regional Science* and the *Review of Economics and Statistics*, among other scholarly journals. He has presented his research at many conferences around the world, including the prestigious World Economic Forum in Davos, Switzerland.

Joan Wright is a former graduate research assistant in the Department of Resource Economics at the University of Nevada, Reno. Her primary areas of research were geographic information systems and linkages to rural economic development.

1 Targeted regional economic development

Introduction and overview

Stephan J. Goetz, Steven C. Deller, and Thomas R. Harris

Introduction

Academic economists have long frowned on government-directed develop-ment programmes that seek to recruit or develop particular industries within local communities. The standard argument is that public sector decision-makers are ill-equipped to cherry-pick industries with strong future potential, and many examples exist of inefficient and wasteful uses of taxpayer funds to recruit businesses from elsewhere. The escalating public expenditures per job created in the automobile industry exemplify the high and growing public cost of such industrial recruitment efforts. A common related argument is that there simply are too few business owners seeking new locations in a given year, compared to the large number of communities offering industry location incentives, to justify or make worthwhile the recruitment effort. Nationally, and indeed internationally, the debate about the proper role of government in economic development culminated in the so-called Washington Consensus of the 1980s. This consensus, which has since fallen apart, held that "getting policies and prices right" at the national level and allowing markets to function freely would place countries on a path of economic growth and prosperity. Even if this prescription was necessary and sufficient as a national policy, it made no allowance for regional or local variations within countries.

In a forum published in *Economic Development Quarterly*, Buss (1999a, 1999b) dismissed industry targeting strategies as wasteful and ineffective "central planning".[1] Pointing to a selected set of failed firm-targeting efforts, Buss concluded that such activities are methodologically flawed, not grounded in economic theory, and are mere political acts, in addition to being based on poor data. Nevertheless, in his rejoinder to criticisms by Wiesel (1999) and Finkle (1999) published in the same forum, Buss conceded that targeting efforts will continue as a political necessity, and he presented a number of suggestions for improving future studies, which we review in more detail in Chapter 20.

While the academic debate continues within economics and related social sciences about the value of public policies aimed at promoting specific forms of local or regional economic development, concerned citizens and in particular elected officials face tremendous pressures to "do something" about the economic situation of the local economy. Peter Eisinger (1988, 1995) argued that strong political incentives exist for politicians to invest in subsidies and other targeted economic growth strategies because of the need to show short-term and immediate impacts. The ability to attend ribbon-cutting ceremonies and "take credit" for businesses moving into their districts has powerful political appeal for elected leaders. The work of Michael Porter (1998, 2000) has reinforced this push toward proactive intervention in many important ways.

In this second-best environment, economists can play an important role by helping decision-makers to better understand the fundamentals of their local economies, with the goal of choosing those strategies that potentially are most productive (and least damaging) in the medium to long runs. Furthermore, a few notable – and in some ways path-breaking – recent publications shed new light on the issue of targeted development. This new work also suggests that the time has come to reevaluate the role of the public sector in identifying potential businesses to target for development.

At the same time, most of the discussion of targeting regional economic development (TRED) has been heavily biased toward recruitment in the spirit of the first wave of economic development policy. As we will discuss in detail throughout this volume, equating targeted economic development efforts with recruitment is too narrow of a view. We will see that well-crafted targeting analysis can help focus energies on existing businesses and the promotion of new businesses through entrepreneurship in the spirit of the second wave of economic development policies. By combining the *process* of targeting analysis with the *contents* of the analysis, powerful insights into the regional economy can be gained. We suggest that the TRED exercise can be as much an educational tool as it is the foundation of a technical report delivered to community leaders.

Key recent developments in the literature

An important recent study on the possible merits and demerits of industry targeting is that by Greenstone and Moretti (2004), who use counterfactual analysis to find a 1.5 per cent increase in earnings above trend in counties that succeeded in attracting a major manufacturing plant, and a 1.1 per cent increase in property values above trend in these counties. This result is in stark contrast to the conventional wisdom that holds that the net benefit to communities of giving subsidies for the purpose of attracting plants is, at best, zero and at worst, negative and that such activities on balance reduce the welfare of the local population. Although this study has been sharply criticized, for example by Markusen (2007) for the methods used and conclusions drawn, it has caused some economists to rethink their long-held beliefs on these kinds of interventionist activities.

Another important recent publication is Baumol et al.'s (2007) *Good Capitalism, Bad Capitalism, and the Economics of Growth and Prosperity*. These authors identify four types of capitalism (pp. 60–61): entrepreneurial, big-firm, oligarchic, and state-guided. Briefly, small and innovative firms play a major role in the first form of capitalism, and large firms in the second form. Under oligarchic capitalism, a small number of individuals have wealth and political influence. State-guided capitalism consists of government extending its role beyond merely providing public goods to many citizens and removing barriers to entry for businesses. Baumol et al. argue that this form can succeed as well, and point to booming Asian economies that have grown rapidly primarily through export-led growth that was encouraged or "guided" by the state (p. 67).

There are of course important potential pitfalls to such state-guided capitalism, and it may work best where a known production frontier exists toward which firms within a nation – or region – can be nudged. Once that frontier has been reached, it is less clear that the government can *necessarily* do a better job than private businesses of identifying "the next big thing". In other words, predicting the whims of consumer demands or the next production innovation is difficult, and the danger always exists that vested interests in protected industries succeed in extending those protections indefinitely. At the same time, there is at least one important precedent under which the United States government not only decided on an industry that would be a winner but also created that industry from scratch and made sure that it would succeed – *space exploration*. The benefits of these original public investments for American consumers have been significant, and continue to this day, for example, through the ongoing miniaturization of technology. Similarly, the prospect of private space exploration today would be unthinkable had it not been for this initial public investment.

One of the communities that benefited enormously from the Space Age – the region surrounding Cape Canaveral in Florida – is now bracing for the end of the Shuttle programme in 2010. Although private space-related businesses are expected to employ some of the up to 10,000 individuals who may lose their jobs in the region, local government leaders are pursuing other firms and sectors that could build on the existing local human and capital resources. This is an example of proactive targeted regional economic development, where government seeks to act well before the local firms are lost or move elsewhere.

Another success story – especially in terms of initially unexpected indirect or secondary impacts – is that of the UPS sorting hub in Louisville, Kentucky. At the time when the city was bidding for UPS to locate its facility in the community, and rearranged air corridors around the airport to accommodate the shipping company, to the detriment of local residents who were exposed to noise pollution, few observers foresaw that major manufacturers of electronic goods would establish repair operations in the community. It turned out to be more cost effective for them to locate such facilities at this transshipment point, and so the city of Louisville has benefited from a size-able expansion of employment in the ostensibly unrelated equipment repair sector. In other instances, major recruitment projects have turned out to be white elephants. For example, the city of Indianapolis lost $320 million in direct subsidies when United Airlines shut down its aircraft maintenance facility in 2003.

Last, the work of Michael Porter (e.g., 1998, 2000) has led to an explosion of interest in cluster development. Clusters in turn are intrinsically and inseparably tied to space, or regions, just as they are tied to or built on specific industries. Thus, there is a close logical connection between the emergence of clusters and targeted regional economic development. The idea of clusters can be traced to the writings of early classical economists such as Marshall (1930). Later, cluster studies were developed more fully in Europe (Asheim et al. 2006: 6) – primarily in Italy – and they were also applied to food system subsectors by agricultural economists through the structure-conduct-performance model (e.g., Marion 1986). This is not to diminish the contribu-tions of Porter, as he almost singlehandedly spurred the interest in thinking differently about economic development (Maskell and Kebir 2006). One important outgrowth of this new thinking is the concerted movement away from the former approach of "shoot anything that flies, claiming anything that lands" (Rubin 1988) to more strategic behavior in identifying the specific types of industry that should be promoted at the local and regional levels.

Porter's work has also drawn attention to the idea that regions matter, and that they to some extent control their own destinies even as they are con-strained by the rules of cumulative causation and path dependence (Arthur 2007). In the US at least, regions have in many ways become *the* primary level at which economic development now occurs in practice. In particular, Scott and Storper (2003) refer to certain regions within countries as launching pads for innovation and "most advanced" types of development. And these regions, as well as regional analyses, are becoming more rather than less important as globalization continues.

The rationale for Targeted Regional Economic Development (TRED) and this book

Policy-makers and economic development practitioners are now asking the more focused question: in what types of industry does our region have a competitive advantage? The analytical tools that are available to policy-makers and practitioners for practical targeting purposes range from the relatively simple, such as the location quotient approaches promoted by Porter to statistically derived probability models, to interlinkage models based on input-output analysis. Despite the explosion of interest in this area, however, these various tools have until now not been presented within a single volume that describes both the underlying analytical principles and provides examples of each. The intent of this volume is, first, to review the current thinking in industry targeting policy; second, to discuss the socioeconomic theoretical foundations of industry targeting; third, to present alternative methods of identifying industries for targeting in different community settings; and fourth, to think more seriously about the process through which the analysis is undertaken and used by the community.

This edited volume builds on a series of workshops and working papers organized by the Northeast Regional Centre for Rural Development (NER-CRD)[2] at Pennsylvania State University in collaboration with the Rural Policy Research Institute (RUPRI) at the University of Missouri, at the request of stakeholders in the community of scientists. Through the coordinated efforts of NERCRD and RUPRI, specifically the Community Policy Analysis Network (CPAN) within RUPRI, a network of university-based researchers and extension education specialists has been developed and provides the foundation of this book.[3]

In this book we do not advocate industrial recruitment efforts at any cost, and certainly not at the cost of neglecting other local economic development strategies. We do believe, though, that there are tangible benefits to communities in thinking through the possible alternatives for local economic development, including gap analyses, and to applying the tools presented here. As we mentioned earlier, and as Shields et al. note in Chapter 3, we live in a second-best world that is driven by political considerations, and there is a benefit to reducing the potential damage that can be done by blindly recruiting firms. In other words, it is better to shoot at fewer targets. Indeed, many if not most of the industries that should be targeted for promotion may already be present in the region, and strategies of retention, expansion, and entrepreneurship may be highly effective.

This book follows in the spirit and intent of previous efforts of the researchers and extension educators who make up CPAN. This work is best represented in the volume *Community Policy Analysis Modeling* (2006), edited by Thomas G. Johnson, Daniel Otto, and Steven C. Deller. The intended audience for the present book is researchers and community development educators located in universities, state agencies, and public policy centres, and economic development practitioners.

Targeted economic development, or in our construct, Targeted Regional Economic Development (TRED), has a long and rich tradition both among academic economists and in the more practical policy world of economic development practitioners. As Deller and Goetz outline in more detail in Chapter 2, targeted development efforts have historically been thought about within the context of industry recruitment that can be traced back to the Mississippi Balancing Agriculture with Industry (BAWI) policies of the 1930s. In an effort to rebuild the state's economy after the Great Depression, Mississippi aggressively marketed itself to manufacturing firms from the northern states with offers of cheap labour and land, coupled with low taxes and limited regulations. Initial attempts at recruitment took what might be considered a "shotgun" approach and did little to discriminate between types of industries or firms. A job was a job and all comers were welcomed.

Over time, as firm location theory was refined (e.g., Deller, Chapter 4), insights were gained into factors that influenced where industries are mostly likely to locate. As academic empirical work on firm location moved forward, our understanding of where certain industries might locate expanded as well. Alongside the expanding academic literature, numerous attempts were made to build tools to help state and local economic development practitioners target select industries that had higher probabilities of locating within their region.

Goode and Hastings's (1989) Northeast Industrial Targeting (NIT) and Economic Development Database (EDD) System was a pioneering early effort to provide rigorous, community-specific estimates of locational probabilities of different industries. Supported by NERCRD, this work represented a rigorous movement away from more simple descriptive tools such as location quotient and shift-share analyses to more comprehensive and systematic examinations of how local factors affect industrial location. The work was described in publications such as the *Wall Street Journal* and became widely known across the nation. This earlier work has now evolved in many ways to include agglomeration factors in the analysis (Gabe, Chapter 6), to examine more detailed industries than was the case earlier (e.g., Leatherman and Kastens, Chapter 7), and to take advantage of recent developments in econometrics (e.g., Davis and Harris, Chapter 9). In many ways, the primary purpose of this book is to take stock of developments in this subject area, many of which were spawned by the work of Goode and Hastings.

TRED is a collection of analytical tools aimed at helping users to quantify regional competitive or comparative advantage(s). This advantage is in the spirit of Porter's work and "clusters". TRED does not presume that we can pick winners more effectively than the market, or firms, can. Instead, it provides a framework for thinking about local markets, economies, and regions. As we have already noted, TRED has historically served as a foundation for targeted firm recruitment (first-wave strategies) but within the spirit of Porter it also provides focus to second-wave strategies (BR&E and entrepreneurship strategies) and third-wave strategies (public-private partnerships and regional collaboration).

More specifically, the basis of the first wave of economic development was that government can pick winners. In the presence of market failure, doing so could increase social welfare. Porter challenged the "old model" of picking winners by introducing a new analytical framework (his "diamonds"). In the third wave, the role of government (community) is to build private-public partnerships and facilitate networking, discussions, and institution building that can leverage competitive market advantages, all of which are consistent with the arguments Porter set forth.

Yet Porter primarily uses just one tool – location quotients – in his work. In this book, we compile in one place a suite of different analytical tools. Each tool has strengths and weaknesses, which are identified by the authors. The book is designed to provide basic information for local decision-makers and concerned citizens. How they use that information is up to them. At best, we can outline strategic planning efforts to help them think through the process. In the end, the buzz surrounding Porter's work creates a critically important "teachable moment", and our experience has shown that communities can benefit tremendously from the simple process of starting to have discussions around the issues addressed here.

Outline of the book

The remainder of this introductory chapter briefly describes the contents of the work that follows. The book is divided into three parts: I: Policy Background; II: Empirical Modelling Approaches; and III: Applications and Case Studies. Part I sets the stage for why TRED, or industry targeting, is particularly relevant today. Historical background materials provide a foundation for an in-depth discussion of current policy approaches. Special attention is given to the notion of "cluster development" as advanced by Porter. The chapters provide a general appreciation of the tone of current policy debates.

In Chapter 2, Historical Description of Economic Development Policy, Deller and Goetz sketch a broad overview of key policies ranging from tax incentives that started after the Great Depression with Mississippi's BAWI policy to the current competition for firms and jobs between the states. It also covers the more recent emphasis on entrepreneurship and business retention and expansion, as well as the current philosophies of collaboration and partnership building within and across communities. This chapter outlines in detail the "waves" of economic development policies at the state and local levels.

Shields, Barkley, and Emery, in Chapter 3, Industry Clusters and Industry Targeting, provide an overview of the industry cluster strategy for regional economic development and the role of industry targeting in helping communities and states identify innovative clusters and design policies for cluster growth. They first define industry clusters and summarize advantages and disadvantages to a clustering strategy. Next, they introduce the concept of industry targeting and then apply it to industry cluster development, focusing on their role in micropolitan or rural economic development. This is an important distinction, as rural areas do not offer the interindustry networking opportunities (urbanization economies) available in metropolitan areas. Thus, access to cluster-related benefits takes on added importance to micropolitan businesses and communities.

Deller then provides an Overview of the Theory Behind TRED in Chapter 4. He reviews alternative theories of firm location and expansion decisions in a nontechnical manner, and then describes basic distinctions between cost minimization and demand maximization, giving special attention to the differences between manufacturing, service, and retail types of businesses. He gives special attention to the lack of a solid theoretical foundation for our understanding of why firms cluster. Deller also discusses how policies can, or cannot, influence the location and expansion decisions of firms.

Woodward and Guimarães provide a critical review of Michael Porter's work in Chapter 5, Porter's Cluster Strategy and Industrial Targeting. As they note, the "Porter Approach" has received significant attention in the formulation of state economic development and is only now reaching the community level. Through the idea of clusters, many communities are starting to see the value of collaboration and partnership building within and across communities (i.e., the third wave of development). This chapter provides a critical review of the Porter Approach, emphasizing how communities may or may not find the approach to be useful.

Much of the modern theory of economic growth and development focuses on the role of agglomeration economies, or the role of internal and external economies of scale. Modern endogenous growth theory, particularly in a spatial setting, predicts that scale economies drive economic growth and development. For larger metropolitan areas, such economies are inherent to the regional economy. But for most communities, scale works against them. Gabe's Chapter 6, Impact of Agglomerations on the Economy, reviews the current thinking about agglomerations and how policy at the local level can be affected. His study is based on data from the State of Maine.

In Part II, Empirical Modelling Approaches, we provide in-depth reviews of current empirical methods that are being used within the industrial targeting framework. The reader will gain an understanding of the different empirical approaches that can be used to work with communities that are interested in industrial targeting. The chapters provide sufficient detail to allow readers to replicate each of the approaches. The first three chapters use econometric methods, the next three draw on the tool of input-output and value chain analysis, and the last two employ the Analytical Hierarchy Process (AHP) and so-called matching methods.

Leatherman and Kastens, in Chapter 7, Modelling the Probability of Manufacturing Activity in the Great Plains, estimate the probability that a specific type of manufacturing activity locates within a given Great Plains county. They report probabilistic models, paying special attention to how these statistical tools can be used to help better understand what drives manufacturing firm location decisions and how communities can craft policies to change those probabilities.

Chapter 8, Regional Variation in the Location Choices of Goods- and Services-Producing Industries, by Cader, Leatherman, and Crespi, examines the location choices of goods- and services-producing firms in regions characterized by varying rural/urban status. They employ a conditional logit model in their estimation and focus on the importance of clustering and the role of economic spillovers in industry location and firm profitability.

Davis and Harris use a double hurdle firm location model and data from ten Montana counties in Chapter 9, An Application of a Double Hurdle Firm Location Model: The Example of Montana. Using the notion of market thresholds, this chapter focuses on probabilistic models for predicting the location decisions of manufacturing firms. In addition, the authors review simpler and more direct methods. This chapter complements the previous chapter by Cader et al.

IMPLAN (Impact Analysis for Planning) is a widely used modelling system and database that allows for the construction of detailed input-output (IO) models for individual counties or any combination of counties. Several applied researchers have creatively adapted IMPLAN to undertake industry targeting studies. The next three chapters review in detail some of the alternative approaches of using IO and IMPLAN specifically for TRED analysis.

Chapter 10, Targeting Industry Clusters for Regional Economic Development: The REDRL Approach, by Barkley and Henry, describes how one institution, the Regional Economic Development Research Laboratory's (REDRL), identifies clusters for TRED purposes. The authors outline a sequential process for developing a primary list of industries for targeted development. The region's industries must pass five screens to be selected as a targeted cluster: substantial local presence as indicated by number of establishments and employees, growing industry employment in the region, relative regional specialization in the industry, and local employment growth that exceeds the national industry average. Next, industry value chains are identified to determine if linked industries are good prospects for targeting. Finally, the identified high-potential industry clusters are rated according to workers' wages, potential future employment growth, import substitution potential, average plant size, and linkages to the local economy.

Hughes, in Chapter 11, Rural-Urban Economic Linkages: Implications for Industry Targeting Recommendations, employs input-output analysis to identify and examine rural-urban economic linkages and, among other contributions, highlights the potential benefits of regional collaboration. After discussing important underlying concepts including central place theory, core-periphery models, and backwash/spread effects in rural areas, he develops specific recommendations from his results for industry targeting in rural communities.

In Chapter 12, Regional Cluster Analysis with Interindustry Benchmarks, Feser, Renski, and Koo show how so-called value chains based on national trading patterns among industries can be used for interindustry benchmarking purposes with the goal of identifying regional clusters. Feser et al. compare their approach with other methods of cluster identification and discuss specific insights that can be gained from this type of analysis, along with possible pitfalls. Their chapter concludes using data from Maine for illustrative purposes, along with a brief discussion of strengths and weaknesses of the benchmarking method.

One of the limitations of using industry targeting or cluster analysis to help form economic growth and development policies for communities is that the analysis and potential recommendations may be sterile in that they do not reflect the culture or values of the community. The next two chapters discuss these limitations and offer methods for incorporating community values into the analysis.

Chapter 13, Targeting with the Analytic Hierarchy Process, by Johnson, shows how industrial targeting studies can be designed to better reflect local community preferences by employing the Analytical Hierarchy Process (AHP). This includes interviewing local residents to identify the region's preferences for economic, social, environmental, and other outcomes. Cardinal weights are then assigned to alternative local economic development impacts and the results used to identify most-preferred strategies.

In Chapter 14, The Community Business Matching Model: Combining Community and Business Goals and Assets to Target Rural Economic Development, Cox, Alevy, Harris, Andreozzi, Wright, and Borden point out that community economic development often involves trade-offs among competing economic and community goals. The Community Business Matching (CBM) model provides a framework for communities to examine their goals and identify desirable tradeoffs. A community can use CBM to prioritize its goals and identify the assets available to help it achieve these goals. The CBM model fits these goals and assets to business profiles in order to ascertain which economic development prospect best reflects the desires of the community.

One of the central objectives of this book is to provide the reader not only with insights into the theoretical foundations of targeting and the empirical methods, but also with a basic understanding of the approaches for using the analysis to affect policy. Part III presents various applications in the form of case studies and also highlights concrete processes and methods for working within communities.

Goetz, Shields, and Wang in Chapter 15, Identifying Food Industry Clusters: A Comparison of Analytical Tools, compare the results that are obtained by applying various cluster identification methods to the same region and set of industries, rather than using a single tool to identify a potentially clustered industry within a given county or region. Their application is to food industry clusters in the Northeastern US, and the tools used range from location quotients to input-output analysis. They employ the Local Moran statistic, a spatially explicit measure of local association that is based on a spatial weights matrix. This is argued to be especially useful for capturing county-level spillovers of economic activity in the food industry.

In Chapter 16, Targeted Industry Analysis in a "Comprehensive" Economic Development Extension Program, Nelson, Woods, Homm, and Doekson outline a broad framework for working within communities in the area of economic development. Using the "blueprints" framework, they outline a collection of educational tools. They use industry targeting and cluster analysis as a focal point for a broader discussion of community economic development.

Chapter 17, TRED as an Educational Tool, by Deller, Leatherman, and Shields, outlines a community educational programme in which TRED analysis serves as a catalyst for community engagement. The authors discuss one potential educational programme that is based on their experience in programme design and delivery within a university extension setting. Specifically, they develop the idea of using tools from community visioning and economic development strategic planning as a method for implementing the TRED analysis as an educational tool. In this chapter, the notion of process is front and centre.

Chapter 18, Industry Targeting: Theoretical Underpinnings and Practical Applications by Hughes, critically reviews the theoretical basis of applied TRED. Although IMPLAN has seen widespread use throughout the US, the construction of such detailed models requires strong assumptions, in both model construction and database development. This chapter focuses on the inherent limitations of using IO models built on secondary data. The author reviews the strengths and weaknesses of IMPLAN and explores the impact of potential modelling errors on industrial targeting analysis.

A central tenet of IO analysis is the identification of interindustry linkages. In addition, in the construction of these models, detailed estimates of industry imports and exports are needed. In Chapter 19, Import Substitution and the Analysis of Gaps and Disconnects, Deller shows how "gaps" and "disconnects" can be developed and applied at the community level. Gaps exist where firms must import goods and services into the region because they are not available from local suppliers. Disconnects exist when local suppliers and consumers (businesses) are not connected in the supply chain, but goods and services that are imported are actually available from local suppliers.[4] In the spirit of industry targeting, the "gaps" are the potential industry for attention. The author outlines the methods and provides applications.

The final chapter presents a conclusion and summarizes what we have learned. One of the most important lessons from this work is that the process of implementing a TRED programme can create enormous public value (Kalambokidis 2004) simply by virtue of getting community elected leaders and their stakeholders to think systematically and methodically about their local community and its economic system. The chapter also outlines future research, policy, and educational directions.

Notes

1 Somewhat ironically, at the time he wrote his article, Buss was in Washington, DC, "working on public policies for high-growth firms" (author biographical information for Buss 1999a and 199b). Presumably it is acceptable for social scientists and analysts to work on public policy for high-growth firms, but not for communities that are losing firms.

2 The NERCRD is one of four Regional Rural Development Centres established under the Rural Development Act of 1972 and supported under the authority of section 2(c)(1)(B) of Public Law 89–106, as amended (7 U.S.C. § 450i(c)), which

enables the USDA/Cooperative State Research, Education, and Extension Service (CSREES) to support research, extension, or education activities. The NERCRD serves 12 states and the District of Columbia. Any opinions expressed in this volume are solely those of the authors and do not necessarily reflect those of the funding agencies.

3   We are referring to the community-based educators who serve as crucial links between the new research generated within the national system of land grant universities and the evolving economic and social development needs of communities (often counties).

4   This is especially important in an environment of rising fuel prices that lead to higher transportation costs.

References

Arthur, W.B. (2007) *Increasing Returns and Path Dependence in the Economy*, Ann Arbor: University of Michigan Press.

Asheim, B., Cooke, P., and Martin, R. (2006) "The rise of the cluster concept in regional analysis and policy: a critical assessment", in B. Asheim et al. (eds) *Clusters and Regional Development: Critical Reflections and Explorations*, London: Routledge.

Baumol, W.J., Litan, R.E., and Schramm, C.J. (2006). *Good Capitalism, Bad Capitalism, and the Economics of Growth and Prosperity*, New Haven: Yale University Press.

Buss, T.F. (1999a) "The case against targeted industry strategies", (Forum), *Economic Development Quarterly*, 13(4): 339–56.

——. (1999b) "To target or not to target, that's the question: a Response to Wiewel and Finkel", *Economic Development Quarterly*, 13(4): 365–70.

Eisinger, P. (1988) *The Role of the Entrepreneurial State*, Madison: University of Wisconsin Press.

——. (1995) "State economic development in the 1990s: politics and policy learning", *Economic Development Quarterly*, 9: 146–58.

Finkle, J.A. (1999) "The case against targeting might have been more . . . targeted", *Economic Development Quarterly*, 13(4): 361–64.

Goode, F.M., and Hastings, S.E. (1989) "The effect of transportation service on the location of manufacturing plants in nonmetropolitan and small metropolitan communities", in William R. Gillis (ed), *Profitability and Mobility in Rural America: Successful Approaches to Tackling Rural Transportation Problems*, University Park: Penn State University Press.

Greenstone, M., and Moretti, E. (2004) "Bidding for industrial plants: does winning the million dollar plant increase welfare?" Unpublished manuscript (mimeo), January.

Johnson, T.G., Otto, D., and Deller, S.C. (editors). (2006) *Community Policy Analysis Modeling*, Oxford: Blackwell.

Kalambokidis, L. (2004) "Identifying the public value in extension programs", *Journal of Extension*, 24(2). Online. Available HTTP: <http://www.joe.org/joe/2004april/a1.shtml>.

Marion, B.W. (and NC 117 Committee). (1986) *The Organization and Performance of the U.S. Food System*, Lexington, MA: Lexington Books.

Markusen, A. (editor) (2007) *Reining in the Competition for Capital*, Kalamazoo, MI: W.E. Upjohn Institute for Employment Research.

Marshall, A. (1930) *Principles of Economics*, 8th Edn., originally published 1890, London: Macmillan.

Maskell, P., and Kebir, L. (2006) "What qualifies as a cluster theory?" in B. Asheim, P. Cooke, and R. Martin (eds) *Clusters and Regional Development: Critical Reflections and Explorations*, London: Routledge.

Porter, M.E. (1998). *On Competition*, Cambridge, MA: Harvard Business School Press.

——. (2000) "Location, competition and economic development", *Economic Development Quarterly*, 14: 23–34.

Rubin, H. (1988) "Shoot anything that flies; claim anything that falls", *Economic Development Quarterly*, 2: 236–51.

Scott, A.J., and Storper, M. (2003) "Regions, globalization, development", *Regional Studies*, 37: 579–93.

Wiesel, W. (1999) "Policy research in an imperfect world: response to Terry F. Buss, 'The case against targeted industry strategies,' " *Economic Development Quarterly*, 13(4): 357–60.

Part I
Policy background

Part 1

2 Historical description of economic development policy

Steven C. Deller and Stephan J. Goetz

Introduction

In this chapter, we provide a broad historical overview of economic development policy, ranging from tax incentive programmes that are generally recognized as starting with the Mississippi Balance Agriculture with Industry (BAWI) policies of the Great Depression era and the modern competition between the states for new firms, to the focus on entrepreneurship and business retention and expansion, along with the current philosophies of collaboration and partnership-building within and across communities and regions. We outline the "waves" of economic development policies at the state and local levels, leading up to the current state-of-the-art of economic development thinking. The primary focus is on the history of development ideas related to targeted economic development.

Economic development as a field of study did not come into being until after WWII (Malizia and Feser 1999). With many former colonies becoming independent nations, coupled with the desire to rebuild after the widespread destruction suffered during the war and a strong desire not to repeat the economic hardships of the Great Depression, significant attention was focused on economic growth and development. At least internationally, much of this early work targeted agricultural economic development, because the agricultural sector dominated the economies of the former colonies. The expertise of American agricultural economists was sought in developing countries around the world, and many seminal publications were written in these early years, including 1979 Nobel Laureate T.W. Schultz's *Transforming Traditional Agriculture* (1976), and, later, publications such as Mellor's *The New Economics of Growth – A Strategy for India and the Developing World* (1976) and Eicher and Staatz's (various editions) *Agricultural Development in the Third World*.

For the first time, focused questions of what could be done to promote targeted economic growth were being raised after WWII by academics interested in policy analysis. Prior to WWII, the governments of most countries generally played only a minor role in economic development. Most discussions focused on short-term macro policies to minimize the negative impacts of swings in the business cycle. Indeed, much of the Keynesian Revolution and the New Deal were aimed at policy options to address short-term economic fluctuations. A few key examples explain this growing interest in state intervention in economic development:

- The Great Depression raised questions about the robustness, resilience, and stability of private markets.
- The apparent success of Soviet central planning, as well as the success of the US Marshall Plan in Germany.
- The example of India developing a plan for economic growth and development immediately after independence. In fact, with newfound freedoms, many former colonies embraced nationalism and the desire to be proactive.
- The apparent economic success of Japan after WWII.
- Within the US, the apparent success of state policies such as the Mississippi Balance Agriculture with Industry (BAWI).

Even so, there are a few key historical examples of targeted economic growth policies even before WWII. The English Corn Laws of the 19th century (1815) restricted trade in grain and were designed to keep the country's agriculture out of a depression. The state of New Jersey offered tax incentives in 1791 to industrialist Alexander Hamilton to influence the location of a manufacturing plant. The famed Erie Canal, completed in 1825, is one of the first public investments in infrastructure and was justified in terms of offering a cheap and safe way to transport agricultural products to markets. Further, in the name of economic development, the state of Pennsylvania by 1844 had invested over $100 million and placed promoters of the state on the boards of directors of more than 150 corporations.

During the rapid expansion of the railroads throughout the Great Plains, communities aggressively competed with one another for railroad access. There are numerous examples of rail lines zigzagging between small communities that aggressively pursued rail service but were subsequently abandoned due to the lack of freight. The railroads likewise opened up the American frontier to extraction of natural resources. It is important to distinguish between policies targeted at specific sectors (such as certain kinds of manufacturing) and those targeted broadly at all businesses. Opponents of targeting are willing to concede that general public sector intervention may be desirable, if it does not favor any one particular sector. In the case of railroads, the primary sector that benefited was natural resources, but it is difficult to argue today that the railroads were unwise investments from a national perspective.

Other examples from the distant past include the opening of Western lands to homesteaders in the 19th century, and tariffs that were used to protect New England textile mills. The Morrill Act of 1862 created the Land Grant system of public universities with the goal of educating people in agriculture, home economics, mechanical arts, and other professions that were vital to the economic foundation at the time. This was followed by the Smith-Lever Act of 1914, which created the Cooperative Extension Service within the Land Grant system for the purpose of extending the educational mission of the Land Grants to all residents, not just those on campus at the universities. The Highway Act of 1916 was aimed specifically at "getting farmers out of the mud". The states of Alabama, Florida, North Carolina, and Maine all created economic development agencies between 1923 and 1927. Florida and Arkansas passed "right-to-work" legislation that prohibited closed-union shops. This was an attempt to provide businesses with greater flexibility in the face of strong trade unions, which were widely perceived as "anti-business". Even so, most of the states' efforts were narrowly focused on infrastructure investment awarded through federal public works programmes. The notion of strategic planning for economic development was weakly imposed on the states as a partial condition for receiving federal New Deal public works dollars. But with the start of WWII, the nation's focus shifted and all economic development strategic planning efforts disappeared.

As we have seen, while the notion of subnational economic development efforts was not unknown prior to WWII, it was not an area of study or a focal point of policy until the 1950s. As such, the intent of this chapter is to provide a broad overview of economic growth and development thinking with a primary focus on the past 50 years. There are two main sections, with one focusing on international developments and the other on domestic thought. Woven into this chapter is an emphasis on how changing theoretical understanding has affected practical policy implementation.

Patterns in international development

Although international economic development patterns are discussed in other texts, we provide a cursory overview here to show how this field also has informed domestic development thinking. This is important for many of the TRED tools that are discussed in this volume, because the methods of analysis and policy formations set in the international discussion also influenced domestic thinking. There are three basic stages or eras of thought, including primarily an internal focus through import substitution, an external orientation based on export-base theory, and the so-called Washington Consensus on free trade.

1 Internally focused import substitution strategies

One of the early tenets of economic development was the idea that nations could "catch up" with more advanced countries and become more self-sufficient if they protected so-called infant industries. The government basically selected industries to protect, usually by imposing tariffs or quotas on imported goods. This afforded the chosen industries temporary protection, which allowed them to develop workers' skills and experience and expand productivity by achieving economies of scale so as to be able to compete with imports. Although this argument is most commonly associated with developing countries, primarily in Central and South America, the underlying idea was first proclaimed by Alexander Hamilton in 1791.

As reviewed by Burton (1998), many developing countries after WWII rejected the efficiency and effectiveness of the capitalist economic system because of the lingering effects of the Great Depression and the perceived success of the Soviet economy. In this environment, the governments of many developing countries elected to take a more proactive role in promoting economic growth and development. Because many of these economies were dependent on agriculture and resource-extractive industries, governments naturally turned to examining ways to grow these industries. Given the popularity of the Rostow-Kuznets stages of growth theory at the time, a natural conclusion was to promote mechanization that would lead to increased labour productivity and hence income levels. But rather than looking to import the manufactured goods to foster this mechanization process, policies such as trade restrictions through tariffs and quotas and manipulation of exchange rates were crafted to encourage local manufacturing. The belief was that, by creating stronger internal linkages through import substitution policies as the traditional sectors, such as agriculture, grew, the manufacturing sectors would automatically develop as well. As with many "new" economic ideas, the notion of focusing on import substitution was not new. Indeed, the "Buy Oregon" and "Buy Chicago" and other "buy local" programmes date back to the 1920s (Persky et al. 1993).

Infant industry protection is a clear example of a government picking a winner, generally using non-economic criteria to select the industry. In practice, politically influential industries that tell the best stories are likely to be chosen. While this strategy can be effective in moving countries or regions forward, the danger exists that the protective barriers will remain in place indefinitely. More specifically, once incentives or flows of economic rents have been created in an economy, it is politically difficult to remove them. A key test is to assess whether or not the industry in question has a reasonably good chance of ever overcoming whatever disadvantage it currently has in competing with world prices.

Over time, the notion of import substitution fell from grace for a number of reasons. First, there was scant evidence that the policies were proving effective in fostering economic growth and development. Second, there was little theoretical or practical understanding of how the various forms of protection should or could be implemented. This was particularly true for the new political leaders in Central and South America. Third, the methods and data required for effective planning, such as methods for identifying the specific industries to target and how to foster internal growth once the trade barriers were put in place, were not fully developed. While the broad concept of import substitution may have made sense, the knowledge of how to effectively implement the policies was lacking. Finally, as we describe below, the Washington Consensus pushed many of the Central and South American counties that favoured the strategy of import substitution to abandon the policy.

From a purely theoretical perspective, Krueger (1993), among others, argues that economic growth is derived through learning and innovation in a Schumpeterian manner. By creating artificial protections, firms lose the market force motivation to learn and innovate. In essence, the protected industries that are to be the foundation for economic growth become inefficient and wasteful.

Deller (Chapter 19) describes how this import substitution approach can be used in modern TRED by analysing gaps and disconnects in the local economy. The context here is a bit different, because individual regions within the United States are unable to impede free trade in goods and services. The idea of building stronger local linkages between industries, however, is at the core of and perfectly consistent with Porter's notion of clusters and the building of networks of interconnected firms. Import substitution at the local level is aimed not so much at protecting targeted industries, but at identifying opportunities to build stronger linkages and promote expansion from within (Persky et al. 1993). At a subnational level, the theoretical objections advanced by Krueger (1993) do not apply because the policy intent, strategies, and tools are fundamentally different.

Another important idea that needs to be mentioned here is the induced innovation model of agricultural development (Hayami and Ruttan 1971). This model is built on the idea that technologies for particular industrial sectors are developed endogenously within different nations, reflecting local factor endowments. Instead of letting markets alone determine which technologies ought to be developed, subtle pressures coming from various interest groups influence and set the public science and technology research agenda that leads to the development of new tools and techniques. In a sense this, too, is a model of targeted economic development and it explains fairly well the path toward development in countries as diverse as Japan and India.

The modern notion of value chains, and their optimal exploitation, also has very clear and important antecedents in the international economic development literature, starting with the fundamental importance of backward- and forward-linkages as outlined by A.O. Hirschman. Mellor (1976) devotes an entire chapter to the subject of rural growth linkages, which are examined in this volume by Hughes (Chapter 11) and also by Feser and Isserman (in press). As we also mentioned in Chapter 1, the idea of linkages within and across subsectors of the US food system was one of the key contributions of the North Central-117 Research Committee effort, as documented in Marion (1986).

2 Export-focused strategies

Another critically important idea in economic development thinking has been the promotion of exports from an area with incentives given to certain industries. This idea is at the very heart of economic base theory within a nation, whereby inflows of new money into a regional economy set off a chain reaction of economic multipliers, but the same notion holds at the national level. The most prominent examples are the so-called Asian Tiger economies of Hong Kong, South Korea, Singapore, and Taiwan. In retrospect, however, the role of the government may have been much less important in terms of picking winners than it was to setting the proper institutional and economic environment that allowed businesses in these nations to flourish (Baumol et al. 2007; World Bank 1993).

More nuanced scholarship has also investigated the types of goods or commodities that are exported. In the case of pure natural resources, such as coal mining in West Virginia and other Appalachian states, a general consensus is that these regions benefit relatively little from the resource. The reason is that most of the value-added occurs out of state and incentives for local residents to invest in skills and higher education have been limited because the jobs available in natural resource-based industries were high-paying but required very little formal education. This is also known as the "curse of natural resources". In the case of developing countries, an important concern historically has been that of secularly declining terms of trade for primary commodities relative to the types of goods exported. At the time of this writing, however, these historical concerns have been completely reversed, with prices of many commodities experiencing all-time highs in real terms. This shows how quickly ideas can become obsolete as a result of changing economic conditions.

While the export base model remains in widespread use, particularly in software such as IMPLAN, some have argued that the theory retains less and less relevance because exports of primary goods or raw commodities are less and less important to overall economic well-being in countries such as the US. This ignores the fact, however, that the US continues to export widely in other sectors, including financial instruments, legal contracts, software, and the like, and these exports continue to drive domestic economic growth. The German export growth miracle has also flourished in an environment that was less "free" or capitalistic than is the case in countries such as the US due in part, it is believed, to the fact that firms and industries in that nation both collaborate and compete, making them more efficient.

In the end, the promotion and protection of export-based industries remains a focal point of many if not most targeted regional economic development efforts. There remains a widely held opinion among many local politicians that economic growth means attraction of a manufacturing plant. In rural areas, agriculture is still perceived as the engine of economic growth and is fervently protected and promoted. For example, the feverish promotion of bio-energy such as ethanol in the US Midwest is viewed as creating an export-focused manufacturing base that adds value to agricultural products such as corn.

3 Washington Consensus

With the election of the Reagan and the Thatcher administrations, a considerable shift occurred in the political philosophies surrounding economic development policies. There was growing evidence that the import substitution policies of Central and South America were not working. For example, Goldar (1986) found that those industries that were targeted for import substitution policies had significantly slower growth in total factor productivity (TFP) than those industries that were not the focus of import substitution policies. In addition, as Burton (1998) noted, the "boom" of Korea and Taiwan, which pursued export-oriented strategies, was drawing attention and challenging the idea of import substitution. In addition, during the late 1970s and early 1980s, with the exception of a few East Asian countries, the economies of many developing nations collapsed. Finally, political pressure increased from many US corporations, particularly in the auto industry, stating that foreign trade policies were detrimental to domestic growth and stability. In short, the economic havoc of the late 1970s and early 1980s, coupled with the Reagan-Thatcher administrations embracing of conservative economic values, created an environment for changes in economic policies. The collapse of the Soviet Union basically sealed this philosophical change.

As we noted above, our theoretical understanding of the economic growth and development process returned a focus on Schumpeter's notion of innovation, learning, and entrepreneurial behaviour. The relatively new endogenous growth theory of Lucas (1988) and Romer (1986) emphasizes the power of competitive market forces in motivating firms to learn and innovate to gain a competitive advantage over its competitors. The implication is that any policies that hinder competitive market forces also stifle economic growth and development.

The strength of the Washington Consensus was fully realized in the policies adopted by the World Bank (WB) and the International Monetary Fund (IMF). As outlined by Williamson (1993), these two powerful development organizations established a series of criteria against which developing counties are judged. In order to receive WB or IMF support, in terms of either technical assistance or more importantly financial aid, counties must demonstrate that they are implementing policies that are moving in the direction dictated by these criteria. In addition, as Gore (2002) noted, countries that did not embrace the policies embodied in the Washington Consensus found themselves increasingly isolated in the globalizing economy.

Williamson (1993), who is credited with coining the phrase "Washington Consensus", outlined 10 of these criteria. Countries must demonstrate that they are imposing *fiscal discipline*. Budget deficits including at the levels of subnational governments, state enterprises, as well as central banks should be small enough to be financed without inflationary pressures. Indeed, an operating deficit should be no more than 2 per cent of GDP. Countries must also show proper priorities in *public expenditures*. Policy reforms must be put in place to redirect public expenditures away from administration, defence, subsidies, and what in the US would be called pork projects, toward economic growth-focused areas such as infrastructure, education, and health care. *Tax policies* should focus on low marginal rates on a broad base, and capital gains taxes should be low, to discourage capital flight. *Financial markets* should be liberalized so that market forces determine interest rates and allow financial resources to flow to their highest and best use. Preferential loan policies toward privileged borrowers should be eliminated. Attempts to protect or manipulate *exchange rates* should be minimized, to eliminate distortions and uncertainty. *Trade policies* should be liberalized and markets opened to free trade. This is the embodiment of free trade agreements such as NAFTA. *Direct foreign investment* should be encouraged. Foreign firms should be able to enter domestic markets and compete with domestic firms on an equal footing. Nationalized industries should be *privatized*. Based on a Niskanen-Buchanan-type view of public sector bureaucracy, government-run industries are inherently inefficient, and stifle learning and innovation. This is sometimes referred to as the Leviathan hypothesis, or more colloquially, "bloated government". Countries should embrace *deregulation* and abolish regulations that impede new firm formation and competition. Regulations should be limited to ensuring environmental protection, worker safety, and proper functioning of key sectors including financial institutions. Finally, a well-defined notion of *property rights* must be in place, where ownership of resources is clearly defined and contracts are enforceable.

The implications for economic development policy are clear and straightforward. Minimize the role of government, get the rules right and in place, and allow competitive market forces to play out. The policy of free-trade and *laissez-faire* are front and centre. As Buss (1999a and 1999b) argued, these philosophies spilled over into subnational economic development efforts and the notion of targeted regional economic development came under attack.

There is, however, a significant and growing backlash against the Washington Consensus (Gore 2002). Opponents argue that the narrow focus on growth in GDP does not take into account issues of equality and the human dimension of growth. The underlying idea that "a rising tide lifts all boats" is not unequivocally supported by the available research, and the strong evidence of rising income inequality challenges the "fairness" of competitive markets as the solution to growth and development (Kanbur 2008; World Bank 2008). In addition, the Consensus does not adequately deal with issues of market failure and externalities. Sugden and Wilson (2002) argue that what they deem as the failure of the Washington Consensus development agenda might fundamentally derive from a failure to engage people in the decisions and processes surrounding their development. The political backlash and dwindling support has perhaps caused the extreme positions embodied in the Washington Consensus to be relaxed (Sugden et al. 2006). Much like a pendulum, economic development philosophies have swung from one extreme of fierce protection to the other extreme of wide-open markets. The pendulum is slowly moving away from either extreme, partly as a result of Porter's argument that cluster development can be a viable economic development strategy. There is a role for public policy, if it is intelligently implemented.

Patterns in domestic development

In a detailed review of economic development within the US, Eisinger (1988) suggests that most subnational policies have been "supply-side based". The more widely used policies include financing of private development through public revenue bonding to take advantage of the tax-exempt status of public bonds, state loans and loan guarantees for construction, local tax exemption or moratoria on land or capital improvements, and public provision of industrial land sites. Many of these efforts were piecemeal and targeted toward larger firms. While the 1980s witnessed a return of strategic planning for economic development, states and local governments tended to implement efforts in a piecemeal manner that reflected political criteria and preferences over economic viability.

Federal policies for economic development since WWII have tended to be less episodic than those before WWII. Many of the early federal policies were in the broad area of urban renewal, such as Title I of the 1949 Housing Act. Here the federal government provided financial resources to help redevelop "slum" areas or other area of urban blight. A loophole in the law meant that the renewal did not necessarily have to be focused on residential redevelopment, and many of the cleared blighted areas were instead targeted for commercial development. Title II of the 1949 Housing Act allowed for the creation of public housing. Ironically, because of the concentration of crime that followed large public housing projects such as the Robert Taylor Homes in Chicago, most of those public housing projects are now being dismantled. The 1959 Housing Act increased the fiscal resources that were initially provided in the 1949 Act, and explicitly opened the loophole by allowing all of the monetary resources to be used for broader urban redevelopment efforts. Many of the programmes made available in the Housing Acts along with other miscellaneous programmes were combined into community block grants through the 1974 Housing and Community Development Act.

In 1953, the federal government established the Small Business Administration (SBA) with the central mission of helping to promote small business development through counselling, loans and loan guarantees, and grants. Unlike most other federal programmes of the time, the SBA was not intended to provide support to state and local economic development efforts, but rather to provide services directly to small businesses. While the SBA has been criticized, particularly during the Reagan Administration, as being too disjointed, scattered, and insufficiently funded to affect the larger economy, it remains a centerpiece of federal small business development.

The Economic Development Administration (EDA) was established by the Public Works and Commerce Development Act of 1965 with the stated mission "to lead the federal economic development agenda by promoting innovation and competitiveness, preparing American regions for growth and success in the worldwide economy". This is accomplished primarily through the use of federal dollars to support infrastructure investments (Title I), grants, loans and loan guarantees for industry (Title II), aid in planning at the regional and local level (Title III), and special grants to local communities for economic readjustment in response to economic emergencies such as the closure of a major employer (Title IV). It should be noted that in the US the EDA has been a major proponent and supporter of Porter and his work on clusters. While the EDA offers a range of services and programmes, it does have a history of tunnel vision with respect to certain economic development ideas. For example, in the late 1970s, it actively promoted the development of industrial parks to the detriment of other policies, and today it has embraced clusters with equal fervour.

In a discussion of US rural development policy, Honadle (2001) notes that the US Department of Agriculture (USDA) has historically been designated as the lead federal agency vested with advocating for and administering programmes in rural areas. Much of US rural development policy has been focused on promoting and stabilizing the agricultural sector, because the economic base of rural areas has historically been agricultural. While this was perhaps true before WWII, most rural areas outside of the Central Plains have now diversified into manufacturing, tourism and recreation, and service-based industries. Rural development policy has generally not reflected that fundamental shift, however. Honadle (2001) and Shaffer (2001) observe that, outside of farm support programmes, rural development policy has also been fragmented and piecemeal. Part of this is due to the vaguely worded Rural Development Act of 1972, which basically required the President to form a coherent policy. Again, the US Department of Agriculture was charged with implementing any subsequent policies. Each administration has either ignored the mandate, such as the Reagan Administration, or embraced the challenge with initiatives such as the National Rural Development Partnerships, as in the case of the first Bush Administration. Many observers believe that the enormous diversity of rural America continues to pose profound challenges to formulating a coherent rural policy in this nation. The many interests in rural areas are simply too diverse to be able to rally stakeholders around a single and effective policy. Quite the opposite is true in the case of commodity policies, for example.

Consistent with the international political philosophies embodied in the Washington Census was the emergence of the New Governance School, which was best captured by the work of Osborne and Gaebler (1992). The idea captures the concept of the National Rural Development Partnerships, which challenged the existing paradigm about what and how government should operate. Rather than implementing a top-down rural development policy that could not possibly reflect the diversity of rural America, the National Partnerships were aimed at building stronger public-private partnerships within each state. Initially, the State Rural Development Councils were to provide a forum for federal, state, and local agencies vested with economic development responsibilities to build stronger connections.

Shaffer (2001: 78) outlined the rationale for the initiative as:

> The heart of this proposal is that the NRDP and SRDCs represent key dimensions in articulating a national rural policy. First, they provide a forum for a sustained dialogue among public, private, tribal and non-governmental entities that have historically represented rural interests at both the national and state level. Second, since they are not a new funding source, the NRDP and SRDCs represent a way for all of the parties to engage in a new way of doing business. Third, they personify the diverse coalition needed to move a rural agenda forward.

This captures many of the paradigms of New Governance as outlined by Osborne and Gaebler (1992). There are some success stories associated with the State Councils, such as in Kansas, where a number of granting agencies realized that each agency was asking for basically the same information from the applicants in their application forms. Nevertheless, each agency used different forms, thereby creating considerable governmental red tape. Through the Kansas State Council, the involved agencies streamlined the application procedures and allowed applicants for grants and funding to use one form for multiple agencies.

Unfortunately, as is the case with most public policies, the sustainability of the Rural Development Councils hinged on the political support of not only the White House but also state governors. Because this was a Republican initiative originating from the first Bush Administration, many Democratic governors were reluctant to participate. Over time as administrations changed, political support waned. The Clinton Administration was only lukewarm to the idea, and as Democratic governors replaced Republicans, political support faded further, in some states more than in others. As advanced by Eisinger (1998), economic development initiatives identified with one administration, whether at the national or state level, are seldom embraced by subsequent administrations.

Eisenger (1995) eloquently argued that the political structure of the US creates strong incentives to take a very short-term view of economic development policies. There is a strong disincentive to embrace policies of political rivals, such as the former president or governor. There are also strong incentives to embrace policies that have short-term immediate political payoffs, such as the recruitment of a major employer. Policies that do not garner media headlines and may have economic success in the long term, such as entrepreneurship or the expansion of smaller firms, are not supported politically. The State Rural Development Councils were aimed at creating institutions that went beyond political gamesmanship, but without political support the Councils were bound to fail.

Waves of development policy

The notion of targeting economic development has a rich and well-developed tradition within the academic literature and has been a major emphasis of regional economic development policies (Reeder 1995). Within the academic literature, the foundation for targeting policies can be found in the introduction of space within microeconomics, the location of the firm, and the concepts of spatial markets (see Deller, Chapter 4). Given that manufacturing was the driving force behind the economy during this time, much of the work focused on the location decisions of manufacturing firms. The economic concept that firms pick a location to minimize the costs of production had a direct and important implication on economic development policies. During the Great Depression of the 1930s, many state governments became frustrated with the lack of response to the economic crisis and felt the need to respond to local economic distress. The first state-level programme was the Mississippi Balance Agriculture with Industry (BAWI) Act, which built aggressively on the idea of export base theory (as it was known at the time) and firms' costs of production. Mississippi promoted itself as a low-cost alternative location to manufacturing firms located in the northeastern states. Advancing the idea of cheap labour, land, and tax costs, Mississippi was successful in recruiting many northeastern firms.

Perhaps more important than and beyond a mere marketing effort, the BAWI introduced the notion of tax incentives aimed at firms that would relocate into Mississippi. The dire economic conditions at the time, coupled with the early success of the BAWI programme, along with the relatively new theoretical advances in economics, resulted in numerous states adopting similar types of policies. In essence, the foundation for a new "war between the states" was effectively laid. In one of her latest publications, *Reining in the Competition for Capital*, Markusen (2007) draws five major conclusions about this war.

1   The competition for capital and resulting jobs among jurisdictions is becoming more intense around the world, and the process is least regulated or controlled within the United States.
2   The emergence of site consultants, as an institutional innovation (see above), plays an important role in the growing use of incentives to compete for firm locations. Sometimes these consultants work "both sides of the market simultaneously" (p. viii).

3 Economists recommendations or views on this matter range from completely banning or outlawing incentive competition; allowing the market to work along the lines of Tiebout's sorting; and that using properly established incentives will create beneficial outcomes in the form of welfare improvement.

4 Opportunity costs tend not to be considered at all in the incentives "game".

5 While policy reforms to limit such competition have succeeded in other parts of the world, the same is unlikely to happen in the US in the foreseeable future.

As outlined in Shaffer et al. (2006), the progression of state and local economic development policies can be described in terms of "waves". The strategy of industry recruitment, or "smokestack chasing", embodied in the Mississippi BAWI approach is often reviewed to as the first wave. Today three waves of strategy development have been acknowledged, and the search for the next or fourth wave has become akin to the search for the golden grail in economic development. Because of the impact of Porter's cluster concepts, one could reasonably argue that clusters are the fourth wave. Beyond tax abatements, other first-wave strategies include offering low-cost sites, low-interest loans, and training funds, to name a few. The second wave of economic development strategies emphasized homegrown economic activity (entrepreneurship, expansion, and retention). Activities associated with these types of strategies were increasing investment capital for local firms, development of incubators, technical assistance for local firms, revolving loan funds, and tax increment financing.

The second wave of economic development strategies emphasized homegrown economic activity (expansion and retention). Much of this refocus in policies can be traced to the work of Birch (1979, 1981), who asked a very simple question: does economic growth flow from large or small firms? His conclusion pointed to small firms. This caused many economic development policy-makers and practitioners to question not only the effectiveness of recruitment efforts but also the role of small businesses in their own portfolio of policies. Many development agencies reevaluated their efforts and found that they could be more efficient and effective if they focused on small to medium-sized businesses that were already in their communities. Activities associated with these types of strategies were increasing investment capital for local firms, development of incubators, technical assistance for local firms, revolving loan funds, and tax increment financing.

Third-wave economic development strategies emphasize public-private partnerships. Here the focus is on increasing competitiveness. In third-wave strategies, government agencies and economic development organizations worry about creating networks to leverage capital, investing in human resources, and high-skill and well-paying jobs. Reasons for emphasizing third-wave development strategies are that the delivery of economic development service was fragmented and the customers were expected to incur the cost of integrating across government silos. Third-wave strategies attempt to integrate different programmes for the customer. Another key feature of third-wave strategies was to allow for differentiation instead of assuming that *one-size-fits-all* strategies (endemic to first- and second-wave thinking) were sufficient. Yet other reasons for third-wave strategies include issues of scale, in particular the concept of agglomeration economies. The notion of agglomeration economies within a spatial world is at the core of the Porter approach to economic cluster development. Some have suggested that Porter's cluster development is the fourth wave of development, yet others maintain that it is but one dimension of the third wave.

Focus on business climate

A phrase that is widely used in economic development but seldom fully understood is that of business climate. The phrase, much like culture or sub-urban sprawl, has no clear definition, although everyone knows what it means. The typical connotation of business climate focuses on taxation levels and the regulatory climate. Generally, lower taxes and a weaker regulatory climate translate into a better business climate, although residents and businesses do understand clearly that superior public services such as clean parks, high levels of public safety, and well-maintained roads come at a cost. In other words, the focus of business climate discussions is on the public sector's role in economic development and growth, while implicitly acknowledging Tiebout's key insight about how consumers or residents choose their desired locations by trading off different variables.

While taxation levels and the regulatory climate are important, they represent only a small part of the components that define a community's business climate. In the broadest sense, a community's business climate speaks to the attitudes of the community toward change, experimentation, entrepreneurship, institutional capacity, and communication levels. Business climate is a specific way in which to discuss what Cornelia and Jan Flora (1990, 1993) call entrepreneurial social infrastructure and Putnam refers to as social capital (see also Rupasingha et al. 2002, 2006). This specifically relates to the rules that govern how a community functions. These can be formal rules that are established by governments and informal rules that are established by the culture of the community. Formal rules range from land use, signage, and environmental regulations to workplace safety and child labour laws. Informal rules are dictated by society and culture and speak to what is socially acceptable and not acceptable.

Business climate speaks to both formal and informal rules. Unfortunately, because the formal rules are determined and enforced by government, it is easy to focus attention on only those rules. In essence, formal rules are written down and can be easily pointed to in economic development discussions. Informal rules, or the culture of the community, are more difficult to pin down, debate, and alter in the short term, when business decisions are often made. For example, in some communities, failure is frowned upon and to fail breaks an informal rule. This type of informal rule can place a serious barrier on entrepreneurial activity. The research suggests that most successful entrepreneurs fail three to five times before their businesses are successful. If failure is unacceptable in the community, what does this say about the business climate within the community?

Alternatively, for some communities, the culture of success is ill-defined. Rising above the average of the community is discouraged and success is not rewarded. There is a perverse peer pressure not to succeed. Communities in which being average is expected have a poor business climate regardless of what the public sector does in terms of taxation and regulatory policy. These types of expectations within the community are powerful forces and can overpower any public policy. Goetz and Freshwater (2001) provide state-level estimates of entrepreneurial climate using the notion of Solow residuals calculated from an econometric model of entrepreneurial activity.

A narrower way of thinking about the business climate of a community hinges on the quality of the relationship between the private and public sectors in pursuing community economic development. What is the nature of the partnership? Is it harmonious or turbulent? While there is rarely complete agreement between business and government, high-quality business climates foster a situation in which businesses accept their social responsibilities and government supports legitimate business needs. In essence, the business climate is but one small part of the overall culture of the community. Unfortunately, the full richness of this relationship is often collapsed into the simplistic tax burden issue.

Many communities have found that informal business visitation programmes, in which a small team of elected officials visit local business owners, can vastly improve the business climate of the community. Here the visitation team simply introduces itself to the business owners, extends its appreciation for the businesses' contribution to the community, and asks how the community can help the businesses. This builds a stronger sense of community, which in itself enhances the business climate. In addition, informal business visitation programmes can identify potential problems within the set of formal rules that local public officials may be in a position to address.

In the end, business climate speaks to the social capital of the community, the ability of the public and private sector to work together, and the flexibility of rules, both formal and informal, to be adjusted when economic opportunities present themselves. Is the public sector willing to listen to the concerns of the private sector? Is the private sector willing to compromise on their plans if they reduce the well-being of the residents of the community? If there are barriers to change imposed from outside the community, such as federal regulations, can the public and private sectors form partnerships to address these barriers?

Within the business literature, this type of partnership is parallel to the relationship between workers and management. Do workers and management approach their positions as "us versus them"? A wealth of new age business management studies speaks to the importance of team work where workers and managers work in teams to improve the efficiency, productivity, and profitability of the business. In essence, the business climate of the community is an exact parallel to this notion of teams within business.

Rules are a key component of community economic development. In the most basic sense, they govern how we bring markets and resources together through decision-making across space. Rules are the social, political, and legal tenets that must be accounted for in the use of resources, in economic exchanges, and in the distribution of rewards. They define what is possible, and what is illegal, which behaviours are acceptable and which are unacceptable, which benefits and/or costs are legitimate public issues and which are private. Rules and institutions define who receives the income generated from the use of resources, thus facilitating or hampering economic development. Economic institutions provide decision rules for adjusting and accommodating conflicting demands among different interest groups within society.

Concluding thoughts

Economic development policy has a long history, with early efforts in the US dating back to colonial times. But subnational efforts did not really come into focus until after WWII. As we have seen, many of the policy approaches have changed over time as our understanding of the growth and development process has changed and matured. Some analysts have talked in terms of waves of strategies. But, unfortunately, economic development policies have tended to be piecemeal, subject to fads and to extreme political pressures. The overriding question boils down to this: what is the proper role of government? (Krueger 1993.)

First, the government must do what the private sector cannot do. This includes defining rules such as contract law, private property rights, patent laws, and, increasingly, intellectual property rights. It also must define and regulate institutions such as the courts. Second, government should step into the market when private firms will fail or not enter at all. This includes public infrastructure investments, investments in education including K–12, technical schools, universities, and continuing educational opportunities, and the promotion of basic research where questionable returns on investment may hinder private firms from investing. Third, government inevitably finds itself "picking winners" in the name of economic growth and development. Clearly, this is the most controversial aspect of past and present economic development thought and practice.

References

Baumol, W.J., Litan, R.E., and Schramm, C.J. (2007) *Good Capitalism – Bad Capitalism and the Economics of Growth and Prosperity*, New Haven and London: Yale University Press.

Birch, D. (1979) *The Job Generating Process*, Cambridge, MA: MIT Programme on Neighborhood and Regional Change.

——. (1981) "Who creates jobs?" *Public Interest*, Fall: 3–14

Burton, H.J. (1998) "A reconsideration of import substitution", *Journal of Economic Literature*, 36(2): 903–36

Buss, T.F. (1999a) "The case against targeted industry strategies" (Forum), *Economic Development Quarterly*, 13(4): 339–56.

——. (1999b) "To target or not to target, that's the question: a response to Wiewel and Finkel", *Economic Development Quarterly*, 13(4): 365–70.

Eicher, C.K., and Staatz, J.M. (1998) *Agricultural Development in the Third World* (Third Ed.), Baltimore, MD: Johns Hopkins University Press.

Eisinger, P.K. (1998) *The Rise of the Entrepreneurial State: State and Local Economic Development Policies in the United States*, Madison: University of Wisconsin Press.

——. (1995) "State economic development in the 1990s: politics and policy learning", *Economic Development Quarterly*, 9: 146–58.

Feser, E., and Isserman, A. (in press) "The rural role in national value chains, *Regional Studies*.

Flora, C.B., and Flora, J.L. (1990) "Developing entrepreneurial rural communities", *Sociological Practice*, 8: 197–207.

——. (1993) "Entrepreneurial social infrastructure: a necessary ingredient", *Annals, American Association of Political and Social Sciences*, 529(September): 48–58.

Goetz, S.J., and Freshwater, D. (2001) "State-level measures of entrepreneurship and a preliminary measure of entrepreneurial climate", *Economic Development Quarterly*, 15(1): 58–70.

Goldar, B. (1986) "Import substitution, industrial concentration and productivity growth in Indian manufacturing", *Oxford Bulletin of Economics and Statistics*, 48(2): 143–64.

Gore, C. (2002) "The rise and fall of the Washington Consensus as a paradigm for developing countries", *World Development*, 28: 789–804.

Hayami, Y., and Ruttan, V.W. (1971) *Agricultural Development, an International Perspective*, Baltimore: Johns Hopkins University Press.

Honadle, B.W. (2001) "Rural development policy in the United States: beyond the cargo cult mentality". *Journal of Regional Analysis and Policy*, 32: 93–108.

Kanbur, R. (2008) "Globalization, growth and distribution: framing the questions", Working paper no. 5, Washington, DC: Commission on Growth and Development, The World Bank.

Krueger, A.O. (1993) "Virtuous and vicious circles in economic development", *American Economic Review*, 83(2): 351–55.

Lucas, R.E. Jr. (1988) "On the mechanics of economic development", *Journal of Monetary Economics*, 22: 3–42.

Malizia, E.E., and Feser, E.J. (1999) *Understanding Local Economic Development*, New Brunswick, NJ: Center for Urban Policy Research.

Marion, B.W., and the NC 117 Committee. (1986) *The Organization and Performance of the U.S. Food System*, Lexington, MA: Lexington Books.

Markusen, A. (editor) (2007) *Reining in the Competition for Capital*, Kalamazoo, MI: W.E. Upjohn Institute for Employment Research.

Mellor, J.W. (1976) *The New Economics of Growth: A Strategy for India and the Developing World*, Ithaca, NY and London: Cornell University Press.

Osborne, D., and Gaebler, T. (1992) *Reinventing Government: How the Entrepreneurial Spirit is Transforming the Public Sector*, Reading, MA: Addison-Wesley.

Persky, J., Ranney, D., and Wiewel, W. (1993) "Import substitution and local economic development", *Economic Development Quarterly*, 7(1): 18–29.

Reeder, R. (1995, Sept.) "Industrial targeting", in *Business Assistance and Rural Development*, pp. 51–65, Washington DC: Economic Research Service, Rural Economy Edition, US Dept. of Agriculture.

Romer, P. (1986) "Increasing returns and long-run economic growth", *Journal of Political Economics*, 94: 1002–38.

Rupasingha, A., Goetz, S.J., and Freshwater, D. (2002) "Social and institutional factors as determinants of economic growth: evidence from the United States counties, *Papers in Regional Science*, 81: 139–55.

——. (2006) "The production of social capital in US counties", *Journal of Socio-Economics*, 35: 83–101.

Schultz, T.W. (June 1976) *Transforming Traditional Agriculture (World Food Supply)*, Ayer Co Pub.

Shaffer, R.E. (2001) "Building a nation rural policy and the National Rural Development Partnership", *Journal of Regional Analysis and Policy*, 31: 77–91.

Shaffer, R.E., Deller, S.C., and Marcouiller, D. (2006) "Rethinking community economic development", *Economic Development Quarterly*, 20: 59–74.

Sugden, R., and Wilson, J.R. (2002) "Economic development in the shadow of the consensus: a strategic decision-making approach", *Contributions to Political Economy*, 21: 111–34.

Sugden, R. Wei, P., and Wilson, J.R. (2006) "Clusters, governance and the development of local economies: a framework for case studies", in C. Pitelis, R. Sugden, and J.R. Wilson (eds), *Clusters and Globalisation*, pp. 61–95, Northampton, MA: Edward Elgar.

Williamson, J. (1993) "Democracy and the 'Washington Consensus' ", *World Development*, 21: 1329–36.

World Bank. (1993) *The East Asian Miracle: Economic Growth and Public Policy*, New York: Oxford University Press.

——. (2008) "The growth report: strategies for sustained growth and inclusive development (final report)", Commission on Growth and Development, Washington, DC. Online. Available HTTP: <http://www.growthcommission.org/index.php?option=com_content&task=view&id=96&Itemid=169> (accessed June 11, 2008).

3 Industry clusters and industry targeting

Martin Shields, David Barkley, and Mary Emery

Introduction

The US economy is undergoing a well-documented structural change as a result of market globalization, revolutionary technological changes, and advances in production practices. Innovation, adaptability, and entrepreneurship are recognized as keys to the sustainable development of companies and regions in the New Economy where product life cycles are short and competition is intense (Acs 2002). A popular public policy response to the new competitive environment is to create "regional production systems" within which existing businesses become more productive and new business start-ups are encouraged.

Porter (2001) argues that a firm's productivity will be enhanced if it operates in a regional business environment characterized by a concentration of competing and cooperating firms, high quality and specialized inputs, supporting industries and institutions, and sophisticated and demanding local customers. Many state and local programmes designed to foster these regional production systems focus on the promotion of existing or emerging industry clusters (NGA 2002). Porter et al. (2004: 63) even propose that "viewing regional economies in terms of clusters is central to understanding the competitiveness of rural areas and how it can be improved". Chapter 5 by Woodward and Guimarães contains a more detailed discussion and critique of Porter's influential work.

In this chapter, we provide an overview of the industry cluster strategy for regional economic development and the role of industry targeting in helping regions and states identify innovative clusters and design policies for cluster growth. Our discussion first defines industry clusters and provides a summary of the advantages and disadvantages to a clustering strategy. Next, we introduce the concept of industry targeting and the applications of industry targeting to industry cluster development. Our discussion of industry clusters and targeting focuses on their role in the economic growth of smaller regions. This is an important distinction as smaller cities and rural areas may not have sophisticated the interindustry networking opportunities (urbanization economies) available in larger metropolitan areas. Thus, access to cluster-related benefits takes on added importance to micropolitan businesses and regions.

Although the term "cluster" has entered the vernacular relatively recently, the notion of targeting industries as an economic development strategy for small regions is not new (see, e.g., Chapter 2). Indeed, rural areas have long emphasized business recruitment as an important component of their development efforts. One important question, then, is how does a targeted industry cluster strategy differ from previous efforts, if at all? We discuss this question in detail in our concluding comments.

Why industry clusters?

Industry clusters identified

Porter (2001: 7) defines clusters as "geographically close groups of interconnected companies and associated institutions in a particular field linked by common technologies and skills". An important aspect is that spatial concentration enhances national and global competitive advantages across firms. These advantages arise from a variety of interfirm spillovers of factors such as technology and knowledge, as well as region-level agglomeration effects, such as shared input suppliers.

Although industry clusters are common in smaller regions, each cluster is unique because of differences in sizes, core industries, and interfirm relationships. For example, a cluster may consist of firms engaged in producing similar products, such as log homes (Montana) or houseboats (Kentucky). Establishments in these "horizontally" organized clusters benefit from the availability of a pool of skilled and specialized labour (Kim et al. 2000). Clusters also may comprise establishments in value chains (car assembly plants and suppliers) or firms linked by their reliance on similar specialized services (e.g., research and development facilities or education and training services). Finally, McCann (1995) suggests that some industry clusters result from establishments independently selecting the same location because that location provides proximity to a shared resource or market. In this case, the establishments may have little interaction and experience few benefits from locating near one another.

Markusen (1996) also proposes that industry clusters may be categorized into four general types according to their industrial structure: Marshallian, hub-and-spoke, satellite platforms, and state-anchored clusters (Table 3.1). Marshallian clusters are composed primarily of locally owned, small- and medium-sized businesses in the more information and technology intensive industries. The information technology cluster in New York is one example.

Hub-and-spoke clusters are dominated by one or several large firms surrounded by related input suppliers and service providers. The Toyota Motor Manufacturing plant in rural Georgetown, Kentucky is a notable example of this. After the plant opened in 1988, the region witnessed a significant

Table 3.1 Markusen's typology of industry clusters

Cluster Type	Characteristics of Member Firms	Intracluster Interdependencies	Employment Growth Prospects
Marshallian	Small and medium locally owned firms	Substantial interfirm trade, collaboration, strong institutional support	Dependent on synergies, economies provided by cluster
Hub-and-spoke	One or several large firms with numerous smaller suppliers and service firms	Cooperation between large firms, smaller suppliers on terms of large firms	Dependent on growth prospects of large (hub) firms
Satellite platforms	Medium and large branch plants	Minimum interfirm trade, networking	Dependent on region's ability to recruit, retain branch plants
State-anchored	Large public or non-profit entity and related, supplying service firms	Restricted to buy-sell relationships between public entity, suppliers	Dependent on region's ability to expand political support for public facility

Source: Markusen (1996).

increase in local suppliers related to the automotive giant. Satellite platforms consist primarily of the branches of large multiplant companies. These differ from hub-and-spoke clusters, in that the branch plants tend to be relatively large and independent. Thus, the availability of local input suppliers is not as critical.

Finally, in the case of state-anchored industry clusters, the local regional economy is dominated by a large public activity (e.g., university, military base, or government office) and the supplier and service sectors that develop around them. Notable small communities include Corvallis, Oregon and State College, Pennsylvania, where large state universities serve as the economy's lifeblood, through both direct impacts and technology related spin-offs.

As we show in Table 3.1, each of the above cluster types offers different interfirm interdependencies and prospects for growth. Each cluster type also requires a different policy focus for improving the competitiveness of the cluster.

Industry cluster advantages and shortcomings

Targeted industrial development programmes at the industry cluster level are founded on the perception or belief that cluster growth will provide greater local economic development benefits than less focused efforts (Barkley and Henry 1997). Three principal advantages accrue to establishments in clusters and their host regions that enhance the competitiveness of both the firms and regions:

- Industry clusters provide production and marketing cost savings (localization economies) to member firms. Sources of potential cost savings include access to specialized input and service providers; a larger pool of trained, specialized workers (for example, software engineers in Silicon Valley); and public infrastructure investments and financial markets geared to the needs of the industry.
- Industry clustering provides establishments with a greater ability to focus on their core activities and to adopt new production technologies and organizations (NGA 2002). Highly competitive product markets mandate rapid adaptability to market changes, and clusters provide a more conducive environment for change.
- Industry clustering facilitates the development of linkages, cooperation, and collaboration among area firms. Interfirm networking enhances information sharing in marketing, new product development, and technological upgrading. Rosenfeld (2002: 7) argues that "Innovation, imitation, and entrepreneurship are what propel virtually all competitive clusters". Intracluster networking helps provide the knowledge spillovers critical to product development and new firm spinoffs. The importance of clusters to new firm start-ups is supported by Gabe's (2003) findings that new business activity in an industry is positively associated with the region's industry cluster size.

The potential benefits from cluster development have encouraged many states and regions to structure their industrial development programmes around clusters. For example, Pennsylvania has identified nine industry clusters that are the focus of the Commonwealth's workforce development programmes. This strategy, however, has three potential pitfalls and shortcomings.

First, regions will have difficulty "picking winners", i.e., identifying industry clusters that best fit their local economies. The successful development of a competitive industry cluster is most probable if a regional competitive advantage exists, often the result of past industry location patterns. Yet, potential problems facing smaller regions are summed up by Porter et al. (2004: 61), who acknowledge that "There is still no rich understanding of the composition and evolution of rural economies at the industry cluster level ...". A further complication to "picking winners" is that the political process will be "too inclusive" rather than "too selective" when selecting industries for cluster promotion (Peck and McGuinness 2003). The consequence is a dilution of resources available for cluster development programs. For example, Pennsylvania's targeted industries encompass nearly 69 per cent of the Commonwealth's total employment.

The second shortcoming is that many regions, especially smaller ones, have clusters in declining industries or no clusters at all. For such regions, it may not be prudent, or even possible, to pursue cluster strategies. In these situations, Rosenfeld (2002: 13) suggests that development practitioners look for local connections to clusters in adjacent regions or "re-orienting the central theme of the cluster from some commonality of the production process to a commonality related to knowledge, innovation or entrepreneurship".

The third shortcoming is that a focus on cluster development may lead to imbalanced economic development across the region or within segments of the population. Martin and Sunley (2003: 28) argue that "[t]he danger of a cluster-based approach to policy is that it detracts from the need to take a more holistic view of regional development". In their simplest formulations, cluster policies fail to account for other sources of economic prosperity as identified in the literature, such as innovation (Acs 2002), entrepreneurship (Acs and Armington 2003), human capital (Mathur 1999), local quality of life (Deller et al. 2001; Florida 2002), and social capital (Sobe, 2002; Rupasingha et al. 2005). As such, Feldman and Francis (2004: 135) recommend that "[r]ather than target specific industries or technologies, effective state policy might focus on creating conditions that would allow firms to grow and prosper". DeBreschi and Malerba (2001) are more specific and argue that cluster development policies should focus on improving local education and labour quality, infrastructure improvements, and small business development.

In summary, the benefits provided by a successful cluster development strategy will be realized only if the strategy addresses the above shortcomings. A well-designed industry targeting programme can increase the likelihood of cluster development by helping regions identify (1) existing or potential innovative clusters; (2) industries linked to the selected clusters through value chains, labour pools, and technologies; and (3) programmes to enhance innovation and entrepreneurship within the clusters. Next, we provide an overview of targeting methods that regions may adopt to better position themselves to take advantage of cluster-based growth.

Cluster targeting and policy

Over the past 10 years or so, the cluster concept has taken hold among both economic development policy-makers and practitioners. Responding to the 2001 national economic downturn and increased worker insecurity as a result of globalization, it appears that these long-known ideas are moving beyond political rhetoric. Nowadays, key phrases of the cluster vernacular – such as value-chains and agglomeration effects – roll off the tongues of governors, economic development agency heads, and local leaders. Indeed, numerous states and regions have identified key industry clusters to serve as cornerstones of their economic development efforts. For example, like Pennsylvania, Iowa has identified clusters to serve as the basis of its economic development strategy, focusing on bioscience, advanced manufacturing, and information solutions.

Alongside theoretical advances, the cluster concept has enjoyed myriad practical innovations – primarily identification methods. From the resurgence of interest in location quotients to the emergence of neural network analysis, researchers and consultants implement both tested and new techniques in order to help regions recognize local sectors with competitive advantages that can serve as growth engines. In practice, these sectors can range from traditional resource-extractive industries to high-tech manufacturing, from financial services to retail trade.

From a policy perspective, the driving force behind cluster analysis is the desire to identify the sectors, industries, and processes that propel a regional economy. Here, the focus is as much on the cluster's competitive structure (such as interfirm relationships and local capacity) as it is on the products themselves. Once identified, cluster-specific economic policies can be designed to strengthen their performance or tap their potential. For example, a region promoting a food manufacturing cluster might use its workforce development funds to put together a food safety training curriculum for incumbent workers. Or, an industrial development corporation trying to lure a new business might focus its efforts on firms with business service needs similar to those already in place. Here, the goal is to enhance the efficiency of existing resources and processes.

Consequently, one outcome of the rise of cluster-based economic development is a renewed interest in economic targeting. In its modern variant, targeting is the process of identifying the sectors or clusters that are most likely to prosper in a region, given the region's characteristics. Although methods vary, most targeting programmes generally have two components. The first is a means to identify clusters that have a high potential for locating or expanding in the area. In this respect, analysts assess detailed sector trends, particularly with an eye toward how clusters line up with regional characteristics.

The second component is more subjective; it involves narrowing candidates to sectors that provide attractive local economic development impacts, such as future job growth, high wages, contributions to the local tax base, and minimal negative environmental impacts. After assessing potential sectors, regions decide which of these characteristics are most important and target clusters accordingly. In the end, targeting efforts aim to identify a small set of clusters that are the best match given a region's specific capabilities and preferences. These can include both existing and new industries.

Although often derided as "smokestack chasing", a well-defined targeting strategy enables regions to focus their economic development activities. Such efforts usually include recruitment, but also may rely on local business retention and expansion activities, and entrepreneurship, incubation, and small business development programs. Thus, targeting permits a more efficient use of limited economic development resources.

As we already noted, the fact that it is very difficult to "pick winners" is well known. Still, thousands of economic development practitioners and state and local policy-makers work every day on exactly that. Although regional economists tend to look unfavourably on these efforts, there is no reason to expect that this longstanding practice will disappear any time soon.

Accordingly, analysts interested in having a "real world" impact may need to accept a less-than-optimal outcome. Although this is perhaps a disheartening result for purists seeking an ideal solution, policy relevance is an important virtue as well. And, fundamentally, working in this context is not that much of a compromise. Because efficiency remains one of the pillars of economics, regional economists still have much to contribute. For example, they can bring their quantitative skills to bear in helping regions pare down the seemingly infinite list of potential candidates into a more manageable set – call it "conditional efficiency" (i.e., the best outcome in an imperfect world). In the remainder of this chapter, we describe some of the key components of such efforts. More detail is given in the chapters that follow.

Using location quotients in cluster targeting analysis

The location quotient (LQ) is, perhaps, the most prevalent method in use today for identifying existing and potential clusters. A common application of LQs is identifying a region's importing and exporting industries. An exporting industry not only meets the local demand for its products, but also produces enough so as to sell outside of the region. An importing industry is one in which local production levels are insufficient to meet local demand.

The LQ approach is appealing in that it is both intuitive and easy to calculate from readily available data. In practice, this analysis is most informative when using the most disaggregated employment data available for the region (NAICS 3- or 4-digit). The basic formula for the location quotient is:

$$LQ = (\%LEi/\%NEi) = \text{per cent of local employment in industry i divided by the per cent of national employment in industry i.}$$

Simply put, the LQ identifies how local industries stack up against national averages.

When interpreting the data, an LQ greater than 1.0 indicates that the economy is self-sufficient, and may even be exporting the good or service of that particular industry. Any exporting industry might be a strong candidate for further development. Used in conjunction with local expertise, the LQ can help identify industry clusters. Strategies centred on LQ analysis tend to complement their identification methods with qualitative techniques, such as focus groups and interviews with industry experts. This process can help policy-makers interpret aspects of the quantitative research, develop a better picture of the relationships among local industries, and identify similar workforce or infrastructure needs.

Despite its popularity, LQ analysis has several drawbacks in both application and concept. From a practical standpoint, comprehensive LQ analysis relies on data that may not be available for small regions. For example, disclosure rules may mean that employment data are not available in sufficient detail to conduct meaningful cluster analysis. Specifically, government regulations prohibit disclosing employment data when individual firms might be identified. As an example, if there are only one or two firms operating in a particular industry in a given region, the government will not disclose this data through published sources. As this is fairly common in small and rural regions, potential clusters may be missed if analysts lack in-depth knowledge about the economy under scrutiny.

But conceptual problems may be of greater concern. By construction, LQs focus on single industries. Thus, whereas LQ analysis might help identify industries that are regional strengths, LQs do not necessarily identify clusters. This is an important distinction in that the cluster development concept is much broader than the industry development concept. The latter tends to focus on the needs of individual firms, whereas the former considers the entire value chain, the competitive structure within the region, and various local information networks.

Recognizing these shortcomings, analysts weave the LQ approach into more sophisticated cluster identification efforts. For example, David Barkley and Mark Henry's approach at Clemson University (Chapter 10) follows three main steps:

1 Use the LQ to identify industry concentrations within which the region has experienced recent employment growth.
2 Construct value chains for the industry clusters selected in Step 1. Using input-output models, identify industries in the value chains with the greatest linkages to the local industry concentrations.
3 Rank the selected industries from Steps 1 and 2 by expected economic and fiscal impacts on the local economy. Methods for estimating and evaluating impacts are detailed in a recent book on community impact simulation models (Otto et al. 2006).

One key component of their analysis is the use of relative local employment growth rates as a way to identify "promising" industries. An industry with a comparatively high growth rate may indicate an area of competitive advantage.

Fostering serendipity

Despite recent advances in cluster identification methods, the fact remains that most techniques in use today classify, at best, historical and current strengths of the local economy. For example, a typical application of the location quotient method might identify an industry cluster as having an LQ greater than 1.2. By this criterion, in order for any cluster to reveal itself, it must already have a relatively strong presence.

Such an analysis, though useful, can be incomplete or (misleading) for a number of reasons. First, like a mutual fund, past performance is no guarantee of future success – a lesson confirmed by many long-lost rural manufacturing industries. Consequently, relying solely on established industries can be a limiting, or even wrong-headed, strategy.

A related effect of requiring a strong historical presence is that most cluster identification methods are incapable of identifying emerging or potential industries. In today's economy, being first matters. Because most cluster identification algorithms depend on detailed published government employment data, which is often released one year or more after it is collected, it may take several years to recognize important trends.

As a result, cluster analysts often arrive "too late". Rather than helping regions build advantages, the analysts' role is generally one of trying to explain why the cluster emerged. Often unable to do so, we commonly attribute cluster emergence to "serendipity", a wholly unsatisfactory concept.

Furthermore, cluster methods are not predictive. Although analysts have developed a comprehensive set of tools for identifying existing clusters, they offer precious few methods for identifying nascent clusters. In particular, few current approaches look at existing fundamentals of the regional economy with an eye toward identifying hitherto nonexistent clusters. In the dynamic global economy, however, it is likely that economic growth in small regions will be driven by emerging industries at least as much as by existing ones. As a result, the practice of economic development also requires methods for identifying potential. Simply put, regions can no longer count on "getting lucky".

Shields and Vivanco (2003) confront this issue in their "back-of-the-envelope" method for identifying new opportunities for aggregate employment growth in Pennsylvania. They compare employment trends in rural Pennsylvania with rural counties in "similar" states to identify the local industries that are not doing as well as their peers. In pinpointing the industries, three criteria had to be satisfied:

1   The industry needed to exhibit positive employment growth at the US level from 1990 to 2000.
2   The aggregate industry employment growth rate in the rural counties of the comparison states had to exceed the US average.
3   The aggregate industry employment growth rate for the US had to exceed the aggregate growth rate for rural Pennsylvania counties.

In a nutshell, this analysis identifies Pennsylvania industries that are being greatly outperformed by both comparison places and the US. While a methodological cousin of the Barkley and Henry approach, the Shields and Vivanco (2003) model focuses on new targets rather than existing strengths, in essence asking "why not here?"

For more sophisticated efforts, econometric models offer a promising method for identifying emerging or potential industries. For example, Goode and Hastings (1989) and Leatherman et al. (2002) modelled business location decisions taking into account most of the variables identified as important in business growth. Goode and Hasting's Northeast Industrial Targeting system modeled the requirements of 69 aggregate regional manufacturing sectors, using 730 non-metropolitan communities in the northeast United States. Leatherman and Kasten's Plains Economic Targeting System (PETS, see Chapter 7) matches industry requirements of 78 industry sectors to the characteristics of 414 counties in the six Great Plains states. In both models, results were used to identify the industries that offer the highest probability of success for each region, with subsequent development efforts focused on those industries.

Typically, economic development professionals apply these results to industrial attraction strategies. Today, the challenge many small cities and regions face requires developing strategies to help existing business use these results to expand existing markets or products. In such cases, the resources that go into attending conventions and making calls now go into taking time to visit local firms and creating coaching relationships that help them be more resourceful in understanding and using the results of the analysis.

Concluding comments and a reality check

Are clusters simply "old wine in new bottles"? In other words, what is it that distinguishes cluster development from its failed predecessors? This is a valid question. Prima facie, the cluster targeting strategy can be characterized as an effort to identify the sectors that are the sources of local competitive advantage. Once identified, limited local economic development dollars are spent to grow these sectors. This appears to be analogous to historical rural development initiatives aimed at attracting branch manufacturing plants.

But the cluster approach is much richer. In Chapter 5, Woodward and Guimarães introduce the "Porter Diamond", a diagram that captures the key relationships among firms, suppliers, and institutions that characterize economic clusters. The cluster approach to economic development policy recognizes all of these actors and builds appropriate strategies for each of their interactions. For example, it sets the stage for active dialogue between local businesses and government organizations, such as workforce development centers, and between supplier networks and regional universities. Overall, then, a cluster effort is much more holistic than policies built around individual firms.

In the remainder of this book, other authors introduce various methods for identifying and evaluating the efficacy of clusters. However, it is important to recognize that choosing the targeted industries is as much a political decision as an economic one. Comprehensive industry targeting programmes are likely to involve business, labour, environmental organizations, and government, each with their own goals, interests, and stakeholders. And these may often be at odds. For example, commercial and residential real estate developers may favor large-scale business attraction efforts, because such growth will likely push up the value of land as new people and businesses move into the region. Municipal officials in smaller regions, however, might feel political pressure from current residents to "maintain the local quality of life", which often translates into opposition to growth.

Thus, analysts need to be mindful that analysis is just one component of efforts to identify clusters that may succeed locally and in the national or global market place. Achieving consensus among interested parties, or at least enough agreement to enact and carry out expensive public programs, remains a major challenge. Accordingly, an important part of any targeted regional cluster initiative is an inclusive strategic plan.

References

Acs, Z.J. (2002) *Innovation and the Growth of Cities*, Northampton, MA: Edward Elger.

Acs, Z.J., and Armington, C. (2003, January) "Endogenous growth and entrepreneurial activity in cities", US Bureau of Census paper CES 0-3-02, Washington, DC: US Bureau of Census.

Barkley, D.L., and Henry, M.S. (1997) "Rural industrial development: to cluster or not to cluster?" *Review of Agricultural Economics*, 2: 308–25.

Breschi, S., and Malerba, F. (2001) "Geography of innovation and economic clustering", *Industrial and Corporate Change*, 4: 817–33.

Deller, S.C., Tsai, T-H., Marcouiller, D.W., and English, D.B.K. (2001) "The role of amenities and quality of life in rural economic growth", *American Journal of Agricultural Economics*, 2: 352–65.

Feldman, M.P., and Francis, J.L. (2004) "Homegrown solutions: fostering cluster formation", *Economic Development Quarterly*, 2: 127–37.

Gabe, T. (2003) "Local industry agglomeration and new business activity", *Growth and Change*, 1: 17–39.

Goode, F.M., and Hastings, S.E. (1989) "The effect of transportation service on the location of manufacturing plants in nonmetropolitan and small metropolitan communities," in William R. Gillis (ed), *Profitability and Mobility in Rural America: Successful Approaches to Tackling Rural Transportation Problems*, University Park: Penn State University Press.

Johnson, T.G., Otto, D., and Deller, S.C. (editors), (2006) *Community Policy Analysis Modeling*, Oxford: Blackwell.

Kim, Y., Barkley, D.L., and Henry, M.S. (2000) "Industry characteristics linked to establishment concentrations in nonmetropolitan areas", *Journal of Regional Science*, 2: 231–59.

Leatherman, J., Howard, D.J., and Kastens, T.L. (2002) "Improved prospects for rural development: an industrial targeting system for the great plains", *Review of Agricultural Economics*, 24: 59–77.

Markusen, A. (1996) "Sticky places in slippery space: a typology of industrial districts", *Economic Geography*, 3: 293–313.

Martin, R., and Sunley, P. (2003) "Deconstructing clusters: chaotic concept or policy panacea?" *Journal of Economic Geography*, 3: 5–35.

Mathur, V.K. (1999) "Human capital-based strategy for regional economic development", *Economic Development Quarterly*, 3: 203–16.

McCann, P. (1995) "Rethinking the economics of locations and agglomerations", *Urban Studies* 563–577.

National Governors Association (NGA) (2002) *A Governor's Guide to Cluster-Based Economic Development*, Washington, DC. Online. Available HTTP: <http://www.nga.org>.

Peck, F., and McGuinness, D. (2003) "Regional development agencies and cluster strategies: engaging the knowledgebase in the north of England", *Local Economy*, 1: 49–62.

Porter, M.E. (2001) *Cluster Innovation: Regional Foundations of U.S. Competitiveness*, Washington, DC: Council of Competitiveness.

Porter, M.E., Katels, C.H.M, Miller, K., and Bryden, R.T. (2004) *Competitiveness in Rural and U.S. Regions: Learning and Research Agenda*, Cambridge, MA: Institute for Strategy and Competitiveness, Harvard Business School.

Rosenfeld, S.A. "Creating smart systems: a guide to cluster strategies in less favored regions", paper presented at European Union-Regional Innovation Strategies, April 2002.

Shields, M., and Vivanco, C. (2003) *Rural Pennsylvania's "New-Economy": Identifying the Causes of Growth and Developing New Opportunities*, Center for Rural Pennsylvania.

Sobel, J. (2002, March) "Can we trust social capital?" *Journal of Economic Literature*, 139–54.

4   Overview of firm location theory and TRED

Steven C. Deller

Introduction

The use of targeted regional economic development (TRED) is based on theoretical understandings of how regional economies are structured and how firms make location and expansion decisions. Firms make these decisions so as to maximize profits through minimizing the costs of operations while maximizing the demand for their goods and services (Shaffer et al. 2004). All of this takes place within a spatial setting. Targeted development policies as well as the analytical tools that are employed to identify potential industries to target for attention have generally focused on the two special cases of the general profit maximization problem. In classical location theory associated with Weber, Lösch, Hirschman, and Vernon, these include cost minimization and demand maximization. This is the underlying theoretical framework for the work of Leatherman and Kastens (Chapter 7), Cader et al. (Chapter 8), and Davis and Harris (Chapter 9). Firms can be grouped into these two special cases depending on the nature of the structure of demand. For some types of firms, the location of the firm itself does not influence the demand for its products. These types of firms make location and expansion decisions based solely on costs of production. As Deller and Goetz (Chapter 2) outline, the first "wave" of economic development policies focused on these types of firms, primarily basic-type industries from export-base theory such as manufacturing, by trying to market themselves as low-cost locales and by offering tax and other cost-related incentives. The policy of "smokestack chasing" is strongly rooted in the theory of firm location through cost minimization.

For other types of firms, such as retail and many service firms, the location decision has a strong impact on the revenue-generating capacity of the firm. The microeconomic foundations of central place theory tell us that in a spatial world there will be a unique and predictable pattern of these types of firms across the economic landscape. Increasingly, many communities are attempting to rebuild downtowns by targeting businesses on the basis of the firm location theory of demand maximization. Targeting tools such as threshold analysis (see, for example, Deller and Harris 1993; Hustedde et al.

1993), trade area analysis (see, for example, Deller et al. 1992), spatial analysis in the spirit of Reilly's Law of Retail Gravitation and Huff Probability Contours (see, for example, Holden and Deller 1993), are all based on this common theoretical foundation.

An aspect of firm location that relates to regional uniqueness is based on the productivity and availability of primary factors of production. The importance of primary factor resources provides a basis for the concept of *regional comparative advantage*. As outlined by Woodward and Guimarães (Chapter 5), this notion complements the notion of clusters. Traditionally, these have been identified to include land, labour, and capital. Regional advantages begin to surface when we relax the spatial assumption of a featureless plane to account for differences in the endowments of primary factors of production. Factor endowments, factor productivities, and factor markets differ from one region to the next. In this classical regional advantage framework, different factor resource endowments and productivities lead to relative factor scarcities. These factor productivity advantages reflect unique characteristics of a region's land, labour, and capital endowments. For example, advantages in land productivity can reflect climate, growing season, and/or soil characteristics. Advantages in labour productivity could reflect high skill levels and/or large workforce numbers. Advantages in financial capital productivity could reflect lower regional investment risk because of safer, more secure, or supportive political systems. Where factor resources are more productive, the natural tendency is for increased specialization to occur based on production that relies on those factors that are relatively more productive.

The framework of comparative advantage in factor resources provides another reason why regions tend to exhibit production cost differences. In regions with highly productive and large labour forces, this relative production advantage leads to a cost advantage as outlined below in the discussion of cost minimization. Likewise, regions endowed with rich land resources and low-risk capital enjoy relative advantages. With increased specialization, trade can act to aggregate regional advantages to higher overall levels of productivity across space. The benefit of trade is to allow increased consumption of the good in which the region is relatively disadvantaged in producing. This is the standard argument for free trade where prices for all goods and services equilibrate to the point where the region most advantaged in production determines the price of the goods and services sold.

The scope of comparative advantage within classical location theory involves several key issues. First is a region's natural endowment of factor resources. These include the initial endowment and availability of land, labour, and capital. They reflect the existing climatic conditions (temperature, precipitation) and topography (mountains, rivers, etc.). Next are favourable production (firm) conditions outlined earlier in this chapter that focus on production inputs (backward linkages or cost-minimizing components) and markets for outputs (forward linkages or demand maximization components). Also as discussed earlier, transportation considerations of regions (such as infrastructure) lead to transportation and marketing cost advantages. Proximity to centres of research leads to technological advantages. Good examples of this can be found where research parks founded by institutions of higher education provide centers of innovation and lead the development of high-technology sectors.

In a more latent way, two additional aspects delineate the scope of regional comparative advantage. First, as outlined above, institutional advantages can exist that speak to issues of production risk. These include the underlying stability of political institutions building on our often overlooked rule of law and order. Regions without sound and equitably enforced legal structures often suffer from economic disadvantage. The second latent aspect that relates to the scope of regional comparative advantage is quality of life. Amenity factors of regions affect how individuals make locational decisions. Also, firms can use a region's amenity base as an issue in location and thereby affect where labour and capital become employed.

Regional advantages play a part in the previously described process of a firm's decision to maximize profits through minimizing costs and maximizing revenues. The initial endowment and underlying productivity of factor resources combined with the availability of these resources and the knowledge of their use lead to competitive opportunities for firms and increased specialization of regional output. Indeed, these regional comparative advantages are an integral part of the notion of clusters discussed in more detail later in this chapter. But it is important to note, as Asheim et al. (2006) observed, that the notion of clusters is not a competing theory of the neoclassical view of firm location but rather is complementary. Indeed, Porter makes links with the classical location theory associated with Weber, Lösch, Hirschman, and Vernon, concluding that "[t]he economic theory of location shows how firms will locate close to each other to gain access to the broadest array of customers" (Porter 1990: 789).

The general neoclassical profit maximization problem

The most general problem facing the firm is a situation in which its consumers and suppliers are scattered across a homogenous economic plane that is not complicated by natural barriers such as mountains, rivers, or valleys that create transportation bottlenecks, or institutional barriers such as political boundaries. The firm is faced with the locational choice that places the firm somewhere on the economic plane in a manner that maximizes profits. The firm does this by minimizing the transportation costs of shipping input supplies to the firm and maximizing the potential market demand for their good or service. The profit maximization approach to location decisions declares that businesses select the site from which the number of buyers whose purchases are required for maximum sales can be served at the least possible total costs (Gabszewicz and Thisse 1986;

McCann 2002). It is important to note that this site need not be the lowest total cost site possible, but rather a site from which monopolistic control over buyers makes this site more profitable than a lower cost site. An individual business can offer a delivered price to buyers at less than competitors' prices. This approach recognizes the interaction between demand for the firm's product and the cost of production in site selection. Typically, the firm believes one of these factors is more important than the other, and it focuses on either maximized revenue or minimized costs first. Other factors enter the decision only after that initial choice has been made.

To help see how the profit maximization problem facing the firm plays out, let's formalize the problem and examine two special cases: cost minimization and demand maximization. Assume that a single firm produces one good, using a number of inputs shipped from different locations, and the output is shipped to a number of markets. This firm produces a good that is also offered for sale by a large number of competing firms; hence, the firm is in a market that can be described as competitive. In our spatial world, however, firms have some flexibility in setting their own prices. In a spatial world, firms compete through effective prices, where effective prices reflect not only the costs of production but also transportation costs. For example, the effective price paid by a consumer for a pint of milk is composed of two parts: the price at the store plus the cost of travelling to the store to make the purchase. Stores offering milk for sale compete directly by paying attention to the price at the store, but embedded in the price to the consumer is the cost of travelling to the store. The consumer selects the store with the lowest travel cost, which is likely to be the store closest to the customer.

To formalize the firm's problem, we define demand, production and transportation costs using the following terms:

Π = profit
P_i = price charged at market $i = 1 \ldots m$
$D_i(P_i)$ = demand for the firm's product at market $i = 1 \ldots m$
s^i = spatial location of market $i = 1 \ldots m$
$t(s,s^i)$ = cost of transporting one unit of the good from firm location s to market location s^i
f = fixed costs facing the firm to produce the good
v = constant marginal cost of producing one unit of the good
x_i = production inputs from market $i = 1 \ldots n$
$d(s,s^i)$ = cost of transporting one unit of input x_i from market location s^i to firm location s
$q(x_i)$ = output level of the firm

The firm produces one good (q), which is sold in m separate markets (s^i) and uses n separate inputs (x_i) shipped from different markets. In a spaceless or aspatial world, the firm's maximized profits are:

$$\Pi = \sum_{i=1}^{m} P_i D_i(P_i) - f - vq(x_i) \tag{1}$$

The firm has one decision: what price (P_i) to charge at each separate market. Once a price has been established, say P^*, the amount of the good sold at each market is determined by its respective demand function $D_i(P^*)$. Total revenue is simply the sum of all sales across the m separate markets, or $\Sigma 3_{I=1\,\ldots\,m} P_i D_i(P_i)$. Total cost of production is the fixed cost of production (f) plus marginal cost (v) times the quantity produced (q), or $f + vq(x_i)$. What we have is simply price times quantity minus costs of production.

Placing the firm in a spatial world where it must balance not only prices (P_i) at each of the output markets, but also transportation costs of shipping both inputs to the firm and output to markets, makes for the more relevant problem to targeting efforts. The firm does this by selecting a location (s) somewhere on our economic plane that minimizes transportation costs. Transportation costs can be expressed as:

$$\sum_{i=1}^{m} t(s,s^i) D_i(P_i) + \sum_{i=1}^{n} d(s,s^i) x_i \tag{2}$$

which is the sum of total transportation costs of shipping the firm's product to m separate markets plus the total transportation costs of shipping n inputs to the firm from n separate markets. This is traditionally known as Weber's problem.

To better understand the transportation problem, assume that the firm has three output markets $(m = 3)$ as well as three input markets $(n = 3)$ and that those markets overlap. Graphically the firm is looking at what is known as the Weber triangle on our economic plane (Figure 4.1) (McCann 2002). The firm is selecting a location (s^*), somewhere between the three markets (s^1, s^2, s^3), that will maximize profits. In this simple example, the firm is shipping inputs from three markets $(d(s, s^i))$ to a centrally located physicality, and then shipping its product to – in this case – the same three markets $(t(s,s^i))$.

All the terms needed to formally state the general profit maximization problem are now defined:

$$\Pi = \sum_{i=1}^{m} P_i D_i(P_i) - f - vq(x_i) - \sum_{i=1}^{m} t(s, s^i) D_i(P_i) - \sum_{i=1}^{n} d(s, s^i)x_i \tag{3}$$

where the firm selects a set of prices (P_i) that maximize demand at each market and a location (s) that minimizes transportation costs. The number of output markets (m) need not be equal to the number of input markets (n) and the cost of transporting output $(t(s,s^i))$ need not be the same as the cost of

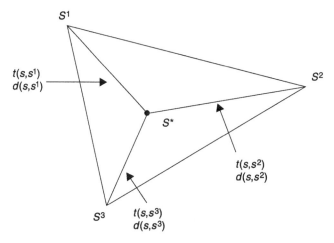

Figure 4.1 Transportation on an economic plane – Weber's problem.

shipping inputs ($d(s,s^i)$). The problem can be made even more general by allowing for multiple outputs (q_i) and multiple firm locations (e.g., multiple plants) (s^j).

When thinking about the location problem, one must keep in mind that the profit maximization problem as expressed in equation (3) is a general theory of firm location with transportation costs, or space, between the firm and its suppliers ($d(s,s^i)$) as well its customers ($t(s,s^i)$). In the profit maximization approach, the firm has not necessarily made its final decision when it identifies the transportation cost minimizing location s^*. By lifting the strict assumption of a homogenous economic plane and allowing for some economic variations across locations, the cost-minimizing firm is said to go through a two-step process. Here, the first step centres on the general location based on transportation costs. The important thing to remember is that once transportation costs are minimized, the firm's attempt to minimize factor of production costs may result in a new location. Once this decision is made, it must pick a specific location. Consider, for example, a cheese producer who decides to locate in the upper Midwest. Once this first decision is made, the producer must find a specific plant location within the region. This is the second step of the two-step process.

One way to think about the second step of the location process is through the use of spatial cost curves, or what are widely referred to as isocosts. Spatial cost curves are a spatial representation of total cost including transportation, labour, land, and capital costs. Space cost curves represent variations in total costs and profitability over space. Any location at which total costs exceed total revenues does not represent a viable long-term location.

Consider Figure 4.2, where a set of hypothetical isocosts are superimposed on the Weber triangle. Each isocost is akin to a production isoquant or

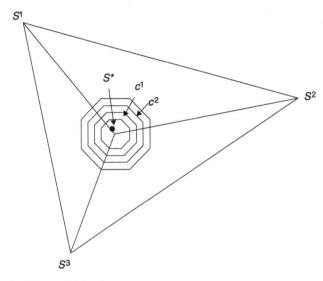

Figure 4.2 Profit maximizing isocosts.

indifference curve from the individual utility maximization problem. The cost to the firm is identical at each site along a particular isocost. At all points along spatial (iso-) cost curve c^1, the cost to the firm is the same. But we do not know *a priori* the relationship between the separate isocost curves; specifically, c^2 may be greater than or less than c^1. Because of variations in labour, land, and capital markets, there may be a specific location on c^2 that represents lower overall costs to the firm than the transportation cost minimizing location s^*, or a closer site on c^1.

It is in this second stage of the location decision-making process that communities often have some influence on firm location decisions. Communities can offer high-quality infrastructure, skilled labour, building locations, and generally high quality of life characteristics, and not only offer low cost alternatives for the firm but, more importantly, offer a viable comparative advantage over other locations.

This approach to location decisions indicates that communities must be sensitive to the total cost of production in one community compared with other communities. Thus, the community seeks to keep transportation rates low or to offset higher transportation costs by reducing the nontransportation costs such as wages, land, and taxes. The community may attempt to create some agglomeration economies through a fully serviced industrial park. This neoclassical approach to firm location has served as a backbone to many traditional industrial targeting studies as well as policies aimed at attracting or promoting certain types of businesses. As outlined in detail in other chapters in this volume such as Leatherman and Kastens (Chapter 7), Cader et al. (Chapter 8), and Davis and Harris (Chapter 9), a wealth of studies have documented which types of factors are more attracted to different types of firms. Communities or regions that have the "right" mix of certain factors are said to have a comparative advantage with respect to that particular type of firm or industry. Policies can then be crafted to build on these factors or address weaknesses in other factors.

The neoclassical approach to firm location theory is not without its critiques. The first and most obvious is the strong set of assumptions on which the theory is based. Location decisions are being made by a profit-maximizing firm located on a homogenous economic plane. Firms and customers have perfect information and can fully process that information. In addition, firms are perfectly mobile and able to enter and exit spatial markets at no cost. The approach, while abstract, provides a rigorous framework to begin to think about space in an industry-targeting setting. As a deductive theory of location it provides an excellent foundation for more in-depth analysis.

Our current economy, however, is characterized by large-scale, mass production operations that are part of complexly organized, multiproduct and multiestablishment businesses. With a multiproduct, multilocation, multidivisional firm, the questions of optimality are complicated by optimality for the total firm or a particular division, total product line or a particular product, internal flows of inputs or markets being served, or the interest of management or the owners. The firm's multiple objective function includes objectives other than profit maximization. These other objectives arise partially from the interaction between the firm and the communities (society).

Behavioural approach

The neoclassical profit maximization approach yields models with relatively low predictive powers. This is particularly troublesome for targeted regional economic development policies. If the neoclassical approach to firm location has a mixed history in empirically predicting actual location decisions, then policies based on those studies are likely to fall short. This weakness of the neoclassical approach has not only generated strong critique of the many industry-targeting policies but also caused researchers to think in new ways about firm location decisions. Porter's notion of industry clustering is in some sense the newest way of thinking about firm location.

There are several reasons for the low predictive ability of neoclassical firm location theory. First, the theory, but more importantly the empirical studies based on the theory, do not handle personal preferences and psychic incomes or costs related to location decisions. These personal considerations cause the decision-maker to maximize total (money and psychic) satisfaction rather than only monetary profit. Second, the theory assumes that the individual making a location decision has perfect knowledge about the future, which is, of course, not possible. Differences in opinion about risk and profit potential associated with various locations lead to different location decisions. A risk-averse owner or firm with limited financial resources may choose a site with less potential profit but less risk of loss. Third, location decisions are typically made infrequently during the career of a business owner or manager. This infrequency, coupled with imperfect knowledge, often yields site selection criteria such as long-run sales growth with reasonable profits or space for expansion. The cost of acquiring additional information about alternative sites deters the business from further inquiry. The result is the selection of a satisfying rather than a profit-maximizing site.

The behavioural approach proposes a significant relaxation of these assumptions (Pellenbarg et al. 2002). It allows for personal goals other than profit maximization; inadequate and inappropriately used information; and uncertainty about current and future conditions of markets, rivals, and inputs. The approach uses game theory and the concept of bounded rationality to analyse location decisions. The behavioural approach attempts to explain why the selection of certain sites appears to be irrational.

The behavioural approach explicitly permits the decision-maker to seek objectives other than profit maximization in making location decisions. These alternative objectives could be market penetration or share, some minimal return, or expansion within some geographically bounded area to maintain management control. The different objective function takes the form of seeking a satisfactory, rather than maximum, level of some monetary or non-monetary goal. Thus, the firm no longer necessarily seeks the location yielding maximum profits, but a location meeting some minimal profit standard.

Including non-monetary elements in the firm's location choice makes the analysis both more realistic and more complex. The more realistic dimension occurs because it reduces the range of possible locations. Most sites fail to provide the non-economic characteristics desired, such as a view of the mountains or simply being the owner's hometown. The firm calculates costs and rivals' responses for a limited number of sites, not all possible sites. The more complex dimension optimizes objective functions that may or may not include non-economic criteria. From an industry-targeting perspective, this element of the behavioural approach is particularly troublesome because it does not lend itself to easy empirical analysis. It does, however, justify targeting policies that are based on what can be called a revealed preference approach: focus on industries that are already located within the community or region because they have revealed a preference for operating within that area.

Relaxing the assumption of complete geographical and temporal knowledge by the firm permits uncertainty and risk to enter the location decision.[1] Locational uncertainty and risk occur in many forms. National uncertainty and risk appear as imperfect insight about future general price changes, economic growth, interest rates, and federal monetary and fiscal policies. Regional uncertainty and risk include population shifts, regional response to national economic changes, and how input suppliers may respond to shocks. Local uncertainty and risk may involve labour-management relations, water supply, or local governmental actions. Firm uncertainty and risk include the type of production processes, location of competition, and continued availability of inputs.

The firm's intelligence and experience filters much of the apparent chaos and gives patterns to events. Relatively precise estimates of the probability of occurrence of some events (e.g., uncertainty becomes a risk) may even be available. Uncertainty causes the firm to produce a continuum of conditional decisions rather than a single location decision. The behavioural approach argues that the firm does not have full and complete information even without uncertainty (Pellenbarg et al. 2002). Bounded rationality says the human limitations of the decision-maker within the firm prevent all the information available from being absorbed. Furthermore, decision-makers are more sensitive to some sources of information than others. These sources are business associates, friends, family, and some media. The decision-maker's own receptiveness, experiences, and perspectives further filter the flow of information.

Decision-makers have a tendency to repeat prior successful decisions, which can be useful in thinking about TRED efforts. For communities, this means that businesses continue to use the same production technique or location rather than trying new ones. Townroe (1979) described three management conditions associated with location decisions: first, lack of experience with the type of decision and no precedents to follow; second, ignorance of all the relevant location possibilities; and third, uncertainty about what decision criteria to use. Location decisions are made in a dynamic environment in which the firm and community affect each other. This learning and adaptation process is continuous. The adaptation may arise as altered production scheduling and processes, reduced sales, and profits, and may result in relocation or closure. Townroe (1979) argues that the adjustment/adaptation process occurs because of unforeseen circumstances at the time of the initial decision, or because inadequate information was sought and used, critical factors for operation were not fully accounted for and, finally, poor judgment was used initially.

Access to information and the ability to process that information varies greatly by size of the firm and the distance of the potential location options. Larger firms generally have greater access to information or have the resources to gather the necessary information. On the contrary, small firms may find the cost to gather all the necessary information about all possible locational sites to be prohibitive. In addition, firms generally have more information about sites that are in close proximity to their existing locale. Limited information, limited ability to process information, perceptions, and uncertainty all lead to a large spatial bias in location decision-making. In essence, conditions at a more distant location are less well known than those prevailing at closer locations. As a result, firms may not be as freely mobile as presumed in the classical profit maximization problem.

The policy implications from a targeting perspective are straightforward: policies aimed at reducing uncertainty and risk by providing pertinent and timely information and reasonable stability in local rules and regulations are vital. There is little if anything the community can do about how firms process information and form risk trade-offs. The behavioural approach, however, is a deductive theory of the location problem. As such, although it is intuitively appealing, it does not lend itself to rigorous testing. In other words, it is difficult to build an empirical industry targeting study on the behavioural approach. As Scott (2000) argues, a major drawback to the behavioural approach is that it focuses too much on sociological, psychological, and other "soft" variables while ignoring the economic foundation of the classical profit maximization approach (Pellenbarg et al. 2002). In the discussion of Porter's cluster approach, we will see that the same critique could be applied around vital concepts like trust, reputation, and honesty in business relationships.

Institutional approach

The classical profit maximization and behavioural approaches both have one common theme: the firm is at the centre of the location decision-making process (Pellenbarg et al. 2002). The firm has to take into consideration both economic and non-economic factors in decision-making. What is overlooked is that the economic processes involved in firm location and expansion decisions are greatly influenced by society's cultural institutions and value systems. In essence, economic development decision-makers emphasizing targeting efforts must look not only at the economics of the firm but also at the social, cultural, and political context in which the firm makes its decisions.

Much of the location decision-making process involves negotiations between businesses, owners of the land, labour unions, and local governments for access to local infrastructure. The institutional approach focuses on the rules that set the parameters for negotiations and contract law as well as the negotiating power of the firm. Larger firms have greater negotiating leverage than smaller firms. State-level economic development policies are often targeted toward larger firms and firms have become accustomed to seeking incentives from state and local governments. Unfortunately, many TRED policies have state economic development agencies effectively bidding against each other in attempts to influence firm location and expansion decisions. This creates asymmetry of information in the location decision process. The firm knows whether or not a subsidy is truly necessary to make the site either profitable or the site of first choice. The community does not have this information, and thus there is a constant danger that it will over-subsidize the already profitable decision. Although the cost effectiveness of these state-level policies has been widely challenged, larger firms can and do exert market power in negotiations.

Smaller and medium-sized firms focus mostly on two types of institutions: local governments and real estate markets. Local governments can have significant impacts on the location decisions of firms. They determine land use laws such as zoning regulations and building codes and in many cases have the power to deny the necessary permits for the firm to move forward. From a conceptual point of view, local governments can and do affect the structure of the isocosts discussed in the cost minimization approach (Figure 4.2). In the name of economic development, local governments often will try to provide flexibility in zoning, access to public infrastructure, and fiscal incentives. Local governments can have a significant impact on the nature of local economic development by choosing how to structure and whether to enforce these local rules. While one might see common themes in this theoretical approach and Porter's notion of clusters, the institutional approach here focuses more narrowly on the "rules of the game" and the power differential between large and small firms to use those rules to their advantage.

Industry clusters

A relatively recent insight into firm location theory, and a common theme throughout this volume, is the concept of industry clusters. Di Tommosa et al. (2006) note that the literature on why firms cluster can be grouped into two main categories: the first is embodied in neoclassical firm location theory and the second emphasizes the advantages arising from what is historically referred to as agglomeration economies. Industrial clusters are geographic concentrations of interconnected companies, specialized suppliers, service providers, firms in related industries, and associated institutions in a particular field that compete but also cooperate (Enright 2000; Fesher and Sweeney 2002; McCann 2002; Porter 1995; Steiner 2002). A cluster is a geographically bounded concentration of independent businesses with active channels for business transactions, dialogue, and communications, and that collectively shares common opportunities and threats. The relevant geography can be a single city, or a region, or a state, or even national or multinational in nature. The geography relates to distance over which informational, transactional, and other efficiencies occur. The boundaries of clusters are flexible and are more art than an exact science. Clusters provide a constructive and efficient form for dialogue among private businesses, their suppliers, their customers, governments, and other institutions.

Clusters typically encompass an array of linked industries and other entities important for competition. Some of these include the following: suppliers of specialized inputs such as components, machinery and services; providers of specialized infrastructure such as rail and power; they extend downstream and laterally to manufacturers of complementary products; and they can be companies and industries related by skills, technologies, or common inputs. They can be institutions such as governments and universities, and standard-setting agencies, think tanks, and vocational training providers. They can also be trade associations. The role of government in cluster development is really to remove obstacles, relax constraints, or eliminate inefficiencies in production and enhance productivity growth. The emphasis is on dynamic improvement more than market share.

Clusters are critical to competition because modern competition depends on productivity. It does not depend on access to inputs or scale of individual enterprises. Productivity depends on how companies compete, not on the particular fields in which they compete. Competition is employing sophisticated methods, or using advanced technology, or offering unique products and services. Clusters can affect competition in three general ways. One, they can increase the productivity of companies based in the area. Two, they can increase competition by driving the direction and pace of innovation that underpins future productivity growth. Three, clusters affect competition by stimulating the formation of new businesses that expand and strengthen the cluster itself.

As Woodward and Guimarães (Chapter 5) discuss at length, the weakness of the notion of clusters made popular in the public policy realm by Porter (1990, 1995) is the lack of a coherent theoretical foundation. Nooteboom (2006: 137) observes that "although there has been much written about clusters, we still know little, theoretically and empirically, about how clusters develop and evolve". In their attempt to lay the theoretical foundation for clusters, Malmberg and Power (2006) make use of the term "cluster head-ache" and point to Webster's Revised Unabridged Dictionary, which defines agglomeration as 1) the act or process of gathering into a mass, or 2) a confused or jumbled mass. It is the latter definition that most accurately reflects the state of the art related to the theoretical foundation of clusters. Paniccia (2006) concludes that clusters has turned into a "chaotic concept" because its main proponent, Porter, put forth a concept that lacked precise conceptual boundaries. One is reminded of Krugman's (1991a) sarcastic physicist who claimed "what you are telling me is that firms agglomerate because of agglomeration affects". One could easily replace the term agglomeration with clusters and adequately summarize the state of the theoretical foundation for clusters. This observation leads Sugden et al. (2006: 61) to conclude "that the majority of existing methodologies for the analysis of clusters tend to centre on relatively superficial features".

The notion of clusters as outlined by Porter is not a new concept within economics and many (e.g., Asheim et al. 2006; Henry and Pinch 2006) trace its origins to Marshall's (1890/1930, 1919) analysis of "industrial districts". Pitelis et al. (2006: 20) note that "Marshall viewed the industrial district as greater than the sum of its parts, and highlighted increased specialization, external economies and collective efficiency as factors conducive to the industrial district's growth". Sugden et al. (2006) as well as Asheim et al. (2006) argue that industrial clusters have long been acknowledged within regional science in the form of Perroux's (1950, 1955/1971, 1988) notion of "centres" or "poles" of growth and innovation. Here Perroux uses the Schumpeterian idea of innovative "swarming" into a geographic centre on the economic landscape. Ozawa (2000: 227) goes one step further and argues that the notion of agglomeration economies and clusters can be traced to Adam Smith: "Adam Smith (1776) already introduced the concept of industrial agglomeration by conceptualizing the growth of a manufacturing town".

Although Ozawa (2000) is correct in that Smith does speak to the notion of agglomeration, his observation points to a distinction within the economics literature between urban economics and cluster analysis. In Krugman's (1991a, 1991b, 1995, 1999) seminal work on the "new economic geography", he asks a very basic question: why does a network of small hamlets form into a system of large cities? By introducing space into endogenous growth theory, Krugman offers a deductive theory of agglomeration economies (Fujita et al. 1999; Fujita and Thisse 2002). But Krugman's "new economic geography" addresses a fundamentally different question than Porter's question as to why clusters form. One falls cleanly into urban economics, whereas the other is more of an industrial organization question. This subtle but important distinction offers one insight into why the theoretical foundation of clusters is so troublesome.

Some (e.g., Asheim et al. 2006) maintain that stylized deductive theories offer little help in understanding the socio-institutional processes and factors that are stressed in Porter's and others' notions of clusters. Specifically, the role of "social capital" and the notion of trust and confidence in relationships, reputation, tradition, and communally established norms cannot be easily captured in mathematically focused deductive theories (Dupuy and Torre 2006). Gilly and Perrat (2006) maintain that the dynamics of clusters are driven by the idea of a process: how do institutions link together with each other as well as with businesses and how do economic actors compete or cooperate with one another within a specific geographic location? The conflict can be summarized as the fundamental differences between deductive theories of firm behaviour that dominate economics and case-study-based deductive theories that tend to dominate the thinking in business academics. On the other hand, although inductive based theories provide nice descriptive stories, it is difficult to generalize and provide rigorous testable hypotheses. Malmberg and Power (2006: 52) conclude that "[t]he cluster approach provides a way to describe the systematic nature of an economy". We are back to Krugman's sarcastic physicist.

One complicating factor in trying to develop an underlying theoretical foundation for clusters is the wide ranging and at times contradictory definitions of clusters (Belussi 2006). A sampling of definitions includes:

- Porter (2000: 254): "A cluster is a geographically proximate group of interconnected companies and associated institutions in a particular field, linked by commonalities and complementaries."
- Rosenfeld (1997: 4): "A cluster is very simply used to represent concentration of firms that are able to produce synergy because of their geographic proximity and interdependence, even though their scale of employment may not be pronounced or prominent."

- Feser (1998: 20): "Economic clusters are not just related and supporting industries and institutions, but rather related and supporting institutions that are more competitive by virtue of their relationships."
- Roelandt and Den Hertog (1999: 9): "Clusters can be characterized as networks of producers of strongly independent firms (including specialized suppliers), linked to each other in a value-adding production chain."
- Enright (1996: 191): "A regional cluster is an industrial cluster in which member firms are in close proximity to each other."
- Lundvall and Borras (1997: 39): "The region is increasingly the level at which innovation is produced through regional networks of innovators, local clusters and the cross-fertilizing effects of research institutions."
- Maskell (2001: 925): "The term cluster is used synonymously in the literature together with industrial agglomeration or localization, while the term industrial district . . . is often applied when wishing explicitly to emphasize values and norms shared by co-localised firms."[2]
- Cooke and Huggins (2002: 4): "Clusters are geographically proximate firms in vertical and horizontal relationships, involving a localized enterprise support infrastructure with shared developmental vision for business growth, based on competition and cooperation in a specific market field."
- Pitelis (2001: 2): "Clusters are agglomeration of firms in a particular activity, usually with a geographical dimension, with horizontal and (preferably also) vertical intra- and (preferably) inter-sectoral linkages in the context of a facilitatory socio-institutional settings, which co-operate and compete (co-opete) in (inter)national markets."
- Maskell and Kebir (2006: 30): "Clusters may be defined as non-random geographical agglomeration of firms with similar or closely related complementary capabilities."

Although one can see common themes across the range of working definitions of clusters, there does not appear to be a clear convergence onto core concepts that are not so vague as to be useless in practice. Indeed, Malmberg and Power (2006) argue that Porter's attempt to refine his notion of clusters by offering different definitions has caused more confusion than additional insights.

As Henry and Pinch (2006) and Asheim et al. (2006) noted, another complicating factor is the puzzling assortment of terms used including "districts" (Marshall 1919, 1890/1930), "clusters" (Porter 1990, 1995, 2000), "new industrial space" (Scott 1988), "industrial districts" (Third Italy) (Becattini 1989, 1990; Brusco 1989, 1990; Paniccia 2002), "local and regional innovation systems" (Asheim and Gertler 2005; Cooke 1998, 2001), "neo-Marshallian nodes" (Amin and Thrift 1994), "learning regions" (Asheim 1996, 2001; Florida 1995; Morgan 1997), "associational economies" (Cooke and Morgan 1998), "milieu" (Campagni 1991), "innovation milieu" (Longhi 1999; Maillat 1995), and "nexus of untraded interdependencies" or "local production systems" (Crouch et al. 2001; De Propris and Driffield 2006; Storper 1995).

In an attempt to shed light on this range of terms, Paniccia (2006) offers six separate terms, or cluster types, ranging from "canonical industrial districts" to "science-based or technological agglomeration" and provides a systematic categorization of characteristics across 16 factors such as firm ownership structure, firm size, and urban setting.

For many of these terms, each author is examining a specific situation, in the spirit of case studies, and is describing unique characteristics of the region under study. Although there are several commonalities across each of these "terms" and underlying thinking, each introduces subtle differences that add more confusion than insights. Whereas Paniccia's (2006) grouping of cluster types helps lay out the complexity of characteristics, it falls short of providing a unifying theoretical context. Steiner (2006) concludes that because of wide socio-institutional differences across settings of the case studies, there is strong diversity in clusters both in form and content. What works in one regional cluster may not work in another.

In addition to competing and at times confusing definitions of clusters and the arbitrary use of different terms, the cluster literature appears to be moving forward, or perhaps more appropriately sideways, by the introduction of "typologies" of clusters as opposed to unifying theories (e.g., Asheim et al. 2006; Bottazzi et al. 2002; Enright 2000; Pitelis and Pseiridis 2006). Webster's Revised Unabridged Dictionary define a *topology* as "[t]he art of, or method for, assisting the memory by associating the thing or subject to be remembered with some place". One could reasonably argue that Porter's Diamond is nothing more than a topology to describe the factors that are associated with industrial clustering and falls short of a coherent theory. Paniccia (2006) describes his grouping of different types of clusters as a topology of clusters and provides more of a listing of different characteristics than a theoretical foundation. We return to Malmberg and Power's (2006) argument that cluster theory is inductive in nature and provides a framework for telling a nice story. Indeed, in an attempt to lay the foundation for what qualifies as a cluster theory, Maskell and Kebir (2006) argue that for the theory to be convincing it must do more than provide a compelling account (i.e., story) for the benefits of collocation.

Simmie (2006) concludes that Porter's notion of clusters is just an extension of traditional agglomeration economies and Marshall's districts. It offers no analytical criteria for establishing the geography of clusters, no explanation for why some clusters thrive and others stagnate and fail, and no rigorous hypotheses that can be systematically tested. We are again left with Krugman's sarcastic physicist. Birkinshaw (2000) concludes that Porter's notion of clusters is so generic and vague that any policy recommendations are equally generic and vague. Henry et al. (2006) are a bit more forgiving and argue that the confusion, "chaotic concepts", and "cluster headaches" are more a reflection of a "work in progress" around an immature concept. Krugman's original challenge, which motivated his development of the "new economic geography", has yet to be answered in terms of cluster development.

Conclusions

In this chapter, I have laid the theoretical foundation for targeted regional economic development methods. Using traditional neoclassical firm location theory, many of the empirical tools outlined in other chapters of this volume are rooted in a solid foundation. The notion of isocosts within the traditional Weber problem offers not only a theoretical foundation but also a range of testable hypotheses that can help inform policy. Once we move to the notion of agglomeration economies and clusters in particular, our theoretical footing becomes slippery. In the broadest sense, the traditional Weber profit maximization problem is a deductive theory whereas agglomeration and clusters are an inductive theory. Unfortunately, the "new economic geography" has failed to bridge the gap when we move from the formation of cities to the formation of industrial clusters. The question is whether the two lines of work will converge to a unified, rigorous, and testable theory. The challenge will be to capture vague notions of trust, confidence in relationships, reputation, culture, and historical relationships within a deductive theory.

Notes

1   There are important differences between risk and uncertainty. Risk is associated with events where the economic agent does not know the outcome but can form probabilistic statements about the outcomes. Uncertainty is associated with events where no probabilistic assessments can be made. To use Secretary of Defense Donald Rumsfeld's statement, "we know what we know (certainty), we know what we don't know (risk), and we don't know what we don't know (uncertainty)".
2   Notice the overlap here with the institutional approach discussed in the previous section. Recall that the institution approach is more narrowly focused on the power of larger firms over smaller to "bend the rules" to better position themselves. This concept is independent of the notion of clusters and agglomeration economies.

References

Amin, A., and Thrift, N. (1994) *Globalization, Institutions and Regional Development in Europe*, Oxford: Oxford University Press.

Asheim, B. (1996) "Industrial districts as 'learning regions': a condition for prosperity?" *European Planning Studies*, 4(4): 379–400.

——. (2001) "Learning regions as development coalitions: partnerships as governance in European workfare states?" *Concepts and Transformation: International Journal of Action Research and Organizational Renewal*, 6(1): 73–101.

Asheim, B., Cooke, P., and Martin, R. (2006) "The rise of the cluster concept in regional analysis and policy: a critical assessment", in B. Asheim, P. Cooke, and R. Martin (eds) *Clusters and Regional Development: Critical Reflections and Explorations*, pp. 1–29, London: Routledge: London.

Asheim, B., and Gertler, M. (2005) "The geography of innovation: regional innovation systems", in J. Fagerberg, D. Mowery, and R. Nelson (eds) *The Oxford Handbook of Innovation*, pp. 291–317, Oxford: Oxford University Press.

Becattini, G. (1989) "Sectors and/or districts: some remarks on the conceptual foundations of industrial economics", in E. Goodman and J. Bamford (eds) *Small Firms and Industrial Districts in Italy*, pp. 123–35, London: Routledge.

——. (1990) "The Marshallian industrial districts as a socio-economic notion", in F. Pyke, G. Becattini, and W. Segenberger (eds) *Industrial Districts and Inter-Firm Co-operation in Italy*, Geneva: ILQ.

Belussi, F. (2006) "In search of a useful theory of spatial clustering: agglomeration versus active clustering", in B. Asheim, P. Cooke, and R. Martin (eds) *Clusters and Regional Development: Critical Reflections and Explorations*, pp. 30–49. Routledge: London.

Birkinshaw, J. (2000) "Multinational corporate strategy and organization: an internal market perspective", in N. Hood and S. Young (eds) *The Globalization of Multinational Enterprise Activity and Economic Development*, pp. 55–79, New York: St. Martin's Press.

Bottazzi, G., Dosi, G., and Fagiolo, G. (2002) "On the ubiquitous nature of agglomeration economies and their diverse determinants: some notes", in A. Curzio and M. Fortis (eds) *Complexity and Industrial Clusters*, Heidelberg: Physica.

Brusco, S. (1989) "A policy for industrial districts", in E. Goodman and J. Bamford (eds) *Small Firms and Industrial Districts in Italy*, pp. 259–69, London: Routledge.

——. (1990) "The idea of the industrial district", in F. Pyke, G. Becattini, and W. Segenberger (eds) *Industrial Districts and Inter-Firm Co-operation in Italy*, Geneva: ILQ.

Campagni, R. (1991) "Introduction: from the local 'milieu' to innovation through cooperation networks", in R. Campagni (ed.) *Innovation Networks: Spatial Perspectives*, pp. 1–9, London: Belhaven.

Cooke, P. (1998) "Introduction: origins of the concept", in H. Braczyk, P. Cooke, and M. Heidenreich (eds) *Regional Innovation Systems*, pp. 2–25, London: UCL Press.

——. (2001) "Regional innovation systems, clusters and the knowledge economy", *Industrial and Corporate Change*, 10(4): 945–74.

Cooke, P., and Huggins, R. (2002) "High technology clustering in Cambridge", in A. Amin, S. Goglio, and F. Sforzi (eds) *The Institutions of Local Development*, London: IGU.

Cooke, P., and Morgan, K. (1998) *The Associational Economy*, Oxford: Oxford University Press.

Crouch, C., Le Gales, P., Toglian, C., and Voelzkow, C. (2001) *Local Production Systems in Europe: Rise or Demise?* Oxford: Oxford University Press.

Deller, S.C., and Harris, T.R. (1993) "Estimation of minimum market thresholds using stochastic frontier estimators", *Regional Science Perspectives*, 23(1): 3–17.

Deller, S.C., McConnon, J.C., Holden, J., and Stone, K.E. (1992) "The measurement of a community's retail sector", *Journal of the Community Development Society*, 22: 68–83.

De Propris, L., and Driffield, N. (2006) "FDI, clusters and knowledge sourcing", in C. Pitelis, R. Sugden, and J.R. Wilson (eds) *Clusters and Globalisation*, pp. 133–58, Northamption, MA: Edward Elgar.

Di Tommosa, M.R., Paci, D., Rubini, L., and Schweitzer, S.O. (2006) "Is distance dead? high-tech clusters, analysis and policy perspectives", in C. Pitelis, R. Sugden, and J.R. Wilson (eds) *Clusters and Globalisation*, pp. 196–214, Northampton, MA: Edward Elgar.

Dupuy, C., and Torre, A. (2006) "Local clusters, trusts, confidence and proximity", in

C. Pitelis, R. Sugden, and J.R. Wilson (eds) *Clusters and Globalisation*, pp. 175–95, Northampton, MA: Edward Elgar.

Enright, M.J. (1996) "Why local clusters are the way to win the game", *World Link*, 5: 24–25.

——. (2000) "The globalization of competition and the localization of competitive advantages: policies towards regional clustering", in N. Hood and S. Young (eds) *The Globalization of Multinational Enterprise Activity and Economic Development*, New York: St. Martin's Press.

Feser, E. (1998) "Old and new theories of industrial clusters", in M. Steiner (ed) *Clusters and Regional Specialization*, London: Pion.

Fesher, E.J., and Sweeney, S.H. (2002) "Theory, methods and a cross-metropolitan comparison of business clusters", in P. McCann (ed.) *Industrial Location Economics*, Northampton, MA: Edward Elgar.

Florida, R. (1995) "Toward the learning region", *Futures*, 27: 527–36.

Fujita, M., Krugman, P., and Venables, A. (1999) *The Spatial Economy: Cities, Regions and International Trade*, Cambridge, MA: MIT Press.

Fujita, M., and Thisse, J.F. (2002) *Economics of Agglomeration: Cities, Industrial Location and Regional Growth*, Cambridge: Cambridge University Press.

Gabszewicz, J.J., and Thisse, J.F. (1986) "Spatial competition and the location of firms", in J.J. Gabszewicz, J.F. Thisse, M. Fujita, and U. Schweizer (eds) *Location Theory*, New York: Harwood Academic.

Gilly, J.P., and Perrat, J. (2006) "The institutional dynamics at work in territories: between local governance and global regulation", in C. Pitelis, R. Sugden, and J.R. Wilson (eds) *Clusters and Globalisation*, pp. 159–174, Northampton, MA: Edward Elgar.

Henry, N., and Pinch, S. (2006) "Knowledge clusters", in C. Pitelis, R. Sugden, and J.R. Wilson (eds) *Clusters and Globalisation*, pp. 114–32, Northampton, MA: Edward Elgar.

Henry, N., Pollard, J., and Benneworth, P. (2006) "Putting clusters in their place", in B. Asheim, P. Cooke, and R. Martin (eds) *Clusters and Regional Development: Critical Reflections and Explorations*, pp. 272–91, London: Routledge.

Holden, J.P., and Deller, S.C. (1993) "Analysis of community retail market area delineation techniques: an application of GIS technologies", *Journal of the Community Development Society*, 24(2): 141–58.

Hustedde, R., Shaffer, R., and Pulver, G. (1993) *Community Economic Analysis: A How To Manual* (RRD141), Ames, IA: North Central Regional Center for Rural Development.

Krugman, P. (1991a). *Geography and Trade*, Cambridge: MIT Press.

——. (1991b) "Increasing return and economic geography", *Journal of Political Economy*, 99: 483–89.

——. (1995) *Development, Geography and Economic Theory*, Cambridge: MIT Press.

——. (1999) "The role of geography in development", *International Regional Science Review*, 22: 142–61.

Longhi, C. (1999) "Networks: collective learning and technology development in innovative high technology regions: the case of Sophia-Antipolis", *Regional Studies*, 33: 333–42.

Lundvall, B., and Borras, S. (1997) "The globalizing learning economy: implications for innovation policy", Report from DG XII, Commission of the European Union.

Maillat, D. (1995) "Territorial dynamics, innovation milieu and regional policy", *Entrepreneurship and Regional Development*, 7: 157–65.

Malmberg, A., and Power, D. (2006) "True clusters: a severe case of conceptual headache", in B. Asheim, P. Cooke, and R. Martin (eds) *Clusters and Regional Development: Critical Reflections and Explorations*, pp. 50–68, London: Routledge.

Marshall, A. (1919) *Industry and Trade*, London: Macmillan.

——. (1930) *Principles of Economics* (8th edn, originally published in 1890), London: Macmillan.

Maskell, P. (2001) "Towards a knowledge based theory of the geographical cluster", *Industrial and Corporate Change*, 10(4): 921–43.

Maskell, P., and Kebir, L. (2006) "What qualifies as a cluster theory?" in B. Asheim, P. Cooke, and R. Martin (eds) *Clusters and Regional Development: Critical Reflections and Explorations*, pp. 30–49, London: Routledge.

McCann, P. (2002) "Classical and neo-classical location-production models", in P. McCann (ed.) *Industrial Location Economics*, Northampton, MA: Edward Elgar.

Morgan, K. (1997) "The learning region: institutions, innovation and regional renewal", *Regional Studies*, 31: 491–504.

Nooteboom, B. (2006) "Innovation, learning and cluster dynamics", in B. Asheim, P. Cooke, and R. Martin (eds) *Clusters and Regional Development: Critical Reflections and Explorations*, pp. 137–63, London: Routledge.

Ozawa, T. (2000) "Small- and medium-sized MNCs, industrial clusters and globalization: the Japanese experience", in N. Hood and S. Young (eds) *The Globalization of Multinational Enterprise Activity and Economic Development*, pp. 225–48, New York: St. Martin's Press.

Paniccia, I. (2002) *Industrial Districts: Evolution and Competitiveness in Italian Firms*, Cheltenham: Edward Elgar.

——. (2006) "Cutting through the chaos: towards a new typology of industrial districts and clusters", in B. Asheim, P. Cooke, and R. Martin (eds) *Clusters and Regional Development: Critical Reflections and Explorations*, pp. 90–114, London: Routledge.

Pellenbarg, P.H., van Wissen, L.J.G., and van Dijk, J. (2002) "Firm migration", in P. McCann (ed.) *Industrial Location Economics*, Northampton, MA: Edward Elgar.

Perroux, F. (1950) "Economic space, theory and applications", *Quarterly Journal of Economics*, 64: 89–104.

——. (1955/1971) "Notes on the concept of growth poles", in T. Livingstone (ed.) *Economic Policy for Development: Selected Readings*, Oxford: Oxford University Press.

——. (1988) "The pole of development's new place in a general theory of economic activity", in B. Higgins and D.J. Savoie (eds) *Regional Economic Development*, Boston: Unwin Hyman.

Pitelis, C.R. (2001) "Cluster diagnosis", Presentation at Netwin Project in London, December.

Pitelis, C.R., and Pseiridis, A. (2006) "A conceptual framework for firm cooperation and clusters, and their impact on productivity", in C. Pitelis, R. Sugden, and J.R. Wilson (eds) *Clusters and Globalisation*, 17–60, Northampton, MA: Edward Elgar.

Pitelis, C., Sugden, R., and Wilson, J.R. (2006) "Introduction", in C. Pitelis, R. Sugden, and J.R. Wilson (eds) *Clusters and Globalisation*, pp. 1–16, Northampton, MA: Edward Elgar.

Porter, M.E. (1990) *The Competitive Advantage of Nations*, New York: The Free Press.

—— . (1995) "The competitive advantage of the inner city", *Harvard Business Review*, (May/June): 55–71.

—— . (2000) "Location, competition and economic development", *Economic Development Quarterly*, 14: 23–34.

Roelandt, T., and Den Hertog, P. (1999) "Cluster analysis and cluster-based policy making in the OECD", in *Boosting Innovation: The Cluster Approach*, Paris: OECD.

Rosenfeld, S. (1997) "Bringing business clusters in the mainstream of economic development", *European Planning Studies*, 5: 3–23.

Scott, A.J. (1988) *New Industrial Spaces: Flexible Production Organization and Regional Development in North America and Western Europe*, London: Pion.

—— . (2000) "Economic geography: the great half-century", *Cambridge Journal of Economics*, 24(4): 483–504.

Shaffer, R., Deller, S.C., and Marcouiller, D. (2004) *Community Economics: Linking Theory and Practice*, Oxford: Blackwell.

Simmie, J. (2006) "Do clusters or innovation systems drive competitiveness?" in B. Asheim, P. Cooke, and R. Martin (eds) *Clusters and Regional Development: Critical Reflections and Explorations*, pp. 164–87, London: Routledge.

Smith, A. (1776/1908) *An Inquiry into the Nature and Causes of the Wealth of Nations*, London: Routledge; and New York: E.P. Dutton.

Steiner, M. (2002) "Clusters and networks: institutional settings and strategic perspectives", in P. McCann (ed.) *Industrial Location Economics*, Northampton, MA: Edward Elgar.

—— . (2006) "Do clusters 'think'?: an institutional perspective on knowledge creation and diffusion in clusters", in B. Asheim, P. Cooke, and R. Martin (eds) *Clusters and Regional Development: Critical Reflections and Explorations*, pp. 199–217, London: Routledge.

Storper, M. (1995) "The resurgence of regional economics, ten years later: the region as a nexus of untraded interdependencies", *European Urban and Regional Studies*, 2(3): 191–221.

Sugden, R., Wei, P., and Wilson, J.R. (2006) "Clusters, governance and the development of local economies: a framework for case studies", in C. Pitelis, R. Sugden, and J.R. Wilson (eds) *Clusters and Globalisation*, pp. 61–95, Northampton, MA: Edward Elgar.

Townroe, P.M. (1979) "The design of local economic development prices", *Town Planning Review*, 50(April): 148–63.

5 Porter's cluster strategy and industrial targeting

Douglas Woodward and Paulo Guimarães

Introduction

In December 2003 Harvard Business School professor Michael Porter unveiled a new economic development strategy for the state of South Carolina, akin to dozens prepared for regions across the world. In the presentation and a related report, Porter (in conjunction with the Monitor Group, a consultancy) asserted that "South Carolina has pursued a low-cost economic strategy, emphasizing its abundant and flexible workforce, good physical infrastructure, and responsive government in order to attract manufacturing operations" (South Carolina Council on Competitiveness 2005). Porter's central thesis was that the traditional approach to economic development was wrong. In turn, he challenged South Carolina to reassess and overhaul economic development policy, and to promote the role of clusters in raising regional productivity and innovative capacity. Passionately and persuasively, he championed his alternative approach to regional economic development. A new private-sector group, the Council on Competitiveness (renamed "New Carolina"), was launched to activate and oversee the strategy, similar to other groups formed around the world in the wake of cluster studies.

Porter's presentation resonated in a region battered by globalization and witnessing sluggish job and wage growth. As is true in many states, foreign imports have steadily eroded South Carolina's traditional industrial base. Bedrock industries such as textiles and apparel have declined continually since the mid-1970s. As a result, the state government targeted new industries like automobiles, along with the promotion of foreign direct investment. Subsequently, targeted incentives had some success in the early 1990s, notably with the attraction of a major BMW plant. With related suppliers, the automotive plant is responsible directly and indirectly for over 17,000 jobs (Schunk and Woodward 2003). This clearly helped to revitalize the former textile region. Yet since 2000, South Carolina had not progressed in relative terms, with per capita income stagnating at 82 percent of the US average. Aggregate manufacturing employment has continued to plummet, even as the national economy overall has continued to expand.

Following his 2003 address, which was critical of targeted incentives, Porter was given a special honour by the state legislature and hailed as nothing less than the "guru" of economic development by private sector leaders. A similar story could be repeated for regions across the world. Indisputably, Porter has become the early 21st century's most prominent champion of economic development. His message – the old model is wrong – makes sense in all areas feeling the effects of globalization and industrial restructuring. In turn, cluster strategies have proliferated. They serve as the basis for economic development policy in countries as dissimilar as Japan, Finland, Estonia, Portugal, Singapore, Costa Rica, Nicaragua, Mexico, Libya, and Rwanda. Since the early 1990s, European regional development authorities have been especially active in implementing cluster-related programs (Sölvell et al. 2003). Public and private development organizations like USAID have helped spread the policy in less-developed countries (see Mitchell Group 2003). At the state and local level in the United States, Porter's influence has inspired ubiquitous competitiveness councils designed around cluster development. Overall, more than 1,400 cluster initiatives have been identified worldwide (Sölvell et al. 2003).

Porter's phenomenal impact as a cluster analyst and advocate deserves attention. In copious case studies, books, and articles, he stresses that the cluster approach represents the organizing principle for economic progress. Many regional and urban scholars agree that clusters represent a "pervasive aspect of modern economies" (valuable reviews can be found in Bergman 1998 and Bergman and Feser 1999).

The focus of this chapter is on regional cluster strategy and its compatibility with the kind of industrial targeting practice discussed throughout this book. We will see that Porter's extensive research does not advance any novel or advanced techniques for targeting industries. Moreover, there is some confusion about Porter's policy among regional development analysts and practitioners. Most tend to view cluster strategies and industrial targeting as identical.

While Porter contends that all clusters matter (and is critical of targets), some seem to matter more than others; for example, Porter emphasizes the importance of traded (economic base) clusters. To identify promising regional traded clusters, Porter and associates have engaged in a comprehensive regional mapping project covering many US regions. To be sure, the project is not meant to pinpoint the clusters that can develop in particular areas; it only suggests where existing regional strengths may lie. Nevertheless, empirical cluster identification is accomplished through a modified location quotient approach, mostly for industries. This measure is a familiar part of targeted screening approaches, as discussed by Barkley and Henry (Chapter 10) later in this book.

Porter's approach raises a policy conundrum for regional targeting, particularly for policies designed to attract high-technology industries. His actual argument is that it is not *what* a region produces, but *how* productively and efficiently it produces higher-value products. By extension, getting the right industry mix through targeting does not really matter, for firms in any industry can develop innovative, competitive clusters and continuously upgrade productivity. In fact, Porter often states that "there are no low-tech industries, only low-tech firms." It would follow that there is no need for industrial targeting. Instead, Porter argues for public–private collaboration to promote regional cluster externalities, which he believes exist everywhere from inner cities to rural communities. Nevertheless, the search for promising industry targets remains the rationale used by many state and local policy-makers – even in their embrace of the cluster framework.

The next section presents a review of cluster development strategy. Here we describe cluster theory and summarize key elements of the Porter approach. We then contrast the Porter policy prescriptions with traditional industrial targeting. Since Porter claims nothing less than to change the fundamental direction of policy, there is a strong need for clarification. We will then argue that Porter's "new direction" for development policy actually reverts to a form of industrial targeting. That is, where he sees his policy as an alternative, we maintain that it is actually entirely compatible with, if not a complement to industrial targeting. In the third section we contrast clusters and industrial targeting techniques, including discussion of empirical problems with measuring clusters. We close the chapter with a summary and conclusion.

Porter-style clusters

Understanding and identifying regional competitive advantage is the major theme of this book. Porter pioneered the modern theory of competitive advantage. His early contributions, however, were concerned with firm (not regional) advantage (Porter 1998: Ch. 1). Having established a strong reputation as a business operational strategist in the 1970s and 1980s, he turned his research to country-wide and then regional competitiveness (Porter 1998: Ch. 7). By and large, his approach emerged inductively from a series of cross-national case studies that are still cited and widely read (Porter 1990). Among his many prodigious achievements since writing *The Competitive Advantage of Nations*, Porter has constructed an annual international ranking of micro-level competitiveness (World Economic Forum 2007) and it is conceivable that similar measures could be developed for regions. In any event, the argument for microfoundations – placing firm strategy as the basis for understanding national and subnational economic policy – represents a noteworthy achievement.

In a series of articles and books, Porter (1990, 1996, 1998, 2000, 2003) moved beyond firm strategy to argue that localized clusters are central to microeconomic competitiveness. Generally, his cases and articles do not build on conventional economic theory or empirical findings (an exception is Porter 2003). The findings are mostly derived case studies of developing and developed countries, including analyses of urban and rural development. The series of analyses began with country-wide case studies in which Porter

(1990) argues that competitive advantage is not just determined by macro-economic conditions alone, the focus of most national economic policy. While arguing that macroeconomic stability (low inflation, stable currency) is necessary for competitiveness, Porter says it is not sufficient. In some cases, macroeconomic factors such as exchange rate depreciation provide an ephemeral advantage at best.

Porter argues that the long-run microeconomics of competitive advantage, unlike macroeconomic policy considerations, are too often ignored, or taken as given. In this connection, it is instructive to contrast his view with conventional comparative advantage theory. In fact, Porter's concept of competitive advantage can be seen as an alternative to textbook microeconomics, where the logic of comparative advantage ultimately leads to regional specialization (and leaves little room for industrial targeting). It is well known that a country's comparative advantage in trade is determined by relative factor endowments such as land, natural resources, labour, and the size of the local population. According to the Heckscher-Ohlin variant of the textbook micro theory, factor intensity is the basis for an area's production cost advantage. A country should specialize and export products that use its abundant factors intensively. Consequently, comparative advantage leads to regional specialization as determined by resource endowments of land, labour, and capital.

No doubt there are factor-driven economies based on abundant labour, suitable land, or natural resources. Yet in contrast to the laws of comparative advantage that lead to specialization, Porter posits that "national prosperity is created, not inherited". Porter (1998) accepts that factor-driven economies represent a stage of competitiveness, but economic development is more influenced by competitive firm behaviour and how policy shapes this behaviour. For example, competitive advantage may be determined by regional policies oriented toward attracting capital investment, which essentially raises the local productivity of factors through capital widening and deepening. In this age of capital mobility, investment targeting strategies characterize many regional and national efforts and there is a widespread belief that governments should compete vigorously for domestic and foreign investment. The rivalry among US states for new capital investment even verges on fiscal fratricide, with escalating incentives offered to companies that make large investments. Targeting of capital-intensive industries remains a highly criticized but still common regional policy (Markusen 2007). While Porter is critical of this approach, typified by South Carolina's aggressive use of incentives to attract BMW, it is conceivable that the approach can be effective in regional transformation. In fact, another leading Harvard Business School professor promoted the Greenville-Spartanburg region as a paragon of successful economic restructuring through foreign direct investment (Kanter 1997). Incentive packages favourable to large capital investments ($120 million in the BMW case) were used to seed what policymakers hoped would be fertile ground for new clusters (Schunk and Woodward 2003).

Over the long-run, however, targeting industries for new capital investment alone will not create competitive economic improvement according to Porter. Instead, Porter's studies reveal that competitive countries and regions require an innovative environment in addition to appropriate incentives and capital investments. Broadly conceived, innovation is the sustaining force in regional competitive advantage. In Porter's view, innovative economies are not only highly efficient, but they also create unique, high value-added products and services. They thrive through constant upgrading of the economic base.

It is hardly controversial to posit that innovative clusters are the goal for regional development in the 21st century. A full review of the substantial literature on cluster benefits is beyond the scope of this chapter (see, for example, Anderson 1994; Bergman and Feser 1999; Doeringer and Terkla 1995, 1996; Feser 1998; Jacobs and De Jong 1992; Jacobs and De Man 1996; Hewings et al. 1998; Hill and Brennan 2000; Roelandt and den Hertog 1999; Steiner 1998; Sternberg 1991). To be sure, spatial concentration concepts similar to clusters have been written about extensively: industrial districts (Bellini 1996; Harrison 1992; Rabellotti 1995), industrial complexes (Czamaski, 1971; Czamanski and Ablas 1979), and growth poles (Darwent 1969). It is also beyond our aim here to critique Porter-style clusters with these and other concepts of spatial concentration, such as industry agglomeration and Marshallian spatial externalities (see Gabe Chapter 6).

Instead we focus on Porter's specific account of spatial clusters as they emerge from his case research. To analysts and observers of regional innovation networks, the cluster case that most commonly comes to mind is California's high-technology Silicon Valley (Saxenian 1996). Silicon Valley is synonymous with the modern innovative milieu. Yet, surprisingly, Porter's lectures and writings point to California's wine-producing Napa Valley as a primary example of an innovating cluster (Porter and Bond 2003). Although wine is the classic example of factor-based comparative advantage theory, the high-value vineyards of Napa Valley are not the result of natural endowments alone – the so-called *terroir* (soil conditions, climate etc.). In lieu of comparative advantage, Porter contends that the success of the California wine region is based on its *competitive* advantages; that is, on the ability of firms to innovate, raise productivity, and create exceptional brands.

The central Porter hypothesis is that competitive, productive firms require a set of supportive microeconomic conditions to thrive, regardless of natural endowments. Porter's emphasis on the importance of raising regional productivity (making regional products and services better, not just cheaper) is readily accepted by policy-makers. He maintains that the best way to raise firm competitiveness is through encouraging collaborative, localized clusters of firms, with private-sector councils of competitiveness taking the lead from government. Clusters are geographic concentrations of interconnected companies in related industries, but also encompass specialized suppliers, financial institutions, universities, and trade associations. Porter takes spatial clustering, no doubt descriptive of successful regional development, and makes it the prescriptive policy for revamping regional development.

Again, this conclusion emerged inductively through case studies, rather than through deductive logic or rigorous empirical analysis. What Porter found in case research is that when clusters take hold, they continually enhance *firm* competitiveness and strategy. Moreover, successful clusters can act as a centripetal force, holding regional firms intact. This helps regions prosper in the face of the centrifugal forces of contemporary globalization – the dispersion of firm activity through outsourcing and offshoring. Potentially, clusters will encourage local competition and new business formation, leading to a virtuous cycle of development. In turn, clusters root firms in the local economy. Consequently, governments are less likely to require incentives to foment economic development.

The Porter "diamond model" suggests how clusters are more than agglomeration economies. Regional cluster strengths can be assessed through four drivers:

- Sophisticated local demand for cluster products and services. That is, for example, the refined, new California cuisine of the 1970s spurred the wine cluster to be more competitive. Tourism adds to the local demand base.
- Local supply inputs from related and supporting industries. For the Napa Valley wine case, which spans the Bay Area around San Francisco, this support includes everything from bottling, labeling, advertising, and finance. Vintners can find appropriate upstream and downstream linkages that are deeply anchored in the local economy. They are supported by academic institutions such as the University of California at Davis and locally produce the leading trade magazine, the *Wine Spectator*.
- Favourable factor (resource) conditions. California vineyards enjoy a superior *terroir*, but also good infrastructure including highways and ports in close proximity, access to highly developed capital markets in the Bay Area, and a labour force that includes specialized managerial talent and low-wage, migrant grape pickers.
- A competitive context for firm rivalry, further driving productivity. For wine in Napa Valley, entrepreneurial activity is continual and new entrants are omnipresent. Vineyards cover a range of sizes – the competitive structure is not dominated by a few leading wineries. The vintners cooperate through trade associations, but also compete in an intense rivalry around branding.

In short, echoing urban and regional theory, Porter maintains that competitive clusters are not defined by the co-location of firms, but true interrelationships and collaboration. The cluster competitive advantage is not just the result of spatial externalities and agglomeration advantages (discussed in Gabe, Chapter 6). The goals for cluster activation should be enhancing innovation, upgrading the regional resources (especially infrastructure and

the labour force), nurturing local suppliers, strengthening local marketing/
customer relations, and cooperating with educational institutions. Coordinated public-private efforts are crucial to success.

There is widespread consensus now that Porter is essentially correct about
the drivers of regional competitiveness. In their comprehensive review for
the *Web Book of Regional Science*, which covers clusters and related regional
development concepts such as agglomeration economies and growth poles,
Bergman and Feser (1999) said the following about the influence of the
diamond framework:

> Porter's readable account of the sources of national competitive advan-
> tage, which includes a key role for geographic proximity, is largely
> consistent with a growing body of literature on how interdependencies
> between firms, industries, and public and quasi-public institutions affect
> innovation and growth in regional agglomerations ... Nearly every
> analysis of industry clusters begins with – or at least makes some men-
> tion of – Porter's "diamond", a characterization of his four key drivers
> of competitiveness.
>
> (Bergman and Feser 1999: 7)

Porter-sytle clusters versus traditional targeting

As can be gleaned from the discussion so far, Porter argues that given the four
elements of the diamond, the question is not *what* a country or region produces but *how to make what it produces better*. With the same natural regional
endowment, wine can be a highly competitive, differentiated, premium brand
or a low-value, undifferentiated commodity – a boutique varietal or a jug
wine. California's Napa Valley has many alternative uses. Firms, both large
estates and small vintners, thrive in this environment because they create
valuable brands, spurred by collaboration and competition in the wine
cluster, not because of the natural *terroir*.

In theory, any area can develop a myriad of competitive clusters. As the
age-old wine example suggests, they do not need to be the emerging "industries of the future". Regions can prosper by upgrading existing industries and
clusters, not by searching for high-technology saviours. Indeed *all* clusters
matter in Porter's analysis. This may come as a particular surprise to regional
policy-makers looking for industrial targets. Driving home this point, Porter
asserts that "there are no low-tech industries, only low-tech firms". Accordingly, it would appear that there is *no need for industrial targeting* if one
strictly follows Porter.

To clarify further, the following three points encapsulate the differences
between cluster-based economic development vis-à-vis traditional targeted
industry policies. These points are summarized from Porter (1998: 248–49),
where he discusses "clusters versus industrial policy":

- Traditional policy targets "desirable industries and/or sectors"; whereas Porter's policy emphasizes that all clusters can contribute to prosperity.
- Regional industrial policy has been oriented toward tilting outcomes in favour of particular companies; while cluster policy should support all companies, domestic or foreign, that enhance local productivity.
- Industrial policy distorts regional competition through industry subsidies, protection, and promotion; on the other hand, cluster-based policy stresses easing obstacles and limits to productivity through collaborative efforts.

Rejecting "the old model" of industrial policy is not easily accomplished. The problem is that after cluster consultants present their findings, regional cluster committees lose focus and coordination efforts fizzle (see Deller, Leatherman and Shields Chapter 18). Even accepting the basic tenets of Porter's theory, regional policy-makers still want to know which clusters matter most, want to target emerging industries, and generally believe that what a region produces (not just how) is essential to strategic development policy. "All clusters matter" does not appear to be a strategy.

To be sure, Porter (2003) does believe that "traded" (export-oriented, or economic base) clusters are more important for regional policy than "nontraded" clusters. In this respect, Porter's approach agrees with traditional industrial policy, in which traded clusters serve as primary drivers and regional clusters are anchored through backward and forward linkages. In regional science, these linkages to traded cluster are uncovered through input-output analysis (see Deller, Chapter 19 and Hughes, Chapter 11). However, Porter rejects input-output analysis. In his case research, the important connections are not backward and forward linkages, but interfirm networks that are hard to quantify.

Presumably, policy-makers could qualitatively assess the strengths and weaknesses of cluster development through the prism of the diamond. Yet in any rigorous or consistent way, it is hard to measure and compare local demand conditions, related and supporting industries, the context for firm rivalry, and factor conditions. The problem is empirical. In the next section we will show that as a practical consequence it is only possible to measure the strength of traded, or export-based clusters with industry-level data. Even Porter's cluster analysis reverts back to the techniques used in targeting industries, as shown in Barkley and Henry's application to South Carolina (Chapter 10).

Empirical problems with traded clusters

In the last section we found that despite real insights, Porter's model puts forth no new empirical methods that can help identify potential clusters, as would be expected by policy-makers and practitioners of regional development. In this section, we will see that Porter's empirical definition of clusters in fact relies on industry employment, plainly an imperfect measure of clusters. These traded industries or clusters can be seen in the cluster-mapping initiative sponsored by Harvard University's Institute on Strategy and Competitiveness (2007).

The cluster mapping project, which covers most regions of the United States, suggests where existing strengths may lie. Porter and associates revert to identifying clusters as economic-base industries, using standard location quotients (LQs) familiar to regional analysts. In regional mapping by the Harvard Institute for Strategy and Competitiveness clusters are presented in bubble charts, with the bubble diameter representing employment size. The vertical axis measures industries (clusters) that have shares of national employment greater than the regional average share. These are said to be as strong clusters. Growth in the share of employment is shown on the horizontal access. Thus, strong industries (clusters) appear in the upper right-hand quadrant, with high location quotients and growing employment shares.

The LQ, a widely used technique for identifying regional industrial targets, is actually a misleading way to look at clusters. Its appeal is due to its simplicity, requiring data that are usually easily obtained from published official statistics. Typically, location quotients are calculated for each industry by computing the ratio between the regional employment share for the industry under study and that industry's national share of total employment. Hence, the location quotient for industry i in region j is given by

$$LQ_i = \frac{(E_{ij}/E_{in})}{(E_j/E_n)}$$

where E designates employment and the subscripts i, j and n designate industry, region and national, respectively. It is well-known that a location quotient above one indicates that the region has a higher share of employment in that industry than the nation as a whole.

With location quotients, most analysts are merely looking for measures of regional specialization, not clusters. They set up an arbitrary thresholds for determining specialization, sometimes 1.25 (Malizia and Feser 1999) or other times values as high as three (Isaksen 1996; Malmberg and Maskell 2002), assuming that LQs above the threshold constitute evidence of regional specialization in that industry.

Relying solely on the employment LQs for regional cluster mapping is problematic because of the serious pitfalls associated with the measure. By construction, the LQ measures the relative importance of the industry, thus providing no indication about the absolute size of that industry. This means that it becomes possible to obtain high values of the LQ for industries that have a small presence in the local economy, particularly if industries are being analysed at a fine level of aggregation. Hence, to overcome this limitation it is common to restrict attention to industries that have a significant dimension, usually industries that have a share of employment in the local economy that is above a predetermined level. In Porter's cluster mapping project, the bubble size suggests which industries are larger, but some may be declining in employment (like textiles and apparel in South Carolina). These would not be likely cluster targets.

Another significant limitation of the LQ for measuring cluster strength is its inability to differentiate between external and internal scale economies. The LQ will be the same whether the industry employment in region j is due to the existence of a single large establishment, or due to the existence of several smaller sized establishments. Evidently, a large LQ in the first situation is not due to the existence of an industry cluster or evidence of agglomeration economies. Ellison and Glaeser (1997) brought attention to another problem with indices such as the LQ. Because of the discrete nature of the phenomenon being measured it is possible to observe spurious concentration, that is, concentration (clustering) that occurs by chance alone. Thus, the higher number of firms in the region under study may be a result of chance and the measuring index should account for that. An obvious way to deal with this problem is to implement statistical tests for the LQ using bootstrapping or other approaches (Moineddin et al. 2003; O'Donoghue and Gleave 2004). As discussed earlier, applied researchers and economic development practitioners tend to use arbitrarily defined cutoff points.

Despite its limitations, the LQ is still a valid approach if the focus is on the identification of a global pattern of regional specialization. In Chapter 10, Barkley and Henry adumbrate a more elaborate procedure for targeting industrial clusters. Like Porter's Cluster Mapping Project, they include regional specialization through employment location quotients and local employment growth greater than the national industry average. But they include additional criteria, which are useful for policy.

Beyond the location quotient, it is important to recognize that cluster strengths can be better informed by empirical work on agglomeration. That is, when information is available at a finer level of aggregation, it may be possible to use measures of agglomeration for cluster identification (see also Gabe's discussion in Chapter 6). Empirical agglomeration techniques attempt to quantify the discrepancy between the distribution of employment across regions in a particular industry compared with the distribution of overall economic activity. Examples of these measures are Hoover's location coefficient and the spatial Hirschman-Herfindahl index. Following the publication of Ellison and Glaeser (1997), the new EG index rapidly became the standard for measuring the level of industrial agglomeration. Ellison and Glaeser constructed a theoretically grounded index of agglomeration and claimed several advantages over existing agglomeration indices. Distinct advantages of the EG index over other approaches include the following:

- It accounts for the size distribution of establishments (that is, the EG purges the effect of scale economies on agglomeration).

- It accounts for the inherent randomness in the spatial distribution of firms; it is comparable across industries.
- It is insensitive to the level of spatial aggregation at which data are collected.

Nevertheless, like the LQ, the EG index poses problems if used as a basis for cluster identification and targeting. Feser (2000) found that in applied work the EG index was sensitive to the level of spatial aggregation. Guimarães et al. (2007) showed by example that the EG index could lead to counterintuitive results. One finding is particularly relevant to cluster mapping: applications of the EG index that employ regional employment data instead of plant count data (as suggested by Ellison and Glaeser) offered no statistical advantage and led to higher imprecision in measuring levels of industrial agglomeration. Guimarães et al. (2007) proposed an alternative index of agglomeration consistent with the theoretical framework of Ellison and Glaeser (1997), but with different statistical properties. This index has the added advantage of offering a statistical test of significance of the agglomerations.

All agglomeration measures discussed so far treat space as discrete. In discrete space, there may be situations when methods will fail to identify localized firm clusters. Measures of spatial agglomeration that treat space as continuous overcome these problems (Feser and Sweeney 2000; Duranton and Overman 2005). But in cluster mapping, analysts rarely have detailed information about the actual location of each establishment. However, it is still possible to account for the impact of agglomerations that spill over neighboring spatial units using methods from the spatial statistics and econometrics literature. These methods include techniques that account for the existence of spatial autocorrelation such as the Moran's I index and measures of local association like the Getis-Ord statistic (Arbia 2001; Feser and Sweeney 2000; Guillian and Le Gallo 2006).

Our point is that to advance beyond the LQ, cluster mapping would improve if it were made consistent with techniques for assessing agglomeration (localization) economies. Even then, the measures discussed above are only capable of providing evidence of agglomeration for firms belonging to the same industry and confined to a specific geographical area. This notion of cluster ignores groups of firms from different industrial sectors that have significant interrelations, as emphasized by Porter.

One strategy would be to look for interdependence across sectors and measure the patterns of co-location of the industries. It may be possible to use simple methods such as industry pairwise correlations of employment, as in Latham (1976) or a more sophisticated approach as found in Ellison-Glaeser (1997), with a co-location index that controls for overall economic activity and looks at "excess" co-location. However, each of these methods will only provide indirect evidence of inter-industry relationships.

An alternative approach is regional input-output analysis and industrial complex techniques that can be traced to Isard et al. (1959). This analysis is discussed extensively elsewhere in this book. For cluster identification, one could distinguish between two different approaches based on input-output tables: the "direct value chain analysis" and the "trading pattern analysis" (Hofe and Chen 2006). Direct value chain analysis groups industries into clusters by examining the strength of their input-output transaction links. If the links are above a certain predetermined threshold then the industries are considered to be clustered. This approach is arbitrary, however, because there is no guidance about the cutoff values to be used. The "trading pattern analysis" method looks at similarity of trading patterns across industries. Generally, identification of these patterns is based on multivariate statistical methods such as cluster and principal component factor analysis (Hill and Brennan 2000). Feser and Sweeney (2000) extended this line of work by integrating spatial analysis techniques with information derived from input-output tables in order to test whether linked and related manufacturing enterprises tend to cluster in space. Also noteworthy is the benchmarking approach to industry clusters proposed by Feser and Bergman (2000). These authors identified industrial clusters using detailed information on national inter-industry linkages and propose that these be used as templates to identify potential clusters in US regions. However, Feser and Bergman (2000) caution that this approach should be a first analytical step to more in-depth cluster studies.

To summarize, the employment location quotients employed in Porter's cluster mapping project are rudimentary attempts to quantify traded clusters. However, they have an advantage over more sophisticated approaches because they can be readily calculated and easily explained to non-specialists and used by practitioners who may have limited formal training in economics. They are limited in their usefulness for targeting, however, and not even effective in identifying clusters. At the same time, agglomeration measures and input-output techniques continue to be honed for practical targeting applications (see Hughes in Chapter 11 and Deller in Chapter 19). Whether evaluating cluster specialization or targeting industries, it would seem wise to incorporate recent agglomeration measures designed to overcome inherent problems with the location quotient.

Conclusion

Porter's influence pervades modern regional development policy and thus warrants attention in a book on targeted regional economic development. The precursors of Porter-style clusters date to the origins of regional analysis, with antecedents such as growth poles, industrial complexes, and industrial districts. Yet, as explained in this chapter, Porter's analysis was derived independently through national and regional case studies. In Porter's view, clusters are not industry agglomerations, but inter-industry networks of companies, specialized suppliers, service providers, segments of related industries, and associated institutions (for example, universities and trade associations). Admittedly, such clusters are hard to identify and track over time.

Regarding regional development policy, Porter's popularity derives from his reputation for astute strategic thinking. He alleges that previous development practice has been misguided. From South Carolina to Singapore, policy-makers now believe that competitive economic strategy entails building innovative clusters. Surprisingly, however, Porter rejects cluster initiatives that involve explicit industrial targeting. Instead, he vehemently argues for upgrading the innovative capacity of all clusters, often asserting that policy-makers should not choose among them. He also avows that regions should strengthen established clusters rather than attempt to generate entirely new ones. Finally, Porter's strategy rejects a top-down government agenda that guides development. Instead, he argues that cluster activation should be advanced by the private sector, perhaps with local government acting as a facilitator. Clusters with strong collaborative institutions are likely to be most successful.

Among many maxims, Porter states that 21st century economic development is a "marathon not a sprint". It is hard to disagree that raising regional living standards is a long-run proposition, but government targeting will no doubt continue to play a role in this race. Regions need a roadmap – and clear guidance about the direction for policy initiatives. This chapter has argued that the evolving empirical tools used in industrial targeting can be employed to refine and focus Porter-inspired cluster initiatives. To return to the case discussed at the opening of the chapter, it would be unlikely that South Carolina could ever develop an automotive cluster without direct state government efforts to target the industry in the first place. When successful, government-led industrial targeting efforts may generate the kind of private-sector clusters that eventually may display the competitive characteristics favored in Porter's diamond model. At the same time, we concur with Porter's message: continual innovation, deep supply linkages and supporting institutions, vigorous local firm competition, and enhanced resources (labour, capital, and infrastructure) are going to sustain clusters over the long run. Yet we also agree with other authors in this volume: Intelligently designed and more accurate industrial targeting can help regions identify potential clusters.

References

Anderson, G. (1994) "Industry clustering for economic development", *Economic Development Review*, 12(2): 26.

Arbia, G. (2001) "The role of spatial effects in the empirical analysis of regional concentration", *Journal of Geographical Systems*, 3(3): 271.

Bellini, N. (1996) "Italian industrial districts: evolution and change", *European Planning Studies*, 4(1): 3–4.

Bergman, E.M. (1998) "Industrial trade clusters in action: seeing regional economies whole", in M. Steiner (ed.) *Clusters and Regional Specialization: On Geography, Technology, and Networks, European Research in Regional Science*, vol. 8, London: Pion.

Bergman, E.M. and Feser, E. (1999) "Industrial and regional clusters: concepts and comparative applications", in *The Web Book of Regional Science*, Morgantown: Regional Research Institute, West Virginia University. Online. Available HTTP: <http://www.rri.wvu.edu/WebBook/Bergman-Feser/contents.htm> (accessed 2 May 2007).

Brusco, S. (1986) "Small firms and industrial districts: the experience of Italy", in D. Keeble and E. Wever (eds) *New Firms and Regional Development in Europe*, pp. 184–202, London; Sydney.

Czamanski, S. (1971) "Some empirical evidence of the strengths of linkages between groups of industries in urban regional complexes", *Papers of the Regional Science Association*, 27: 137–50.

Czamanski, S., and Ablas, L.A. (1979) "Identification of industrial clusters and complexes – comparison of methods and findings", *Urban Studies*, 16(1): 61–80.

Darwent, D.F. (1969) "Growth poles and growth centers in regional planning – review", *Environment and Planning*, 1(1): 5–31.

Doeringer, P.B., and Terkla, D.G. (1995) "Business strategy and cross-industry clusters", *Economic Development Quarterly*, 9(3): 225–37.

——. (1996) "Why do industries cluster?" in U.H. Staber, N.V. Schaefer, and B. Sharma (eds) *Business Networks: Prospects for Regional Development*, Berlin: de Gruyter.

Duranton, G., and Overman, H.G. (2005) "Testing for localization using micro-geographic data", *Review of Economic Studies*, 72(4): 1077–1106.

Ellison, G., and Glaeser, E.L. (1997) "Geographic concentration in US manufacturing industries: a dartboard approach", *Journal of Political Economy*, 105(5): 889–927.

Feser, E.J. (1998) "Old and new theories of industry clusters", in M. Steiner (ed.) *Clusters and Regional Specialization*, London: Pion Limitedpp. 18–40.

——. (2000) "On the Ellison-Glaeser geographic concentration index", working paper. Online. Available HTTP: <http://www.urban.uiuc.edu/faculty/feser/publications.html> (accessed 3 May 2007).

Feser, E.J., and Bergman, E.M. (2000) "National industry cluster templates: a framework for applied regional cluster analysis", *Regional Studies*, 34(1): 1–19.

Feser, E.J., and Sweeney, S.H. (2000) "A test for the coincident economic and spatial clustering of business enterprises", *Journal of Geographical Systems*, 2(4): 349.

Guillain, R., and Le Gallo, J. (2006) "Measuring agglomeration: an exploratory spatial analysis approach applied to the case of Paris and its surroundings", REAL Working Paper, no. 06-T-10.

Guimarães, P., Figueiredo, O., and Woodward, D. (2007) "Measuring the localization of economic activity: a parametric approach", *Journal of Regional Science*, 47(4): 753–774.

Harrison, B. (1992) "Industrial districts – old wine in new bottles", *Regional Studies*, 26(5): 469–83.

Hewings, G.J., Schindler, G.R., Israilevich, P.R., and Sonis, M. (1998) "Agglomeration, clustering, and structural change: interpreting changes in the Chicago regional economy", in M. Steiner (ed.) *Clusters and Regional Specialisation*, London: Pion Limited.

Hill, E.W., and Brennan, J.F. (2000) "A methodology for identifying the drivers of industrial clusters: the foundation of regional competitive advantage", *Economic Development Quarterly*, 14(1): 65–96.

Hofe, R., and Chen, K. (2006) "Whither or not industrial cluster: conclusions or confusions?" *The Industrial Geographer*, 4(1): 2–28.

Isaksen, A. (1996) "Towards increased regional Specialisation? the quantitative importance of new industrial spaces in Norway, 1970–1990", *Norsk Geografisk Tidsskrift*, 50: 113–23.

Isard, W., Schooler, E.W., and Vietorisz, T. (1959) *Industrial Complex Analysis and Regional Development: A Case Study of Refinery-Petrochemical-Synthetic-Fiber Complexes and Puerto Rico*. Cambridge: Technology Press of the Massachusetts Institute of Technology.

Jacobs, D., and De Jong, M.W. (1992) "Industrial clusters and the competitiveness of the Netherlands", *De Economist*, 140(2): 233–52.

Jacobs, D., and De Man, A.P. (1996) "Clusters, industrial policy and firm strategy: a menu approach", *Technology Analysis & Strategic Management*, 8(4): 425–37.

Kanter, R.M. (1997) *World Class: Thriving Locally in the Global Economy*, New York: Touchstone.

Latham, W.R. (1976) "Needless complexity in identification of industrial complexes", *Journal of Regional Science*, 16(1): 45–55.

Malizia, E., and Feser, E. (1999) *Understanding Local Economic Development*, New Brunswick, NJ: Center for Urban Policy Research, Rutgers, the State University of New Jersey.

Malmberg, A., and Maskell, P. (2002) "The elusive concept of localization economies: towards a knowledge-based theory of spatial clustering", *Environment and Planning A*, 34(3): 429–49.

Markusen, A. (ed) (2007) *Reining in the Competition for Capital*, Kalamazoo, MI: W.E. Upjohn Institute for Employment Research.

Mitchell Group. (2003) *Promoting Competitiveness in Practice: An Assessment of Cluster-Based Approaches*, Washington, DC: US Agency for International Development. Online. Available HTTP: <http://www.bdsknowledge.org/dyn/bds/docs/254/USAID-Mitchell-Clusters.pdf> (accessed May 7, 2007).

Moineddin, R., Beyene, J., and Boyle, E. (2003) "On the location quotient confidence interval", *Geographical Analysis*, 35(3): 249–56.

O'Donoghue, D., and Gleave, B. (2004) "A note on methods for measuring industrial agglomeration", *Regional Studies*, 38(4): 419–27.

Porter, M.E. (1990) *The Competitive Advantage of Nations*. New York: The Free Press.

——. (1996) "Competitive advantage, agglomeration economies, and regional policy", *International Regional Science Review*, 19(1–2): 85–90.

——. (1998). *On Competition*, Cambridge, MA: Harvard Business School Press.

——. (2000) "Location, competition, and economic development: local clusters in a global economy", *Economic Development Quarterly*, 14(1): 15–34.

——. (2003) "The economic performance of regions", *Regional Studies*, 37(6&7): 549–78.

Porter, M.E., and Bond, G.C. (2003) *The California Wine Cluster*, Harvard Business School, Case 9-799-124. Cambridge, MA: Harvard Business School Press.

Rabellotti, R. (1995) "Is there an industrial district model – footwear districts in Italy and Mexico compared", *World Development*, 23(1): 29–41.

Roelandt, T. J. A., and den Hertog, P. (1999) "Cluster analysis and cluster-based policy-making in OECD countries: an introduction to the theme", in Organisation for Economic Co-operation and Development (ed.), *Boosting Innovation: The Cluster Approach*, OECD Proceedings, pp. 9–23.

Schunk, D.L. and Woodward, D.P. (2003) "Incentives and economic development: the case of BMW in South Carolina", in S.B. White, R. Bingham and E.W. Hill (eds), *Financing Economic Development in the 21st Century*, Armonk, NY: M.E. Sharpe, pp. 145–69.

South Carolina Council on Competitiveness. (2005) *South Carolina Competitiveness Initiative: A Strategic Plan for South Carolina*. Report prepared by the Monitor Company Group for the South Carolina Council on Competitiveness. Online. Available HTTP: <www.competesc.org> (accessed 14 April 2007).

Sölvell, Ö., Lindquizt, G., and Ketels, C. (2003) *The Cluster Initiative Greenbook*, Stockholm, Sweden: Ivory Tower AB.

Steiner, M. (1998) *Clusters and Regional Specialization*, London: Pion.

Sternberg, E. (1991) "The sectoral cluster in economic development policy: lessons from Rochester and Buffalo, New York", *Economic Development Quarterly*, 5(4): 342.

World Economic Forum. (2007) *Global Competitiveness Report 2006–2007*. Online. Available HTTP: <http://www.weforum.org/en/initiatives/gcp/Global%20Competitiveness%20Report/index.htm> (accessed 3 May 2007).

6 Impact of agglomerations on the economy

Todd Gabe

Introduction

Regional and local policy-makers increasingly look to targeting-based strategies to promote and encourage high agglomerations of activity in selected industrial sectors. Such policies are motivated by the recognition that industry agglomeration provides location-specific advantages that are external to individual businesses but are shared by establishments operating in the local industry (Porter 2000). These localization externalities, as discussed by Woodward and Guimarães in Chapter 5, include the availability of a skilled workforce and specialized machinery, and information spillovers concerning product markets and production technologies (Barkley and Henry 1997; Krugman 1991; Marshall 1890). Although many economic development researchers and practitioners believe they exist, location-specific advantages of industry agglomeration are difficult to capture and measure directly. For this reason, past studies have used a variety of indirect indicators related to business performance (e.g., firm location, employment growth, wages) and comparisons of the growth of industries across regions to measure the effects of industry agglomeration (Glaeser et al. 1992; Head et al. 1995; Gibbs and Bernat 1997).

This chapter presents empirical evidence on the location-specific advantages of industry clustering, as well as the effects of industry agglomeration on indicators of growth and development in Maine. First, the importance that businesses place on location-specific advantages associated with industry clusters is examined. These findings are based on surveys of Maine companies operating in the biotechnology industry and the environmental and energy technology industry. Second, results from several recent empirical studies are used to investigate the extent to which firm location, employment growth, and earnings are positively associated with industry agglomeration, and to identify the industries in which agglomeration seems to matter. This analysis is guided by the notion that these indicators of growth and development may capture different aspects of localization externalities. For example, new businesses may locate in an area with a high agglomeration of industry to tap into a skilled labour force or key natural resource. On the other hand, incumbent establishments may grow more rapidly in an area with a high agglomeration of industry than elsewhere because of knowledge spillovers transmitted through repeated dealings with similar firms.

Previous studies have examined the effects of industry agglomeration on firm location, employment growth, and wages (Head et al. 1995; Gibbs and Bernat 1997). Some of these studies distinguish between "static" and "dynamic" localization externalities (Glaeser et al. 1992; Henderson et al. 1995; Sveikauskas 1975). Static localization externalities are the immediate benefits an establishment receives from its close proximity to other businesses in the same industry. These benefits, such as the availability of industry-specific inputs, explain the high geographical concentration of many US industries and the importance of industry agglomeration to firm location (Guimarães et al. 2000; Head et al. 1995; Krugman 1991).

Dynamic localization externalities are the location-specific advantages an establishment accrues over time from repeated dealings with other local businesses in the same industry. These knowledge spillovers explain the high levels of employment growth, productivity, and wages associated with industry agglomeration (Gibbs and Bernat 1997; Henderson 1997). O'hUallachain and Satterthwaite (1992) found a positive relationship between employment growth and industry size, and Henderson et al. (1995) uncovered a positive relationship between employment growth and an industry's share of total local employment. Although the effects of industry agglomeration on rural employment growth reported by Barkley et al. (1999) are somewhat mixed, Henry and Drabenstott (1996) found that industry clusters are a "major source" of manufacturing employment growth in US rural areas.

Maine provides a good case study for an empirical analysis of industry agglomeration in rural areas. Thirteen of Maine's 16 counties are classified as "non-metropolitan", based on USDA's rural–urban continuum, and five of the non-metropolitan counties are "not adjacent" to a metropolitan area. Some of the most agglomerated industries in Maine are logging, ship and boat building and repairing, miscellaneous wood products, water transportation services, sawmills and planing mills, fuel dealers, hotels and motels, and camps and recreational vehicle parks (Gabe 2003). Maine's wood products industries, which rely heavily on the state's natural resources, are typical of the types of sectors that are concentrated in US non-metropolitan areas (Kim et al. 2000). Gibbs and Bernat (1997) found timber and wood products clusters in 183 rural areas, which cover 848 non-metropolitan US counties.

Empirical evidence on industry cluster advantages in Maine

As noted above, some of the commonly cited location-specific advantages of industry agglomeration are a large pool of trained, specialized workers; access to specialized equipment and machinery; and enhanced opportunities for interfirm networking and information sharing. Although these benefits are often difficult for policy-makers to measure, business surveys can be used to assess their importance to firm profitability and growth. Allen and Gabe (2003) and Noblet and Gabe (2006) surveyed Maine businesses in the biotechnology industry and the environmental and energy technology industry. These industries have been targeted by Maine policy-makers as key clusters for growth and development assistance. Given that they are highly agglomerated in the southern part of the state, the industries are ideal candidates for an analysis of industry cluster advantages.

Before looking at some of the survey questions related to industry clustering, a brief description of the two highlighted industries is provided. The Maine biotechnology industry consists of approximately 80 businesses. These companies are engaged in research and development, as well as the manufacturing and provision of a wide variety of products and services. They cover a broad spectrum of the biotechnology industry, from human diagnostics to marine biotechnology to genomics and proteomics. Biotechnology firms are highly concentrated in southern Maine around the city of Portland, but they also operate in 10 of the state's 16 counties. An industry study conducted in 2002 found that these firms generated a combined $432 million in annual sales and directly employed 3,690 workers, which is equivalent to 0.76 per cent of total state employment (Allen and Gabe 2003). Including multiplier effects, the biotechnology industry contributed $685 million in output to the Maine economy in 2002 and supported 7,135 Maine jobs.

Maine's environmental and energy technology industry consists of approximately 688 businesses and organizations. It is quite diverse, comprising firms and organizations engaged in activities ranging from environmental consulting services to the development of non-traditional energy sources. Like the biotechnology industry, the environmental and energy technology industry in Maine is highly concentrated in the southern, more urbanized, part of the state. Two southern Maine counties are home to a combined 45 per cent of industry establishments. Noblet and Gabe (2006) found that Maine's environmental and energy technology industry directly generated an estimated $574.1 million in sales, supported 5,269 full- and part-time jobs, and provided $222.8 million in employee earnings in 2006. Direct employment in the industry is equivalent to 1.1 per cent of total state employment. Counting multiplier effects, the industry contributed $882.7 million in sales to the Maine economy and supported 9,650 jobs that provided $330.9 million in earnings.

The business surveys included several questions that can be used to examine the location-specific advantages of industry clusters. A question relevant to labour market pooling asked firms to indicate "important sources" of workers. As reported in Table 6.1, almost 40 per cent of the biotechnology survey respondents viewed other biotechnology businesses located within the state as an important source of new employees. By comparison, only one-third and one-quarter of the businesses felt that four-year universities located in Maine, and out-of-state businesses, respectively, are key sources of biotechnology employees. Likewise, in the environmental and energy technology

Table 6.1 Important sources of workers for firms in the Maine biotechnology and environmental & energy technology industries

Source:	In Maine (%)	Out-of-State (%)
Biotechnology		
Other businesses	39.4	25.7
4-year universities	33.1	30.1
2-year universities	8.8	2.9
Environmental & Energy Technology		
Other businesses	31.9	23.7
4-year universities	23.7	17.0
2-year universities	14.3	6.6

industry, a higher proportion of firms (32 per cent) felt that other Maine establishments are an important source of workers, compared to out-of-state businesses (24 per cent) and four-year universities located in Maine (24 per cent).

The importance that firms place on the availability of specialized equipment was assessed with a question that asked if this "location issue" affects the establishment's profitability or growth potential. Sixty-nine per cent of the biotechnology firms surveyed felt that the availability of specialized equipment impacted their profitability or growth potential. In terms of the proportion of biotechnology firms that felt it was important, the availability of specialized machinery ranked below business climate factors such as health care costs (92 per cent), Maine's quality of life (85 per cent), and labour costs (82 per cent); and above factors such as access to in-state venture capital (39 per cent), the quality of local primary schools (58 per cent), and distribution and transportation costs (65 per cent).

Compared to the biotechnology industry, a much smaller percentage (30 per cent) of survey respondents in the environmental and energy technology industry believed that the availability of specialized equipment affected their profitability or growth potential. In terms of the proportion of environmental and energy technology companies that felt it was important, the availability of specialized machinery ranked well below factors such as Maine's quality of life (81 per cent), health care costs (79 per cent), and state sales and income taxes (74 per cent) and only slightly above financing issues such as access to in-state venture capital (16 per cent), access to in-state debt financing (23 per cent), and availability of state government funding for research and development (29 per cent).

With respect to the location-specific cluster advantage of knowledge spillovers, the surveys asked whether the business has ever engaged in joint research and development activities or shared technical information with other businesses or organizations (e.g., universities, non-profits). Results from the biotechnology survey, summarized in Table 6.2, show that 58 per cent of the respondents have conducted joint research and development activities, and 56 per cent have shared technical information with other businesses or organizations. However, surprisingly, the survey found that Maine bio-technology companies were more likely to partner with non-Maine busi-nesses than with other Maine businesses for both types of activities (it is possible that these out-of-state businesses may be located across the border in New Hampshire).

By comparison, although environmental and energy technology firms appear less likely than biotechnology companies to share technical informa-tion or conduct joint research and development with any type of partner, Table 6.3 shows that they are more apt to engage in these types of activities with other Maine businesses than with firms from outside the state. A pos-sible explanation for the differences in the in-state versus out-of-state orienta-tion of information-based partnerships of the two highlighted industries is that they rely on different types of knowledge. Howells (2002: 877) suggests that scientific industries, such as biotechnology, "depend more on codifica-tion and the transmission of information via codified 'knowledge' ", which generate spillovers that are "less localized in nature". On the other hand, for industries dominated by engineers – like Maine's environmental and energy technology industry – "learning-by-doing and tacit knowledge are more important", which are displayed through "more localized spillover effects".

These survey results reveal the importance, or in some cases indifference, that businesses place on the location-specific advantages often associated

Table 6.2 Partnerships of Maine biotechnology firms

Cooperative Activity	Other Maine Business (%)	Non-Maine Business (%)	Maine Nonprofit Organization (%)	Maine University Researcher (%)	Total* (%)
Conducted joint R&D	22	39	11	20	58
Submitted joint research proposal	14	18	14	10	31
Coordinated marketing effort	6	20	0	0	21
Shared equipment or personnel	18	2	8	14	32
Coordinated purchase of supplies	6	9	5	0	19
Shared technical information	27	35	18	21	56
Shared facilities and space	18	13	9	16	41

* A summation of cell entries may exceed row totals because some businesses are involved in multiple partnerships and cooperative activities.

Table 6.3 Partnerships of Maine environmental and energy technology firms

Cooperative Activity	Other Maine Business (%)	Non-Maine Business (%)	Maine Nonprofit Organization (%)	Maine University Researcher (%)	Total* (%)
Conducted joint R&D	13	8	4	3	17
Submitted joint research proposal	10	7	4	4	19
Coordinated marketing effort	21	13	2	0	27
Shared equipment or personnel	24	9	4	1	31
Coordinated purchase of supplies	6	1	1	0	8
Shared technical information	38	23	10	7	46
Shared facilities and space	12	1	1	1	19

* A summation of cell entries may exceed row totals because some businesses are involved in multiple partnerships and cooperative activities.

with industry clusters. Maine firms in the two highlighted technology-based industries, which are highly agglomerated within the state, tend to believe that other Maine businesses (at least more so than other sources of employees) are a good place to find workers. This provides modest evidence – although the numbers are not overwhelming – that businesses tap into a locally available skilled workforce. The evidence is mixed on the benefits that businesses derive from the local availability of specialized equipment and machinery. More than two-thirds of the biotechnology firms believe that this business climate factor affects their profitability or growth potential, but only 30 per cent of companies in the environmental and energy technology industry feel it is relevant. Finally, survey results related to knowledge spillovers suggest that businesses in both industries seem to interact with others, especially in research and development activities and the sharing of technical information. However, in the biotechnology industry, these types of interaction are more likely to occur with a non-Maine business than with an in-state partner.

Empirical evidence on industry clusters and local business vitality

The second part of this chapter summarizes recent studies on the effects of industry agglomeration on business location, employment growth, and wages. This section explores the extent to which clusters stimulate economic vitality, and provides insights into the industries that gain a boost from agglomeration. Empirical results are discussed after a general overview of the firm location and establishment growth models used in the analysis. Detailed descriptions of these models are presented elsewhere (Gabe 2003, 2004; Gabe and Bell 2004).

As outlined by Deller in Chapter 4, business location models typically relate the expected profits ($\pi_{i,j}$) earned by establishment i in municipality j to a set of location-specific attributes,

$$\pi_{i,j} = \beta'X_{i,j} + e_{i,j} \tag{1}$$

where β is a vector of parameters, $X_{i,j}$ is a vector of location-specific attributes, and $e_{i,j}$ is a random error term (Carlton 1983; Friedman et al. 1992; Guimarães et al. 2000). Profit-maximizing behavior suggests that establishment i will locate in municipality k if the expected profits in municipality k exceed the expected profits the business could earn elsewhere (e.g., $\pi_{i,k} > \pi_{i,j}$, $\forall j \in J$).

McFadden's (1974) conditional logit model is commonly applied to this type of discrete-choice location problem (Carlton 1983; Coughlin et al. 1991; Head et al. 1995; Leatherman and Kastens, Chapter 7; Cader et al., Chapter 8). However, Guimarães et al. (2003) propose the use of a Poisson regression framework, instead of the conditional logit model, to analyse business location decisions (see also Davis and Harris, Chapter 9). The number of businesses that began operations in each municipality is estimated using a Poisson regression model in which the likelihood of observing n_j new businesses is:

$$f(n_j) = (e^{-\lambda_j} \lambda_j^{n_j})/n_j! \text{ and } \ln \lambda_j = \beta'X_j, \tag{2}$$

where β is a vector of parameters and $X_{i,j}$ is a vector of location-specific attributes (Coughlin and Segev 2000; Greene 2000). Along with the industry agglomeration variable (i.e., location quotient), the vector $X_{i,j}$ contains the municipality's distance to the nearest interstate highway, population size, local labour costs, and several local government spending variables. The government spending variables were included in the empirical model to examine the effects of local fiscal policy on business location, which was the focus of the original paper (Gabe and Bell 2004). Analysis presented in this chapter extends the original research with a new emphasis on the importance of industry agglomeration as a location factor. The population size variable accounts for the effect of urbanization economies on location, whereas the distance to an interstate highway measures accessibility to markets.

The business growth model that underlies our empirical analysis is:

$$S_{t'} = [G(S_t, A_t)]d(S_t)e_t \tag{3}$$

$$(\ln S_{t'} - \ln S_t) / d = \ln G(S_t, A_t) + u_t \qquad (4)$$

where S and A are establishment size and age, $G(\cdot)$ is a firm growth function, the subscript t indicates time where $t' > t$ and $d = t' - t$, e is a log normally distributed error term, and u is normally distributed with mean zero and independent of S and A (Evans 1987). This type of model has been used to examine the relationship between firm (employment) growth rates and internal conditions such as business size and age (Hall 1987; Hymer and Pashigian 1962; Simon and Bonini 1958; Singh and Whittington 1975). Previous studies have investigated Gibrat's law, which suggests that firm growth is independent of firm size (Hart and Prais 1956). Jovanovic's (1982) passive firm learning hypothesis, which implies a negative relationship between growth and firm age, has also been tested in many empirical studies (Dunne et al. 1989; Evans 1987; Variyam and Kraybill 1992, 1994).

Equation (4) can be expanded to include industry agglomeration and other regional characteristics that may affect establishment growth:

$$(\ln S_{t;}' - \ln S_t) = \beta_0 + \beta_1 \ln S_t + \beta_2 \ln A_t + \beta_3 (\ln S_t)^2 + \beta_4 (\ln A_t)^2$$
$$+ \beta_5 (\ln S_t) \times (\ln A_t) + \beta_6 \ln LQ + \beta_7 \ln COMP$$
$$+ \beta_8 \ln POP + \beta_9 \ln DIVER + \beta_{10} INDGRO$$
$$+ \beta_{11} \ln CITY\ WAGE + e \qquad (5)$$

where LQ (location quotient) is a measure of industry agglomeration, COMP represents the competitiveness of the local industry, POP is municipality population size, DIVER is a measure of local economic diversification, INDGRO is the logarithmic growth rate of US employment in the establishment's industry, and CITY WAGE is the local wage rate. As in the business location model, population size is included as a measure of urbanization economies, expected to enhance business growth. The economic diversification variable, defined as the percentage of local employment made up by the five largest industries, is used to test the idea that local industrial variety stimulates growth (Glaeser et al. 1992; Jacobs 1969). Following Glaeser et al. (1992), the competitiveness of the local industry is represented by the average size of establishments operating in the industry (relative to the national industry average). Porter (1990) suggests that competition occurring within a local industry encourages innovation and growth, whereas Romer (1986) believes that competition may limit growth because it erodes the market power necessary to capture rents from new innovations.

The dependent variable used in the establishment wages model is the natural logarithm of quarterly wages paid per establishment employee divided by the average quarterly wages earned per worker in the US industry. This is interpreted as a rate by which establishments "over" or "under" pay their workers relative to the national industry average. The employee earnings model uses the same set of explanatory variables as the employment growth model shown in equation 5, although the reasoning behind the inclusion of some of the control variables is slightly different. For instance, employment size is included in the wage model to test the hypothesis that large companies pay higher wages than small businesses (Brown and Medoff 1989; Doms et al. 1997).

The firm location, business growth, and wages models described above are estimated using data on Maine establishments. The firm location analysis focuses on 3,763 new establishments that began operations in one of Maine's 129 most populated municipalities between 1993 and 1995. These businesses were identified using Covered Employment and Wages (ES-202) data. To be counted as a new business, the establishment must have an "initial liability date" between the first quarters of 1993 and 1995, and it must have remained in operation with one or more workers until at least 1996. The empirical analysis of employment growth and wages uses ES-202 data on a sample of 21,775 establishments that employed one or more workers during the first quarter of 1996. A three-year logarithmic growth rate of employment between 1996 and 1999 is examined, as well as wages paid during the first quarter of 1996.

Industry agglomeration is represented in all three of the empirical models by location quotients, a measure of local (i.e., municipality) industry specialization relative to the US economy. As described by Woodward and Guimarães (Chapter 5) and Barkley and Henry (Chapter 10), location quotients are calculated as the percentage of a municipality's businesses in a two-digit SIC industrial category divided by the percentage of US businesses in the same category. Location quotients greater than 1 imply that the region has a specialization in the particular industry.

Table 6.4 summarizes empirical results on the effects of industry agglomeration on business location, establishment growth, and wages. Separate business location models are estimated for 54 two-digit SIC industries, and establishment growth and wages models for 58 two-digit industries. As discussed above, a Poisson estimator is employed to analyse business location. To account for the censored nature of the dependent variable (i.e., establishments that closed have a "growth rate" of −1.0), a Tobit estimator is used to analyse establishment growth. Finally, the analysis of establishment wages uses an ordinary least squares (OLS) estimator. In the table, a "+" sign means that the municipality-industry location quotient has a positive and statistically significant effect on the selected indicator, while a "−" sign means that the industry agglomeration variable has a negative and significant effect on the indicator. Cells are left blank in cases where the location quotient does not have a statistically significant effect on the indicator of business vitality.

Other results from the analysis of business location, discussed in more detail by Gabe and Bell (2004), suggest that local spending on educational instruction and operations – but not educational administration – encourages business location. In addition, businesses are attracted to areas with a large population, whereas fewer establishments begin operations in areas located

Table 6.4 Effects of industry agglomeration on location, growth, and wages

Industry	Location	Growth	Wages
General contractors and operative builders			+
Heavy construction, except building			
Special trade contractors		+	
Food and kindred products			
Textile mill products	+		
Apparel and other textile products			
Timber and wood products	+		
Furniture and fixtures		+	–
Paper and allied products	NA		
Printing and publishing		+	+
Chemicals and allied products	+		
Rubber and miscellaneous plastics products			
Leather and leather products		–	
Stone, clay, and glass products			+
Fabricated metal products			
Industrial machinery and equipment	+		
Electronic and other electronic equipment			
Transportation equipment	+		
Instruments and related products	NA	+	
Miscellaneous manufacturing industries	+		
Local and interurban passenger transit			
Trucking and warehousing	+	+	
Water transportation			
Transportation by air	NA		
Transportation services			
Communication	+	+	
Electric, gas, and sanitary services		+	
Wholesale trade – durable goods			
Wholesale trade – nondurable goods	+		+
Building materials and garden supplies			
General merchandise stores		+	
Food stores		+	
Automotive dealers and service stations		+	
Apparel and accessory stores	+	+	
Furniture and homefurnishings stores	+		
Eating and drinking places		+	
Miscellaneous retail	+		

(Continued overleaf)

Table 6.4 Continued

Industry	Location	Growth	Wages
Depository institutions			
Nondepository institutions			+
Security and commodity brokers			
Insurance carriers			–
Insurance agents, brokers, and service		+	
Real estate	+	+	+
Holding and other investment offices			
Hotels and other lodging places	+		+
Personal services	+	+	
Business services		+	+
Auto repair, services, and parking			
Miscellaneous repair services			
Motion pictures			
Amusement and recreation services			
Health services	+		
Legal services			
Educational services			
Social services		+	
Museums, botanical, zoological gardens	NA		
Membership organizations			+
Engineering and management services	+		

Notes: "+" means that the municipality-industry location quotient has a positive and significant effect on the indicator. "–" means that the municipality-industry location quotient has a negative and significant effect on the indicator. Cells are left blank in cases where the location quotient does not have a statistically significant effect on the indicator of growth or development. NA indicates that results are not available for the sector.

far away from an interstate highway. As discussed in the original firm growth paper (Gabe 2004), several of the control variables unrelated to local industry agglomeration have a significant effect on establishment employment growth and wages. Establishment size and age were found to have a negative effect on employment growth, which is consistent with other studies on the topic (Evans 1987; Dunne et al. 1989; Variyam and Kraybill 1992, 1994). Also found in other studies, establishment size has a positive effect on the wages paid by a business (Brown and Medoff 1989; Doms et al. 1997).

The empirical results suggest that all three indicators are, to some degree, positively associated with industry agglomeration. Agglomeration clearly appears to matter, according to at least one indicator of growth or development, in 35 of the 58 two-digit SIC industries. Industry agglomeration encourages business location in 17 of 54 industries, it promotes establishment growth in 17 of 58 industries, and agglomeration increases establishment wages in nine of 58 industries. On the other hand, industry agglomeration has a negative effect on employment growth in one industry, and it decreases wages in two industries.

The municipality-industry location quotient has a positive effect on all three indicators of growth and development in just one industry, "real estate". Industry agglomeration has a positive effect on two of the three indicators in the "printing and publishing", "trucking and warehousing", "communication", "wholesale trade – nondurable goods", "apparel and accessory stores", "hotels and other lodging places", "personal services", and "business services" industries. Finally, the location quotient has a positive effect on one of the three indicators in 24 of the 58 two-digit SIC industries.

These results demonstrate how the indicators of growth and development used in the study capture different aspects of localization externalities. Recall that static localization externalities, most likely to affect establishment location, are the benefits received immediately on beginning operations near other similar businesses. The "timber and wood products" industry, mentioned earlier in the chapter to exhibit clustering in US non-metropolitan areas, provides a good example of an industry characterized by static localization externalities. Wood product businesses flock to an area with a high agglomeration of industry to immediately take advantage of a key natural resource (i.e., Maine's forests). However, for establishments already in operation, there are no signs of dynamic localization externalities resulting in enhanced growth or wages. Beyond this example, it is interesting to note in Table 6.4 that agglomeration affects employment growth or wages in only six of the 17 industries in which agglomeration encourages location. This suggests that static localization externalities rarely lead to lasting agglomeration benefits after an establishment begins operations.

Results also imply that the way in which agglomeration affects growth and development may vary systematically by industry. Although a full comparison based on multiple industry characteristics is beyond the scope of the current analysis, the average size of US industry establishments serves to illustrate this point. In the 17 industries in which industry agglomeration affects location, the average US establishment employed 31.1 workers. This compares with an average of 23.7 workers per establishment in the 37 industries in which agglomeration does not exert a significant effect on location. On the other hand, the average US establishment employed 23.5 workers in those industries in which agglomeration enhances growth, compared to 30.4 workers in the industries in which agglomeration does not have a significant effect on growth. This suggests that agglomeration affects the location of new businesses in industries with a large average employment size, while agglomeration encourages employment growth of incumbent businesses in industries characterized by small establishments. Whereas Kim et al. (2000) found that average establishment size increases an industry's tendency to agglomerate, these results provide some evidence that average establishment size may also influence the ways in which agglomeration affects location and employment growth.

Once again, the concepts of static versus dynamic localization externalities may shed light on these results. It appears that dynamic localization externalities are relevant to industries characterized by small businesses, which is consistent with the idea of "Marshallian" clusters of small businesses engaging in cooperation and coordination over time (Markusen 1996; Barkley and Henry 1997). On the other hand, static localization externalities are important in industries characterized by large businesses. This suggests that businesses more apt to benefit from internal economies of scale (i.e., large employment size) locate in areas to take advantage of industry-specific inputs, but they do not tend to interact much with other local businesses.

Conclusions

The empirical evidence presented in this chapter illustrates some of the challenges in implementing a cluster-based economic development strategy. As discussed by Woodward and Guimarães (Chapter 5) and Barkley and Henry (Chapter 10), important questions arise in picking which industry to target, creating supportive institutions, and helping "latecomers" catch up with established clusters (Barkley and Henry 1997). Results presented in this chapter expand the list of issues that policy-makers must consider when planning a targeted industrial development strategy.

First, the presence of an agglomerated industry does not always lead to the location-specific advantages commonly associated with clusters. Although researchers and economic development practitioners often talk about the benefits of a pooled labour force, shared equipment and specialized machinery, and knowledge spillovers among businesses, there is no guarantee that these benefits will in fact materialize. Survey results for two agglomerated industries in Maine provide modest support for the benefits of a pooled labour force: that is, establishments feel that other businesses in the state are an important source of workers. The evidence related to the benefit received from the availability of specialized machinery is mixed: nearly 70 per cent of biotechnology businesses felt that this affected their profitability or growth potential, whereas only 30 per cent of companies in the environmental and energy technology industry perceived this to be a benefit. Finally, the survey results show that businesses in both industries are likely to share technical information and conduct joint research and development activities with others, but these activities are not necessarily confined to a small geographical area defined by political boundaries.

Another challenge facing policy-makers revealed in the second part of the chapter is that the effects of clusters on local economic vitality differ widely across industries. This suggests that multiple indicators should be used to measure the success of agglomeration-based strategies. The results show that agglomeration encourages location in some industries, especially those made up of large businesses. These static localization externalities arise from industry-specific inputs present in the cluster as well as increased information about business opportunities, which Porter (2000) suggests lowers "entry barriers" to business location. On the other hand, agglomeration tends to stimulate the growth of incumbent establishments in industries characterized by small businesses. This paints a picture of cooperation and coordination among small businesses operating in "Marshallian" clusters.

These results do not imply that local industries made up of large companies will outperform small business industry clusters in terms of supporting new business activity. Using a similar dataset on business location in Maine, Gabe (2003) shows that more new business activity occurs in industry clusters comprised of small establishments than in clusters made up of large companies. This finding, considered along with the analysis presented in this chapter, suggests that although agglomeration is an important location factor in industries characterized by large businesses, small business clusters are generally more conducive to new business activity. The results do not show, however, whether or not large businesses (attracted by industry agglomeration) tend to seek out clusters made up of small establishments.

Gabe's (2003) study also found that, along with average employment size, the average age of establishments in an industry cluster has a negative effect on business location. Likewise, previous analysis found that industry cluster "age" has a negative effect on business employment growth and wages (Gabe 2004). These results show that newly formed clusters are more likely than mature clusters to generate static and dynamic localization externalities. Thus, when implementing and evaluating a targeted economic development strategy, policy-makers should consider attributes of the targeted industry (e.g., average business size) as well as characteristics of the local cluster itself (e.g., age and business size). This multidimensional approach will better illuminate the impact of agglomerations on the local economy.

References

Allen, T., and Gabe, T. (2003) "The business climate for biotechnology in Maine", Maine Agricultural and Forest Experiment Station, University of Maine, Miscellaneous Report 432.

Barkley, D., and Henry, M. (1997) "Rural industrial development: to cluster or not to cluster?" *Review of Agricultural Economics*, 19: 308–25.

Barkley, D., Henry, M., and Kim Y. (1999) "Industry agglomerations and employment change in non-metropolitan areas", *Review of Urban and Regional Development Studies*, 11: 168–86.

Brown, C., and Medoff, J. (1989) "The employer size-wage effect", *Journal of Political Economy*, 97: 1027–59.

Carlton, D. (1983) "The location and employment choices of new firms: an econometric model with discrete and continuous endogenous variables", *Review of Economics and Statistics*, 65: 440–9.

Coughlin, C., and Segev, E. (2000) "Location determinants of new foreign-owned manufacturing plants", *Journal of Regional Science*, 40: 323–51.

Coughlin, C., Terza, J., and Arromdee, V. (1991) "State characteristics and the location of foreign direct investment within the United States", *Review of Economics and Statistics*, 73: 675–83.

Doms, M., Dunne, T., and Troske, K. (1997) "Workers, wages, and technology", *Quarterly Journal of Economics*, 112: 253–90.

Dunne, T., Roberts, M., and Samuelson, L. (1989) "The growth and failure of U.S. manufacturing plants", *Quarterly Journal of Economics*, 104: 671–98.

Evans, D. (1987) "Tests of alternative theories of firm growth", *Journal of Political Economy*, 95: 657–74.

Friedman, J., Gerlowski, D., and Silberman, J. (1992) "What attracts foreign multinational corporations? evidence from branch plant location in the United States", *Journal of Regional Science*, 32: 403–18.

Gabe, T. (2003) "Local industry agglomeration and new business activity", *Growth and Change*, 34: 17–39.

—— . (2004) "Establishment growth in small cities and towns", *International Regional Science Review*, 27: 164–86.

Gabe, T., and Bell, K. (2004) "Tradeoffs between local taxes and government spending as determinants of business location", *Journal of Regional Science*, 44: 21–41.

Gibbs, R., and Bernat, G. (1997) "Rural industry clusters raise local earnings", *Rural Development Perspectives*, 12: 18–25.

Glaeser, E., Kallal, H., Scheinkman, J., and Shleifer, A. (1992) "Growth in cities", *Journal of Political Economy*, 100: 1126–52.

Greene, W. (2000) *Econometric Analysis*, 4th edn, Upper Saddle River, NJ: Prentice Hall.

Guimarães, P., Figueiredo, O., and Woodward, D. (2000) "Agglomeration and the location of foreign direct investment in Portugal", *Journal of Urban Economics*, 47: 115–35.

—— . (2003) "A tractable approach to the firm location decision problem", *Review of Economics and Statistics*, 85: 201–4.

Hall, B. (1987) "The relationship between firm size and firm growth in the US manufacturing sector", *Journal of Industrial Economics*, 35: 583–606.

Hart, P., and Prais, S. (1956) "The analysis of business concentration: a statistical approach", *Journal of the Royal Statistical Society*, 119: 150–81.

Head, K., Ries, J., and Swenson, D. (1995) "Agglomeration benefits and location choice: evidence from Japanese manufacturing investments in the United States", *Journal of International Economics*, 38: 223–47.

Henderson, V. (1997) "Externalities and industrial development", *Journal of Urban Economics*, 42: 449–70.

Henderson, V., Kuncoro, A., and Turner, M. (1995) "Industrial development in cities", *Journal of Political Economy*, 103: 1067–90.

Henry, M., and Drabenstott, M. (1996) "A new micro view of the U.S. rural economy", *Economic Review*, 81: 53–70.

Howells, J. (2002) "Tacit knowledge, innovation and economic growth", *Urban Studies*, 39: 871–84.

Hymer, S., and Pashigian, P. (1962) "Firm size and rate of growth", *Journal of Political Economy*, 70: 556–69.

Jacobs, J. (1969) *The Economy of Cities*, New York: Vintage.

Jovanovic, B. (1982) "Selection and the evolution of industry", *Econometrica*, 50: 649–70.

Kim, Y., Barkley, D., and Henry, M. (2000) "Industry characteristics linked to establishment concentrations in nonmetropolitan areas", *Journal of Regional Science*, 40: 231–59.

Krugman, P. (1991) *Geography and Trade*, Cambridge, MA: MIT Press.

McFadden, D. (1974) "Conditional logit analysis of qualitative choice behavior", in P. Zarembka (ed.), *Frontiers in Econometrics*, New York: Academic Press.

Markusen, A. (1996) "Sticky places in slippery space: a typology of industrial districts", *Economic Geography*, 72: 293–313.

Marshall, A. (1890) *Principles of Economics*, London: Macmillan.

Noblet, C., and Gabe, T. (2006) "Business climate for Maine's environmental and energy technology sector", Department of Resource Economics and Policy, University of Maine, Staff Paper 565.

O'hUallachain, B., and Satterthwaite, M. (1992) "Sectoral growth patterns at the metropolitan level: an evaluation of economic development incentives", *Journal of Urban Economics*, 31: 25–58.

Porter, M. (1990) *The Competitive Advantage of Nations*, New York: Free Press.

—— . (2000) "Location, competition, and economic development: local clusters in a global economy", *Economic Development Quarterly*, 14: 15–34.

Romer, P. (1986) "Increasing returns and long-run growth", *Journal of Political Economy*, 94: 1002–37.

Simon, H., and Bonini, C. (1958) "The size distribution of business firms", *American Economic Review*, 48: 607–17.

Singh, A., and Whittington, G. (1975) "The size and growth of firms", *Review of Economic Studies*, 42: 15–26.

Sveikauskas, L. (1975) "The productivity of cities", *Quarterly Journal of Economics*, 89: 393–413.

Variyam, J., and Kraybill, D. (1992) "Empirical evidence on determinants of firm growth", *Economics Letters*, 38: 31–6.

—— . (1994) "Managerial inputs and the growth of rural small firms", *American Journal of Agricultural Economics*, 76: 568–75.

Part II

Empirical modelling approaches

A. Location probability and attractive score models

7 Modelling the probability of manufacturing activity in the Great Plains

John C. Leatherman and Terry L. Kastens

Introduction

Despite the fact that many rural regions have been buoyed by urban expansion, attraction for rural amenities, and high energy and commodity prices, many regions within rural America continue to struggle with population loss and economic decline. Persistent pockets of poverty in the South and Appalachia, natural resource dependence in many Western states, and continuing agricultural dependence in the Midwest have left many rural communities and regions without prospects for growth. This certainly is true in the Great Plains region of the United States, where traditional economic sectors (agriculture, energy, and manufacturing) are insufficient to sustain many rural communities. The dearth of alternative employment opportunities has led workers and their families to seek opportunities in larger population centres, leaving behind rural communities with stagnant or declining population and economic bases.

For those who remain, the desire for new economic opportunity is intense. New business recruitment is among the highest priority local economic development strategies for many communities. Despite the competitive and high-risk nature of industrial recruitment, it has a place in the toolbox of local economic development strategies. The challenge is one of making wise choices in targeting the expenditure of scarce local resources to market the community to prospective employers.

In this chapter, we provide an overview of an industrial targeting system used to help local officials improve decision-making related to selection of targets for business recruitment. The Plains Economic Targeting System (PETS) consists of a series of econometric equations that match industry input and market requirements with community characteristics to generate a probability of new business location over a given time period. The original system matched location requirements for 78 industry sectors to local characteristics for 414 counties in six states (Leatherman et al. 2002). Further, the coefficients generated for a given county were transformed into marginal impacts, providing important information relating to local policies that can improve the probability of attracting a given industry.

While PETS provides insight into prospect probabilities, it does not offer any indication of the likely scale of activity (number of jobs), the quality of new employment, or any other important location factor not considered in the analysis. Additional information will be needed to determine both the location needs of specific sectors as well as the type of costs or benefits that would accrue to the community resulting from any specific activity.

Here, we focus on a subset of the system's output related to manufacturing activity included in the model. The system is offered as one among several methods outlined in this volume not only to help local officials better understand realistic development opportunities, but also to provide a better understanding of prospects for promoting interindustry networks. The chapter proceeds with a brief discussion of business recruitment strategies. The factors influential to economic growth and the methods used to create PETS are then presented. Use of the system is illustrated by presenting the output for a single place, and by discussing regional and industry linkages. Finally, the implications for rural economic development strategies are addressed.

Industry targeting strategies

Targeted industry marketing has been used as an economic development strategy for decades (Sweet 1994; Deller and Goetz, Chapter 2). Over time, it has evolved from a general community marketing approach to one that carefully selects targets based on industry growth prospects, potential benefits to the community, and the extent to which the community can provide the production inputs, market access, and overall business climate conducive to a firm or an industry's success (McClenahen 1996). Careful targeting is necessary given the cost of effective marketing, the high degree of competition between places, and the limited number of desirable growth opportunities.

The process of industry targeting typically begins by ranking industry sectors according to their relative attractiveness to the community (Boyle 1994; McKee 1994). Attractiveness criteria can include historic and projected growth patterns, size, profitability, and other factors. Those industries ranking high in attractiveness are evaluated in terms of their location criteria, such as labour, energy, or transportation needs. The community then performs a self-evaluation to determine its competitive position in meeting those needs.

A variety of analytic techniques has been used in the target selection process. All are designed to help the community narrow the range of potential targets to a relative few likely and/or desirable prospects. Industry location quotients have long been used to determine which sectors are growing most rapidly. Analysing backward and forward interindustry linkages has been used to identify targets for import substitution (Anderson and Johnston 1992; Hefner and Guimarães 1995; Deller, Chapter 19). Recently, cluster analysis has been used to identify regional growth opportunities (Feser et al. 2000; Kim et al. 2000; Stough et al. 2000). Other work has focused on spatial competition (Bresnahan and Reiss 1991; Thill 1992). To help project potential community impacts, various measures such as payroll per employee and employment per establishment have been devised (Whaley and LaCroix 1997). Finally, techniques such as the analytical hierarchy procedure also have been used to assist in determining community preferences for growth alternatives (Cox et al. 2000; Johnson, Chapter 13).

Location models are among the tools available to assist in the process of evaluating community competitiveness for various industry sectors. These models match industry location requirements to community characteristics. Over the past two decades, considerable research has been conducted to identify the location requirements of different industry sectors (Kusmin 1994). The factors identified in these location studies become the inputs into location models that can consider a wide variety of potential industry targets.

An earlier version of the industry targeting system used here was built in the mid-1980s (Goode and Hastings 1989). The Northeast Industrial Targeting (NIT) and Economic Development Database (EDD) systems matched industry requirements with community characteristics for 69 aggregate manufacturing sectors for 730 non-metropolitan communities in the northeastern United States. The PETS draws from Goode's modelling procedures, but incorporates a number of important modifications in adapting it to the Great Plains, exploiting its information potential, and updating it by acknowledging a wider variety of economic growth targets.

The probability-type model described here built on Goode's original work and expanded sectoral consideration to encompass a wider variety of economic activity, including transportation, trade, and service activities. Following on this effort, Davis Reum and Harris (2006 and Chapter 9) overcome some of the methodological challenges inherent in limited data availability by using a double-hurdle procedure in constructing their model for Western states' manufacturing activity (also see Gabe, Chapter 6).

A conceptual model of business growth

Conceptually, it is assumed that for a given place, the probability of business growth is a function of key community attributes coupled with industry input and market requirements:

$$\text{business growth} = f(\text{community economic conditions, social climate, infrastructure, labour force, and market access}) \quad (1)$$

Community economic characteristics

The literature on economic growth suggests a number of variables that might be considered in transforming the conceptual model in equation (1) into an empirical specification. Location factors can be categorized as including tax variables, government expenditure variables, labour market variables, education, market access, demographic characteristics, regional characteristics, industrial composition effects, and additional variables (Kusmin 1994). A description of the variables selected for PETS is found in Table 7.1. The effects of any of the variables would be expected to differ depending on the sector modelled. For example, higher local expenditures for education might negatively affect manufacturing while having a positive impact on business services.

Bartik (1991, 1992) found that local tax rates generally had a negative effect on economic growth for communities, with the highest rates occurring in metropolitan areas. Overall, the effects of local taxes appear to depend on the mix of taxes, the use to which taxes are put, and the opportunity for interlocal (interstate) competition on the basis of taxes (Fox and Murray 1990;

Table 7.1 Variables incorporated into the Plains Economic Targeting System

Dependent variable
Business growth (1 if positive growth in the number of establishments for a given sector between 1986 and 1994, 0 otherwise)

Independent variables
Community economic conditions
Per capita total local government (county) tax revenues
Percentage of county employment in agriculture
Percentage of county employment in manufacturing
Percentage of county employment in services
Median value of housing ($/house)
Lagged industry growth (1 if growth in 1977–84 (1985–94 in predictive models) for a given sector, 0 otherwise)
Five state variables (1 if the county is in that state, 0 otherwise; Kansas as the excluded category)

Community social attributes
Percentage of families below poverty level
Local per capita expenditures for public safety
Median age of county residents

Community infrastructure
Local per capita expenditures for highways
Presence of an interstate highway (1 if present, 0 otherwise)
Presence of a commercial airport (1 if present, 0 otherwise)

Industry input/market conditions
Total county population
County population density (persons per square mile)
Metro influence (1 if Beale Code 1–5, 0 if Beale Code 6–9, all counties over 75,000 population excluded)
Percentage of age ≥25 population with more than a high school education
Local per capita expenditures for education
County labour force participation rate (% of total population included in the labour force)
County average earnings per job (%)

Gabe and Bell 2004; Kusmin 1994; Newman and Sullivan 1988). County industrial composition effects reflect potential linkages with input providers or markets, or the presence of agglomeration economies (Bartik 1989; Carlton 1983; Fox and Murray 1990; Kusmin et al. 1996; Smith et al. 1978; Wasylenko 1991). The value of housing in a community was also hypothesized to be an important community characteristic, reflecting land costs or a personal amenity important to business owners and managers. The state variable reflects the laws, policies, and institutions unique to each state as well as the influences of other factors not specified in this system (Bartik 1989; Holmes 1998; Schmenner et al. 1987). Finally, the lagged growth variable reflects the presumption that industry performance in one time period has a carryover effect to the next period.

The lagged growth variable in many respects mirrors the efforts inherent in the clustering perspectives of prevalence today. The desirability of clustering is for purposes of fostering a regional network of economic activity that feeds into a regional momentum of economic activity. In this system, it is simply presumed that past economic performance helps propel current economic performance with no assertion of any causal genesis. Nonetheless, to the extent lagged growth performance is found to be predictive of future economic probabilities, at least indirect support is offered for the notion that such network/agglomeration economies are important to foster and capture.

Community social climate

Several indicators of a community's social climate were incorporated into the system. Local rates of poverty may have either positive or negative effects, presumably reflecting wage conditions in the labour market for individual sectors (Killian and Parker 1991; Kusmin 1994; Porterfield 1990). The age distribution (median age) may provide signals relating to the overall labour market (Killian and Parker 1991; Wasylenko and McGuire 1985). Finally, county per capita expenditures for public safety were assumed to reflect local needs and preferences for public goods and services (Bartik 1989; Gabe and Bell 2004), another indicator of social climate.

It might be noted that government tax and expenditure data discussed elsewhere among the explanatory variables are likely to reflect certain countervailing effects in business location decisions. On balance in the literature, it is generally accepted that although taxes typically have a negative effect in business location decisions, the spending they support often has a positive impact. The challenge in a future modelling exercise will be to craft "net" measures where it makes sense to try to capture the net effect on balance of these types of investments.

Community infrastructure

The quality and extent of a community's infrastructure is generally considered an important location variable. County per capita expenditures for highways (Kusmin 1994; Kusmin et al. 1996), the presence of an interstate highway (dummy variable) (Carlino and Mills 1987; Fox and Murray 1990; McHugh and Wilkinson 1988), and the presence of a commercial airport (dummy) (Fox and Murray 1990; Kusmin et al. 1996; Porterfield 1990) were seen as providing important signals related to public infrastructure.

Industry input (labour force) and market requirements

Specific industries have both input and market access requirements that were seen as important location determinants. Input determinants included in this system related primarily to qualities of the local labour force. County per capita expenditures for education, educational attainment (percentage of population with greater than high school education) (Bartik 1989; Killian and Parker 1991; Kusmin et al. 1996; Porterfield 1990), labour force participation rate, and average wage rates (Fox and Murray 1980; Kusmin et al. 1996) were incorporated into the study. Similarly, market access is important to many types of business activities (Dorf and Emerson 1978; Kusmin 1994). Total population, proximity to a metropolitan area (Dorf and Emerson 1978; McNamara et al. 1988; Mead 1982), and population density (Schmenner et al. 1987) were considered.[1]

It may be worth noting at this point in the review of explanatory variables that our modelling system is very much intended to be a "practitioner's tool" as opposed to a rigorous theoretically driven modelling system. We included all factors where comparable data exists and for which previous research had shown was related to business location decisions. We then let the data "speak" to what's actually important. Further, in our system, we permit all of the explanatory variables to remain regardless of significance so long as we logically justify their inclusion at the start versus the alternative approach of retaining only the best fitting model for each industry. Admittedly, the approach is left to the modeller to select on the basis of his or her belief structure about appropriate modelling techniques.

Aggregate business sectors represented in the economic targeting system

PETS incorporates economic activity associated with 78 aggregate industries (or business sectors) viewed as having growth potential in rural areas, and includes manufacturing (38 industries); transportation, communication, and public utilities (5); wholesale trade (20); finance, insurance, and real estate (7); and business services (8). This inclusiveness recognizes the rural growth potential associated with a wider range of activities. Most other studies have been limited to manufacturing activity and, more recently, business services (Porterfield 1990). The industry sectors included represent an aggregation scheme intended to balance the need for specificity of industry identity and sufficient data to generate likely probabilities and reasonably reliable effects based on statistically significant coefficients.

The scheme began with county-level activity specified at a four-digit Standard Industrial Classification (SIC) level. The US Census Bureau's *County Business Patterns* was used to count the number of positive business changes for each of the 414 study area counties between 1986 and 1994 (US Department of Commerce 1986, 1994). Where the increased industry counts were insufficient, industries were aggregated within the same numeric range. For example, within the class 2000, there was sufficient activity to leave 2010, 2020, 2030, and 2040 disaggregated at a three-digit level, while all other sectors in the 2050–2999 range were aggregated to the 2000 not elsewhere classified (nec) SIC.

"Sufficient activity" was determined on the basis of the perceived relevance of an industry sector to the Great Plains region. Whereas Goode (1989) clustered manufacturing activity into sectors until 100 instances of increase in number of establishments were counted, the Great Plains region does not have nearly as much activity to allow such a threshold while retaining any useful specificity. Some sectors that represent important rural sectors were left disaggregated despite relatively small numbers of additional establishments. Increases in the number of establishments within sectors ranged from 11 to 283. Forty-one sectors had more than 100 additional establishments, 23 had between 50 and 100 additional establishments, and 14 had less than 50. The manufacturing sectors included in the discussion here are shown in Table 7.2.

Methods used to create the economic targeting system

To summarize the methods used to construct the PETS, 1980 county characteristics were used to explain economic growth occurring between 1986 and 1994. The parameter estimates from the 1980 model were inserted into a predictive equation containing 1990 county characteristics to generate probabilities of industry growth between 1995 and 2003. Finally, the coefficients from the second model were used to derive the marginal impacts associated with each of the independent variables.

The Great Plains generally encompasses an area extending northward from northern Texas to western Minnesota and west to eastern Montana (Rowley 1998). PETS includes 414 counties in North Dakota, South Dakota, Nebraska, Kansas, Oklahoma, and the northern Texas panhandle region with a 1980 population of less than 75,000 each. Because the PETS is intended to project activity in rural counties, 16 counties with population greater than 75,000 were excluded. The study area is shown in Figures 7.1a–7.1d.

The dependent variable for the PETS model was binary. Counts of the

Table 7.2 Manufacturing sectors represented in the PETS system

Industry Sector	Standard Industrial Class
Non-durable goods manufacturing	
Food and Kindred Products	2000
Meat Products	2010
Dairy Products	2020
Preserved Fruits and Vegetables	2030
Grain Mill Products	2040
Textile Mill Products	2200
Apparel and Other Textile Products	2300
Timber and Wood Products	2400
Millwork, Plywood and Structural Members	2430
Furniture and Fixtures	2500
Household Furniture	2510
Paper and Allied Products	2600
Printing and Publishing	2700
Newspapers	2710
Commercial Printing	2750
Chemicals and Allied Products	2800
Industrial Inorganic Chemicals	2810
Agricultural Chemicals	2870
Petroleum and Coal Products	2900
Durable goods manufacturing	
Rubber and Misc. Plastics Products	3000
Leather and Leather Products	3100
Stone, Clay, and Glass Products	3200
Concrete, Gypsum, and Plaster Products	3270
Primary Metal Industries	3300
Fabricated Metal Products	3400
Fabricated Structural Metal Products	3440
Industrial Machinery and Equipment	3500
Farm and Garden Machinery	3520
Construction and Related Machinery	3530
Metalworking Machinery	3540
Special Industry Machinery	3550
General Industrial Machinery	3560
Industrial Machinery, Nec	3590
Electronic and Other Electric Equipment	3600
Electronic Components and Accessories	3670
Transportation Equipment	3700
Instruments and Related Products	3800
Miscellaneous Manufacturing Industries	3900

total number of establishments at the four-digit SIC level were taken for each of the 414 counties in the study area for the years 1986 and 1994. A county was given a score of 1 if the total number of businesses within an industry sector increased between the two time periods, and 0 if the number remained unchanged or declined. Industry sectors were then aggregated to the final 78

PETS Region and Probabilities for Food and Kindred Products (SICS 2000) Location, 1995-2003

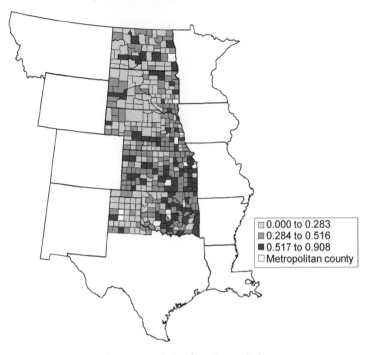

Metropolitan counties were excluded from the analysis.

Figure 7.1a PETS region and probabilities for food and kindred products (SIC 2000) location, 1995–2003.

for each county. Thus, the dependent variable consisted of a zero/one score for the 78 industry sectors in each of the 414 PETS counties.

The independent variables described above consisted of 23 community characteristics for each county thought to be important to business location decisions. Explanatory variables were constructed from the 1980 and 1990 US Census of Population and other sources. The proximity to metro area variable was based on the 1993 rural/urban continuum codes developed by the US Department of Agriculture's (USDA) Economic Research Service (Butler and Beale 1994). The codes range from zero for major metro core counties to nine for the most remote rural counties. The variable was structured as a binary variable with counties coded one through five (zero-coded counties were excluded in the model) counted as a one, and counties coded six to nine counted as a zero. The 24th variable was the lagged business growth variable, counted as one if there was a positive change in the industry sector being modeled in the period 1977 to 1985 and zero otherwise.

The procedures used to generate predicted probabilities are generally based

PETS Region and Probabilities for Printing and Publishing (SIC 2700) Location, 1995-2003

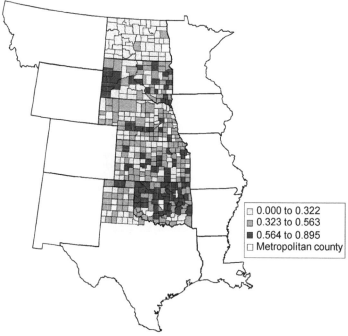

- □ 0.000 to 0.322
- ▦ 0.323 to 0.563
- ■ 0.564 to 0.895
- □ Metropolitan county

Metropolitan counties were excluded from the analysis.

Figure 7.1b PETS region and probabilities for printing and publishing (SIC 2700) location, 1995–2003.

on those outlined in Goode (1989, 1993). Whereas Goode used an ordinary least squares regression procedure, the PETS equations were estimated using a logistic regression procedure due to the binary (0/1) nature of the dependent variable. Each estimated equation was of the form:

$$\text{Prob}(G^{86-94}_{i,k} = 1) = \frac{e^{(a_i + b_{i,1} C^{80}_1 + b_{i,2} C^{80}_2 + \ldots b_{i,23} C^{80}_{23} + b_{i,24} G^{77-85}_{i,k})}}{\{1 + e^{(a_i + b_{i,1} C^{80}_1 + b_{i,2} C^{80}_2 + \ldots b_{i,23} C^{80}_{23} + b_{i,24} G^{77-85}_{i,k})}\}} + \varepsilon_{i,k}, \tag{2}$$

where:

$G^{86-94}_{i,k} = 1$ if the number of businesses increased for industry i in county k over the period 1986–1994, 0 otherwise.

$C^{80}_{1,k} \ldots C^{80}_{23,k}$ are the values of 23 community characteristics in 1980 for counties 1 through k.

$G^{77-85}_{i,k}$ is the lagged dependent variable measuring industry growth over the period 1977–1985 for the ith industry in county k.

PETS Region and Probabilities for Rubber and Misc. Plastics Products (SIC 3000), 1995-2003

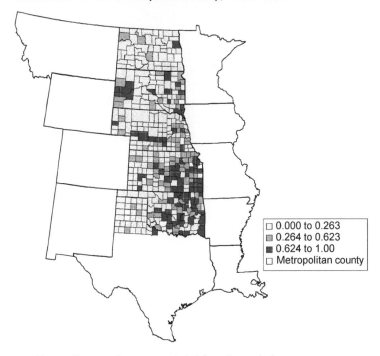

☐ 0.000 to 0.263
▨ 0.264 to 0.623
■ 0.624 to 1.00
☐ Metropolitan county

Metropolitan counties were excluded from the analysis.

Figure 7.1c PETS region and probabilities for rubber and misc. plastics products (SIC 3000) location, 1995–2003.

$a_i, b_{i,1} \ldots B_{i,24}$ are the parameters to be estimated for equation (industry sector) i.

$\varepsilon_{i,k}$ is the model i error for county k (assumed logistically distributed).

Using maximum likelihood, equation (1) was independently estimated for each of $I = 78$ industries

The resulting parameter estimates were then incorporated into a predictive equation of the same form as equation (2), along with 1990 values for the independent variables. While Goode set nonsignificant parameter estimates to zero and retained the significant parameter values to create an implicit weighting system, PETS retained all parameter estimates regardless of significance. Expected probabilities of an increase in the number of establishments during the next eight-year period, 1995–2003, were generated using:

$$P^{95\text{--}03}_{i,k} = \frac{e^{(\hat{b}_0 + \hat{b}_{i,1}C_1^{90} + \hat{b}_{i,2}C_2^{90} + \ldots + \hat{b}_{i,23}C_{23}^{90} + \hat{b}_{i,24}G_{i,k}^{86\text{-}94})}}{\{1 + e^{(\hat{b}_0 + \hat{b}_{i,1}C_1^{90} + \hat{b}_{i,2}C_2^{90} + \ldots + \hat{b}_{i,23}C_{23}^{90} + \hat{b}_{i,24}G_{i,k}^{86\text{-}94})}\}},$$ (3)

Industrial Machinery and Equipment (SIC 3500), 1995-2003

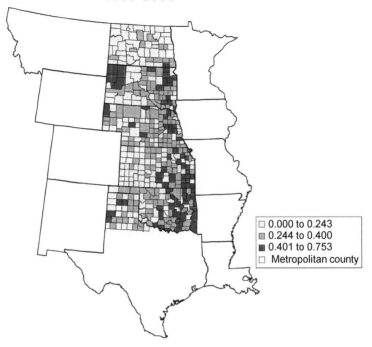

0.000 to 0.243
0.244 to 0.400
0.401 to 0.753
Metropolitan county

Metropolitan counties were excluded from the analysis.

Figure 7.1d PETS region and probabilities for industrial machinery and equipment (SIC 3500) location, 1995–2003.

where:

$P_{i,k}^{95-03}$ is the predicted probability of an increase in the number of industry i establishments in county k between 1995 and 2003.
$C_{i,k}^{90} + \ldots + C_{23,k}^{90}$ are the values of 23 community characteristics in 1990 for counties 1 through k.
$G_{i,k}^{86-94}$ is a lagged industry growth variable for the ith industry in county k.
$\hat{b}_0$ and $\hat{b}_1 - \hat{b}_{24}$ are the parameter estimates derived from the 1986–1994 model in equation (2).

To better understand the influence of each independent variable on expected growth, the parameter estimates in equation (3) were used to derive marginal impacts. The marginal impact is defined as the expected change in probability of growth associated with a one-unit change in some explanatory variable. For a particular industry model, say industry i, the change in probability of growth for county k associated with a one-unit change in the nth variable, $B_{i,k,n}$, is calculated as (suppressing the 95–03 superscript):

$$B_{i,k,n} = \hat{b}_{i,n} * P_{i,k} * (1 - P_{i,k}),$$ (4a)

where $\hat{b}_{i,n}$ is taken from the ith estimated equation in the group of equations described by equation (2) and $P_{i,k}$ is taken from equation (3).

To obtain a measure of the expected marginal impact of the nth variable on growth in the ith industry across all counties (a total of K counties, here 414), as might be needed to establish a more general understanding of the impact of the nth variable on growth for industry i, a simple average of the marginal impacts in equation (4a) is constructed:

$$B_{i,n}^* = 1/K * \sum_k B_{i,k,n}.$$ (4b)

Similarly, to generalize across industries (a total of I industries, here 78) as well as counties, the following expected marginal impact of the nth variable is constructed:

$$B_n^{**} = 1/(I*K) * \sum_i \sum_k B_{i,k,n}.$$ (4c)

Of course, other levels of generality can easily be obtained by appropriately constructing the average marginal impact.

Because the marginal impact as calculated in equation (4a) is only correct for a very small change in the independent variable, it is not appropriate to apply that expected change to the relatively large change associated with jumping from zero to one for a binary independent variable (e.g., building a commercial airport where none had existed). Thus, for a binary independent variable, the marginal impact associated with moving from zero to one was calculated as the difference in the predicted probability associated with the independent variable evaluated at one, less the predicted probability when it was evaluated at zero.

To evaluate the predictive utility of the system, two models were created based on an earlier version of PETS. The first counted the change in number of business establishments for each of the 78 sectors between 1977 and 1985 in the study region regressed on the 1980 independent variables. The second counted the change in the number of business establishments for each of the sectors between 1986 and 1994 regressed on the 1980 independent variables. The predictions generated by the two models were compared to the actual changes in the two periods. By a slight degree, the predictions for the future period, 1986–1994, were more accurate than the earlier period. This provided at least some evidence that current conditions could be used to predict future activity and that the change over at least this period was not so great as to suggest vast structural changes in economic relationships.

As we indicated earlier, the importance of the lagged growth effect implies that whatever local or regional network/agglomeration effect that may in some measure have influenced industry performance in one time period helps to propel it into the next period. This is, in spirit, the same influence cluster approaches seek to capture in fostering a regional economic cluster.

Outlook for a single county

The Plains Economic Targeting System is intended to assist officials at the local level identify the most likely prospects for new economic development. Use of the system is illustrated by the case of Smith County, Kansas, a remote rural county (5,947 population) on the Nebraska border in north central Kansas.

Selected industry growth probabilities for Smith County manufacturing are shown in Table 7.3. The rank shows where among the 78 total sectors considered each of the manufacturing activities falls. The probabilities reflect the relative likelihood there will be an increase in the number of establishments within an identified industry sector between 1995 and 2003. In the case of Smith County, the overall probability of new manufacturing activity was fairly low. The system predicted there was only about a 30 per cent chance that a new manufacturing establishment of the highest-ranked manufacturer would appear between 1995 and 2003. The best manufacturing prospects include stone, clay, and glass products; industrial machinery and equipment; and printing and publishing.

If Smith County officials wanted to know how to improve their probability for a given prospect, or were otherwise interested in a strategy of adding to or diversifying the existing economic base, they might be interested in examining the marginal impacts associated with specific sectors. For illustration, the marginal impacts of four of the highest-probability manufacturing sectors are shown in Table 7.4, together with Smith County's 1990 independent variable values. The state marginal impacts generally indicate that Smith County compares somewhat unfavorably to counties in other states for these manufacturing activities. Local officials also can determine that their county's small population size may hinder their efforts. They may want to think about strategies to mitigate the generally strong negative effects associated with local poverty. It also appears that their heavy dependence on agricultural employment would not especially hurt their chances for attracting several of these activities. Taken together, the information related to marginal impacts may help local officials develop strategies about points of emphasis for marketing or programmes to mitigate the negative conditions that may exist.

An additional potential application of PETS could be to inform local business retention and expansion (BR&E) programmes. To the extent we

Table 7.3 Manufacturing prospect industries for Smith County, KS, 1995–2003

Rank Order	Probability of Growth	Industry SIC Code	Industry Sector Description
13	0.323	3200	Stone, Clay and Glass Products
16	0.280	3500	Industrial Machinery and Equipment
17	0.273	2700	Printing and Publishing
23	0.208	2710	Newspapers
24	0.206	2510	Household Furniture
25	0.200	3400	Fabricated Metal Products
26	0.199	3590	Industrial Machinery, Nec
27	0.194	2000	Food and Kindred Products
31	0.156	2040	Grain Mill Products
32	0.148	3000	Rubber and Misc. Plastics Products
34	0.139	3270	Concrete, Gypsum and Plaster Products
35	0.128	3700	Transportation Equipment
36	0.114	2500	Furniture and Fixtures
39	0.108	2400	Timber and Wood Products
41	0.093	2750	Commercial Printing
42	0.092	3900	Misc. Manufacturing Industries
43	0.086	2300	Apparel and Other Textile Products
48	0.066	2430	Millwork, Plywood & Structural Members
49	0.063	2010	Meat Products
52	0.048	3800	Instruments and Related Products
53	0.048	2600	Paper and Allied Products
54	0.037	3600	Electronic and Other Electric Equipment
56	0.036	2030	Preserved Fruits and Vegetables
57	0.034	2800	Chemicals and Allied Products
61	0.025	3440	Fabricated Structural Metal Products
62	0.022	3540	Metalworking Machinery
63	0.021	3300	Primary Metal Industries
64	0.020	3550	Special Industry Machinery
65	0.013	2200	Textile Mill Products
69	0.006	3670	Electronic Components and Accessories
70	0.006	2900	Petroleum and Coal Products
74	0.003	3560	General Industrial Machinery
75	0.002	2870	Agricultural Chemicals
76	0.002	3100	Leather and Leather Products
77	0.000	2810	Industrial Inorganic Chemicals
78	0.000	2020	Dairy Products

observe sectors with high probabilities of additional establishments appearing, we would presume those that are currently present in the economy will have future expansion opportunities. Further, to the extent we find these activities have characteristics deemed desirable for local development purposes (e.g., Johnson, Chapter 13), these sectors also may become the foci for cluster development efforts.

Table 7.4 Marginal effects in decimal form and significant growth variables for highest-probability manufacturing industries for Smith County, KS, 1995–2003

Independent variable	1990 Smith County value	SIC 3200: Stone, Clay and Glass Products	SIC 3500: Industrial Machinery and Equipment	SIC 2700: Printing and Publishing	SIC 2510: Household Furniture
North Dakota	0	-0.41121	-0.29888	0.34437	0.14333
South Dakota	0	0.18713	0.19354	0.33229	0.02555
Nebraska	0	-0.00293	0.11334	0.36688	0.00599
Oklahoma	0	0.09918	0.01385	0.50104	-0.06188
Texas	0	0.09599	0.11135	-1.22910	-1.11399
Metro effect	0	-0.13309	-0.04685	-0.15742	0.09051
Interstate	0	0.02270	0.00831	0.07718	0.03107
Airport	0	-0.01274	-0.03623	0.06709	-0.03697
Population (per 1,000)	5,947	0.00535	0.00768	0.00399	0.01141
Population density (per square mile)	6.6	-0.00026	0.00226	0.00232	0.00165
Families below poverty (%)	13.0	-0.02056	-0.01655	-0.04510	-0.02905
Total per cap. local govt. revenue ($)	$542	-0.00024	-0.00038	0.00016	-0.00016
Local per cap. expend. highways ($)	$202	0.00004	-0.00044	-0.00121	-0.00085
Local per cap. expend. education ($)	$519	0.00011	0.00000	0.00016	0.00028
Local per cap. expend. public safety ($)	$28	0.00011	0.00165	0.00012	0.00039
Population with some college (%)	66.3	-0.00288	-0.00127	-0.00759	-0.01040
Median age in county	42.9	-0.00129	-0.00099	-0.02312	0.00003
Average county wage ($)	$8.68	-0.00339	0.00603	0.04667	-0.00839
Labour force participation rate (%)	53.4%	0.00725	0.00746	0.00465	0.00754
Housing value (per house)	$18,300	-0.00219	-0.00139	-0.00087	-0.00996
Agricultural employment (%)	30.7%	0.00101	-0.00062	0.01105	0.00457
Manufacturing employment (%)	5.9%	-0.00245	-0.00254	0.00755	0.00813
Service employment (%)	25.7%	0.00806	-0.00159	-0.02062	0.00163

Building networks of economic activity

Additional insights can be derived from the PETS system by considering the relationships of manufacturing activity. Porter emphasizes the notion of building networks of interrelated activities in pursuit of economic clusters. We consider the probabilities generated by PETS for all counties and all industries. First, we consider the geographic proximity of industry sectors by the relative probabilities. The probabilities for a sampling of manufacturing sectors for all study counties are mapped in Figure 7.1. Overall, the probabilities range from zero to 100 per cent. Mapping the probabilities allows a visual analysis of the spatial aggregation of county prospects for this activity. In general, the probability of new activity of this type occurring follows the population distribution found in the states considered. Further, the spatial proximities observed make intuitive sense considering transportation routes, sectoral employment patterns, and commodity production patterns known to exist in states included. In contrast to the Porter notion that state policies for the most part are irrelevant, we note fairly distinct patterns of both heightened and lower probability levels that coincide with state boundaries.

Taking the interindustry relationships one step further, the correlation coefficients between each of the manufacturing sectors and each of the other 78 industries in the model are provided in Figure 7.2. This aspatial view suggests both the potential spin-off effects of industry location, and the necessary production input "infrastructure" likely to be needed by an activity.

Here, without regard to any specific geographic locale, we observe what activities tend to be found together. Looking at it from the two sides, it would help to suggest that if a given activity were present, what other activities might want to be in close proximity to it (might follow it). We might then suggest that a desirable target industry is one that tends to be connected to a lot of other activities. Conversely, it might suggest the other industries that may need to be present in order to be successful in attracting a given target.

Given the relatively large number of observations (counties) included in the model, a correlation was significant at a relatively low level, about 0.11. To gain insight, we group them by the strength of their association in Figure 7.2. Reading down a column, the density of the shading observed shows the extent to which the manufacturing activity is likely to attract other economic activities. Reading across the rows and noting the shading density shows what other economic sectors are likely needed within reasonable geographic proximity if a locality would hope to attract a prospect.

Among those manufacturing activities likely to attract a larger number of associated activities, commercial printing, chemical and allied products, rubber and miscellaneous products, and fabricated metals tend to be strongly associated with a large number of other activities. Conversely, those sectors with fairly weak linkages to other activities include several food products and multiple agriculture-related manufacturers. Considering the services and other inputs generally required by manufacturers, business services and

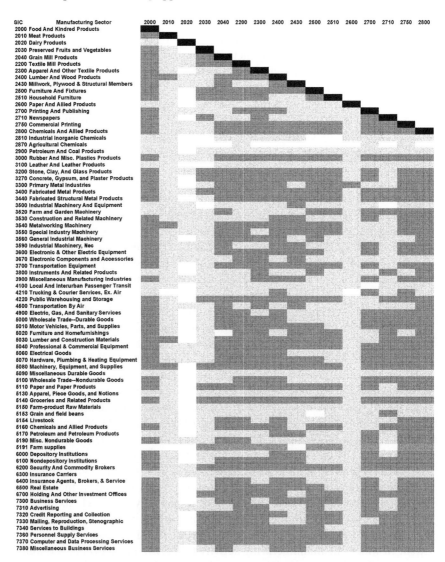

Figure 7.2 Manufacturing activity correlations with 78 PETS industries.

transportation services are among those most strongly associated. Thus, if networks are the key to economic competitiveness, our correlation matrix suggests the activities are likely to foster dense networks in the region.

Conclusion

In this chapter, we presented and discussed an industry targeting system for the Great Plains region. The system calculates the probability of new industry

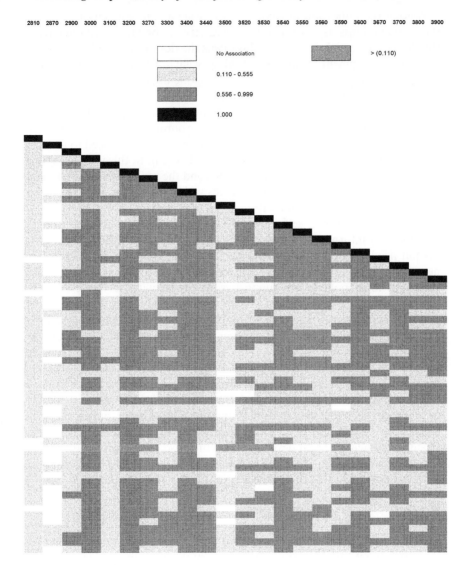

establishments at the county level for 78 business sectors. In addition to an overall probability, the system estimates the marginal impacts associated with a number of community and regional characteristics generally thought important to business growth. Further, the system incorporates information associated with a wider variety of economic sectors possessing growth potential in rural communities beyond manufacturing. The system will be of direct benefit to local officials eager for new economic opportunity in a generally lagging region of the country.

Among the important attributes of the system is its capacity to consider the marginal impacts associated with a variety of community characteristics that influence growth prospects. This opens the door to a broader discussion of local development strategies regarding what might be done to improve prospects by investing in education, reducing the impacts of local poverty, or focusing on the quality of housing stock.

Even among the variables for which it appears there is little a community can do, local policy strategies may exist. For example, if an industry is sensitive to the labour force participation rate, this may suggest a need to focus on helping a prospective employer recruit needed labour. In this way, the system provides rich possibilities for education beyond the simple notion of "smokestack chasing", while at the same time answering important questions asked in virtually every rural community.

The system is not a self-sufficient decision-making system, nor would it be the only information needed to select industry targets. Additional information needed prior to selecting a target include its potential positive and negative impacts to the community, its growth prospects, the extent to which state and local policies are supportive of the activity, its place within a regional economic system, the degree to which spatial competition may exist, and the community's preference for development alternatives (see other chapters in this volume). Effective local action still depends on an intimate understanding of the industries that are the focus of local efforts. There is potential to append these types of information to the probabilities and marginal impacts generated with this type of targeting system.

The Plains Economic Targeting System holds potential as a useful tool to improve the practice of local economic development and a powerful educational "hook" to open discussion about rural community goals and strategies to achieve local development. For those concerned about broader regional economic prospects, the system provides insight into the factors that influence economic growth and the relationships inherent in economic activity.

Note

1 Goode (1986, 1989) demonstrated the efficacy of using more refined input and market access variables to explain sectoral growth. The refinements he developed represented a formidable data management task, and were not incorporated into the current version of this system.

References

Anderson, D., and Johnston, S.A. (1992) "A linkage approach to industrial location", *Growth and Change*, 23: 321–34.

Bartik, T.J. (1989) "Small business start-ups in the United States: estimates of the effects of the characteristics of states", *Southern Economic Journal*, 55: 1004–18.

———. (1991) *Who Benefits from State and Local Economic Development Policies?* Kalamazoo, MI: W.E. Upjohn Institute for Employment Research.

——. (1992) "The effects of state and local taxes on economic development: a review of recent research", *Economic Development Quarterly*, 6: 102–10.

Boyle, M.R. (1994) "Economic development targeting in the nineties", *Economic Development Review*, 12: 13–22.

Bresnahan, T.F., and Reiss, P.C. (1991) "Entry and competition in concentrated markets", *Journal of Political Economy*, 99: 977–1009.

Butler, M.A., and Beale, C.L. (1994) *Rural-Urban Continuum Codes for Metro and Nonmetro Counties*, ERS Staff Report No. 9425, Washington, DC: US Department of Agriculture.

Carlino, G.A., and Mills, E.S. (1987) "The determinants of county growth", *Journal of Regional Science*, 27: 39–54.

Carlton, D.W. (1983) "The location and employment choices of new firms: an econometric model with discrete and continuous endogenous variables", *Reviews in Economics and Statistics*, 65: 440–49.

Cox, A.M., Alwang, J., and Johnson, T.G. (2000) "Local preferences for economic development outcomes: analytical hierarchy procedure", *Growth and Change*, 31: 341–66.

Davis Reum, A., and Harris, T.R. (2006) "Exploring firm location beyond simple growth models: a double hurdle application", *Journal of Regional Analysis & Policy*, 36: 45–67.

Dorf, R.J., and Emerson, M.J. (1978) "Determinants of manufacturing plant location for nonmetropolitan communities in the west north central region of the U.S.", *Journal of Regional Science*, 18: 109–20.

Feser, E.J., Renski, H., and Sweeney, S.H. (2000) "Labor pools or value added chains as the basis for the geographic clustering of businesses", Paper presented at the Southern Regional Science Association annual meeting, Miami Beach, FL, 13–15 April 2000.

Fox, W.F., and Murray, M.N. (1990) "Local public policies and interregional business development", *Southern Economic Journal*, 57: 413–27.

Gabe, T.M., and Bell, K.P. (2004) "Tradeoffs between local taxes and government spending as determinants of business location", *Journal of Regional Science*, 44: 21–41.

Goode, F.M. (1986) "The efficacy of more refined demand variables in industrial location models: note", *Growth and Change*, 17: 66–75.

——. (1989) "Rural industrial location versus rural industrial growth", *Annals of Regional Science*, 23: 59–69.

——. (1993) "The role of interindustry linkages in an industrial targeting model", in D.M. Otto and T.G. Johnson (eds.), *Microcomputer-Based Input-Output Modeling: Applications to Economic Development*, Boulder, CO: Westview.

Goode, F.M., and Hastings, S.E. (1989) "An evaluation of the predictive ability of the Northeast Industrial Targeting (NIT) and Economic Development Database (EDD) system", unpublished, State College: Pennsylvania State University.

Hefner, F.L., and Guimarães, P.P. (1995) "Backward and forward linkages in manufacturing location decisions reconsidered", *Reviews in Regional Studies*, 24: 229–44.

Holmes, T.J. (1998) "The effects of state policies on the location of manufacturing: evidence from state borders", *Journal of Political Economy*, 106(41): 667–705.

Killian, M.S., and Parker, T. (1991) "Education and local employment growth in a changing economy", in *Education and Rural Economic Development: Strategies for the 1990s*, ERS Staff Report No. AGES 9153, Washington, DC: US Department of Agriculture.

Kim, Y., Barkley, D.L., and Henry, M.S. (2000) "Industry characteristics linked to establishment concentrations in nonmetropolitan areas", *Journal of Regional Science*, 40: 231–59.

Kusmin, L.D. (1994) *Factors Associated with the Growth of Local and Regional Economies: A Review of Selected Empirical Literature*, ERS Staff Report No. AGES 9405, Washington, DC: US Department of Agriculture.

Kusmin, L.D., Redman, J.M., and Sears, D.W. (1996) *Factors Associated with Rural Economic Growth: Lessons from the 1980's*, ERS Technical Bulletin 1850, Washington, DC: US Department of Agriculture.

Leatherman, J.C., Howard, D.J., and Kastens, T.L. (2002) "Improved prospects for rural development: an industrial targeting system for the Great Plains", *Reviews in Agricultural Economy*, 12: 59–77.

McClenahen, J.S. (1996, October 6) "Selective pursuit", *Industry Week*, 245: 35–38.

McHugh, R.J., and Wilkinson, J.T. (1988) "The determinants of country growth", *Journal of Regional Science*, 28: 271–73.

McKee, D. (1994) "Target industry marketing: strategy and techniques", *Economic Development Review*, 12: 4–12.

McNamara, K.T., Kriesel, W.P., and Deaton, B.J. (1988) "Manufacturing location: the impact of human capital stocks and flows", *Reviews in Regional Studies*, 18: 42–48.

Mead, A.C. (1982) "A simultaneous equations model of migration and economic change in nonmetropolitan areas", *Journal of Regional Science*, 22: 513–27.

Newman, R.J., and Sullivan, D.H. (1988) "Econometric analysis of business tax impacts on industrial location: what do we know and how do we know it?" *Journal of Urban Economics*, 23: 215–34.

Porterfield, S.L. (1990) "Producer services: a viable option for rural economic development?" paper presented at the Southern Regional Science Association annual meeting, Washington, DC, March 1990.

Rowley, T.D. (1998) "Sustaining the Great Plains", *Rural Development Perspectives*, 13: 2–6.

Schmenner, R.W., Huber, J.C., and Cook, R.L. (1987) "Geographic differences and the location of new manufacturing facilities", *Journal of Urban Economics*, 21: 83–104.

Smith, E.D., Deaton, B.J., and Kelch, D.R. (1978) "Location determinants of manufacturing activity in rural areas", *Southern Journal of Agricultural Economics*, 10(July): 23–32.

Stough, R.R., Kulkarni, R., Riggle, J., and Trice, M. (2000) "Some new cluster analytic methods and advising state technology policy", paper presented at the Southern Regional Science Association annual meeting, Miami Beach, FL, 13–15 April 2000.

Sweet, D.C. (1994) "Targeting software as a tool for today's economic development professional", *Economic Development Review*, 12: 65–68.

Thill, J-C. (1992) "Spatial competition and market interdependence", *Papers in Regional Science*, 71: 259–75.

US Department of Commerce. (1986) *County Business Patterns* (CD-ROM), Washington, DC: US Department of Commerce, Bureau of the Census.

——. (1994) *County Business Patterns* (CD-ROM), Washington, DC: US Department of Commerce, Bureau of the Census.

Wasylenko, M. (1991) "Empirical evidence of interregional business location decisions and the role of financial incentives in economic development", in H.W. Herzog and A.M. Schlottmann (eds.), *Industry Location and Public Policy*, Knoxville: University of Tennessee Press.

Wasylenko, M., and McGuire, T. (1985) "Jobs and taxes: the effect of business climate on states' employment growth rates", *National Tax Journal*, 38: 497–511.

Whaley, J.W., and LaCroix, S.S. (1997) "Advanced targeting simplified", *Economic Development Review*, 15(Fall): 11–1.

8 Regional variation in the location choice of goods- and service-producing industries

Hanas A. Cader, John C. Leatherman, and John M. Crespi

Introduction

One focus of many targeted regional economic development (TRED) modelling initiatives is to understand how evolving economic conditions affect prospects for urban and rural places. The urban/rural (metropolitan/non-metropolitan) dichotomy often is used as the basis for measuring differential economic performance. Whereas empirical studies have shown that metro areas consistently outperform non-metro areas, it is not yet known whether the rapid economic growth in the late 20th century has significantly altered the economic trajectory of rural areas. It is commonly believed, however, that recent advancements in telecommunications and transportation systems have affected non-metro area economic performance. However, it is not yet known whether these new economic conditions make it easier or more difficult for rural and less densely populated areas to attract or promote economic growth and development. Technological change leads to innovation with the likely result being better economic performance. Schumpeter (1939) argued that technological change is an important element in economic growth and the argument is that rural areas may not be positioned to promote or effectively adopt such change.

One perspective is that spillovers foster regional economic growth. These spillovers are industry-specific externalities that include, but are not limited to, product and process innovations. The link between regions or locations and the source of technical change is implied by cluster growth perspectives. Locations closer to the sources of technological advancements are likely to benefit from spillovers that result from technical change (Cassar and Nicolini 2003). For example, research parks and businesses that specialize in relatively high technology are typically located close to universities and empirical evidence supports the notion that technological spillovers contribute to economic growth in these regions (Anselin et al. 1997).

The availability of advanced telecommunication infrastructure is increasingly a key factor in location choice decisions and may open markets for rural areas. Malecki (2001) found that telecommunication infrastructure was among the top five criteria used in industry location decisions, and Lawless and Gore (1999) reported it was the leading criterion in location decisions. Given recent technological advancements in telecommunication industries, and the cost advantages associated with non-metro economies, traditional goods- and service-producing industries have drawn renewed attention as a possible source for further improving rural economic conditions. It is reasonable to hypothesize that advances in communication technology and improved transportation systems have altered the location of the goods- and service-producing industries across metro and non-metro regions.

There is a renewed interest among economists to examine the impacts of firm location choices in the context of technological advancements in tele-communication industries. In this chapter, we examine the location choices of goods- and service-producing industry firms in a metro/non-metro continuum in 1990, 1996, and 2002, using location, industry, and establishment characteristics. This period brackets a time of rapid development and ascension of new information and telecommunications technologies, as well as the relative "peaks and valleys" in US economic performance. By examining the location choice patterns of firms in three distinct time periods and across three different regions, we may gain insight into the impacts of general economic conditions on regional economies and the factors that influence firm location choice decisions during times of recession and economic expansion.

From an empirical standpoint, we seek to answer several related questions. What were the key factors that influenced a firm's location choice decision? Given the location's characteristics, what is the likelihood of a similar firm selecting the same location? What was the discrete influence of specific characteristics from among a bundle of characteristics represented in a site? How general are these influences across different regions? If we can provide insights into these fundamental questions for a specific region, we can provide insights into policies that can effect change.

This research provides insights into how regional prospects have changed during a period of rapid technological innovation. Within the spirit of targeted regional economic development (TRED), we seek to better understand how the dispersion of economic activity may be changing both the scale and scope of regional economic activity. The geographic scale of economic clusters and what it means to be a "cluster" may itself be evolving. Indeed, by better understanding the evolving location choices of economic activities, we can begin to ask questions about the nature and extent of economic linkages and activities across space. One might hypothesize that the very notion of economic activities being tightly clustered geographically may be weakening as economic activities disperse across space to more distant locations offering discrete firm advantages. Our concern is what this may mean for the welfare and prospects of rural places and regions.

The remaining sections of this chapter are structured as follows: in the next section, we review the literature on modelling industry location choices. We then specify the empirical model and present a regional classification system. The section following discusses the data and variables used in this study. The empirical estimation and results and conclusions and policy implications are presented in the final two sections.

Modelling industry location choices

Modelling industrial location choices is a complex undertaking. Debate about the appropriate theoretical and empirical modelling procedures is far from settled. Selecting the best location for a firm's business operation depends on many implicit and explicit factors, particularly in the context of a global marketplace. The objective of a firm is driven by its competitive strategy (the customer's needs the firm intends to satisfy) and returns on investment (see for example Deller Chapter 4). An array of factors influences a firm's location choice apart from a firm's investment, technology, and demand for the product. These factors include market accessibility, physical and telecommunication infrastructure, cost of inputs and other related services, and the incentives that are provided by state or local governments. From a modeller's point of view, it is important to determine which factors are crucial in influencing a firm's location choice decision. This is particularly important from a TRED perspective because the results of these empirical studies form the foundation on which policy recommendations are based. Further, we are interested in understanding the extent to which economic activities remain geographically clustered versus dispersing across space.

The discrete nature of the outcome (selecting one location over other locations in the region) limits the use of conventional regression models. Binomial and multinomial models are commonly used discrete choice models. The decision being a rational choice process, the modelling can be guided by economic theory. Given the discrete nature of the choice decisions, count data models are likewise commonly used in empirical studies.

Discrete choice models

The modelling of firm location choice begins with selecting from among regions wherein a firm chooses a particular location as its most desirable operating site. In choosing a particular location, there are location-specific factors that were attractive to the firm. These location-specific factors along with other factors are used to model location choice decisions of firms using discrete choice models.

For example, probit or ordered probit (Basile et al. 2003), tobit (Devereux et al. 2004), logit or mutinomial logit (Gunther et al. 1998), conditional logit (Guimarães et al. 2000), negative binomial (Coughlin and Segev 2000), and poisson (Guimarães et al. 2004) models have been used in this empirical work. Theoretical and empirical investigations continue and are supported by advances in econometric techniques (Guimarães et al. 2004; the Harris/Davis chapter 9). With more sophisticated computer power, large volumes of data and complex spatial dependency models are being applied.

Random utility maximization models

An industry will seek a location within a region where it has the greatest competitive advantage or has potential to maximize expected profit. It is assumed that there are i = 1, 2, . . ., I industries, and the firms in those industries can choose to locate in j = 1, 2, . . ., J regions. Industry i has an expected profit in location j (π_{ij}) and an expected profit in location k (π_{ik}). Firms in the industry are likely to choose location j only if $(\pi_{ij}) \geq (\pi_{ik})$. The expected profit of industry i in location j (π_{ij}) is assumed to be a linear function of industry, establishment, and regional characteristics (Z), estimated coefficients (α and β), and an industry location-specific error term (ε).

$$\pi_{ij} = f(Z). \tag{1}$$

$$\pi_{ij} = \alpha + \beta'Z + \varepsilon. \tag{2}$$

If the error terms in equation (2) are assumed to be independently and identically distributed according to the Weibull distribution, then the odds ratio of the probability of choosing location i over location j can be represented by a conditional logit (McFadden 1974). McFadden's (1974) conditional logit distribution provides a basis for modelling industrial location decisions. An indicator variable is used to identify firms in industry i choosing location j $(m_{ij} = 1)$ otherwise $(m_{ij} = 0)$. The probability of a firm in industry i choosing j is defined as p_{ij}^*, and the probability of finding the firm at any other location is $(1 - p_{ij}^*)$.

Model and regional specifications

Conditional logit model

The conditional logit model (CLM) has been considered to be superior among choice models given its ability to accommodate alternative location choices, including the present location of existing firms. The merits of the CLM stem from its grounding in microeconomic theory: the resulting econometric model is based on a random utility maximization framework. The choice characteristics are considered in modelling the location choice of firms rather than individual characteristics. In the CLM, the individual establishment's industry location choices are modeled using industry, establishment, and community characteristics as explanatory variables.

If it is assumed that a firm's selection of a particular location is choice-specific rather than industry-specific, the conditional logit model is considered to be the more appropriate than a multinomial logit model (Greene 2000: 862). Using the CLM approach described in Greene (2000), the probability for firm i choosing location j can be written as:

$$\pi_{ij}^* = \frac{\exp \{a + \beta'Z + \varepsilon\}}{\sum_{j=1}^{J} \exp \{a + \beta'Z + \varepsilon\}}. \tag{3}$$

Although the estimated parameters and their level of significance are important, this may not provide accurate information about specific variables' impacts on the probabilities of choosing one location against another. The marginal effect of a variable can be estimated by differentiating equation (3) with respect to the variable

$$\frac{\partial \pi_{ij}^*}{\partial Z} = (\Omega (a + \beta'Z + \varepsilon)) \, (1 - \Omega (a + \beta'Z + \varepsilon)) \, \beta, \tag{4}$$

where $(\Omega (a + \beta'Z + \varepsilon))$ is the probability density function of CLM.

Regional specification

The US Bureau of the Census uses a dichotomous system to classify geographic areas as Metropolitan Statistical Areas (MSA) and non-metropolitan areas. A metropolitan area is defined as a collection or one or more cities with a population greater than 50,000; all other areas are classified as non-metropolitan (Morrissey 1987).

The counties that are in an MSA are considered to be metro counties (here designated as county type = 1); counties that are immediately adjacent to metro counties are identified as metro-adjacent counties (county type = 2); all other counties are classified as non-metro counties (county type = 3). Applying this classification system to Kansas yields 17 metro counties, 21 metro-adjacent counties, and 67 non-metro counties. Specific county designations are presented in Table 8.1.

Table 8.1 County type, modified urban influence code, and interstate highway

| Name | URINF | | | Name | URINF | | |
	MSA	Code*	Hwy.		MSA	Code*	Hwy.
Allen	2	6	0	Linn	1	2	0
Anderson	2	6	0	Logan	3	9	0
Atchison	2	5	0	Lyon	2	5	1
Barber	3	9	0	Marion	2	5	1
Barton	3	7	0	Marshall	3	6	0
Bourbon	2	6	0	McPherson	2	8	0
Brown	2	6	0	Meade	3	9	0
Butler	1	2	1	Miami	1	2	1

County				County			
Chase	2	5	1	Mitchell	3	8	0
Chautauqua	3	9	0	Montgomery	3	7	0
Cherokee	3	8	0	Morris	2	6	0
Cheyenne	3	9	0	Morton	3	9	0
Clark	3	9	0	Nemaha	2	6	0
Clay	3	8	0	Neosho	3	8	0
Cloud	3	8	0	Ness	3	9	0
Coffey	2	6	1	Norton	3	8	0
Comanche	3	9	0	Osage	1	2	1
Cowley	2	3	0	Osborne	3	9	0
Crawford	3	7	0	Ottawa	3	7	0
Decatur	3	9	0	Pawnee	3	8	0
Dickinson	3	8	1	Phillips	3	8	0
Doniphan	1	2	0	Pottawatomie	2	5	0
Douglas	1	2	1	Pratt	3	8	0
Edwards	3	9	0	Rawlins	3	9	0
Elk	2	6	0	Reno	2	3	0
Ellis	3	7	1	Republic	3	9	0
Ellsworth	3	8	1	Rice	3	8	0
Finney	3	7	0	Riley	2	5	1
Ford	3	7	0	Rooks	3	9	0
Franklin	1	2	1	Rush	3	9	0
Geary	2	5	1	Russell	3	8	1
Gove	3	9	1	Saline	3	7	1
Graham	3	9	0	Scott	3	8	0
Grant	3	8	0	Sedgwick	1	1	1
Gray	3	9	0	Seward	3	7	0
Greeley	3	9	0	Shawnee	1	2	1
Greenwood	2	6	0	Sheridan	3	9	0
Hamilton	3	9	0	Sherman	3	8	1
Harper	2	4	0	Smith	3	9	0
Harvey	1	2	1	Stafford	3	9	0
Haskell	3	9	0	Stanton	3	9	0
Hodgeman	3	9	0	Stevens	3	8	0
Jackson	1	2	0	Sumner	1	2	1
Jefferson	1	2	0	Thomas	3	8	1
Jewell	3	9	0	Trego	3	9	1
Johnson	1	1	1	Wabaunsee	1	2	1
Kearny	3	9	0	Wallace	3	9	0
Kingman	2	4	0	Washington	3	9	0
Kiowa	3	9	0	Wichita	3	9	0
Labette	3	7	0	Wilson	3	8	0
Lane	3	9	0	Woodson	3	9	0
Leavenworth	1	2	0	Wyandotte	1	2	1
Lincoln	3	9	1				

* Modified Urban Influence Code in 1996, 1 = most urban and 9 = most rural.

Notes: Counties within an MSA (metro) = 1; metro-adjacent = 2; non-metro non-adjacent = 3. Highway 1 = presence.

Industry specification

In this study, industries are classified either as goods-producing or service-producing. All industry data are specific to a four-digit Standard Industry Classification (SIC), the most detailed industry-scale level in the SIC system. Industry counts are specific to the state of Kansas.

Goods-producing industries

Goods-producing industries include manufacturing, construction, and agricultural services. A total of 401 industries are included in the goods-producing industry group. Table 8.2 contains a list of industries that were identified as goods-producing industries.

Service-producing industries

Service-producing industries include services; retail trade; wholesale trade; finance, insurance, and real estate; and transportation, communications, and public utilities. A total of 339 industries constituted the service-producing industry category. Table 8.3 presents the list of industries that were identified as service-producing industries.

Data and variables

The response and explanatory variables can be grouped into two categories. The first group of variables is specific to industries (to either the goods-producing industry or the service-producing industry), and the other variables are common to both industries. The number of establishments in the region, average establishment size, industry clustering, and vertical integration are the variables included in the former category. Population density, quality of the labour force, and county employment growth rate are included in the latter group. Table 8.4 presents the sources and description of data. Summary statistics for the goods-producing industry variables, service-producing industry variables, and the common variables are presented in Tables 8.5, 8.6, and 8.7, respectively.

Sources and description of data

Kansas county-level establishment data were obtained from the US Department of Labor, Bureau of Labor Statistics' Quarterly Census of Employment and Wages programme (ES-202) files for the period 1990–2002. The ES-202 data file tracks monthly employment and quarterly wages of all employers with employees eligible for unemployment insurance compensation. The response variable was the count of establishments that choose to locate in a particular county within a region (e.g., metro, metro-adjacent, non-metro). If

Table 8.2 Standard Industry Classification (SIC) codes for the goods-producing industries

SIC	SIC	SIC	SIC	SIC	SIC	SIC	SIC	SIC
711	2023	2231	2599	2843	3262	3423	3537	3635
721	2024	2241	2611	2844	3263	3425	3541	3639
722	2026	2251	2621	2851	3264	3429	3542	3647
723	2032	2254	2631	2861	3269	3431	3543	3648
724	2033	2257	2652	2865	3271	3432	3544	3691
741	2034	2258	2653	2869	3272	3433	3545	3692
742	2035	2259	2655	2873	3273	3441	3546	3694
751	2037	2261	2656	2874	3274	3442	3547	3728
752	2038	2262	2657	2875	3275	3443	3548	3812
761	2041	2269	2671	2879	3281	3444	3549	3821
762	2043	2273	2672	2891	3291	3446	3552	3822
781	2044	2281	2674	2892	3292	3448	3553	3823
782	2045	2282	2675	2893	3295	3449	3554	3824
783	2046	2284	2676	2895	3296	3451	3555	3827
1521	2047	2295	2677	2899	3297	3452	3556	3829
1522	2048	2297	2678	2911	3299	3462	3559	3841
1531	2051	2411	2679	2951	3312	3463	3561	3842
1541	2052	2421	2711	2952	3313	3465	3562	3843
1542	2053	2426	2721	2992	3315	3466	3563	3844
1611	2061	2429	2731	2999	3316	3469	3564	3845
1622	2062	2431	2732	3011	3317	3471	3565	3851
1623	2063	2434	2741	3021	3321	3479	3566	3861
1629	2064	2435	2752	3052	3322	3482	3567	3873
1711	2066	2436	2754	3053	3324	3483	3568	3911
1721	2067	2439	2759	3061	3325	3484	3569	3914
1731	2068	2441	2761	3069	3331	3489	3581	3915
1741	2074	2448	2771	3081	3334	3491	3582	3931
1742	2075	2449	2782	3082	3339	3492	3585	3942
1743	2076	2451	2789	3083	3341	3493	3586	3944
1751	2077	2452	2791	3084	3351	3494	3589	3949
1752	2079	2491	2796	3085	3353	3495	3592	3951
1761	2087	2493	2812	3086	3354	3496	3593	3952
1771	2091	2499	2813	3087	3355	3497	3594	3953
1781	2092	2511	2816	3088	3356	3498	3596	3955
1791	2095	2512	2819	3089	3357	3499	3599	3961
1793	2096	2514	2821	3211	3363	3511	3612	3965
1794	2097	2515	2822	3221	3364	3519	3613	3991
1795	2098	2517	2823	3229	3365	3523	3621	3993
1796	2099	2519	2824	3231	3366	3524	3624	3995
1799	2111	2521	2833	3241	3369	3531	3625	3996
2011	2121	2522	2834	3251	3398	3532	3629	3999
2013	2131	2531	2835	3253	3399	3533	3631	
2015	2141	2541	2836	3255	3411	3534	3632	
2021	2211	2542	2841	3259	3412	3535	3633	
2022	2221	2591	2842	3261	3421	3536	3634	

Source: US Department of Commerce.

Table 8.3 SIC codes for the service-producing industries

SIC	SIC	SIC	SIC	SIC	SIC	SIC	SIC
4111	4932	5113	5521	5995	7021	7515	8412
4119	4939	5131	5531	5999	7032	7519	8422
4121	4941	5136	5541	6011	7033	7521	8611
4131	4952	5137	5551	6019	7041	7532	8621
4141	4953	5139	5561	6021	7211	7533	8631
4142	4959	5141	5571	6022	7212	7534	8641
4151	4961	5142	5599	6029	7213	7536	8651
4173	4971	5143	5611	6035	7215	7537	8661
4212	5012	5144	5621	6036	7216	7538	8699
4213	5014	5145	5632	6061	7217	7539	8711
4214	5015	5146	5641	6062	7218	7542	8712
4215	5021	5147	5651	6081	7219	7549	8713
4221	5023	5148	5661	6082	7221	7622	8721
4222	5031	5149	5699	6091	7231	7623	8731
4225	5032	5153	5712	6099	7241	7629	8732
4226	5033	5154	5713	6311	7251	7631	8733
4231	5039	5159	5714	6321	7261	7641	8734
4311	5043	5162	5719	6324	7291	7692	8741
4412	5044	5169	5722	6331	7299	7694	8742
4424	5046	5171	5731	6351	7311	7699	8743
4432	5047	5172	5734	6361	7312	7911	8744
4449	5048	5181	5735	6371	7313	7922	8748
4481	5049	5182	5736	6399	7319	7929	8811
4482	5051	5191	5812	6411	7322	7933	8999
4489	5052	5192	5813	6512	7323	7941	
4491	5063	5193	5912	6513	7331	7948	
4492	5064	5194	5921	6514	7334	7991	
4493	5065	5198	5932	6515	7335	7992	
4499	5072	5199	5941	6517	7336	7993	
4512	5074	5211	5942	6519	7338	7996	
4513	5075	5231	5943	6531	7342	7997	
4522	5078	5251	5944	6541	7349	7999	
4581	5082	5261	5945	6552	7352	8111	
4729	5083	5271	5946	6553	7353	8211	
4731	5084	5311	5947	6712	7359	8221	
4741	5085	5331	5948	6719	7361	8222	
4783	5087	5399	5949	6722	7363	8231	
4785	5088	5411	5962	6726	7378	8243	
4789	5091	5421	5963	6732	7381	8244	
4911	5092	5431	5983	6733	7382	8299	
4922	5093	5441	5984	6792	7383	8322	
4923	5094	5451	5989	6794	7384	8331	
4924	5099	5461	5992	6798	7389	8351	
4925	5111	5499	5993	6799	7513	8361	
4931	5112	5511	5994	7011	7514	8399	

Source: US Department of Commerce.

Table 8.4 Description of variables and data sources

Descriptor	Dependent Variable	Source
Firm or establishment	Annual average counts with 1 indicating location in a region and 0 otherwise.	ES-202 data
Independent Variables		
Population Density	Population density: population per square mile	Woods and Poole Economics, Inc.
Labour Quality	Quality of the labour force: Percent of employees in knowledge industries	ES-202 and Beck (1992)
Estab. Size	Average industry establishment size: total county employment/total number of establishments	ES-202 data
Ind. Clustering	Industry clustering: location quotient (LQ) $$LQ = \frac{\dfrac{\text{County industry employment}}{\text{Total county employment}}}{\dfrac{\text{National industry employment}}{\text{Total national employment}}}$$	ES-202 and County Business Patterns
Vert. Integration	Vertical integration: indirect output multiplier in million dollars	IMPLAN software (MIG, Inc., 1999)
Co. Employment	County employment growth in percentage	ES-202 data
Highway	Presence of an interstate highway in the region's county	State Highway Map
Urbanization	Measure of urbanization: Modified 1993 Urban Influence Code	USDA Economic Research Service

a firm chose a county in a particular region, the location choice indicator variable for that county was assigned a value of one (1), and all the other counties in that region were assigned a zero (0). If a firm had two branches in different counties, each was considered a separate business entity, creating two different establishment location choices. There were three groups of explanatory variables representing community/regional, industry, and establishment characteristics. All three groups of variables were used in all models to explain the location choice decision of firms in metro, metro-adjacent, and non-metro counties.

The location choice decisions were examined from 1990 to 2002 in all three regions for service-producing and goods-producing industries. The results reported here are for 1990, 1996, and 2002 to avoid a proliferation of results presentation. These years were selected because the represent perhaps the extremes in national economic performance. At the start of the 1990s, the US economy had been in a relatively long but mild economic recession, which ended in 1991. From 1992 on, the economy started to take off. By the mid-1990s, the economy's performance was at its peak. Economic performance again started to slow dramatically in 2000, and by 2002 the economy once again was in a short-term recession. Summary statistics for the data are presented in Table 8.5 and Table 8.6 for service-producing and goods-producing industries, respectively.

Population density (POP) was considered a potentially important variable in firm location decisions. Coughlin and Segev (2000) suggested that population density can be used as a proxy for either economic urbanization or land costs.

The quality of the labour force (QUAL) reflects the knowledge and skill level of the community. Firms are likely to move to locations where the

Table 8.5 Summary statistics for the goods-producing industry

Region	Variable	Mean	Std. Dev.	Minimum	Maximum
Metro	Number of Establishments	7,562	670	6,709	8,474
	Average Establishment Size	17.5	223.2	0.0	23,960.5
	Industry Clustering	1.526	0.166	1.323	1.756
	Vertical Integration	0.240	0.034	0.209	0.325
Metro-Adjacent	Number of Establishments	1,884	118	1,732	2,064
	Average Establishment Size	16.4	79.3	0.0	2,963.7
	Industry Clustering	1.595	0.181	1.357	1.865
	Vertical Integration	0.433	1.065	0.105	3.815
Non-metro	Number of Establishments	3,265	174	3,032	3,577
	Average Establishment Size	15.5	102.9	0.0	3,229.0
	Industry Clustering	1.595	0.206	1.291	1.902
	Vertical Integration	0.196	0.066	0.150	0.378

Source: Calculations found in Table 8.4.

Table 8.6 Summary statistics for the service-producing industry

Region	Variable	Mean	Std Dev	Minimum	Maximum
Metro	Number of Establishments	29,490	1,248	27,805	31,506
	Average Establishment Size	12.8	78.8	0.0	8,093.0
	Industry Clustering	2.211	0.201	1.948	2.540
	Vertical Integration	0.287	0.036	0.228	0.363
Metro-Adjacent	Number of Establishments	7,047	255	6,452	7,469
	Average Establishment Size	11.6	57.4	0.0	4,306.0
	Industry Clustering	2.141	0.186	1.923	2.454
	Vertical Integration	0.223	0.029	0.172	0.275
Non-metro	Number of Establishments	13,261	482	12,421	14,270
	Average Establishment Size	9.6	32.3	0.0	2,107.2
	Industry Clustering	2.074	0.199	1.823	2.401
	Vertical Integration	0.241	0.062	0.144	0.382

Source: Calculations found in Table 8.4.

Table 8.7 Summary statistics for the common variables

Region	Variable	Mean	Std. Dev.	Minimum	Maximum
Metro	Population Density	196.2	304.5	8.1	1072.7
	Quality of the Labour Force	35.95	6.36	24.34	55.22
	County Empl. Growth Rate	1.31	5.23	−27.91	22.58
Metro-Adjacent	Population Density	27.1	25.05	3.79	112.56
	Quality of the Labour Force	33.98	8.63	21.32	67.42
	County Empl. Growth Rate	0.74	4.93	−12.74	27.05
Non-metro	Population Density	12.4	14.6	1.8	74.9
	Quality of the Labour Force	36.74	8.37	11.97	63.16
	County Empl. Growth Rate	0.67	11.26	−76.09	285.58

Source: Calculations found in Table 8.4.

required quality of labour is readily available. College educational attainment had been used as a proxy (Pigeon and Wray 1999). In this research, the percentage of workers in high-knowledge industries[1] was used as a proxy for quality of the labour force.

Average industry establishment size (SIZE) for industry i was estimated by summing county employment by industry and then dividing by total county establishments by industry. The average establishment size is an important variable that would indicate which types of establishments were most frequently found in a particular region. It was hypothesized that non-metro regions are attractive to smaller business establishments.

The location quotient was used as a proxy measure of industry clustering (CLUS) within counties. The location quotient measures the relative share of county industry employment to national share of employment in that industry. As noted by Woodward and Guimarães in Chapter 5, although the location quotient is widely used within our context, it is far from an ideal measure. The location quotient for industry i in region j is given by:

$$LQ_i = \frac{(E_{ij} / E_{in})}{(E_j / E_n)},$$

where E designates employment and the subscripts i, j and n designate industry, region, and national, respectively. It is well known that a location quotient above 1 indicates that the region has a higher share of employment in that industry than the nation as a whole.

Vertical integration (INT) measures both upstream and downstream relationships. These inter- and intraindustry relationships are likely to affect availability of inputs for firms' production processes. Vertical integration may arise for a variety of reasons (improved efficiency, technological economies, etc.). Some of the potential disadvantages associated with vertical integration are the creation of barriers to entry and expansion of competitors (Waterson 1993), which may have implications for new establishment entry. Regional social accounting matrices were constructed from the IMPLAN economic modelling system (MIG, Inc., 1999) and used to track interindustry transactions by industry sector. The indirect multiplier, which measures the strength of interindustry linkages, was used as a proxy for vertical integration (Ribeiro and Warner 2004).

Growth rates of county employment (CEMP) represent local economic growth conditions for existing industries. Conditions can be either favourable or unfavourable depending on the relative industry employment share in the county. County employment growth was estimated using total employment in all industries in a county that were reported in the ES-202 data files.

The presence of an interstate highway (HIGHWAY) has long been considered as an important factor is location choice decisions.[2,3] Interstate highways are an important element in the larger multimodel transportation system that links urban centers and various other transportation modes. The highway variable is an indicator variable (1 if present, 0 otherwise). The presence or absence of interstate highways in a county is reported in Table 8.1.

Urbanization (URBA) promotes regional economic growth. Indicator variables were used based on the Urban Influence Code (Coughlin and Segev 2000). A modified Urban Influence Code (Beale code) was used to represent the rural-urban continuum ranging from one to nine.[4] The value one (1) indicated the most urban and nine (9) was the most rural. Definitions for the Urban Influence Code used here are presented in Table 8.8.

Table 8.8 Modified Urban Influence Codes

Code	Definition
Metropolitan	
1	Central and fringe counties of metro areas of 400,000 population or more
2	Small – Counties in metro areas of fewer than 400,000 population nonmetropolitan counties
Non-metropolitan	
3	Adjacent to a large metro area with a city of 10,000 or more
4	Adjacent to a large metro area and without a city of at least 10,000
5	Adjacent to a small metro area with a city of 10,000 or more
6	Adjacent to a small metro area and without a city of at least 10,000
7	Not adjacent to a metro area and with a city of 10,000 or more
8	Not adjacent to a metro area and with a city of 2,500 to 9,999 population
9	Not adjacent to a metro area and with no city or a city with a population less than 2,500

Empirical estimation and results

The model described in equation (4) was estimated using a maximum likelihood estimator. The multinomial discrete choice procedure was chosen. The
location choice of an industry (e.g., goods-producing) in a year (e.g., 1990)
for a particular region (e.g., metro) was estimated independently from other
industries, years, and regions. The error term in the model was assumed to be
independent and identical with a type I extreme value distribution. These
results present a broader picture of aggregation industries and regions. For
example, one model was estimated (i.e., goods producing industry) for the
entire non-metro region in a particular year (i.e., 1990), and represent the
results for the combined 67 counties. The goods producing industry alone
consists of 391 industry sectors at the four-digit SIC. The coefficients from
the CLM for goods-producing industries and the marginal effects of the
variables on the location choice of firms in metro, metro-adjacent, and non-
metro regions are presented in Tables 8.9 and 8.10. The results for service-
producing industries are presented in Tables 8.11 and 8.12. Although, the
models were estimated for metro, metro-adjacent, and non-metro regions, the
discussion is primarily focused on the non-metro region for ease of exposition
and comprehension.

Most of the coefficient estimates (Tables 8.9 and 8.11) are significantly
different from zero (5 per cent significance level). The marginal impacts
(Tables 8.10 and 8.12) of population density and labour force quality on the
probability of a goods-producing firm choosing the region were generally
quite small, whereas the influence of an interstate highway and urbanization
were somewhat larger. Given the direction and the magnitude of marginal
impacts, it is possible to indicate which industries were attracted to each
region.

The results are discussed in two sections, primarily focusing on industries
suitable for rural economic development (the non-metro counties) in Kansas.
The first section focuses on the factors that had a persistent impact across
industries and over time. For example, a one unit increase in population
density was likely to increase the probability of a goods-producing and a
service-producing firm locating in the non-metro region by about 3.5 per cent
and 3.3 per cent, respectively, in 2002. Although policy-makers have little
ability to influence the demography of a region, this highlights the importance of population density in firm location decisions, an effect that was
persistent through time and across space.

The quality of the labour force was also expected to have a positive impact
in all regions. It was true, however, only in the metro region. The negative
impact of labour force quality in the metro-adjacent and non-metro regions
indicates that for goods- and service-producing industries seeking locations
in these regions, a low-skill, low-wage workforce may be more attractive
than a higher quality labour force. Counties or regions with a relatively
less-educated labour force can still target goods- and service-producers of a

Table 8.9 Coefficients for the goods-producing industries

Variables	Metro			Metro-Adjacent			Non-metro		
	1990	1996	2002	1990	1996	2002	1990	1996	2002
Pop. Density	0.002*	0.001*	0.002*	0.012*	0.017*	0.016*	0.019*	0.02*	0.018*
	(0.00)	(0.00)	(0.00)	(0.002)	(0.002)	(0.002)	(0.002)	(0.001)	(0.001)
Labour Quality	0.056*	0.095*	0.102*	-0.048*	-0.051*	-0.038*	-0.02*	-0.035*	-0.013*
	(0.005)	(0.006)	(0.005)	(0.006)	(0.006)	(0.007)	(0.004)	(0.004)	(0.004)
Estab. Size	-0.011	0.019*	0.039*	0.017*	-0.004	0.004	0.001	-0.005	-0.003
	(0.007)	(0.002)	(0.002)	(0.005)	(0.003)	(0.004)	(0.004)	(0.003)	(0.002)
Ind. Clustering	0.656*	0.01	-0.869*	-0.332*	-0.289*	0.455*	-0.036	-0.213*	-0.064
	(0.149)	(0.039)	(0.076)	(0.119)	(0.076)	(0.067)	(0.065)	(0.032)	(0.042)
Vert. Integration	-0.305*	-0.2*	-0.288	-0.059*	-0.051*	-1.611*	-0.006*	-0.002	-1.164*
	(0.021)	(0.012)	(0.256)	(0.014)	(0.01)	(0.211)	(0.002)	(0.001)	(0.126)
Co. Employment	-0.137*	0.027*	0.065*	-0.082*	-0.013*	0.037*	0.005	-0.002	-0.011*
	(0.004)	(0.008)	(0.009)	(0.015)	(0.005)	(0.011)	(0.005)	(0.001)	(0.004)
Highway	0.663*	1.409*	0.988*	0.184*	0.069	0.058	0.24*	0.112*	0.116*
	(0.079)	(0.077)	(0.066)	(0.071)	(0.075)	(0.08)	(0.05)	(0.049)	(0.046)
Urbanization	-1.038*	-1.559*	-1.153*	-0.115*	-0.237*	-0.138*	-0.441*	-0.362*	-0.315*
	(0.181)	(0.045)	(0.051)	(0.035)	(0.026)	(0.026)	(0.041)	(0.032)	(0.033)
Log Likelihood	-14072	-15117	-17534	-4793	-5059	-5555	-11780	-12363	-12398

* Significance at the 0.05 probability level.

Note: The values in parentheses are standard errors.

Table 8.10 Marginal effects of the variables for the goods-producing industries

	Metro			Metro-Adjacent			Non-metro		
	1990	1996	2002	1990	1996	2002	1990	1996	2002
Pop. Density	0.009	0.006	0.009	0.066	0.091	0.091	0.037	0.038	0.035
Labour Quality	0.308	0.526	0.562	-0.267	-0.285	-0.209	-0.040	-0.069	-0.027
Estab. Size	-0.060	0.105	0.215	0.092	-0.024	0.024	0.001	-0.010	-0.007
Ind. Clustering	3.631	0.055	-4.811	-1.839	-1.598	2.517	-0.071	-0.417	-0.127
Vert. Integration	-1.690	-1.107	-1.596	-0.327	-0.281	-8.917	-0.012	-0.004	-2.323
Co. Employment	-0.759	0.148	0.360	-0.453	-0.074	0.207	0.010	-0.004	-0.021
Highway	3.671	7.801	5.468	1.016	0.381	0.323	0.476	0.220	0.232
Urbanization	-5.747	-8.629	-6.386	-0.637	-1.312	-0.766	-0.875	-0.708	-0.628

Table 8.11 Coefficients for the service-producing industries

	Metro			Metro-Adjacent			Non-metro		
	1990	1996	2002	1990	1996	2002	1990	1996	2002
Pop. Density	0.003*	0.002*	0.001*	0.018*	0.023*	0.024*	0.012*	0.013*	0.017*
	(0.00)	(0.00)	(0.00)	(0.001)	(0.001)	(0.001)	(0.001)	(0.001)	(0.001)
Labour Quality	0.068*	0.07*	0.072*	-0.047*	-0.057*	-0.042*	-0.02*	-0.025*	-0.022*
	(0.003)	(0.003)	(0.003)	(0.003)	(0.003)	(0.003)	(0.001)	(0.001)	(0.001)
Estab. Size	-0.194*	-0.01	0.072*	-0.052*	-0.049*	-0.055*	0.038*	0.053*	0.111*
	(0.012)	(0.007)	(0.006)	(0.01)	(0.014)	(0.008)	(0.008)	(0.007)	(0.006)
Ind. Clustering	0.608*	-0.453*	1.837*	-0.797*	0.51*	-0.681*	-0.257*	0.093*	0.015
	(0.111)	(0.085)	(0.076)	(0.121)	(0.108)	(0.117)	(0.045)	(0.047)	(0.047)
Vert. Integration	-30.175*	-8.279*	-14.67*	-10.239*	-1.678*	-4.239*	-1.234*	-1.176*	-3.142*
	(1.00)	(0.527)	(0.631)	(1.082)	(0.558)	(0.554)	(0.262)	(0.198)	(0.279)
Co. Employment	-0.179*	-0.053*	0.014*	-0.024*	-0.005*	-0.005	0.014*	-0.001*	0.007*
	(0.002)	(0.003)	(0.005)	(0.004)	(0.002)	(0.004)	(0.002)	(0.00)	(0.002)
Highway	0.866*	1.385*	0.447*	0.147*	-0.121*	-0.086	0.238*	0.233*	0.059*
	(0.035)	(0.038)	(0.031)	(0.031)	(0.032)	(0.046)	(0.02)	(0.021)	(0.022)
Urbanization	-1.102*	-2.149*	-2.702*	-0.317*	-0.222*	-0.206*	-0.495*	-0.397*	-0.211*
	(0.04)	(0.026)	(0.033)	(0.017)	(0.014)	(0.014)	(0.019)	(0.016)	(0.019)
Log Likelihood	-62944	-66551	-67989	-22495	-22872	-22026	-62167	-59161	-55988

* Significance at the 0.05 probability level.

Note: The values in parentheses are standard errors.

Table 8.12 Marginal effects of the variables for the service-producing industries

	Metro			Metro-Adjacent			Non-metro		
	1990	1996	2002	1990	1996	2002	1990	1996	2002
Pop. Density	0.014	0.009	0.004	0.097	0.128	0.134	0.025	0.025	0.033
Labour Quality	0.375	0.390	0.398	-0.257	-0.314	-0.234	-0.042	-0.050	-0.045
Estab. Size	-1.076	-0.057	0.396	-0.288	-0.269	-0.307	0.077	0.104	0.222
Ind. Clustering	3.367	-2.506	10.170	-4.415	2.822	-3.772	-0.526	0.182	0.031
Vert. Integration	-167.058	-45.834	-81.219	-56.687	-9.289	-23.471	-2.528	-2.312	-6.273
Co. Employment	-0.988	-0.296	0.080	-0.133	-0.026	-0.027	0.029	-0.003	0.013
Highway	4.794	7.670	2.475	0.812	-0.668	-0.477	0.488	0.457	0.117
Urbanization	-6.102	-11.896	-14.961	-1.752	-1.227	-1.138	-1.014	-0.780	-0.421

certain type, perhaps implying something about the type of cluster development suitable for these types of locales. Based on the marginal impacts for 2002, service-producing industries were, in fact, attracted to metro-adjacent and non-metro regions.

The presence of an interstate highway (HIGHWAY) was expected to have a positive impact on all industries over time, as it facilitates the movement of people and the goods. The results showed that an interstate increased the probability of goods- and service-producing industry location in all regions, with the exception for service industries in the metro-adjacent region in 1996 and 2002. It might be speculated we are observing a "congestion penalty" for service-producing industries by the latter time periods. The persistent positive impact for goods-producing industries in all regions indicates that an interstate highway was relatively more important for these firms. The 2002 marginal effect suggests that the upgrade of a highway to interstate standards could increase the probability of a goods-producing firm choosing a non-metro location by 23.2 per cent compared to 11.7 per cent for a service-producing firm.

Urbanization has a positive impact in all regions and industries (for this variable, as the numbers increase, the level of urbanization decreases). The direction of the marginal impacts indicates that urbanization was likely to increase the probability of both goods- and service-producing firms. The magnitude of the marginal effect, however, showed that service-producing industries were especially likely to be benefit from urbanization, specifically in the metro-adjacent region (transportation penalties notwithstanding). As a region becomes more urbanized, there is greater demand for goods and services. One finds the demand for services to be relatively greater compared to the demand for goods. Similarly, county employment growth generally had a positive impact on goods- and service-producing firms choosing the non-metro region, except in 1996. For service-producing industries, it had a persistent negative impact.

Considering these results thus far in total, the picture to emerge would seem to be one that suggests agglomeration economies and levels of demand are key overall drivers in industry location decisions, a result with unhappy consequences for remote rural areas. Somewhat contradictory findings across the regions for transportation and labour force quality make for interesting speculation. Transportation is hugely important for rural areas, but has its limits in the urbanizing metro-adjacent counties. The findings for labour force quality in the non-metro region suggest that with the appropriate infrastructure in place, rural areas may be attractive for lower skilled service-type activities. Thus, building out cluster-based strategies focusing on back-office type operations may yet be a viable alternative to firms considering outsourcing certain functions.

The second set of variables considered is those more specific to industries. For example, based on the 1996 and 2002 estimates, average establishment size had a negative impact on goods-producing industries choosing a non-metro location. One unit increase in the establishment size was likely to decrease the probability of a goods-producing firm locating in the non-metro region by about 1 and 0.7 per cent, respectively. A similar increase would result in an increase in the probability of a service-producing industry firm location 10.4 and 22.2 per cent. Thus, the effect of concentration in within industry sectors is quite different and may imply the influence of larger national and international trends affecting these industries. With increasing customization and just-in-time deliveries, smaller goods-producers may seek closer quarters with their markets, whether that is an urban market or a major manufacturing activity somewhere. Service industries, perhaps because of newer telecommunication technologies, do have the ability to locate in low-cost locations and, in fact, may do quite well in a rural locale.

Our clustering variable is of particular relevance to our discussion within the context of TRED and clustering approaches. Once again, we observe quite different results across industries in the non-metro region. Our results show that industry clustering was more important for service-producing industry location than for goods-producing industry location. The 1996 and 2002 marginal effect estimates show that a unit increase in industry clustering was likely to result in an increase in service-producing firms choosing a non-metro location by about 18.2 and 3.1 per cent, respectively. Yet, a similar increase in goods producing industries resulted in about 41.7 and 12.7 per cent reduction of the probability of a goods-producing firm choosing a non-metro location. We might conclude that service-type activities attract more in-kind activity, whereas a similar increase in the number of goods-producing industries may lead to a crowding-out effect for other goods-producing firms. This implies that clustering strategies based broadly on service activities would have the greatest potential for rural regions.

Although we expected a positive impact associated with vertical integration in the likelihood of goods- and service-producing firms choosing a location, it had the largest negative impact of all the variables in all regions and years. The result for the goods-producing industry reinforces the notion of the clustering of interrelated goods-producing activities rather than firms internalizing related functions if the objective is increased employment and economic opportunity. The negative impact for the service-producing industry contradicts the positive impact associated with the industry clustering variable for service-producing firms. A general weakening of service linkages such as those measured by economic multipliers has occurred. This is due to the fairly ubiquitous trend toward increasing use of imported inputs to production, the overseas outsourcing of many business activities, and the internalization of many functions that previously had been purchased from outside suppliers. Thus, it is not surprising that a relatively large (one unit) increase in a county indirect output multiplier would lead to a large employment decline overall. It may, in fact, indicate a relatively noncompetitive industry in a globally competitive marketplace.

Conclusions

In this chapter, we focused on the location choice decisions of goods- and service-producing industries in metro, metro-adjacent, and non-metro regions in three economically distinct time periods. A conditional logit approach was used in modelling location choice decisions. Selected industry, establishment, and community characteristics were used to explain the location decisions of firms. Population density, urbanization, and highways were three important characteristics that have a positive impact on goods- and service-producing industry firms' choosing a non-metro location. Enhancing highway infrastructure would likely attract more goods- and service-producing firms to the non-metro region. Service-producing, however, would seem to hold greater promise for rural areas where lower cost labour, transportation system enhancements, trends toward the concentration of service activities, clustering, and vertical integration all are associated with service-producers seeking non-metro locations.

From the standpoint of building out clustering strategies, rural areas and regions will best position themselves by marketing their communities as a viable alternative to outsourcing back-office service operations. This may require some adjustment in conceptualizing what it means to be "clustered". Although the Porter-type conceptualization might suggest relatively compact "bubbles" of economic activity on a map, it may well be that much larger and geographically dispersed clusters can exist through the web of connections represented by advanced telecommunications. The traditional rural advantages of lower cost factor inputs and high quality of life can yet remain its competitive strength as it continues pursuit of economic opportunity in a globally competitive environment.

Notes

1   An industry is identified as a high-knowledge industry if the industry has more than 40 per cent of occupations in managerial, professional and technical positions (Beck 1992).
2   This acknowledges that there is no way to definitively know whether the presence of highways leads to growth, or whether growth leads to more highways. In either instance, the two invariably exist together.
3   Many would now argue that the information superhighways of today is even more important than the concrete highways of yesterday. And, if so, why did we not include information related to the spread of Internet or cellular service in our model? Although we agree with the relative and growing importance of telecommunications infrastructure, we are aware of no reliable and detailed information source chronicling the growth and spread of these technologies that dates to the early 1990s. The state and federal government only began publishing these data beginning after the turn of the century.
4   In the original 1993 coding system, metropolitan counties were defined by a population of one million or more. This criterion was scaled back to 400,000 for this research because of the paucity of such counties in Kansas.

References

Anselin, L., Varga, A., and Acs, Z. (1997) "Local geographic spillovers between university research and high technology innovations", *Journal of Urban Economics*, 42: 422–48.

Bartik, T.J. (1985) "Business location decisions in the United States: estimation of the effects of unionization, taxes, and other characteristics of states", *Journal of Business and Economic Statistics*, 3(1): 14–22.

Basile, R., Giunta, A., and Nugent, J.B. (2003) "Foreign expansion by Italian manufacturing firms in the nineties: an ordered probit analysis", *Journal Review of Industrial Organization*, 23(1): 1–24.

Carlton, D.W. (1983) "The location and employment choices of new firms: an econometric model with discrete and continuous endogenous variables", *Review of Economics and Statistics*, 65(3): 440–49.

Cassar, A., and Nicolini, R. (2003) "Spillovers and growth in a local interaction model", Unitat de Fonaments de l'Anàlisi Econòmica (UAB) and Institut d'Anàlisi Econòmica (CSIC) Working Papers, no. 574.03.

Coughlin, C.C., and Segev, E. (2000) "Location determinants of new foreign-owned manufacturing plants", *Journal of Regional Science*, 40: 323–51.

Devereux, M. P., Griffith, R., and Simpson, H. (2004) "Agglomeration, regional grants and firm location". Working paper. The Institute for Fiscal Studies, London, UK.

Greene, W. (2000) *Econometric Analysis*, 4th edn, Englewood Cliffs, NJ: Prentice Hall.

Guimarães, P., Figueiredo, O., and Woodward, D. (2004) "Industrial location modeling: extending the random utility framework", *Journal of Regional Science*, 44(1): 1–20.

Gunther F.C., Liu, W.K., Bhaskaran, R., Rothmayer, A.P., Devereux, M.P., and Griffith, R. (1998) "Taxes and the location of production: evidence from a panel of US multinationals", *Journal of Public Economics*, 68(3): 335–67.

Lawless, P., and Gore, T. (1999) "Urban regeneration and transport investment: a case study of Sheffield 1992–96", *Urban Studies*, 36: 527–45.

Malecki, E. (2001) "Going Digital in Rural America", in M. Drabenstott (ed.), *Exploring Policy Options for a New Rural America*, Kansas City: Center for the Study of Rural America, Federal Reserve Bank of Kansas City, 49–68.

McFadden, D. (1974) "Analysis of qualitative choice behaviour", in P. Zarembka (ed.), *Frontiers in Econometrics*, New York: Academic Press.

MIG, Inc. (1999) *IMPLAN Professional, Version 2.0: User's Guide, Analysis Guide, Data Guide*, Stillwater: Minnesota IMPLAN Group, Inc.

Morrissey, E.S. (1987) *The Non-metro Working Poor – A Profile of Family Heads*, Washington, DC: US Department of Agriculture.

Pigeon, M., and Wray, L.R. (1999) "Did the Clinton rising tide lift all boats?" *Challenge*, 42(3): 14–33.

Ribeiro, R., and Warner, M. (2004) *Measuring the Regional Economic Importance of Early Care and Education: The Cornell Methodology Guide*, Ithaca, NY: Department of City and Regional Planning, Cornell University.

Schumpeter, J.A. (1939) *Business Cycles*, vol. 2, New York: McGraw-Hill.

Waterson, M. (1993) "Vertical integration and vertical restraints", *Oxford Review of Economic Policy*, 9(2): 41–57.

9 An application of a double hurdle firm location model

The example of Montana[1]

Alison Davis and Thomas R. Harris

Introduction

As noted in other chapters in this volume, particularly by Gabe (Chapter 6), Leatherman and Kastens (Chapter 7), and Cader et al. (Chapter 8), firm location and operation is thought to be influenced by economic, demographic, environmental and social factors. For the most part, how important each is to the final decision is unique to the firm's industry. Firms have a clear profit motive and all else equal, they seek locations where costs are minimized so as to maximize profits. In 1929, Alfred Weber identified several factors that influence industry location, including product weight and shipping distances, proximity to raw materials, and wages. Goode and Hastings (1989), as an extension to the work by Weber and Lösch (1954), hypothesized that transportation services as well as agglomeration effects would play important and different roles for different types of manufacturing plants in both metropolitan and non-metropolitan areas. They found that both the transportation and accessibility measures were important influences in location decisions but these impacts varied across manufacturing sectors and metropolitan and non-metropolitan areas. Today these types of factors still drive location decisions, but they are not all inclusive. Other aspects of a community, including demographic variables, social climate, and the community's infrastructure, are also important.

It is critical for a community to understand the forces that drive development. If economic conditions, such as local wages or taxes, heavily influence business development, policy-makers might entice more firms by implementing policies that are business friendly. If social climate or the community's infrastructure are instead the more important influences, the strategy would be quite different. The strategy might require a more indirect policy, such as allocating tax dollars to target population growth, better school systems, or to lower crime. In the first scenario where economic conditions are at the forefront, a community might lower taxes, whereas in the second, it might increase taxes. Therefore, it is imperative that decision-makers understand what drives firm location decisions.

This chapter builds on Gabe (Chapter 6), Leatherman and Kastens

(Chapter 7) and Cader et al. (Chapter 8) by investigating the importance of economic, demographic, and social factors to the number of manufacturing firms in a region. We focus here on the intermountain western US states. We use the three-digit North American Industrial Classification System (NAICS) to identify the number of manufacturing firms at the county level in 1999. Our findings suggest two hurdles that counties encounter in attracting new firms to the region. First, they must offer a certain set of characteristics to entice firms to even consider the county as a potential market. Second, even if a county meets those standards, firms still may not locate in that region for various other reasons. The factors that affect these two decisions are potentially different.

As opposed to other firm location models in this volume, we used count data models of Poisson, single hurdle, and double hurdle to estimate each of the twenty-one manufacturing sectors. We use industry input, economic and social climate characteristics as explanatory variables. The results suggest that in general industry variables such as population and education drive whether the county is even considered in the first place. Economic variables play only a small role in this first-cut decision, although they play a substantial role in the second decision (once the county is deemed a potential marketplace). These results imply that decision-makers should work to spur population growth and improve school systems, both of which might increase taxes.

Before introducing the conceptual model, we begin with a brief review of past research on the influence of demographic and economic variables on firm location decisions. After describing the conceptual model in section 2, we outline the empirical specification, highlighting the advantages of using a zero-adjusted model over the standard Poisson model, followed by a description of the data used. Following the results of this study, we conclude with some policy implications and apply the results to Montana counties that are used for the community business matching model (Chapter 14).

Literature review

Several studies have investigated the influences of socioeconomic factors on firm location. A brief overview of a few of these studies can be found in Table 9.1. Each study takes a different approach. Some look at the effect of statewide characteristics, others focus on a smaller unit of analysis such as the county, city, or SMSA. Yet others focus on both the county and state levels (e.g., Goetz 1997). This review is by no means inclusive of all studies, but rather highlights some of the key variables in such explorations and some of the inconsistencies in the results. No clear policy implications have yet emerged from this line of research. Thus, local governments are unable to exactly determine the factors that entice a firm to locate in one region versus another.

Bartik (1985) employed a multinomial logit model to determine the

Table 9.1 An overview of selected firm location studies

Study	Variables Studied	Conclusions (Effect on manufacturing activity)
Bartik (1985)	State-specific variables	Land area, unionization, corporate and property taxes were all significant factors
Goetz (1997)	Market access, labor force factors, policy, inputs & agglomeration economies	Effects vary by food sub-industry but in general state fiscal policy, labour costs, educational attainment of workers and population size had expected effects
Gabe and Bell (2004)	Fiscal impacts (local taxes and government spending)	Low taxes are not helpful because they signal low public spending, unattractive to new firms
Guimaraes, Figueiredo, and Woodward (2004)	Labor costs, Land costs, taxes, market size, localization and urbanization economies	Agglomeration[1]: positive influence Property taxes: negative influence Labour and land costs insignificant
Holmes (1998)	Right to work laws (state measures)	Large increase in manufacturing activity when crossing from an anti-business state to a pro-business state
Walker and Greenstreet (1990)	Government incentives	Incentive offerings play a large role in location decisions

[1] Agglomeration was captured with two variables: urbanization economics and localization economies. Urbanization economies are externalities that are common to all firms, measured by the density of manufacturing and service firms in a county. Localization economies are externalities that benefit firms only in the same industry. This was measured by the number of establishments in the same two-digit SIC industry.

importance of state-specific variables in a manufacturing firm's state location decisions. Land area, unionization, and corporate and property taxes were all important factors in location decisions. The same factors remained important when testing each manufacturing sector separately as well as in the aggregate. While some taxes and regulations do vary within state lines, other economic and demographic variables may very greatly among regions in the state. These variations could not be captured in this analysis.

Results are mixed on the impact of fiscal policies on firm location, specifically local taxation. Newman and Sullivan (1988), in their review of the effect of business taxes on industrial location, find no evidence that higher taxes hinder location decisions. They limit their review to metropolitan areas only, however. Gabe and Bell (2004) find evidence that businesses favor communities that spend liberally on public goods and services, even if these expenditures are financed through local taxes. Gabe (Chapter 6) finds that no single indicator adequately predicts establishment growth within all economic sectors. Walker and Greenstreet (1990) investigate the effect of government incentives and assistance on manufacturing, specifically site-specific infra-structure, low-interest loans, training subsidies, and tax breaks. They find that industrial incentives attract new manufacturing firms but the effective tax rate deters businesses, which is inconsistent with Gabe and Bell's result.

Holmes (1998) found that the manufacturing's share of total employment increased by approximately one-third in pro-business stats, compared with anti-business states. The author used a state's right-to-work laws, which deters unionization, to gauge how accommodating an environment was for manufacturing. This measure of a pro-business environment, however, might be too broad, particularly at the state level, to effectively capture the location decisions of individual manufacturing firms.

Chapters in this volume by Leatherman and Kastens and Cader et al. most closely mirror our analysis. Leatherman and Kastens (Chapter 7) investigate the impact of community economic conditions, social attributes, infrastructure, and industry input/market conditions on the growth of manufacturing firms in the Great Plains. Population, poverty levels, and industry employment levels were significant determinants of firm growth. Unfortunately, the model does not capture the magnitude of growth. For example, counties that grew by 200 firms received the same value as a county that grew by only one firm. In addition, counties that lost firms would receive a zero value as would counties where no firm exists.

Cader et al. (Chapter 8) expand on Leatherman and Kastens' study (Chapter 7) by investigating goods-producing and service-producing sectors in Kansas. Population density, urbanization, and highways were three import-ant characteristics for understanding industry firm location there. Results suggest the relative importance of regional trade centers for promoting rural development. As for metropolitan regions, highways continue to play an important role for continued urban development. However, their method shares some of the same concerns as those in Leatherman and Kastens' study.

These chapters provide the motivation for us to extend the analysis of actual firm growth. For comparative purposes, we use similar variables as Leatherman and Kastens within the context of a count model, allowing for the inclusion of total number of firms.

Background and conceptual model

Background

The intermountain western states is a highly rural region. Of the 282 counties in the region, nearly 75 per cent are non-metropolitan. One-half of those counties are also not adjacent to a metro county, and approximately one-fourth are considered completely rural (population of 2,500 or less). Figure 9.1 shows the county population of this region.

Although manufacturing is not as prevalent as in the Midwest and the East, it has seen recent growth in the West. Overall job growth in the rural West outpaced US job growth between 1985 and 1995 by almost 60 per cent (Beyers 1999). Most of this growth occurred in the service industry; however, manufacturing saw some gains, primarily in counties adjacent to metro areas. Manufacturing employment in Western non-metro areas grew by 14.6 per cent compared with 12.3 per cent nationally in non-metro counties. Manufacturing employment in the nation as a whole (both metro and non-metro) declined 5 per cent while in the West, it declined only 2 per cent. Roth (2000) sees the rise of new manufacturing in rural areas as an extension of major advances in telecommunications, which allow firms to locate where they want to be, not where the traditional centers of finance dictate they have to be. In addition, rural manufacturing plants, like metro plants, increasingly rely on new technology to control virtually all phases of their production which often requires more highly trained and skilled workers. Currently, this need for more high-skilled workers may not bode well for rural areas, and rural policy-makers should promote efforts to raise skill levels to help attract new manufacturing firms.

Conceptual model

A wide set of local characteristics are hypothesized to be important to a firm's location. We use many of the characteristics outlined by Leatherman

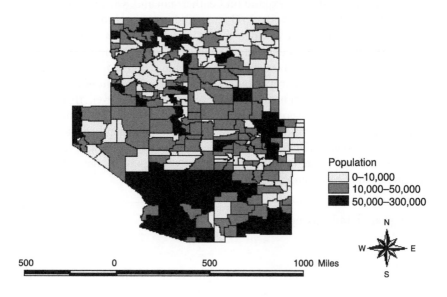

Figure 9.1 1999 population totals for intermountain states.

and Kastens in this volume, which allows for some comparison between the two studies.[2] Among the variables are current economic conditions, community social attributes, community infrastructure, and industry input and market conditions – all of which are thought to help determine the number of firms located within a geographic region. The rationale behind including each of these characteristics and their expected influence on the number of firms is described next.

Current economic conditions

A number of factors likely contribute to economic growth, including taxes, government expenditures, unemployment conditions, and regional characteristics. Here, we examine per capita tax revenue; the percentage of the total employment in agriculture, manufacturing, services, and mining; as well as housing values in the area.

We expect per capita tax revenue (both individual and corporate taxes) to lower the number of firms in the area. This assumption follows from Bartik's (1985) study, in which he found that high state taxes discouraged new manufacturing plants. The four employment variables – agriculture, manufacturing, services, and mining – do not represent all employment in the county, but we expect that clusters of employment will represent both competition and agglomeration. Therefore, the influence on the number of firms will vary depending on the type of manufacturing plant. High levels of agricultural and mining employment are expected to deter manufacturing firms whereas greater existing manufacturing employment is expected to encourage manufacturing firms to locate owing to agglomeration economies. Housing values are thought to be an important community characteristic because they represent the overall economic status of an area.

Community social climate

Two variables capture the social climate of an area: poverty level and age distribution.[3] High poverty levels could have mixed effects on firm location. Areas with high poverty could also have low wages, and less expensive labour could be an incentive for firms to locate. On the other hand, high poverty could signal poor economic conditions and thus a less profitable location. Finally, a lower median age is likely a draw, in that older individuals are less likely to be good candidates for manufacturing jobs.

Community infrastructure

The importance of community infrastructure is measured by the presence of an interstate highway and a commercial airport. Both are expected to be significant positive influences on the number of manufacturing firms in that they increase accessibility from one region to another. This is clearly important for those industries that rely heavily on transportation facilities.

Industry input and market requirements

Industry input factors include the percentage of the population with at least a high school degree, the labour force participation rate, population, population density, annual earnings, and metropolitan influence. The percentage of the population with at least a high school degree is expected to have a mixed effect. More technical manufacturing firms would prefer highly trained workers while less technical firms prefer individuals who work for lower wages. High annual earnings are expected to have a negative influence on firm location because they signal expensive labour. Population is expected to have a large, positive influence on firm location. Although manufacturing firms are not typically "local sellers", they do hire local workers and potentially purchase some of their inputs from local producers. Therefore, population can proxy for available labour as well available resources. Finally, the proximity to a metropolitan area is expected to have a strong positive effect on the number of firms because of the potentially strong nearby market.

Empirical specification

Given the discrete, nonnegative nature of the frequency of firms, a count model seems the most appropriate tool for this analysis. The Poisson regression model stipulates that each y_i is drawn from a Poisson distribution with parameter λ, which can be parameterized to depend on the regressors, x_i. If the probability function for y_i is

$$\text{Prob } (Y = y) = \frac{e^{-\lambda} \lambda^y}{y!} \text{ for } y = 0,1,2, \ldots \tag{1}$$

where Y_i is a potential integer outcome, then $E(Y_i) = \lambda$ and $Var(Y_i) = \lambda$ as well. In this instance λ is parameterized to be $\lambda = \exp(x_i\beta)$. The exponential function is used to ensure non-negativity of the estimated number of firms.

The basic Poisson model accommodates zero entries, suggesting that no firms exist in a location. However, the nature of the data used for this study gives rise to a large number of counties with zero firms for many of the manufacturing sectors (see Table 9.2). Some researchers have used the negative binomial distribution rather than the Poisson to handle the excess zeros. However, the hurdle models do this in a manner that is perhaps more intuitive and allows the decision process to be decomposed into two choices: (1) the choice of a firm to locate in a county at all, and (2) the choice of the number of firms to locate in that county.

The single-hurdle model accommodates many zero observations. It is capable of generating probabilities of counties with zero firms with a single mechanism. However, it cannot tell us why this is so, and thus the possibility that the county is not a suitable market for firms cannot be distinguished from a corner solution.

Let y_i denote the number of firms located in county i observed during a one-year period. Define two vectors of variables, x and z, where x contains variables most likely bearing on the decision on how many firms, n, to locate within county i, and z is a vector of characteristics pertaining to the decision for a firm to locate at all during that year. The number of firms is equal to zero if the random variable $D_i \leq 0$. While it is impossible to have negative firms, D_i merely represents whether there are unobserved impediments which preclude a firm from locating in a county during the year. Adopting the discrete specification, we have Prob $(D_i = 0) = \omega$. ω can be parameterized as a logit, probit, or log-log. In this instance, $\omega = \exp(-\eta)$ where $\eta = \exp(z_i a)$ and a is an unknown vector of parameters.

If the number of firms is positive, then $y_i = y_i^*$ with $E(y_i^*) = \lambda_i = \exp(x_i\beta)$. The single-hurdle model then has a dichotomous probability mass function (PMF) of the form:

Prob $(D_i \leq 0)$;   if $y_i = 0$,   (2)

$PMF(y_i | y_i > 0) \Pr(D_i > 0)$; if $y_i > 0$.

This implies that Prob $(y_i > 0) = 1 - \exp(-\omega)$. The likelihood function in the case of the single hurdle model with Poisson PMF specification is:

$$\lambda = \frac{\displaystyle\prod_{y=0} \exp(-\omega_i) \prod_{y>0} (1 - \exp(-\omega_i))\lambda_i^y}{[(\exp(\lambda_i) - 1)\, y_i!]} \tag{3}$$

The double-hurdle model can allow for two ways of generating zero observations. This model splits the decision into one part that determines the participation decision, and the other part that determines the number of firms. This second stage allows for firms that consider a region a potential marketplace, but we still observe zero firms. Now the probability of a zero observation is:

$\Pr(y_i^* \leq 0) + \Pr(y_i^* > 0) \Pr(D_i \leq 0)$.   (4)

There will be zero firms observed if the county is not a suitable market or if the county is a suitable market but an additional hurdle ($D_i \leq 0$) prevents firms from entering into the county. The PMF of a positive observation reflects that there are a positive number of firms entering and the additional hurdle does not limit firms from entering. It is of the form:

$\Pr(y_i^* > 0)PMF(y_i^* | y_i^* > 0) \Pr(D_i^* > 0)$.   (5)

The Poisson likelihood in this case becomes:

$$\prod_{y=0} [\exp(-\lambda_i) + (1 - \exp(-\lambda_i))\exp(-\omega_i)]$$

$$\prod_{y>0} (1 - \exp(-\omega_i))\exp(-\lambda_i)\lambda_i^{y_i} [y_i!]^{-1} \tag{6}$$

under the assumption that $y_i = y_i^*$ if $y_i^* > 0$ and $D_i > 0$. In this case, the truncated expectation of y is $E(y_i \mid y_i > 0) = \dfrac{\lambda_i}{1 - \exp(-\lambda_i)}$ and the unconditional expectation of y is $E(y_i) = \lambda_i(1 - \exp(-\omega_i))$.

The advantages of the double hurdle model over the single hurdle and Poisson models are clear. The double hurdle model can provide estimates of three different probabilities of participation in the market. The model can predict the probability of non-participation, $\exp(-\omega_i)$, the probability of a corner solution, $(1 - \exp(-\omega_i))\exp(-\lambda_i)$, and the probability of a county acquiring one or more firms, $(1 - \exp(-\omega_i))(1 - \exp(-\lambda_i))$.

Data

We combine data from several sources. The study includes information on 232 counties within the eight intermountain Western states: Arizona, Colorado, Idaho, Montana, Nevada, New Mexico, Utah, and Wyoming. The dependent variable in this study is the total number of firms located in a county, repeated for each of the 21, three-digit manufacturing sectors classified by the NAICS system (311 through 339).[4] Table 9.2 lists the dependent and explanatory variables as well as the source of the data. Table 9.3 provides a description of the dependent variables. In most instances, the variance is substantially larger than the mean, suggesting an overdispersion in the data. However, this is largely attributed to the number of zero counts and thus is well-suited for a zero-altered Poisson model.

We gathered county characteristics used as explanatory variables from several sources. Table 9.4 provides descriptive statistics of the 232 counties in the study. The presence of an interstate highway and commercial airport are dummy variables that take on a value of unity if they exist and zero otherwise.[5] The metro influence is also a dummy variable. If a county has a rural-urban continuum code of five or less (counties with population greater than 20,000), then the variable enters the model with a value of one, and zero otherwise. In addition, we use fixed effects to control for state-specific effects not measurable in the data.

Results

The full set of results is located in the appendix to this chapter. Appendix Table 9.A1 details all of the parameter estimates for the Poisson model for

Table 9.2 Data sources for dependent and independent variables

Dependent Variable	
Number of firms in county in 3-digit NAICS manufacturing sector	US Census Bureau – County Business Patterns
Independent Variables	
Per Capita Tax Revenue	US Census Bureau – 1997 Census of Governments
Percentage Employment in Agriculture	Bureau of Economic Analysis – Regional Economic Accounts
Percentage Employment in Manufacturing	Bureau of Economic Analysis – Regional Economic Accounts
Percentage Employment in Services	Bureau of Economic Analysis – Regional Economic Accounts
Percentage Employment in Mining	Bureau of Economic Analysis – Regional Economic Accounts
Labour Force Participation Rate	US Census Bureau – 2000 Census
Average Home Value	US Census Bureau – 2000 Census
Percentage of Population below Poverty	US Census Bureau – 2000 Census
Percent Population with High School Degree	US Census Bureau – 2000 Census
Median Age of Population	US Census Bureau – 2000 Census
Average Annual Income	US Census Bureau – 2000 Census
Population	US Census Bureau – 2000 Census
Population Density	US Census Bureau – 2000 Census
Metro Influence	ERS 2003 Rural Urban Continuum Codes
Presence of Interstate Highway	Rand McNally Atlas
Presence of Commercial Airport	Rand McNally Atlas

each of the 21 manufacturing industries. Appendix Tables 9.A2 and 9.A3 provide the results from the single-hurdle and double-hurdle models, respectively.[6] Table 9.5 (in text) provides a summary of significant variables that influenced the number of firms locating within a region. For example, in the Poisson model, for 13 of the 21 manufacturing sectors, higher tax revenues were deterrents for firm location. For the most part, the sign and the significance of the coefficients estimated from the Poisson model are consistent with expectations. The results from the Poisson model suggest that firm location is mainly determined by economic conditions, community infrastructure, and industry inputs.

The single-hurdle and double-hurdle models suggest that taxes are not important determinants of the number of firms.[7] Manufacturing and service employment increases the number of firms. The higher the median age, the fewer the manufacturing firms in several of the manufacturing sectors. After including variables that might characterize a hurdle for firm location, it appears that community infrastructure and industry input play an important role in firm location.

Table 9.6 summarizes the variables hypothesized to influence firms that were deterred from locating. The single hurdle is unable to distinguish a lack

Table 9.3 Number and type of firms (dependent variables) in 232 western counties

Industry	Average no. of firms	Variance in no. of firms	No. of counties with zero firms	Maximum no. of firms
Food manufacturing (311)	5.89	191.36	54	142
Beverage and Tobacco manufacturing (312)	0.74	3.02	160	14
Textile Mills (313)	0.38	1.93	193	15
Textile Product Mills (314)	1.46	24.94	150	59
Apparel Manufacturing (315)	1.6	25.77	155	53
Leather and Allied Product Manufacturing (316)	0.51	1.84	178	11
Wood Product Manufacturing (321)	4.23	100.96	80	120
Paper Manufacturing (322)	0.63	8.1	190	36
Printing and Related Products (323)	9.55	139.21	88	469
Petroleum and Coal Products Manufacturing (324)	0.37	1.53	193	13
Chemical Manufacturing (325)	2.78	102.9	122	127
Plastics and Rubber Manufacturing (326)	3.39	192.46	156	172
Nonmetallic Mineral Products Manufacturing (327)	4.48	150.27	66	144
Primary Metal Manufacturing (331)	1.13	16.92	168	48
Fabricated Metal Products Manufacturing (332)	12.09	2181.97	67	618
Machinery Manufacturing (333)	4.66	316.34	108	230
Computer and Electronic Manufacturing (334)	4.92	483.47	144	262
Electrical Equipment, Appliance and Component Manufacturing (335)	1.31	28.66	169	68
Transportation Equipment Manufacturing (336)	2.6	142.62	136	172
Furniture and Related Products Manufacturing (337)	5.67	374.43	98	245
Miscellaneous Manufacturing (339)	9.73	1016.61	99	326

of market participation from participating in the market but still observing a zero response. Three variables consistently appeared to affect zero entry in the single-hurdle model: population, manufacturing employment, and the percentage of the population with at least a high school education. These variables all had the expected effect. As population increases, the area is more appealing for firms, thus lowering the probability of no entries. Areas with high levels of manufacturing employment provide a solid base of employees for future manufacturing firms, making firms more likely to enter. The same holds true for education.

The double hurdle model is capable of distinguishing between zero market participation and those firms that choose to be part of the market but that

Table 9.4 Descriptive statistics of 232 western counties (independent variables)

Variables	Mean	Standard Deviation	Minimum	Maximum
Per Capita Tax Revenue ($)	352.65	322.21	36.32	3220.67
Percentage Employment in Agriculture	0.7	10.4	0	52.6
Percentage Employment in Manufacturing	5.8	5.5	0	34.4
Percentage Employment in Services	24.5	9.5	1.9	85.4
Percentage Employment in Mining	3.6	8.9	0	82.7
Labour Force Participation Rate (%)	59.2	7.9	30.1	83.6
Average Home Value ($1,000s)	113.39	101.86	36.5	1269
Percentage Population below Poverty	10.4	4.9	1	33.5
Percentage Population with at least High School Degree	83.3	6.7	63.6	97
Median Age of Population (years)	36.4	5.1	20.7	48.9
Average Annual Income ($100s)	229.86	48.96	156.84	514.73
Population (1,000s)	71.28	244.04	0.55	3072.15
Population Density (population/sq mileage county)	39.69	126.1	0.4	1218.4
Presence of Interstate Highway	0.49	0.5	0	1
Presence of Commercial Airport	0.32	0.47	0	1
Metro Influence	0.33	0.47	0	1

Table 9.5 Results summary

Variables	Poisson	Single Hurdle	Double Hurdle
Tax Revenue	13/21 negative effect	2/17 negative effect	2/17 negative effect
Agricultural Employment	15/21 negative effect	7/17 negative effect	5/17 negative effect
Manufacturing Employment	14/21 positive effect	15/17 positive effect	13/17 positive effect
Service Employment	3/21 positive effect	7/17 positive effect	10/17 positive effect
Age	9/21 negative effect	7/17 negative effect	8/17 negative effect
Airport	10/21 positive effect	8/17 positive effect	8/17 positive effect
Population	18/21 positive effect	14/17 positive effect	14/17 positive effect
Population Density	21/21 positive effect	14/17 positive effect	17/17 positive effect
Metro Influence	15/21 positive effect	11/17 positive effect	11/17 positive effect

Note: Numbers in cells should be interpreted as: for 13 of the 21 manufacturing sectors, tax revenues were a deterrent to firm location.

Table 9.6 Summary of the results for the hurdle variables

Hurdle Variable	Single Hurdle	Double Hurdle
Population	16/17	16/17
	Negative Effect	Negative Effect
Manufacturing	6/17	1/6
	Negative Effect	Positive Effect
Education	14/17	7/11
	Negative Effect	3 Negative(beverage, printing, plastics)
		4 Positive (computers, nonmetallics, machinery)
Metro		3/4
		2 Positive (Electrical, Textiles)
		1 Negative (Food)
Service		7/9
		Positive Effect
Highway		1/2
		Negative Effect

still do not locate in the region. Table 9.6 shows that population, as expected, is the most influential hurdle. In all but one instance, the larger the population, the more likely firms will locate in the county.[8] The sign and significance of the remainder of the variables were specific to the manufacturing industry. For example, education was a deterrent to entry for the computer, non-metallic, fabricated metals, and machinery industries, but an inducement for the beverage, printing, and plastics industry.

An appealing aspect of the double-hurdle model is that it is possible to calculate the probability that a region will have any firms. Furthermore, it is possible to decompose that probability into two parts. The third column of Table 9.7 provides an estimate of the proportion of counties that do not pass the first hurdle. The proportion of counties with zero firms because the county is considered a non-participant is equal to ω. This was calculated as discussed above for $\omega = \exp(-\exp(z_i \, a))$ where z is the vector of specified hurdle variables. For example, 5.75 per cent of the counties will have zero beverage firms as explained by the level of service employment, population, and the percentage of the population with a high school degree.

The fourth column provides the proportion of counties with zero firms even after the county passed the first hurdle. This was calculated by substituting the parameter estimates back into the equation: $\exp(-\lambda)$ where $\lambda = \exp(x_i\beta)$. Continuing the example above, the results suggest that 63.22 per cent of the counties will have zero beverage firms because of the levels of the x variables. The sum of ω and $\exp(-\lambda)$ should be approximately equal to the percentage of counties with zero firms, which in this instance is equal to 69.96 per cent. This is approximately equal to 68.97 per cent, the estimated percentage of firms with zero beverage firms.

Table 9.7 Expected probabilities of counties with zero firm counts, by manufacturing sector

Manufacturing Sectors	Hurdle Variables Included	Probability of Zero Firms "Out of market"	Probability of Zero Firms "Corner Solution"
Beverage	Service Employment, Population, Education	0.0575	0.6322
Leather	Service Employment, Population, Education	0.2250	0.5383
Printing	Service Employment, Population, Education	0.1123	0.2908
Chemicals	Service Employment, Population, Education	0.3299	0.2162
Plastics	Service Employment, Population, Education	0.4413	0.2418
Computers	Service Employment, Population, Education	0.1594	0.4850
Textile Products	Manufacturing Employ Population, Education	0.4584	0.1856
Non-Metallics	Manufacturing Employ Population, Education	0.1419	0.177
Machinery	Manufacturing Employ Population, Education	0.1475	0.3074
Miscellaneous	Manufacturing Employ Population, Education	0.3122	0.1312
Fabricated Metals	Manufacturing Employ Population, Education	0.1419	0.1771
Food	Service Employment, Population, Metro	0.0856	0.1529
Transportation	Service Employment, Population, Metro	0.4167	0.1745
Textile	Service Employment, Population, Metro	0.1937	0.6469
Electrical	Manufacturing Employ, Population, Metro	0.2333	0.5057
Wood	Highway, Population, Metro	0.18775	0.1565
Furniture	Highway, Population, Education	0.2735	0.1443

In most instances, we gain additional information by using the double-hurdle model. In all but six of the manufacturing sectors, the log likelihood is greater for the double-hurdle models compared with the single-hurdle model. In all instances when the models converged, both models were superior to a simple Poisson count model. It would be advantageous to verify whether a hybrid model, which is a combination of the single- and double-hurdle model, would be the best method. In addition, a negative binomial double-hurdle model might work even better because of the apparent overdispersion, not explained by the excess number of zeros, for several of the manufacturing sectors.

Application to the State of Montana

In conjunction to the application of the Community Business Matching Model (Chapter 14) for selected counties in the state of Montana, we applied the double-hurdle location model to ten Montana counties. Combining results of the double-hurdle location and CBM model would help these rural Montana counties better target economic development efforts.

Table 9.8 shows the probability of at least one manufacturing firm (by NAICS sector) locating in one of the ten Montana counties. It is not surprising that counties such as Yellowstone, Gallatin, and Missoula tend to be the most attractive areas for manufacturing firms. We find a high correlation between the attractiveness of a location and the county's population (see Figures 9.2 and 9.3). The results of the double-hurdle location model clearly show the most important factor is population size, followed by educational level. The importance of population size aligns with Cader et al.'s (Chapter 8) assertion that rural regions are at a disadvantage in the global economy because of lack of critical mass. Sparsely populated areas such as rural Montana should consider forming regional economic development efforts to achieve critical mass.

For the urban or more populated areas of Montana, the double-hurdle model has additional uses. The probability of five or more firms in a given NAICS manufacturing sector locating in a Montana county is shown in Table 9.9, again most applicable to larger urban areas. Such information could help these counties focus their economic development efforts. For

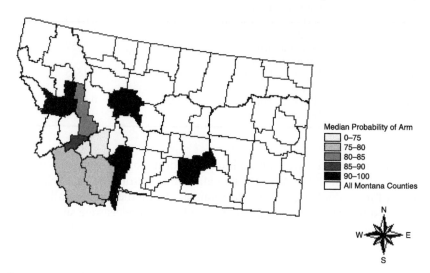

Figure 9.2 Median probability of at least one firm locating in a Montana county.

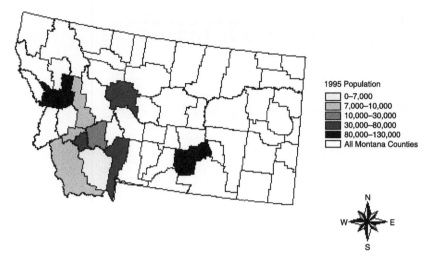

Figure 9.3 Population by county.

example, the probability of five or more beverage sector firms locating in Yellowstone, Gallatin, or Missoula counties is 1.5 per cent, 18.9 per cent, and 38.7 per cent, respectively. Missoula counties, therefore, might want to put more effort than Yellowstone in pursuing these types of industries, or on the other hand, Yellowstone might want to bolster its identified shortcomings. In comparing probability results from Tables 9.8 and 9.9, it is evident how this additional information can assist even urban and populated Montana counties in developing their economic development targets.

Understanding the probability of selected manufacturing firms locating in the area would also be helpful to regional economic development professionals. If the probability of attracting a certain manufacturing sector or additional manufacturing firms is low, this could indicate that more financial or human capital investment is needed in the county or region. It could also signal that it might not be fruitful to spend the time or funds in recruiting certain manufacturing sectors. Employing both the double-hurdle location model and the Community Business Matching Model, economic development practitioners could refine and focus economic development targets and programs.

Conclusions

Local, state, and federal government officials are appointed to identify economic trends or potential opportunities to better promote a sustainable or viable community. The results from this analysis in 10 Montana counties suggest that economic conditions alone, such as tax revenues or average earnings, do not attract firms to an area. Although these factors can be for

Table 9.8 Probability of at least one firm locating in Montana, by county (%)

NAICS Manufacturing Industry	Beaverhead	Cascade	Gallatin	Jefferson	Madison	Missoula	Powell	Yellowstone	Deer Lodge	Silver Bow
Beverage	4.2	11.4	81.0	25.2	0.1	32.2	0.3	4.3	34.9	9.8
Food	83.4	100.0	100.0	58.8	77.3	100.0	88.4	100.0	84.9	69.8
Chemical	78.5	99.1	99.9	78.8	77.6	99.8	94.4	98.8	68.6	52.1
Fabricated Metal	75.2	100.0	100.0	78.3	76.2	100.0	83.9	100.0	89.3	97.8
Computer	87.3	83.9	99.9	82.5	90.6	99.7	93.6	99.9	78.6	52.8
Furniture	100.0	99.9	100.0	100.0	100.0	100.0	100.0	100.0	100.0	99.0
Leather	52.1	42.9	83.2	24.8	35.4	79.6	8.7	98.1	100.0	86.8
Machinery	99.4	95.2	99.8	99.8	97.8	99.8	68.9	99.9	100.0	71.4
Miscellaneous	85.1	100.0	100.0	73.5	70.7	100.0	92.8	100.0	95.8	96.5
Non-metals	77.3	99.9	99.9	72.7	78.4	100.0	86.7	100.0	89.4	74.3
Paper	87.7	56.4	50.6	87.9	91.8	33.0	95.1	100.0	95.2	44.6
Plastics	67.8	89.1	100.0	53.4	54.9	99.9	60.8	100.0	64.1	97.2
Printing	52.8	100.0	100.0	51.1	31.1	100.0	67.8	100.0	74.8	92.4
Textiles	57.7	84.5	91.0	54.8	76.0	94.4	78.6	95.5	64.8	60.3
Transportation	60.6	93.8	99.4	64.3	69.8	98.6	75.9	100.0	100.0	100.0
Minimum	4.2	11.4	50.6	24.8	0.1	32.2	0.3	4.3	34.9	44.6
Maximum	100.0	100.0	100.0	100.0	100.0	100.0	100.0	100.0	100.0	100.0

Table 9.9 Probability of five or more firms locating in Montana by county (%)

NAICS Manufacturing Industry	Beaverhead	Cascade	Gallatin	Jefferson	Madison	Missoula	Powell	Yellowstone	Deer Lodge	Silver Bow
Beverage	0	2.9	18.9	0	0	38.7	0	1.5	0	9.1
Food	4.3	99.9	100	0.4	2.3	100	7.5	100	1.4	33
Chemical	0	51.7	79.7	0	0	74.1	1.4	45.5	0	0
Fabricated Metal	1.4	98.8	99.8	1.8	1.2	100	2.6	100	7.5	34.7
Computer	0	4.6	84.3	0	0	68.7	0	86.4	0	0
Furniture	0.2	79.9	99.4	0.1	0	99.1	0.7	99.7	9.6	45.7
Leather	0	0.1	4.3	0	0	2.9	0	36.9	95	6.3
Machinery	0	20.2	73.6	0	0	75.4	0	87.3	0.1	0.8
Miscellaneous	1.5	100	100	0.3	0.1	100	6.8	100	20.1	25.4
Non-metals	0.5	82.7	80	0.2	0.4	94.8	2	99	3.7	1.5
Paper	0	0.3	0.2	0	0	0	0	99.9	1.1	0
Plastics	0	7.4	88.5	0	0	83.7	0	99.4	0.1	17.1
Printing	0.2	98.4	99.8	0.2	0	100	0.8	100	1.8	12.9
Textiles	0	4.9	10.7	0	0	17.4	0	21	0.1	0.4
Wood	2.3	91.2	94.4	3.2	1.9	93.3	13.2	99.4	98.9	99.9
Minimum	0	0.1	0.2	0	0	0	0	1.5	0	0
Maximum	4.3	91.2	100.0	3.2	1.9	99.1	7.5	10.00	98.9	99.9

government officials to manipulate, a community's infrastructure and industry input characteristics may matter more in firm's decisions to locate there. Thus, the policy implications grow more complex. Rather than simply controlling fiscal policy, government officials should instead target improvements in education and local infrastructure while maintaining a strong population.

Future work could enrich the results of this study. Rather than using actual counts of firms within each region, researchers could look at the influence of these community variables on changes in the number of firms. In addition, it is likely that a firm's decision to locate in an area is related to the locational decisions of other firms. Harris and Shonkwiler (1997) found that the interdependencies of retail business location decisions were important and should not be ignored.

Although we included the influence of nearby metropolitan areas in our analysis, it does not fully capture the importance of spatial relationships. It is possible that non-metro counties that are adjacent to metro counties suffer from spatial competition from the neighbouring metro county. For instance, an interesting question might investigate whether large populations in one area draw away potential demand in a less populous neighbouring region.

Also, although the study area consists of many rural areas, we could extend the analysis by separating the sample into rural and urban areas and exploring the importance of the same economic and community characteristics. It is likely that the influence of these variables would not be the same for the two types of counties. The results from this extension could also be used by policy-makers to entice firms to locate in their community.

Finally, our results show that industrial location analysis and efforts should employ various models. The Community Business Matching Model assists local economic development practitioners in understanding economic sectors that meet local citizen demands and local attributes that meet business needs. But in addition, the double-hurdle location model provides local economic development practitioners with information on the probability of a manufacturing firm's location, which can focus local economic development efforts.

Appendix of parameter estimates for the poisson model, and results from the single-hurdle and double-hurdle models

Table 9.A1 Poisson results

Variables	Food	Beverage	Textiles	Textile Products	Apparel	Leather
Constant	**4.8219**	1.1482	9.637	−0.1396	0.4697	**−20.811**
	(2.292)	(0.268)	(1.450)	(−0.224)	(0.102)	**(−4.074)**
Arizona	−0.0554	0.6687	0.4453	−0.2772	0.8419	**0.9535**
	(−0.116)	(1.147)	(0.619)	(−0.395)	(1.170)	**(1.833)**
Colorado	0.0834	0.6018	−0.3889	0.5841	0.3170	−0.579
	(0.349)	(1.251)	(−0.718)	(1.325)	(0.519)	(−1.317)
Idaho	−0.2025	−0.2830	−1.069	−0.1545	−0.5589	−0.4095
	(−0.723)	(−0.508)	(−1.397)	(−0.331)	(−0.831)	(−0.701)
Montana	0.3627	0.4081	−0.3119	0.1987	0.2859	−0.6361
	(1.445)	(0.979)	(−0.415)	(0.412)	(0.536)	(−1.459)
Nevada	0.3472	0.5532	−1.716	0.673	0.7640	0.6467
	(0.881)	(0.918)	(−1.413)	(1.305)	(1.092)	(0.840)
New Mexico	0.0828	0.2159	0.1588	−0.4577	0.2382	0.3229
	(0.276)	(0.438)	(0.266)	(−0.924)	(0.368)	(0.647)
Utah	**−0.5167**	−0.8159	**−2.031**	−0.1786	−0.4006	−0.8649
	(−1.656)	(−1.319)	**(−2.468)**	(−0.376)	(−0.555)	(−1.408)
Tax Revenues	−0.0007	−0.0005	**−0.00195**	**−0.0012**	−0.0004	**−0.0024**
	(−1.543)	(−0.991)	**(−2.075)**	**(−2.098)**	(−0.806)	**(−3.137)**
Agricultural	−0.0202	**−0.1417**	**−0.11448**	**−0.1215**	**−0.0754**	−0.0175
Employment	(−1.353)	**(−4.008)**	**(−2.226)**	**(−4.015)**	**(−2.609)**	(−0.455)
Manufacturing	**0.0314**	0.0365	0.0346	**0.0515**	0.0227	**0.0745**
Employment	**(2.558)**	(1.471)	(1.138)	**(2.994)**	(1.167)	**(2.784)**
Service	0.0181	0.0079	0.0311	0.0229	0.0209	0.0303
Employment	(1.499)	(0.579)	(0.955)	(1.443)	(1.221)	(1.362)
Mining	**−0.0591**	−0.0259	−0.0178	−0.0708	**−0.094**	0.0128
Employment	**(−2.999)**	(−1.182)	(−0.417)	(−1.641)	**(−2.797)**	(0.482)
Housing Values	−0.0011	0.0006	0.0003	0.0003	0.0012	0.0001
	(−1.311)	(−0.512)	(0.305)	(0.382)	(1.438)	(0.117)
Family Poverty	**−0.0496**	−0.0447	**−0.1597**	0.0085	−0.0311	**0.1200**
	(−2.009)	(−0.897)	**(−2.008)**	(0.384)	(−0.597)	**(2.040)**
Median Age	**−0.0657**	−0.0384	−0.0621	**−0.0343**	**−0.0830**	0.0457
	(−4.095)	(−1.315)	(−1.219)	**(−1.684)**	**(−2.636)**	(1.117)
Highway	−0.1076	0.1132	−0.4293	**−0.4513**	0.0970	0.0093
	(−0.939)	(0.437)	(−1.199)	**(−2.379)**	(0.424)	(0.046)
Airport	**0.3914**	**0.6277**	0.2178	**0.5089**	0.3116	**0.8174**
	(3.057)	**(2.428)**	(0.738)	**(2.867)**	(1.441)	**(2.599)**
Population	**0.0006**	0.00031	0.00014	**0.0009**	**0.0005**	**0.0012**
	(3.475)	(1.162)	(0.319)	**(4.700)**	**(2.129)**	**(3.674)**
Population	**0.0015**	**0.0008**	**0.0034**	**0.0013**	**0.0014**	**0.0018**
Density	**(7.424)**	**(1.809)**	**(4.949)**	**(4.879)**	**(3.968)**	**(4.048)**
Metro	**0.7157**	0.4183	0.5893	0.4248	0.3653	0.1881
Influence	**(4.577)**	(1.342)	(1.296)	(1.635)	(1.143)	(0.492)
Household	−0.0188	−0.0073	−0.0449	−0.0043	0.0146	**0.1634**
Education	(−0.956)	(−0.201)	(−0.971)	(−0.221)	(0.378)	**(3.834)**
Labor Force	0.0065	0.0146	−0.0307	0.0208	0.0009	0.0538
	(0.478)	(0.576)	(−0.922)	(1.084)	(0.042)	(1.459)
Average	−0.0002	−0.0016	−0.0064	−0.0005	0.0024	−0.0049
Earnings	(−0.131)	(−0.413)	(−1.277)	(−0.195)	(0.918)	(−1.198)
Log Likelihood	−551.725	−180.765	−105.84	−217.280	−249.47	−147.678

Note: T-statistics are in parentheses below estimates. Estimates in bold are significant at $a = 0.10$.

Table 9.A1 Poisson results (continued)

Variables	Wood Product	Paper	Printing	Petroleum	Chemical	Plastics
Constant	−0.9039	**−7.9552**	0.4551	6.7866	2.4715	1.0463
	(−0.374)	**(−1.645)**	(0.183)	(1.188)	(0.913)	(0.2664)
Arizona	−0.1635	0.45944	**0.8729**	−0.9242	0.4658	**1.937**
	(−0.526)	(0.408)	**(1.667)**	(−0.776)	(1.110)	**(2.382)**
Colorado	0.2348	1.57294	**0.7186**	0.0415	−0.0995	**1.553**
	(0.979)	(1.624)	**(2.681)**	(0.055)	(−0.335)	**(2.420)**
Idaho	0.2733	0.79762	0.0961	**−1.8528**	**−0.6271**	0.4964
	(1.023)	(0.779)	(0.303)	**(−2.549)**	**(−1.825)**	(0.699)
Montana	0.3334	0.59698	0.2456	−0.2982	0.2279	0.8231
	(1.270)	(0.593)	(0.760)	(−0.460)	(0.805)	(1.300)
Nevada	0.2954	**3.51467**	**1.1465**	−0.6120	**0.6699**	**2.517**
	(0.768)	**(3.171)**	**(2.872)**	(−0.658)	**(1.765)**	**(3.603)**
New Mexico	−0.4391	0.45826	0.5407	−0.2777	−0.1023	0.6055
	(−1.240)	(0.425)	(1.536)	(−0.435)	(−0.271)	(0.8195)
Utah	−0.4110	0.7827	**−0.7727**	−1.1849	−0.6058	0.1909
	(−1.432)	(0.819)	**(−1.918)**	(−1.682)	(−1.623)	(0.278)
Tax Revenues	**−0.0016**	**−0.00302**	−0.0006	**−0.0013**	−0.0003	−0.0007
	(−3.707)	**(−2.457)**	(−1.217)	**(−2.027)**	(−0.072)	(−1.162)
Agricultural	**−0.0823**	−0.11336	**−0.1068**	**−0.2826**	**−0.0527**	**−0.1264**
Employment	**(−4.527)**	(−1.559)	**(−3.821)**	**(−3.074)**	**(−1.845)**	**(−2.843)**
Manufacturing	**0.0558**	0.02863	**0.0391**	−0.0276	**0.0417**	**0.072**
Employment	**(3.838)**	(1.294)	**(2.508)**	(−0.859)	**(2.729)**	**(4.210)**
Service	0.0116	−0.05156	0.0143	0.012	0.0134	0.0038
Employment	(0.838)	(−1.243)	(0.852)	(−0.254)	(0.922)	(0.182)
Mining	−0.0345	**−0.14416**	**−0.0698**	−0.0378	−0.0117	**−0.0938**
Employment	(−1.599)	**(−1.979)**	**(−3.081)**	(−1.261)	(−0.862)	**(−2.222)**
Housing Values	−0.0001	−0.00037	−0.0001	**−0.0299**	−0.009	−0.004
	(−0.249)	(−0.351)	(−0.142)	**(−3.155)**	(−0.882)	(−0.437)
Family Poverty	0.0335	**0.13004**	−0.0235	−0.1091	**−0.0696**	−0.0198
	(1.111)	**(1.713)**	(−0.807)	(−1.587)	**(−1.991)**	(−0.419)
Median Age	0.0216	0.07318	**−0.0559**	−0.0522	**−0.0766**	**−0.0733**
	(1.062)	(1.274)	**(−3.025)**	(−1.054)	**(−3.347)**	**(−2.228)**
Highway	−0.036	0.35771	0.0462	0.0760	−0.0012	−0.1289
	(−0.240)	(0.905)	(0.314)	(0.198)	(−0.027)	(−0.516)
Airport	0.2146	0.27282	**0.5065**	−0.5944	0.149	0.2487
	(1.225)	(1.023)	**(3.227)**	(−1.439)	(0.871)	(1.213)
Population	**0.0009**	**0.00115**	**0.0008**	**0.0007**	**0.0007**	**0.0005**
	(6.881)	**(4.675)**	**(5.187)**	**(2.422)**	**(4.107)**	**(2.777)**
Population	**0.0014**	**0.00249**	**0.0019**	**0.0016**	**0.0015**	**0.0019**
Density	**(5.366)**	**(6.376)**	**(6.029)**	**(2.629)**	**(6.672)**	**(6.363)**
Metro	**0.3924**	**1.88139**	**0.5824**	**1.117**	**1.073**	**4.5265**
Influence	**(1.899)**	**(3.388)**	**(3.077)**	**(2.246)**	**(4.647)**	**(4.226)**
Household	0.0145	0.00315	0.0305	−0.017	0.0135	0.0048
Education	(0.825)	(0.104)	(1.234)	(−0.316)	(0.565)	(0.143)
Labor Force	0.0064	0.05129	−0.0057	0.02812	−0.0245	0.0058
	(0.400)	(1.292)	(−0.362)	(0.623)	(−1.339)	(0.262)
Average	−0.0028	−0.0023	0.0006	0.0004	0.0029	−0.0017
Earnings	(−1.469)	(−0.795)	(0.399)	(0.1118)	(1.512)	(−0.844)
Log Likelihood	*−518.19*	*−104.645*	*−544.048*	*−101.289*	*−306.15*	*−295.993*

Table 9.A1 Poisson results (continued)

Variables	Non-metallics	Primary Metal	Fabricated Metal	Machinery	Computer	Electrical
Constant	−1.51332	−2.21184	−0.33544	0.51549	−3.1274	−7.79763
	(−0.618)	(−0.490)	(−0.119)	(0.174)	(−0.741)	(−0.27)
Arizona	**0.89977**	0.9107	0.68701	0.47589	**1.36242**	**2.02208**
	(2.097)	(1.450)	(1.052)	(0.751)	**(2.391)**	**(1.913)**
Colorado	**0.62445**	0.2782	0.45626	0.29891	**1.03375**	**1.36486**
	(3.041)	(0.504)	(1.299)	(0.931)	**(2.598)**	**(2.542)**
Idaho	−0.07027	0.58757	−0.1431	−0.18691	−0.40424	0.55179
	(−0.294)	(0.974)	(−0.345)	(−0.522)	(−0.850)	(0.167)
Montana	0.23625	0.5938	−0.09824	−0.36353	−0.06434	0.47329
	(1.017)	(1.221)	(−0.265)	(−1.044)	(−0.135)	(0.674)
Nevada	**1.00234**	0.3787	**0.83086**	0.58274	**1.53713**	**2.16497**
	(2.719)	(0.566)	**(1.724)**	(1.140)	**(2.930)**	**(2.775)**
New Mexico	**0.81395**	0.6386	0.16761	−0.51426	0.53505	**1.19049**
	(2.982)	(1.097)	(0.364)	(−1.082)	(1.153)	**(1.862)**
Utah	0.00113	0.7949	−0.26214	**−1.01156**	**−1.24317**	−0.58214
	(0.0190)	(1.469)	(−0.602)	**(−2.494)**	**(−2.274)**	(−0.369)
Tax Revenues	−0.00039	**−0.00156**	**−0.00108**	−0.00098	**−0.00121**	−0.00127
	(−0.932)	**(−2.003)**	**(−2.027)**	(−1.782)	**(−2.042)**	(−0.893)
Agricultural	−0.02741	−0.05697	**−0.05544**	−0.04794	**−0.1236**	−0.10387
Employment	(−1.608)	(−1.225)	**(−2.361)**	(−1.954)	**(−1.944)**	(−0.851)
Manufacturing	**0.02928**	0.0149	**0.04422**	**0.06185**	**0.1032**	0.07301
Employment	**(1.847)**	(0.807)	**(3.234)**	**(3.858)**	**(5.673)**	(1.085)
Service	0.01474	**0.05199**	0.01525	0.01736	**0.0321**	0.02809
Employment	(1.154)	**(2.111)**	(0.829)	(0.983)	**(1.730)**	(0.232)
Mining	−0.01642	−0.02122	−0.02219	−0.02187	−0.04468	−0.00012
Employment	(−1.377)	(−0.590)	(−1.237)	(−1.067)	(−1.114)	(−0.0007)
Housing	−0.00006	−0.00078	−0.00189	−0.00166	0.00086	0.00014
Values	(−0.077)	(−0.695)	(−1.313)	(−1.293)	(1.001)	(0.060)
Family Poverty	−0.02201	−0.05444	−0.01471	−0.02917	−0.00623	0.04584
	(−0.800)	(−0.917)	(−0.440)	(−0.762)	(−0.129)	(0.149)
Median Age	−0.02366	−0.00264	−0.01639	**−0.04612**	**−0.1062**	−0.04151
	(−1.271)	(−0.062)	(−0.764)	**(−1.936)**	**(−3.229)**	(−0.307)
Highway	0.22516	0.36853	−0.00717	−0.09686	**−0.44704**	0.00866
	(1.269)	(1.278)	(−0.048)	(−0.525)	**(−2.110)**	(0.001)
Airport	**0.39633**	0.35641	0.23229	0.13103	**0.76904**	0.35222
	(2.634)	(1.250)	(1.554)	(0.821)	**(4.078)**	(0.478)
Population	**0.00084**	**0.00066**	**0.00082**	**0.00076**	**0.00095**	0.00094
	(5.118)	**(2.403)**	**(5.008)**	**(4.343)**	**(4.010)**	(1.037)
Population	**0.00094**	**0.0012**	**0.00168**	**0.00199**	**0.00242**	**0.00254**
Density	**(4.271)**	**(3.477)**	**(6.867)**	**(6.552)**	**(6.122)**	**(1.988)**
Metro	**0.63135**	**1.28675**	**1.11795**	**1.11127**	**1.08459**	1.09822
Influence	**(3.378)**	**(3.076)**	**(5.905)**	**(4.565)**	**(3.523)**	(1.305)
Household	0.03744	0.0142	0.01709	0.01033	**0.08062**	0.06779
Education	(1.554)	(0.415)	(0.597)	(0.409)	**(2.440)**	(0.617)
Labor Force	−0.01703	−0.0308	0.00834	0.01292	−0.02141	0.02483
	(−1.094)	(−0.977)	(0.467)	(0.694)	(−1.100)	(0.302)
Average	0.00085	0.00213	0.00051	−0.0006	−0.00126	**−0.00548**
Earnings	(0.286)	(0.934)	(0.288)	(−0.241)	(−0.514)	**(−2.369)**
Log Likelihood	*−496.17*	*−193.488*	*−751.232*	*−430.157*	*−308.877*	*−170.761*

Table 9.A1 Poisson results (continued)

Variables	Transportation	Furniture	Miscellaneous
Constant	4.4729	2.32459	−2.08475
	(1.451)	(0.804)	(−0.679)
Arizona	−0.04556	**1.1057**	**0.79174**
	(−0.054)	**(2.446)**	**(1.808)**
Colorado	−0.19308	**0.70887**	**0.59207**
	(−0.402)	**(2.447)**	**(1.867)**
Idaho	**−0.8925**	0.42323	0.13423
	(−1.656)	(1.331)	(0.334)
Montana	−0.39928	0.46432	0.33917
	(−0.739)	(1.558)	(0.988)
Nevada	0.1392	**1.14204**	**1.21974**
	(−0.399)	**(2.800)**	**(2.889)**
New Mexico	−0.90464	**0.90312**	**0.85079**
	(−1.286)	**(2.613)**	**(2.092)**
Utah	**−0.80683**	0.13331	−0.33615
	(−1.6451)	(0.384)	(−0.762)
Tax Revenues	**−0.00132**	**−0.00099**	**−0.001**
	(−2.286)	**(−2.138)**	**(−1.811)**
Agricultural Employment	**−0.11078**	**−0.11133**	**−0.09446**
	(−3.673)	**(−4.803)**	**(−2.831)**
Manufacturing Employment	**0.05083**	0.04267	0.04345
	(3.663)	(3.400)	(2.698)
Service Employment	0.00392	0.018	**0.02876**
	(0.231)	(1.285)	**(1.920)**
Mining Employment	**−0.10425**	**−0.0658**	**−0.0876**
	(−2.929)	**(−2.819)**	**(−3.482)**
Housing Values	−0.00092	−0.00004	−0.00004
	(−0.923)	(−0.051)	(−0.046)
Family Poverty	−0.05202	**−0.05903**	−0.01414
	(−1.140)	**(−1.754)**	(−0.403)
Median Age	0.00104	**−0.0478**	−0.03096
	(0.030)	**(−2.432)**	(−1.201)
Highway	−0.14795	−0.04996	0.17492
	(−0.849)	(−0.352)	(0.974)
Airport	**0.3351**	**0.53179**	**0.55498**
	(1.750)	**(3.762)**	**(3.918)**
Population	**0.0005**	**0.00068**	**0.00079**
	(2.538)	**(3.928)**	**(4.311)**
Population Density	**0.00136**	**0.00136**	**0.00185**
	(4.412)	**(5.861)**	**(6.127)**
Metro Influence	**0.97691**	0.32622	**0.73188**
	(3.646)	(1.907)	**(3.321)**
Household Education	**−0.05732**	0.00474	**0.04942**
	(−2.292)	(0.189)	**(1.883)**
Labor Force	0.03326	0.01034	−0.01238
	(1.478)	(0.632)	(−0.690)
Average Earnings	−0.00112	−0.00286	−0.00015
	(−0.609)	(−1.588)	(−0.074)
Log Likelihood	*−286.867*	*−449.718*	*−597.716*

Table 9.A2 Single hurdle results

Variables	Food	Beverage	Textile Products	Apparel	Leather	Wood Product
Constant	+	−			−	−
Arizona					+	+
Colorado		+				
Idaho						
Montana				−		
Nevada					+	
New Mexico	+					
Utah						
Tax Revenues						−
Agricultural Employment						+
Manufacturing Employment	+		+	+	+	
Service Employment	+	+		+		
Mining Employment	−					
Housing Values	−					
Family Poverty	−				+	+
Median Age	−		−			−
Highway	+			+		
Airport	+		+	+	+	+
Population	+	+	+	+	+	+
Population Density	+	+	+			+
Metro Influence	+	+			+	
Household Education						
Labor Force	−					
Average Earnings		−			−	−
Single Hurdle Variables						
Constant	**4.108**	**1.588**	**5.0092**	**5.1263**	**4.954**	**0.3673**
	(2.731)	**(6.224)**	**(3.435)**	**(3.482)**	**(3.578)**	**(2.476)**
Manufacturing Employment	**−0.0637**	**−0.0187**	−0.02229	0.0066	−0.0079	**−0.3760**
	(−2.777)	**(−1.887)**	(−1.198)	(0.340)	(−0.791)	**(−1.876)**
Population	**−0.0467**	**−0.0086**	**−0.01992**	**−0.1231**	**−0.0078**	**−0.0335**
	(−3.025)	**(−2.862)**	**(−4.714)**	**(−5.459)**	**(−3.315)**	**(−4.565)**
Household Education	**−0.0458**	**−0.5223**	**−0.04536**	**−0.0467**	**−0.0427**	0.4271
	(−2.554)	**(−2.294)**	**(−2.664)**	**(−2.727)**	**(−2.573)**	(1.385)
Log Likelihood	−516.66	−177.811	−215.537	−210.349	−145.37	−495.76

Note: T-statistics are in parentheses below estimates. Estimates in bold are significant at $\alpha = 0.10$.

Table 9.A2 Single hurdle results (continued)

Variables	Printing	Chemical	Plastics	Non-metallics	Fabricated Metal	Machinery
Constant		+		+		
Arizona	+		+	+		
Colorado	+			+		
Idaho						
Montana		+				
Nevada			+	+		
New Mexico				+		
Utah						
Tax Revenues				+		
Agricultural Employment	−				−	−
Manufacturing Employment	+	+	+		+	+
Service Employment						
Mining Employment	−			−		
Housing Values					−	
Family Poverty					−	
Median Age	−	−	−			−
Highway	+					
Airport	+					
Population	+	+		+	+	+
Population Density	+	+	+	+	+	+
Metro Influence	+	+		+	+	+
Household Education				+		
Labor Force		−		−		
Average Earnings			−			
Single Hurdle Variables						
Constant	**5.1508**	**3.9021**	**4.7824**	−0.0800	1.4986	**3.9254**
	(3.392)	**(2.621)**	**(2.818)**	(−0.138)	(0.911)	**(3.064)**
Manufacturing Employment	0.00406	−0.0025	0.0208	0.0006	**−0.0481**	**−0.0519**
	(0.382)	(−0.211)	(1.625)	(0.857)	**(−1.899)**	**(−2.764)**
Population	**−0.0737**	**−0.0483**	−0.041	−0.0542	−0.052	**−0.0284**
	(−3.581)	**(−5.478)**	**(−5.78)**	**(−4.337)**	**(−2.863)**	**(−3.953)**
Household Education	**−0.0524**	**−0.0325**	**−0.0431**	0.0038	−0.0116	**−0.03655**
	(−2.700)	**(−1.788)**	**(−2.109)**	(0.529)	(−0.586)	**(−2.432)**
Log Likelihood	−498.99	−284.11	−254.25	−441.04	−688.88	−400.883

Table 9.A2 Single hurdle results (continued)

Variables	Computer	Electrical	Transportation	Furniture	Miscellaneous
Constant					
Arizona	+	**+**		+	+
Colorado	+	+		+	+
Idaho			−		
Montana				+	
Nevada	+			+	
New Mexico	+			+	+
Utah	−		−		
Tax Revenues			−		
Agricultural Employment	−		−	−	
Manufacturing Employment	+	**+**	+	+	+
Service Employment	+	+	+		+
Mining Employment				−	−
Housing Values	+				
Family Poverty				−	
Median Age	−			−	−
Highway					
Airport	+	**+**		**+**	+
Population	**+**			+	+
Population Density	+	**+**	**+**	**+**	**+**
Metro Influence		**+**		+	+
Household Education	+		−		+
Labor Force	−		+		
Average Earnings		−			
Single Hurdle Variables					
Constant	**5.799**	**1.5371**	**1.2766**	**5.0233**	**5.1619**
	(3.933)	**(9.640)**	**(6.280)**	**(3.262)**	**(3.163)**
Manufacturing Employment	0.00348	−0.0078	−0.0241	0.1542	**−0.0469**
	(0.109)	(−0.511)	(−1.083)	(0.716)	**(−2.188)**
Population	**−0.0623**	**−0.0190**	**−0.0307**	**−0.0687**	**−0.0662**
	(−7.071)	**(−3.852)**	**(−3.561)**	**(−4.147)**	**(−4.839)**
Household Education	**−0.0479**	−0.1944	−0.0175	**−0.0489**	**−0.047**
	(−2.837)	(−0.628)	(−0.599)	**(−2.624)**	**(−2.521)**
Log Likelihood	*−267.60*	*−167.58*	*−260.903*	*−420.103*	*−523.501*

Table 9. A3 Double hurdle results

Variables	Beverage	Leather	Printing	Chemicals	Plastics	Computers
Constant		−				
Arizona			+		**+**	+
Colorado	+	−	+		+	+
Idaho						
Montana		−				
Nevada				+	+	+
New Mexico						
Utah			−		−	**−**
Tax Revenues		−				
Agricultural Employment	−		**−**		−	−
Manufacturing Employment	**+**	+	**+**		**+**	**+**
Service Employment	+	+	+		+	+
Mining Employment		+	−			
Housing Values		+			+	+
Family Poverty	−	+		−		
Median Age	−		−	−	−	**−**
Highway						
Airport		+	+			+
Population		+	+	**+**		+
Population Density	**+**	+	+	+	+	+
Metro Influence			+	+		+
Household Education		+				+
Labor Force				−		−
Average Earnings		−			−	
Double Hurdle Variables						
Constant	**8.7504**	4.4042	**10.8329**	−0.1309	3.3186	**−17.2377**
	(−1.711)	(0.837)	**(3.195)**	(−0.037)	(−1.590)	**(−2.263)**
Service Employment	0.2375	**0.3686**	**0.1863**	−0.0144	**0.0774**	**0.1126**
	(1.740)	**(1.933)**	**(2.768)**	(−0.735)	**(2.700)**	**(2.833)**
Population	**−0.2749**	**−0.2828**	**−0.1016**	**−0.0533**	**−0.0297**	**−0.04377**
	(−1.753)	**(−2.182)**	**(−3.352)**	**(−2.610)**	**(−4.047)**	**(−3.463)**
Household Education	**−0.0029**	−0.1285	**−0.1892**	0.01104	**−.0545**	**0.1908**
	(−2.0813	(−1.609)	**(−3.415)**	(0.249)	**(−2.201)**	**(2.264)**
Log Likelihood	*−168.103*	*−135.37*	*−495.139*	*−293.292*	*−249.28*	*−282.186*

Note: T-statistics are in parentheses below estimates. Estimates in bold are significant at $a = 0.10$.

Table 9.A3 Double hurdle results (continued)

Variables	Textile Product	Non-metallics	Machinery	Miscellaneous	Fabricated Metals
Constant					
Arizona		+		+	+
Colorado		+		+	+
Idaho					
Montana					
Nevada		+		+	+
New Mexico		+		+	+
Utah			−		
Tax Revenues					
Agricultural Employment					
Manufacturing Employment	+		+	+	
Service Employment		+		+	+
Mining Employment				−	
Housing Values					
Family Poverty				−	
Median Age			−	−	
Highway	−				
Airport	+			+	
Population	+	+	+	+	+
Population Density	+	+	+	+	+
Metro Influence	+	+	+	+	+
Household Education		+		+	+
Labor Force				−	
Average Earnings					
Double Hurdle Variables					
Constant	3.424	**−7.1319**	**−26.6389**	2.5031	**−7.1319**
	(1.550)	**(−1.727)**	**(−3.912)**	(1.276)	**(−1.727)**
Manufacturing Employment	−0.0324	0.00156	**0.14244**	−0.032	0.00156
	(−0.747)	(0.015)	**(3.194)**	(−1.081)	(0.015)
Population	**−0.1821**	**−0.0367**	**−0.1521**	**−0.04841**	**−0.0367**
	(−3.095)	**(−1.756)**	**(−3.662)**	**(−2.423)**	**(−1.757)**
Household Education	−0.0122	**0.07862**	**0.3074**	−0.0241	**0.0786**
	(−0.331)	**(1.693)**	**(3.923)**	(−1.067)	**(1.693)**
Log Likelihood	*−197.12*	*−453.175*	*−405.4995*	*−528.078*	*−453.176*

Table 9.A3 Double hurdle results (continued)

Variables	Food	Transportation	Textile		Electrical
Constant	+				−
Arizona			−		+
Colorado			−		+
Idaho		−	−		
Montana					
Nevada			−		+
New Mexico		−	−		
Utah		−	−		
Tax Revenues					
Agricultural Employment		−			
Manufacturing Employment	+	+			+
Service Employment	+		+		+
Mining Employment	−		+		
Housing Values	+		+		
Family Poverty	−				
Median Age	−				
Highway					
Airport	+				+
Population	+	+			+
Population Density	+	+	+		+
Metro Influence	+	+	+		+
Household Education	−	−			
Labor Force		+			
Average Earnings			−		−
Double Hurdle Variables					
Constant	4.9991	1.0282	−7.147	Constant	−0.6280
	(1.585)	(2.848)	(−1.824)		(−0.670)
Service Employment	0.1646	−0.01263	0.21805	Manufacturing	0.0823
	(2.393)	(−0.449)	(1.942)		(1.438)
Population	−0.1637	−0.0732	−0.0417	Population	−0.0557
	(−4.014)	(−3.582)	(−1.555)		(−3.436)
Metro Influence	−0.1065	0.4887	4.332	Metro Influence	2.0853
	(−2.075)	(1.0655)	(2.506)		(3.149)
Log Likelihood	*−507.26*	*−264.75*	*−93.055*	*Log Likelihood*	*−159.93*

Table 9.A3 Double hurdle results (continued)

Variables	Wood		Furniture
Constant			
Arizona			+
Colorado			+
Idaho			+
Montana			
Nevada			+
New Mexico			+
Utah			
Tax Revenues	−		
Agricultural Employment	−		−
Manufacturing Employment	+		+
Service Employment			+
Mining Employment			−
Housing Values			
Family Poverty			−
Median Age			
Highway	−		
Airport			+
Population	+		+
Population Density	+		+
Metro Influence	+		+
Household Education			
Labor Force			
Average Earnings	−		
Double Hurdle Variables			
Constant	−0.17422	Constant	3.9277
	(−0.717)		(1.146)
Highway	**−1.1312**	Highway	0.2088
	(−1.852)		(0.416)
Population	**−0.0268**	Population	**−0.2611**
	(−2.695)		**(−3.268)**
Metro Influence	0.9283	High School	−0.0258
	(1.599)		(−0.674)
Log Likelihood	*−485.741*		*−414.801*

Notes

1 This chapter is based on an original journal article by Reum and Harris (2006).
2 The results will not be directly comparable. Leatherman and Kastens (2008) used a binary logit model for some manufacturing industries, whereas here a count model will be employed for all of the three-digit manufacturing industries in NAICS system.
3 Government expenditures are also expected to be influential in firm location. However the data available aggregated all expenditures into one category and thus was highly correlated with per capita taxes, resulting in a model that would not converge.
4 Not all numbers are used in the system.
5 As determined by the ERS.
6 The single-hurdle models for the following manufacturing sectors did not converge: textiles, paper manufacturing, petroleum and coal manufacturing,

and primary metal manufacturing. The double-hurdle models for the following manufacturing sectors failed to converge: apparel, paper manufacturing, petroleum and coal manufacturing, primary metal manufacturing, and fabricated metal manufacturing.

7   We also included tax variables such as property taxes, corporate income taxes, franchise taxes, and inventory taxes, but they were never significant. Although this may seem counterintuitive, Barkley (1996) found that low local taxes may not provide a locational advantage. Low tax rates might translate into low-quality public services. Manufacturing firms seek skilled labour and thus high-quality schooling (often found in regions with a higher tax base) signals the potential for a well-qualified labour pool.

8   Table 9.6 provide a summary of those variables used in the final analysis after estimating several different combinations of variables thought be significant hurdles. We determined the final set of variables by selecting the model with largest log likelihood.

References

Barkley, D. (1996) "Turmoil in traditional industry: prospects for non-metropolitan manufacturing", in M. Drabenstott and T. Smith (eds), *Economic Forces Affecting the Rural Heartland*, Kansas City, MO: Kansas City Federal Reserve Bank.

Bartik, T. (1985) "Business location decisions in the United States: estimates of the effects of unionization, taxes and other characteristics of states", *Journal of Business and Economic Statistics*, 3(1): 14–22.

Beyers, W. (1999) "Employment growth in the rural west from 1985–1995 outpaced the nation", *Rural Development Perspectives*, 14: 38–43.

Gabe, T.M., and Bell, K.P. (2004) "Tradeoffs between local taxes and government spending as determinants of business location", *Journal of Regional Science*, 44(1): 21–41.

Goetz, S.J. (1997) "State and county-level determinants of food manufacturing establishment growth: 1987–1993", *American Journal of Agricultural Economics*, 79: 838–50.

Goode, F.M., and Hastings, S.E. (1989) "The effect of transportation service on the location of manufacturing plants in non-metropolitan and small metropolitan communities", in William R. Gillis (ed), *Profitability and Mobility in Rural America: Successful Approaches to Tackling Rural Transportation Problems*, University Park: Penn State University Press.

Guimarães, P., Figueiredo, O., and Woodward, D. (2004) "Industrial location modeling: extending the random utility framework", *Journal of Regional Science*, 44(1): 1–20.

Harris, T.R., and Shonkwiler, J.S. (1997) "Interdependence of retail businesses", *Growth and Change*, 24: 523–33.

Holmes, T.J. (1998) "The effect of state policies on the location of manufacturing: evidence from state borders", *Journal of Political Economy*, 106(41): 667–705.

Levinson, A. (1996) "Environmental regulations and manufacturers' location choices: evidence from the census of manufactures", *Journal of Public Economics*, 62: 5–29.

Newman, R.J., and Sullivan, D.H. (1988) "Econometric analysis of business tax impacts of industrial location: what do we know, and how do we know it?" *Journal of Urban Economics*, 23: 215–34.

Reum, A., and Harris, T. (2006) "Exploring firm location beyond simple growth models: a double hurdle application", *The Journal of Regional Analysis and Policy*, 36: 45–67.

Roth, D. (2000) "Thinking about rural manufacturing: a brief history", *Rural America*, 15: 12–19.

Walker, R., and Greenstreet, D. (1991) "The effect of government incentives and assistance on location and job growth in manufacturing", *Regional Studies*, 25(1): 13–30.

Weber, A. (1929) *Theory of the Location of Industries* (Cal Friedrich, trans.), Chicago: University of Chicago Press.

B. Input-output and value chain models

10 Targeting industry clusters for regional economic development

The REDRL approach

David L. Barkley and Mark S. Henry

Introduction

Industry targeting is the process of focusing industrial development pro-grammes and efforts on specific industries or clusters of related industries. The principal objectives of an industry targeting programme are to identify (1) industries that have a high potential for locating or developing in the area and (2) industries that provide attractive local economic development impacts in terms of future job growth, wages paid, and contributions to the local tax base. A targeting approach enables communities to focus their recruitment, retention and expansion, and small business development programmes rather than provide assistance for many different industry types. Thus, targeting permits a more efficient use of the community's limited economic develop-ment resources. This chapter provides an overview of the industry targeting approach developed and used by the Regional Economic Development Research Laboratory (REDRL) of Clemson University. This approach focuses on identifying industry clusters with (1) a high potential for prosper-ing in the study area and (2) significant positive economic impacts on the local economy. The discussion of the REDRL targeting methodology is organized as follows. First, we summarize the advantages and disadvantages of targeting industry clusters as an economic development strategy. Second, we present the screening method for identifying industry clusters and the clusters' value chains. Third, we rank the clusters on the basis of potential impacts on the local economy. The REDRL cluster targeting method was used for the South Carolina secondary wood products (Lamie et al. 1997) and food and fibre industries (Wright et al. 1998), and for manufacturing indus-tries in Anderson County (Barkley et al. 1998), Lancaster County (Barkley et al. 2002), and Florence County (Barkley et al. 2006).

Targeting industry clusters

Industry clusters are "geographic concentrations of interconnected com-panies, specialized supplies, service providers, firms in related industries, and associated institutions" (Porter 2001: 7). Firms in an industry cluster may interact through purchase-sale relationships; interfirm collaboration in product development, marketing, or research; or a shared reliance on specialized services and labour markets (Deller, Chapter 4; Woodward and Guimarães, Chapter 5). Industry clusters are unique as a result of their historical development and the local organizations and institutions that evolved to serve them (Cortright and Mayer 2001). However, commonalities exist among industry clusters that influence their potential for growth and the policies and programmes appropriate for cluster promotion and development. Industry clusters may be classified according to core industry, foundation or economic stimulus for clustering, and intracluster firm structure or organization. The agglomeration of establishments in a location may have resulted from (1) an incidental co-location based on proximity to markets or natural resources (Gordon and McCann 2000); (2) the availability of localization economies derived from specialized goods and services (Bergman and Feser 1999); (3) the evolution of a local value chain (end-market sectors and their primary, secondary, and tertiary suppliers), or (4) the availability of pools of specialized labour (Feser 2003).

Advantages of targeting industry clusters

The targeting of industrial development programmes at specific industry clusters generally will provide greater economic development benefits than those associated with less-focused industrialization efforts. Five principal benefits result from the development of industry clusters in a county or region (Barkley and Henry 1997).

1   *Clustering strengthens localization economies.* The concentration of an industry at a particular location may result in significant cost savings to firms in the cluster. These cost savings are referred to as localization economies. Sources of potential savings include a greater availability of specialized input suppliers and business services; a larger pool of trained, specialized workers; public infrastructure investments geared to the needs of a particular industry; financial markets familiar with the industry; and an enhanced likelihood of interfirm technology and information transfers.

2   *Clustering facilitates industrial reorganization.* The transition in industrial organization from large firms engaged in mass production to small firms focused on specialty production is well documented. This change in industrial structure is attributed to increased global competition and the emergence of new production technologies (e.g., computer-aided manufacturing). Clusters are attractive locations for small, specialized, computer-aided manufacturers for several reasons. First, the adoption of new production technologies is more prominent and easily attained among firms in industry clusters. Moreover, a concentration of firms provides the pool of skilled labour that computer-aided technologies

require. Second, proximity between the more specialized firms and their input suppliers and product markets enhances the flow of goods through the production system, and ready access to product and input markets enables firms to quickly adapt to market changes.

3 *Clustering encourages networking among firms.* Networking is cooperation among firms to take advantage of complementarities, exploit new markets, integrate activities, or pool resources or knowledge. This cooperation occurs more naturally and frequently within industry clusters. Surveys of firms in manufacturing networks show that networks generate significant advantages for firms through cooperation with their counterparts. Networking firms are more likely than non-networking firms to engage in collaboration and information sharing in marketing, new product development, and technological upgrading. The networking firms also report that their competitiveness and profitability are enhanced by interfirm cooperation and collaboration.

4 *Clustering results in larger local economic impacts.* The total employment and income effects associated with attracting a new firm include the direct effects (firm employment and income) and indirect effects (employment and income changes at input suppliers for the new firm). The indirect employment and income changes generally are referred to as the multiplier effects. Programmes supporting cluster development will have relatively large multiplier effects for the local economy because of strong linkages among cluster firms. That is, the total employment and income gains from recruiting (or retaining) cluster members will likely exceed those associated with non-cluster firms of similar size.

5 *Clusters facilitate entrepreneurial activity.* Industry clusters encourage new firm start-ups and growth by fostering innovation and facilitating the commercialization of new products and technologies. Entrepreneurial activity, in turn, leads to further cluster growth through the development of new businesses and new cluster members. Thus, industry clusters and entrepreneurial activity reinforce one another, leading to more rapid local economic development through cumulative causation (Feldman and Francis 2004). The role of entrepreneurial activity in cluster development is especially important in areas where clusters are small or existing clusters are in declining industries.

Disadvantages of targeting industry clusters

The principal shortcoming with an industry targeting approach is the difficulty of "picking winners". A prerequisite to targeting industries is the identification of future regional competitive advantage based on past labour force characteristics, unique regional attributes, and proximity to input and product markets. Industrialization efforts next must identify the industries that best fit the regional competitive advantage. The industry targeting approach also must assess industry prospects for growth, the potential local economic impacts, and the likely environmental and quality of life impacts. This process of picking winners is complicated by the volatility of the marketplace – today's "rapid growth" sectors may be "slow growth" or "declining" industries in the future (Buss 1999).

The second shortcoming to a cluster development strategy is that "late-comer" clusters may not be competitive with larger, established clusters in terms of recruitment, expansion, and new firm development. Early industry clusters may provide localization economies, specialized infrastructure, pools of skilled labour, and institutional support not readily available in newer and smaller clusters. Krugman (1991) suggests, however, that new clusters can compete with existing industry concentrations if the starting positions are not too unequal, firms and workers can move easily, and economies of scale are realized at a relatively small cluster size.

In summary, industry targeting is not an exact science. Industries identified through a targeting study may choose not to locate or expand in the region. Or, firms in a targeted industry may be increasing in size and number but the industry cluster does not provide the anticipated employment and income effects. Thus, the targeting of specific industries for recruitment or retention and expansion does not guarantee that the desired employment and income gains will result. However, industry targeting does increase the probability that the region will be successful in developing an industrial base that provides characteristics desired by the community.

The remainder of this section provides the methods, data, and findings of the REDRL industry clusters targeting approach.

Criteria for selecting industry clusters

The REDRL approach to cluster identification and targeting follows three principal steps:

1   Identify industry concentrations for which the region has experienced recent employment growth.
2   Construct value chains (linkages to input suppliers and product markets) for the industry clusters selected in Step 1, and identify industries in the value chains with the greatest linkages to the local industry concentrations.
3   Rank the selected industries from Steps 1 and 2 by expected economic and fiscal impacts on the local economy.

The industry cluster targeting approach will be demonstrated using the findings of the 1998 study of Anderson County, South Carolina, a small, single-county metropolitan area with total employment of approximately 50,000. Anderson County requested a study focusing on manufacturing industries, and clusters of manufacturing establishments in the county were targeted at the four-digit SIC level. The Anderson County study was selected for review because it permits a retrospective analysis of the targeting methodology.

Step 1: Selection of five screening criteria

1   Three or more establishments in Anderson County in 1996.
2   County industry employment was greater than 200 in 1996.
3   Industry employment in Anderson County increased from 1988 to 1996.
4   An industry specialization index – the location quotient (LQ) – for Anderson County exceeded 1.00 in 1996 or the LQ increased from 1988 to 1996.
5   An industry competitiveness index – the competitiveness differential (CD) component of shift-share analysis – for Anderson County was positive for the period 1988–1996.

Screening criteria 1, 2, and 3 identifies four-digit SIC manufacturing industries that had a significant presence in the county in 1996 and promising employment generation potential (based on 1988–1996 employment growth rates). The LQ and CD criteria are used to identify industries for which Anderson County exhibited a competitive advantage in attracting or developing. An LQ greater than 1 indicates that the region has been, over time, relatively successful in attracting or nurturing employment in a specific industry. An increase in an industry's LQ from 1988 to 1996 indicates that the industry became more important to the local economy compared to the average county in the US. Thus, a high and increasing LQ implies that the region has a competitive advantage in maintaining and attracting employment in that industry. The CD provides an indicator of how well a local industry is performing over a specific time period relative to the nation as a whole. A positive CD indicates that industry employment in the area grew at a more rapid rate than for the nation, or area industry employment declined at a less rapid rate than for the nation. A positive CD, in conjunction with a positive area industry employment growth rate, indicates that the area had a competitive advantage in attracting and generating employment in that industry over the specified time period. Eight Anderson County industry clusters were identified using the above screening criteria (Table 10.1).

Large and expanding industry clusters in the other Upstate counties (Oconee, Pickens, Greenville, Laurens, Spartanburg, and Cherokee) may also be promising manufacturing industries for Anderson County. The presence of an industry cluster in the South Carolina Upstate indicates that the area provides locational characteristics that are attractive to members of these industries. In addition, the availability of Upstate clusters provides advantages to new cluster firms in terms of proximity to product markets and input suppliers, labour familiar with the industry's production process, and the availability of specialized business services. Industry clusters in the South Carolina Upstate counties also were targeted at the four-digit SIC level (Table 10.2).

Table 10.1 Anderson County clusters

	1996		1988–96 US Empl. Change
	Empl.	Estab.	
I. Positive U.S. Employment Change, 1988–1996			
1. SIC 3714 (Motor Vehicle Parts & Accessories)	2312	7	+33.8%
2. SIC 3089 (Plastics Products, NEC)*	259	9	+21.8%
3. SIC 3599 (Industrial Machinery, NEC)*	205	19	+23.3%
4. SIC 2392 (House Furnishings except Curtains & Drapes)	308	3	+6.9%
5. SIC 2273 (Carpets & Rugs)	525	3	+3.9%
6. SIC 2759 (Commercial Printing, NEC)*	228	3	+0.6%
II. Negative U.S. Employment Change, 1988–1996			
1. SIC 2399 (Fabricated Textile Products, NEC)	340	3	−6.0%
2. SIC 2281 (Yarn Spinning Mills)	287	5	−24.0%

Source: ES202 Data Files.

* Does not include Anderson County.

The following screening criteria were used to identify promising Upstate manufacturing clusters.

1   Five or more establishments in the SC Upstate in 1996.
2   Upstate industry employment was greater than 1,000 in 1996.
3   Industry employment in the Upstate counties increased from 1988 to 1996.
4   Industry LQ for the Upstate counties exceeded 1.00 in 1996 or increased from 1988 to 1996.
5   Industry CD of Shift-Share Analysis for Upstate counties was positive for the period 1988 to 1996.

The industry cluster size criteria for an Upstate cluster (five or more establishments, employment exceeds 1,000) are greater than the requirements for an Anderson County cluster (three or more establishments, employment exceeds 200). The size requirements for Upstate clusters were more stringent to focus the study on the most developed clusters in the region. The screening method for Anderson County and the SC Upstate identified 22 industry clusters with high potentials for employment growth in the area – four industry clusters that the Upstate and Anderson County had in common, four clusters unique to Anderson County, and 14 clusters unique to the Upstate counties. The reader will note that Anderson County officials had no input in the selection of the county or regional screening criteria except to designate

Table 10.2 South Carolina Upstate clusters

	1996		1988–96 US Empl. Change
	Empl.	*Estab.*	
I. Positive U.S. Employment Change, 1988–1996			
1. SIC 3714 (Motor Vehicle Parts & Accessories)	1630	12	+33.8%
2. SIC 3089 (Plastics Products, NEC)*	2623	34	+21.8%
3. SIC 3599 (Industrial Machinery, NEC)*	1492	119	+23.3%
4. SIC 2834 (Pharmaceutical Preparations)	1788	3	+10.1%
5. SIC 2653 (Corrugated & Solid Fiber Boxes)	1065	14	+15.4%
6. SIC 2752 (Commercial Printing, Lithographic)	1684	102	+3.1%
7. SIC 2261 (Finishing Plants, Cotton)	3033	25	+37.8%
8. SIC 2673 (Bags: Plastic, Laminated, & Coated)	1680	6	+18.4%
9. SIC 2297 (Non-woven Fabrics)	1334	11	+43.4%
10. SIC 2392 (House Furnishings, except Curtains & Drapes)	2703	12	+6.9%
11. SIC 3566 (Speed Changers, Drives & Gears)	1161	7	+12.9%
12. SIC 2843 (Surface Active Agents)	1038	15	+11.9%
II. Negative U.S. Employment Change, 1988–1996			
1. SIC 3511 (Turbines & Turbine Generator Sets)	1808	4	−0.2%
2. SIC 3562 (Ball & Roller Bearings)	3637	5	−6.5%
3. SIC 2299 (Textile Goods, NEC)	1178	16	−14.9%
4. SIC 3545 (Machine Tool Accessories)	2233	18	−6.9%
5. SIC 3765 (Electronic Capacitors)	3548	5	−16.6%
6. SIC 2821 (Plastics, Materials & Resins)	1195	7	−7.4%

Source: ES202 Data Files.

* Does not include Anderson County.

manufacturing as the industry of interest. Thus, the 22 identified clusters reflect regional comparative advantage and not a local "wish list". The input of local officials was sought to reduce the target industries from 22 industries to 5–10 based on anticipated economic, environmental, and quality of life considerations.

Step 2: Value chains for clusters

Manufacturing industries supplying inputs to or purchasing outputs from the 22 cluster industries may be good candidates for industry targeting and recruiting. Industries linked to the cluster industries may find Anderson County a competitive location if proximity to input suppliers and product markets is desired. Such proximity is especially valued by manufacturers using "just-in-time" inventory replacement or firms producing specialized goods in small-batch production runs.

The IMPLAN database was used to identify the top five inputs suppliers and top five product markets for the 22 industry clusters (see Deller, Chapter 4, for an alternative approach using a similar framework). Manufacturing industries with five or more input or product market linkages to the 22 cluster industries were identified as industries that will find Anderson County an attractive location if the 22 cluster industries continue to develop in the Upstate (Table 10.3).

The manufacturers with the strongest buy-sell relationships to cluster industries include miscellaneous plastics products (SIC 3080); broadwoven fabric mills (SIC 221–226); plastics materials (SIC 2821); cyclic organic crudes and intermediates (SIC 2865); industrial organic chemicals, NEC (SIC 2869); manmade organic fibres (SIC 2824); and yarn-spinning mills (SIC 2281). Plastics materials and yarn spinning mills also were identified as two of the 22 high-potential industry clusters.

The recruitment of manufacturers with strong buy-sell linkages to the 22 cluster industries may be a second phase of a targeted industrial development strategy. Additional development of the identified industry clusters should be the initial focus of the county's industrial development program. Expansion of existing industry clusters will make the area a more attractive

Table 10.3 Manufacturing industries with numerous backward (input) or forward (output) linkages to upstate or Anderson county cluster industries[a]

IMPLAN Sector	SIC Industries in IMPLAN SECTOR	Number of Linkages To Cluster Industries
220	Miscellaneous Plastic Products (308)	9
108	Broadwoven Fabric Mills, Cotton (221) Broadwoven Fabric Mills, Manmade (222) Broadwoven Fabric Mills, Wool (223) Dyeing and Finishing Textiles (226)	8
191	Plastics Materials, Synthetic Resins, Non-vulcanizable Elastomers (2821)[b]	6
190	Cyclic Organic Crudes and Intermediates and Organic Dyes and Pigments (2865) Industrial Organic Chemicals, NEC (2869)	6
194	Manmade Organic Fibers, except Cellulosic (2824)	6
116	Finishers of Textiles, nec (2269) Yarn Spinning Mills (2281)[b] Yarn Texturizing, Throwing, and Winding Mills (2282)	6
162	Paper Mills (262)	5

a Manufacturers listed by IMPLAN as one of the top five input suppliers or product markets for five or more of the cluster industries.

b Industries are classified as Anderson County or Upstate clusters.

location for linked manufacturers, and thus reduce the efforts and incentives required to attract establishments in the linked industries.

Step 3: Ranking industry clusters

The 22 industry clusters selected for the Upstate and Anderson County are good prospects for industrial recruitment because the area provides a competitive advantage for these manufacturers. However, all 22 clusters may not be equally attractive prospects based on the expected economic and fiscal impacts on Anderson County. Insights into the potential county-level impacts associated with successfully recruiting an additional establishment were provided by comparing six characteristics for the cluster industries:

1   *US employment growth rate.* Establishments in industries with rapid national employment growth are more likely to expand and create new jobs more rapidly than establishments in slow growth or declining industries.
2   *Average establishment size.* Industries with large average establishment employment provide greater potential for immediate job generation than industries whose operations require, on average, fewer employees.
3   *Average production worker wages.* Other establishment characteristics held equal, a manufacturing plant paying high wages will provide greater local economic development impacts than a manufacturing establishment offering primarily low-wage jobs.
4   *Fixed assets per employee.* The local fiscal impacts of a new manufacturing establishment are related to (1) the establishment's contribution to public revenues through property taxes paid and (2) public expenditures through increased services required by the establishment's employees. Establishments that contribute to public revenues relative to public expenditures will be preferred to those that add much to public costs relative to tax revenues.
5   *Income multipliers.* Income multipliers for the 22 industries were estimated for the Upstate counties using IMPLAN. The multipliers provide a means of comparing the relative cumulative effect of additional income generated by the cluster industry.
6   *Import substitution.* A location consideration for many manufacturing industries is the size of the local market for the manufacturer's product. One measure of potential local market size is the dollar value of imports of the manufacturer's product to the region. The potential to substitute for Upstate imports may make Anderson County an attractive location for manufacturers. Total Upstate imports by four-digit SIC industry for the 22 manufacturing clusters were estimated using IMPLAN. Total imports were divided by average establishment size to provide an estimate of the number of new local establishments, by industry, the Upstate counties could support based on import substitution.

Summary index of industry characteristics

Comparisons among industry characteristics are complicated by the fact that an industry may rank relatively high on one characteristic but rank low on another. For example, establishments in the yarn-spinning mills industry (SIC 2281) have large average plant sizes but pay relatively low wages to production workers, whereas establishments in the pharmaceutical preparations industry provide, on average, large plant size and high wages. Thus, from a community development standpoint, adding a pharmaceutical preparations plant would be preferred to the attraction of a new yarn spinning mill (everything else held equal).

A ranking of the 22 cluster industries based on four of the six industry characteristics (employment growth rate, mean plant size in terms of employment, assets per employee, and mean wage rate) is provided through the calculation of a summary index. The remaining two industry characteristics (income multipliers and import substitution) varied relatively little among the 22 industries, and thus these characteristics were not included in the calculation of the index. This index is estimated as follows:

1   The national averages for the four industry establishment characteristics are standardized. That is, the 22 values for each characteristic are treated as observations from a standard normal distribution (a distribution with a mean of 0.0 and standard deviation of 1.0). Programmes for the standardization of data are available in most statistics software packages. Standardization of characteristic data permits direct comparisons across industry characteristics that have different measures (for example, employment vs. wages vs. assets).

2   The actual value for the characteristic is replaced by its corresponding standardized value. This standardized value is the number of standard deviations above (+) or below (−) the mean for the 22 industries. Standardized values near 0.0 reflect actual values near the average for the 22 industries. Negative standardized values reflect below average actual values and positive standardized values represent above average actual values. The larger the standardized value (+ or −) the further above or below the characteristic mean. For example, a standardized value of +1.00 or higher places the industry in approximately the top 15 per cent of the 22 industries, whereas a value of −1.00 or lower places the industry in the bottom 15 per cent. An alternative perspective is that the middle 50 per cent of the industries will have standardized values between approximately −0.70 and +0.70.

3   The standardized values for the four industry characteristics are summed for each industry (Table 10.4). This sum represents an unweighted total, that is, each of the industry characteristics is given equal weight in construction of the index. The reader should note that the index rankings reflect the relative potential impacts of only the 22 selected industry

Table 10.4 Standardized distributions of the industry growth rate, mean plant size, assets per employee, and mean wage rate

SIC	Industry	Growth Rate 1988–1996	Mean Plant Size	Assets Per Employee	Mean Wage Rate	Sum
2821	Plastics Materials and Resins	−0.83	0.22	3.99	2.12	5.49
3714	Motor Vehicle Parts and Accessories	1.49	0.76	0.11	1.25	3.61
2834	Pharmaceutical Preparations	0.16	1.84	0.63	0.90	3.53
2297	Non-woven Fabrics	2.03	0.65	0.44	−0.03	3.10
3511	Turbines and Turbine Generator Sets	−0.42	0.94	0.12	2.02	2.66
3562	Ball and Roller Bearings	−0.78	1.81	0.23	0.79	2.05
2843	Surface Active Agents	0.26	−0.59	1.01	0.97	1.65
3566	Speed Changers, Drives, and Gears	0.32	−0.51	−0.20	0.62	0.22
2653	Corrugated and Solid Fiber Boxes	0.46	−0.22	−0.18	−0.11	−0.06
2673	Bags:Plastics, Laminated, and Coated	0.63	−0.13	−0.15	−0.41	−0.07
2261	Finishing Plants, Cotton	1.72	−0.64	−0.42	−0.83	−0.17
3599	Industrial Machinery	0.90	−1.25	−0.53	−0.01	−0.89
3089	Plastics Products, NEC	0.82	−0.63	−0.42	−0.68	−0.92
3675	Electronic Capacitors	−1.35	1.53	−0.48	−0.70	−1.01
2273	Carpets and Rugs	−0.19	0.41	−0.48	−0.89	−1.15
2281	Yarn Spinning Mills	−1.76	1.26	−0.19	−0.99	−1.69
2752	Commercial Printing, Lithographic	−0.24	−1.20	−0.47	0.00	−1.91
3545	Machine Tool Accessories	−0.80	−0.96	−0.46	0.08	−2.14
2392	House Furnishings, NEC	−0.02	−0.54	−0.79	−1.34	−2.70
2759	Commercial Printing, NEC	−0.38	−1.17	−0.64	−0.69	−2.88
2299	Textile Good, NEC	−1.25	−0.67	−0.33	−0.80	−3.05
2399	Fabricated Textile Products, NEC	−0.75	−0.90	−0.77	−1.27	−3.69

Source: ES202 Data Files and 1992 Census of Manufacturers.

clusters. All 22 industries were selected as good candidates for industrial recruitment based on the presence of a growing industry cluster in Anderson County or the Upstate.

Based on the selected industry characteristics, the manufacturing clusters with the most favorable economic and fiscal impact potentials for Anderson County were:

- Motor Vehicle Parts and Accessories (3714)
- Non-woven Fabrics (2297)
- Pharmaceutical Preparations (2834)

- Surface Active Agents (2843)
- Plastics Materials and Resins (2821)
- Turbines and Turbine Generator Sets (3511)
- Ball and Roller Bearings (3562)

The above industries generally ranked average or above average in three or four of the industry characteristics (as indicated by positive values for the standardized measures). In general, however, each of the industries had relative strengths regarding the four characteristics. Plastics Materials and Resins (2812) had high values for assets per employee and mean wage rate. Motor Vehicle Parts (3714) and Non-woven Fabrics (2834) rated highest in terms of past employment growth rates, and Pharmaceutical Preparations (2834) and Ball and Roller Bearings (3562) had the largest average plant size measured in employees. None of the 22 industries dominated the others in all four characteristic categories, thus communities are faced with trade-offs as they select among industry clusters.

How "good" are the targets?

The Anderson County industry targeting study was completed in 1998. The seven years between the study and 2006 is sufficient time to determine if the industries selected by the REDRL clustering methodology were "good" targets for industry recruiting.

Table 10.5 provides the 22 target industries for the South Carolina Upstate and the number of new manufacturing plants established from 1998 to 2005 according to the South Carolina Department of Commerce (SCDOC) records on new plant investments. The SCDOC reported 41 new plant investments in the six-county Upstate area for the period 1999–2005. Twenty-one of these investments were in the four-digit SIC industries selected for targeting and 26 were in the more inclusive three-digit SIC industries that included the target industries. Thus, the REDRL methodology was successful in "predicting" the industry of more than half of the new manufacturing establishments in the Upstate. This result should not be too surprising because the selected clusters were those industries for which the Upstate experienced growth in the recent past, and local economic development options often are path-dependent. That is, the types of businesses that a community nurtures or attracts in the future are influenced by the types of businesses nurtured or attracted in the past. The industry cluster targeting approach takes into consideration an area's historical legacy, and it builds a community's economic future on the foundation of its past successes. This foundation of input and service providers, skilled labour pools, and specialized public services and infrastructure provides the region competitive advantages in promoting job growth in the industry clusters and related industries.

Table 10.5 New establishment start-ups in target industries, Upstate, SC, 1998–2004

SIC	Industry	4-Digit SIC	3-Digit SIC	Total New Establishments in Manufacturing
2821	Plastics Materials and Resins	4	5	
3714	Motor Vehicle Parts and Accessories	5	6	
2834	Pharmaceutical Preparations			
2297	Non-woven Fabrics		1	
3511	Turbines and Turbine Generator Sets	3	3	
3562	Ball and Roller Bearings			
2843	Surface Active Agents			
3566	Speed Changers, Drives, and Gears			
2653	Corrugated and Solid Fiber Boxes			
2673	Bags: Plastics, Laminated, and Coated			
2261	Finishing Plants, Cotton			
3599	Industrial Machinery	1	1	
3089	Plastics Products, NEC	6	7	
3675	Electronic Capacitors			
2273	Carpets and Rugs			
2281	Yarn Spinning Mills			
2752	Commercial Printing, Lithographic			
3545	Machine Tool Accessories	1	2	
2392	House Furnishings, NEC			
2759	Commercial Printing, NEC			
2299	Textile Good, NEC			
2399	Fabricated Textile Products, NEC	1	1	
	TOTAL	21	26	41

Source: South Carolina Department of Commerce.

Conclusion

The REDRL approach to industry targeting encourages communities to focus their industrial development efforts (recruitment, retention and expansion, and small business development) at members of existing and emerging area industry clusters. As such, the industry targeting methods developed for an area have two goals: (1) identify industry clusters that prospered in the region in the recent past, and (2) identify the potential economic impacts resulting from the expansion of each of the selected industry clusters. The results of this approach are a selection of industry cluster targets for which the region has a relative competitive advantage in developing and the resulting economic development impacts are most favourable. Thus, in principle, the targeting approach enables the community to attain the greatest economic development success with its limited resources.

An industry targeting approach that focuses on industry clusters will not be appropriate for all regional industrial development efforts. Industry clusters are geographic concentrations of similar and related industries, and many regions (e.g., rural areas) may not have such concentrations or the clusters present may be in declining industries. In these situations, the targeting approach should be modified to better identify the industries with greatest potential for locating in the region. First, the geographic scope of the study region can be expanded from a county or metro area to a multicounty region such as USDA labour market areas (LMA) or BEA economic areas. Promising industry clusters may be present in the larger region, and these clusters may be reasonable targets for development if spillovers and external economies are valued by members of these clusters.

Second, areas with declining industry clusters may find good targets within the declining sectors. That is, subsets of declining industries may have promising employment generation potentials, and firms in these sectors may find the region an attractive location because of available labour skills and specialized services. For example, the textile industry (an historically important cluster in many Southern communities) has experienced significant job losses and plant closings since 1990. Yet, subsectors of the textile industry (e.g., non-woven fabric mills) and industries closely related to textile (e.g., motor vehicle seating and interior trim manufacturing, surgical appliances and supplies manufacturing, and home furnishings merchant wholesalers) remain relatively strong in terms of employment growth. These subsectors may serve as the cores of emerging clusters and sources of future employment opportunities.

Finally, some regions do not have industry clusters in or near the region. In this situation, the industry cluster targeting approached outlined in this chapter will not be helpful in identifying prospective industries to serve as the region's economic base. For these regions, industry targeting approaches that focus on import substitution (see Deller, Chapter 19) and knowledge-based occupational clusters (Feser 2003) may be useful. Indeed, an in-depth analysis of a region's industrial development potential and prospects would include insights on emerging and expanding clusters, opportunities for import substitution, and pools of skilled and specialized labour resources.

References

Barkley, D.L., Henry, M.S., and Dudensing, R.M. (2006) "Targeting growth opportunities for Florence county", REDRL Research Report 08–2006–01, Regional Economic Development Research Laboratory, Clemson University, Clemson, South Carolina.

Barkley, D.L., and Henry, M.S. (1997) "Rural industrial development: to cluster or not to cluster?" *Review of Agricultural Economics*, 19(2): 308–25.

Barkley, D.L., Henry, M.S., and Warner, M.L. (2002) "Targeting growth opportunities for Lancaster county", REDRL Research Report 10–2002–04, Regional Economic Development Research Laboratory, Clemson University, Clemson, South Carolina.

Barkley, D.L., Henry, M.S., and Wright, S. (1998) "Industry targeting for economic development, Anderson county", EER 170, Clemson University, Department of Applied Economics and Statistics, Clemson University.

Bergman, E.M., and Feser, E.J. (1999) "Industrial and regional clusters: concepts and comparative applications", in *The Web Book of Regional Science*, Regional Research Institute, West Virginia University. Online. Available HTTP: <http://www.rri.wvu.edu/WebBook/Bergman-Feser/contents.htm> (accessed 4 April 2007).

Buss, T.F. (1999) "The case against targeted industry strategies", *Economic Development Quarterly*, 13(4): 339–56.

Cortright, J., and Mayer, H. (2001) *High Tech Specialization: A Comparison of High Tech Centers*, Washington, DC: The Brookings Institute.

Feldman, M.P., and Francis, J.L. (2004) "Homegrown solutions: fostering cluster formation", *Economic Development Quarterly*, 18(2): 127–37.

Feser, E.J. (2003) "What regions do rather than make: a proposed set of knowledge-based occupation clusters", *Urban Studies*, 40(10): 1937–58.

Gordon, I.R., and McCann, P. (2000) "Industrial clusters: complexes, agglomeration and/or social networks?" *Urban Studies*, 37(3): 513–32.

Krugman, P. (1991) *Geography and Trade*, Belgium: Leuven University Press.

Lamie, R.D., Barkley, D.L., Henry, M.S., and Syme, J.H. (1997) "Targeting secondary wood products manufacturing: identifying high impact, high potential sectors", Research Report 97–1, Department of Agricultural and Applied Economics, January.

Porter, M. (2001) *Clusters of Innovation: Regional Foundations of U.S. Competitiveness*, Washington, DC: Council of Competitiveness.

Wright, S., Henry, M.S., and Barkley, D.L. (1998) "Targeting food, fiber, and forestry industries for development of rural South Carolina", Research Report 98–2, Department of Agricultural and Applied Economics, Clemson University, July.

11 Rural-urban economic linkages

Implications for industry targeting recommendations

David W. Hughes

Introduction

Industry targeting based on rural-urban economic linkages has many appealing aspects. Harrison (1996) argued that one appeal is that by highlighting such linkages, policy-makers in smaller communities are forced to realize how much their economy depends on the outside world in general and nearby urban areas in particular. Another appealing facet is that although many urban continue to experience economic growth, numerous rural areas, often within the region, suffer economic decline. Properly constructed rural-urban industry targeting studies seem to hold the potential for enabling the spread of growth from urban to rural areas. Such studies could even, perhaps, help policy-makers relieve some of the negative effects of rapid growth in urban communities. Further, more than a few observers (Weiler et al. 2006, for example) have touted the advantages of regional governance. That is, economic development efforts in which regions (as opposed to single cities or counties) strive to collaborate as one entity are appealing for many reasons. By strengthening economic ties within a region, successful rural-urban linked industry targeting studies would enhance the possibility of successful general cooperative efforts within regions. Industry targeting based on rural-urban economic linkages also has a strong theoretical appeal, because at the heart of regional economics lies the evaluation of economic activity across physical space.

In this chapter I examine the potential for industry targeting efforts based on rural and urban economic linkages. I initially discuss the key theoretical concepts that underlie such linkages, including central place theory, agglomeration economies, core-periphery economic models, and backwash and spread effects. The effort then turns to studies that have explicitly examined trade relationships between urban and rural areas in a detailed manner. Next, I provide a set of stylized facts concerning the potential for industry targeting in both rural and urban areas based on a critical review of the literature. Finally, study results are summarized and final conclusions drawn.

Theoretical constructs

Central place theory (Christaller 1966) defines an ordering of economic activities by communities within a region starting with villages and towns, where only services and retail requiring small markets exist, all the way up to primary cities. The latter are the main suppliers of higher-ordered services, such as health facilities and financial services, to the broader region. The rapid expansion of these higher-ordered services can be an impetus for urban growth, as can earnings growth provided by export-based industries.

An urban core surrounded by a peripheral, largely rural, region extends the central place concept, where the latter depends on the former for higher-ordered goods and services. As suggested by firm location theory, many regions in the periphery specialize in the production of goods in which they have a competitive advantage, often due to local natural resources or to low-cost labour used in routine low-tech manufacturing. As for industry targeting, one could surmise that food processing and other industries that are dependent on periphery-based agriculture or other natural resource-based industries for inputs may locate in the core. However, trade in such commodities may also flow from the periphery to external markets (Parr 1987).

Krugman (1991) argues that the interaction of growing consumer demand and increasing returns in the production of manufactured goods and in transportation systems drives a cumulative process often resulting in a core-periphery economy. Often through accident and history, the core has an early start in the production of manufactured commodities for national or international markets, which is accentuated by scale economies. Workers migrating to the core provide markets for the local production of other goods. Once a critical mass is obtained, a cumulative process of core growth ensues at the periphery's expense. Gabe (Chapter 6) makes a similar argument that agglomeration economies are at the heart of urban economic growth, but less-developed regions suffer from the lack of agglomerative effects.

Growth poles are a related but alternative theoretical model, in which dynamic economic growth in an urban core drives economic activity in the surrounding periphery (Richardson 1979). A growth pole is also a dominant regional central place. The nodal response provides a reversal of core and periphery roles in that economic growth in the core is driven by increasing demand held by a growing periphery economy (Parr 1973). The nodal response implies a relatively fixed pattern of trade between the core and the periphery.

Core economic growth influences economic activity in the periphery through positive spread and negative backwash effects in large part through trade relationships (Barkley and Henry 1997). For example, one spread effect is the backward linkages between sectors of the core economy and their input suppliers in the periphery. Spread effects also include the diffusion of investment, innovation, and growth attitudes from the core to periphery areas.

Core economic growth negatively influences periphery economic development through backwash effects that also have a key trade component such as core service sectors displacing their counterparts in the periphery (Barkley and Henry 1997). An example could be a core health facility specializing in more advanced and complex procedures and thereby drawing an increasing proportion of total regional business. Other backwash effects are the migration of periphery labour and financial capital to the core resulting in depopulation and capital shortages in the periphery.

Economists have tended to disagree on the predominance of spread versus backwash effects in rural areas. Mydral (1957) claimed that backwash effects generally dominate. Hirschman (1958) argued that backwash effects are initially high as resources are pulled into the core, but these eventually ebb, and decentralization characterizes the spatial structure of regional economic activity. Krugman (1991) has argued that a core-periphery economic structure can remain for long periods. However, under the proper conditions, seemingly small changes in economic structure can set off a rapid, cumulative process of import substitution and economic growth in the periphery.

Authors of the most recent studies have based their conclusions on estimations from spatial econometric models (Henry et al. 1997, 2001; Partridge et al. 2007). Their consensus is that spread effects tend to dominate for areas in a periphery close to their urban core. However, for places that are most distant from urban centers, backwash effects are usually more pronounced. This observation is also confirmed by the analysis of Glaeser and Kohlhase (2004), which showed a peaked relationship between manufacturing's share of local economic activity and population density. That is, as areas become less urbanized, manufacturing becomes increasingly important up to a point, but then increasingly less so as population density continues to diminish. Key to our discussion is the reasons *why* manufacturers may seek rural-urban fringe areas. McGranahan (2002) has argued that the location preferences of rural manufacturers are more often based on access to general urbanized economies than to specific urban firms via buying and selling linkages. A study by Dumais et al. (1997) also indicates that in general, interindustry linkages have a significant but small influence of the location decision of manufactures. Further, even certain periphery natural resource producers who are close to urban areas may be able to tap niche household markets in the core for organic products (Holland and Weber 1996) or local food systems (Brown 2003).

Partridge et al. (2007) recently made the persuasive argument that the predominance (or lack thereof) of backwash versus spread effects is location specific. They argue that "the optimal policy mix for governance and rural development would be informed by delineating the geographic range over which either (or neither) dominate" (p. 7). It is against this theoretical backdrop that I examine the potential for both rural and urban areas to target specific industries based on their cross influences.

Particularly important for industry targeting and emphasized here is research examining detailed rural and urban industry trade linkages. Although several studies have estimated such relationships, no study to my knowledge has examined industry targeting based on mutual rural and urban linkages. Theoretical efforts, such as central place and core-periphery theoretical models, and econometric procedures, such as the work by Henry et al. (2001) and by Partridge et al. (2007), provide general frameworks for industry targeting based on rural and urban linkages. A spate of studies based on multiregional input-output models conducted in the 1990s provides more detail concerning the nature of rural and urban trade in a core-periphery model. These studies speak to possible targeting efforts in both rural and urban communities based on mutual and explicit trade linkages.

Industry-level linkages between rural and urban areas

Numerous industry targeting studies have been based on regional input-output models. Such models contain the typical within-region trading relationship described in various chapters (Deller, Chapter 4; Barkley and Henry, Chapter 10; Hughes, Chapter 18; and Johnson, Chapter 13). Multiregional input-output models can be constructed that explicitly account for trading relationships between regions in a detailed manner, by, for example, showing the level of purchases by agricultural firms in a rural periphery from the business service sector in a nearby urban core. Such multiregional models can also be used to estimate interregional multipliers, for example, estimates of increases in economic activity in the periphery (core) as a result of a one dollar increase in sales by various core (periphery) sectors. Multipliers also lead to impact analysis, where, for example, the impact of an increase in sales of $10 million in periphery wood products on various parts of the core economy can be assessed. A related variable is the spillover coefficient (Hamilton and Jensen 1983), "which is the ratio of indirect economic effect in the region where the direct impact does not originate divided by total indirect effect in both regions" (Hughes and Holland 1994: 373–4). Or, the variable measures the impact in the periphery (core) for a given core (periphery) sector, divided by indirect impacts in both the core and the periphery.

By assessing results from these models, including estimated trade relationships, multiplier analysis, and impact results, inferences can be gathered concerning the potential for and direction of industry targeting in both rural and urban areas. Initially emphasized are results of such models that have implications for industry targeting by rural policy-makers.

Results most pertinent for rural industry targeting

Multiregional input-output models provide detailed estimates of trade between rural and urban areas that can be informative for targeting industry studies. Studies examined here include a model of the Seattle economy (as the core) and the rest of Washington State (as the periphery) conducted by

Hughes and Holland (1994), a model of the Portland metropolitan area and its periphery (Waters et al. 1994; Holland et al. 1996), a multiregional model of the northern Nevada economy by Harris et al. (1996), and a core-periphery model of the Monroe, Louisiana Functional Economic Area (FEA) by Hughes and Litz (1996a, 1996b).

Commodity trade provides a key way of examining the strength of linkages between a rural periphery and its urban core. Across all studies, the urban core always formed an important market for periphery exports. In total and for most commodities, external national and international markets were more important. Hughes and Holland (1994) estimated that the Seattle core accounted for 10.8 per cent of all periphery exports, whereas Hughes and Litz (1996a) found that 6.2 per cent of all domestic rural exports were shipped to the urban core in their examination of the Monroe, Louisiana FEA. Waters et al. (1994) estimated that the Portland economy received 8.3 per cent of periphery exports in their study, whereas Harris et al. (1996) estimated that the core accounted for 13.1 per cent of periphery exports in their study of northern Nevada.

In terms of composition, rural to urban trade tended to concentrated in natural resources-oriented commodities (such as meat animals) and primary manufacturing (such as wood products). For example, Hughes and Holland (1994) estimated that primary manufacturing accounted for 65 per cent of rural to urban shipments in the Washington State economy, whereas Hughes and Litz (1996a) found that primary manufacturing and natural resource oriented commodities accounted for 73 per cent of rural to urban shipments in the Monroe, Louisiana FEA. Waters et al. (1994) estimated that primary manufacturing and electric power accounted for 48 per cent of rural to urban trade in the Portland trading region. Examples of estimates for specific sectors in this regard included $880 million in petroleum products for rural to urban trade in the Washington state study, over $19 million in shipments in sawmills and logging camps in the study of the Monroe, Louisiana FEA, and $82 million in rural to urban trade in pulp and paper products in the Waters et al. study for the Portland, Oregon trading region. The northern Nevada study by Harris et al. (1996) showed a concentration of rural to urban trade in services (78 per cent of all such trade) and the Waters et al. study estimated that services accounted for 28 per cent of rural to urban trade. Not surprisingly, these services tended to be concentrated in tourism-type activities, such as $177 million worth of trade in eating and drinking establishments as estimated for the Portland Oregon trading area.

Interregional or between-regional multipliers are other indications of linkages between rural and urban economies. A strong interregional multiplier and spillover coefficient imply that, for example, a given periphery sector has strong backward linkages with the core or that the periphery sector in question is a potential market for core sectors. Core sectors with large interregional multipliers and spillover coefficients could provide significant benefits to their counterpart periphery economies. From a targeting policy viewpoint, periphery leaders would want to work with the leadership in the core in attracting such industries to the core. Core leaders might be able to sell their close connection to input suppliers in the periphery as an advantage to appropriately targeted industries. Further, strong linkages in this regard imply the possibility of developing an industry cluster based on rural-urban linkages.

Among the three studies that provided estimates of interregional multipliers and spillover coefficients (Hughes and Holland 1994; Hughes and Litz 1996; Holland et al. 1996), core sectors with larger than average interregional multipliers and spillover coefficients tended to be either transportation or utilities sectors or, as expected, processors of natural resources. For example, in the Monroe, Louisiana FEA (Hughes and Litz 1996b) study, core sawmills and planning mills had an interregional multiplier of $0.703 in the periphery and a spillover coefficient of 0.405, whereas in the Portland Oregon trade area study (Waters et al. 1994), wood products in the core had an inter-regional multiplier of 0.26 and a spillover coefficient of 0.188. In the same study, core food processing had an interregional multiplier of $0.19 and a spillover coefficient of 0.216. Hughes and Holland (1994) estimated that core grain mill products had an interregional multiplier of $0.36 and a spillover coefficient of 0.35 in Washington State.

Unfortunately, from the viewpoint of periphery policy-makers, core indus-tries with larger than average within-core impacts, and hence logical targets for further development, tended to have relatively small spillover impacts in the periphery. Regressions between the size of interregional multipliers and intraregional multipliers for core industries in the Washington State study were insignificant, whereas the same analysis for the Monroe Louisiana FEA study showed a statistically significant and positive but small relationship between the two variables. In the main, key core sectors, such as aircraft and parts in the Washington State core, tended to have low interregional multi-pliers in the rural periphery. Based on evidence from these limited number of case studies, one implication is that targeting sectors in the periphery on the basis of their provision of key inputs to key players in the core economy may not be a fruitful policy.

Multiplier results were also backed up by the evidence from impact results reported in two of these studies. In this regard, major economic events in the periphery had limited impacts in the core, once again implying a restricted role for industry targeting. In the Monroe, Louisiana FEA study, Hughes and Litz (1996b) examined the impact of a core food-processing sector shock on the periphery economy. Periphery impacts were concentrated in livestock products, retail trade, and real estate and rentals. The spillover coefficient for the shock was 0.127, and the overall impact in the periphery at $2.0 million was not pronounced. A much smaller spillover coefficient of 0.0434 was esti-mated for a core aircraft production shock in the Washington State model (Hughes and Holland 1994), with impact concentrated in petroleum products and eating and drinking places.

An analysis of results must also consider the limitations of the multiregional input-output models. As Holland and Weber (1996) argue, commodity trade in such models often lacks appropriate specification (in fact, this is generalized limitation of all trade models). Using a hypothetical example for trade in food grains, a high-level potential for interregional trade could be indicated, but in reality the producing region is selling rice and the buying region holds demand for wheat. Such lack of detail limits inferences that can be derived from such models. Further, all of these studies are somewhat dated, and do not account for more recent changes in economic structure and trade. For example, in agriculture, local food systems and organic production systems are nascent but growing markets. The studies discussed here do not cover the growth of such markets, and even recent studies could easily miss the potential for rural-urban interaction based on the demand for local foods and perhaps similar systems for other commodities because of problems with commodity definitions.

Results most pertinent for urban industry targeting

Across all studies, the periphery also formed an important market for core exports. However, as found for periphery counterparts, in total and for most commodities, external national and international markets were more important to the core economy. For example, Hughes and Holland (1994) estimated that the periphery accounted for 11 per cent of all Seattle core exports, whereas Hughes and Litz (1996a) found that 15.5 per cent of all urban domestic exports were traded with the rural periphery in their examination of the Monroe, Louisiana FEA. Waters et al. (1994) estimated that the periphery received 20 per cent of Portland core exports in their study, whereas Harris et al. (1996) estimated that the periphery accounted for 5 per cent of core exports in their study of northern Nevada.

Consistent with theory, urban to rural trade in these studies was predominantly concentrated in services. For example, Hughes and Holland (1994) estimated that services accounted for 81 per cent of urban to rural trade in their study of the Washington State economy, whereas Hughes and Litz (1996a) found that services accounted for 85 per cent of such shipments in their study of the Monroe, Louisiana FEA. Waters et al. (1994) estimated that services accounted for 69 per cent of urban to rural trade in the Portland, Oregon trading region. Examples of estimates for specific sectors in this regard included $153 million in engineering and accounting services for urban to rural trade in the Hughes and Holland study, over $41 million in rural periphery consumption of urban hospital services in the Hughes and Litz study, and $199 million in urban to rural trade in insurance and financial services in the Waters et al. study.

As expected, periphery sectors tended to have larger interregional multipliers and spillover coefficients than their urban core counterparts. This result was especially pronounced for the Monroe, Louisiana FEA, the smallest urban core examined by the four studies. For example, in the Monroe study (Hughes and Litz 1996b), periphery finance and insurance had a core inter-regional multiplier of $0.91 and a spillover coefficient of 0.47, whereas periphery business services had a core interregional multiplier of $0.83 and a spillover coefficient of 0.52. For the Washington State study (Hughes and Holland 1994), periphery water transportation was estimated to have a core interregional multiplier of $0.57 and a spillover coefficient of 0.35, whereas periphery business services had a core interregional multiplier of $0.45 and a spillover coefficient of 0.27. Waters et al. (1994) found that core food process-ing in Portland had an interregional multiplier of $0.25, whereas core eating, drinking, and lodging had a periphery interregional multiplier of $0.22 and a spillover coefficient of 0.26.

Impact analysis for all four studies showed reasonably strong backward linkages from key periphery sectors to the core. Spillover coefficients in this regard ranged from 0.3835 in the Monroe FEA study (Hughes and Litz 1996b) examining the impact of periphery agriculture on the core to 0.1344 for the periphery-based spotted owl shock in the Washington State economy (Hughes and Holland 1994). Based on our calculations, a primarily periphery-based spotted owl shock had a spillover coefficient of 0.2665 in the Portland Oregon core (Waters et al. 1994). A reduction in range activity for periphery-based livestock had a 0.1707 spillover coefficient in the urban core in the northern Nevada study (Harris et al. 1996). Robison and Miller (1991) presented data that we used to calculate the spillover coefficients for five small communities in west-central Idaho. Based on the employment multiplier for each community, overall spillover coefficients among the five were as large as 0.764, and the mean of the five spillover coefficients was 0.477. Hamilton et al. (1991) reported spillover coefficients for 26 Arizona agricultural indus-tries into California. Hughes and Holland reported a 20.6 per cent unweighted average spillover for these industries.

As expected, core impacts from periphery-based shocks tended to be concentrated in higher-ordered core services. For example, Hughes and Litz (1994a) found the impact of periphery agriculture in the Monroe, Louisiana FEA was concentrated in core financial services and insurance (at $2.1 million or 14.5 per cent of the total core impact), real estate, and retail trade. The impact of the Washington State spotted owl periphery-based scenario was concentrated in real estate (at $10.2 million), banking and insurance, retail trade, and health services (Hughes and Holland 1994). Walters et al. (1994) found that the impact of the spotted owl scenario for the Portland trade region was concentrated in core business service and wholesaler trade, while core other agriculture and natural resource based industries also received relatively large impacts. In the Harris et al. (1996) periphery-based range shock for northern Nevada, core impacts were concentrated in services (at $0.98 million), manufacturing, financial services, and hay and pasture.

These results hold three implications for industry targeting studies. First, core-provided higher-ordered services have ready-made markets in the periphery, especially in terms of business services and consumer services and retail. Core policy-makers should take these markets into consideration in choosing industry targets. Second, key periphery sectors were large consumers of core financial type services. In making industry targeting decisions, periphery policy-makers need to insure that such core-based services are available for the periphery firms and industries that they opt to target. Finally, it may be possible under conditions of at least fairly rapid growth that periphery could replace these key purchases of core services with their own supplies. Subject to central place theory and threshold demand requirements, however, periphery policy-makers need to approach such an import substitution policy with care. Based on the limited number of case studies examined here, I suspect that such situations may be limited in number.

Limitations of these models also have implications for industry targeting as regards service providers. One limitation is that, as Partridge (2007) states, economic space between rural and urban areas is a continuum, with the expectation that at least certain urban impacts should dwindle for rural areas further from their urban core. Model results emphasized here treat such relationships as point estimates. This aspect is problematic, because rural areas close to urban cores have different problems and prospects than those further from the core. For example, Stabler and Olfert (2001) argue that providers of consumer oriented services and retail activity in isolated rural areas may be to a degree insulated from urban competition. These rural communities may be able to target these services for further development. Alternatively, we can point out that rural areas in the commuting zones of growing urban areas often experience significant population growth. Such areas may also offer certain consumer-oriented services activity as the local population grows and threshold demand levels in terms of population and income are crossed.

Stylized facts for rural-urban linkages and industry targeting

A variety of results from the studies examined here and an examination of major theoretical concepts such as central place theory yield certain stylized factors concerning how rural-urban linkages influence industry targeting studies. These facts are provided in the following list from the perspective of both urban and rural policy-makers.

1   *Periphery markets should be a key, but not an overriding factor, in targeting decisions concerning urban higher-ordered services.* As expected, urban economies provide significant levels of commodities to surrounding rural areas. In targeting certain traded services, especially higher ordered services, urban policy-makers should include the periphery in their market analysis. In this regard, periphery businesses consumed core business services, such as financial services. Periphery households consume higher ordered services, such as hospitals and retail trade. Although substantial

in many cases, these commodity shipments typically do not form the lion's share of their entire market or even export market. Hence, trade with the periphery is an important but still secondary market in core decisions concerning targeting higher ordered services.

2 *Linkages between core processors and periphery natural resource providers provide support for industry targeting recommendations in only a limited number of cases.* In theory, an urban core and the rural periphery could partner in attracting natural resource-based processors in the core. Such linkages could be seen as forming an urban-rural cluster. These potential linkages include rural sells of commodities that are purely natural resources, such as fed cattle sells to an urban-based meatpacker. Another example could be periphery primary product manufacturers, who often process primary inputs too heavy to ship long distances, and whose output could go to core manufacturing for further processing (such as linkages between rural sawmills and urban furniture manufacturing). Such core industries might want primary input providers in close proximity and yet still enjoy urban public services and agglomeration economies – increases in productivity resulting from the proximity of firms to each other – that may not be found in nearby rural areas. A natural resource-based industry, such as an agricultural processor, may also wish to locate in an urban area that could serve as a distribution point.

Urban economies would benefit directly, whereas periphery natural resource providers would benefit indirectly (with a marked share of this impact spilling back into the core). Model results examined here indicate only mixed results for such scenarios. Even if such sectors have a demonstrated potential for to strong and mutually beneficial core-periphery linkages, other concerns remain. Urban-related cost considerations, such as relatively high land cost and congestion, may more than outweigh possible agglomerative type advantages of locating in an urban area. Further, urban areas may not find industries such as meatpackers to be desirable targets because of potential environmental impacts and possible adverse impacts on locally provided public goods (such as roads).

3 *Rural areas on the urban fringe may be able to target industries seeking relatively inexpensive rural-based inputs and urbanized agglomerative effects.* In certain cases, these may form rural-urban economic clusters, which could be enhanced through regional cooperation. A related consideration is the preference of manufacturing to locate in the midrange of population density (neither very densely populated nor too sparsely populated). Gabe (Chapter 6) provides an excellent exposition concerning agglomeration economies. Based on the evidence provided by Glaeser and Kohlhase, Gabe, and elsewhere, clusters and/or agglomerative economies are a function of population density. The upshot is that policy-makers in rural areas that are close to urban areas may have the opportunity to target industries that wish to locate areas that have midrange population density.

4   *Periphery policy-makers need to insure that request core higher ordered services are available for the industry they target.* This need also demonstrates the potential for interregional cooperation. Flipping this issue on its side, industries targeted by rural policy-makers must have access to appropriate inputs often found only in urban areas, such as many business services. In most cases, the periphery lacks the effect demand to provide such services itself, especially for specialized services. Rural policy-makers need to make sure that core service providers can meet the needs of industry that they target for development. Of course, it is often in the interest of core service providers to exploit periphery market opportunities. This interaction between periphery demand and core supply provides an opportunity for regional cooperation based on a win-win proposition. Periphery policy-makers can achieve the policy objective of "landing" or growing leading sectors. Core economic activity in desirable sectors, such as business services, is enhanced because their markets grow.

5   *Periphery and core policy-makers may want to target retail and service sectors that meet the needs of core-based tourism.* Service sectors that provide services to core-based tourism, such as eating and drinking facilities and lodging, can serve as appropriate targets. Of course, rural policy-makers need to wrestle with concerns about the desirability as well as the feasibility of developing tourism markets, given the concerns held by many that tourism mainly developed lower paying and part-time employment and can lead to social disintegration (Albrecht 1998). The core can benefit primarily because it becomes more livable by having nice and interesting nearby rural places to visit. Inasmuch as local quality of life influences economic development, the core economy also benefits.

6   *Selected retail and service sectors may also be appropriate targets for two types of rural areas, those on the fringe of growing urban areas and those that are relatively isolated.* As I previously stated, providers of consumer-oriented services and retail activity in more distant rural areas may be to a degree insulated from urban competitors. Policy-makers in such communities may be able to target these activities for further development. Alternatively, rural areas in the commuting zones of growing urban areas often experience significant population growth. These urban fringe rural communities may offer certain consumer-oriented services and retail as the local population grows and threshold demand levels in terms of population and income are crossed.

7   *Periphery resource-based industries may be able to directly target niche markets based on household demand in urban areas, such as the growing desire for local foods.* Once again, the utility of core consumers is enhanced by such activities. The small but growing demand for organically produced agricultural products and especially for locally produced foods held by urban-based households is a potential industry target for agriculture in rural areas close to urban cores. The demand for both is tied to perceived higher quality and a desire to interact with regional farmers.

There may be other periphery industries, such as wood products, where similar latent demand held by urban households could be tapped as nontraditional targets by rural policy-makers. Once again, core livability and possibly economic attractiveness should be enhanced by such policies, thus laying the groundwork for intraregional cooperation.

8   *Smaller urban areas seem to have stronger linkages with their periphery.* In such areas, the opportunities for industry targeting (and intraregional cooperation) based on rural-urban linkages should be more numerous.

Research implies that interconsecutiveness is much more pronounced when the relationship is between smaller metropolitan areas and surrounding rural communities. Hence, one would expect more targeting opportunities based on rural-urban linkages in those communities than for larger metropolitan areas. We would expect this relationship to become even more pronounced as one goes further down the central place scale. For example, an industry targeting study based on linkages between a smaller city and the surrounding county in which it is located would be expected to show strong and mutually beneficial linkages. Of course, the incentive for intraregional cooperation should also be greater for these smaller urban areas and their surrounding rural hinterlands.

9   *Core-periphery regions have opportunities for mutually beneficial cooperation in many areas.* Applications of cluster development, such as the Porter Diamond (as discussed in Woodward and Guimarães in Chapter 5), are built on cooperation between industry, government, and other components of a regional economy. The theory discussed here emphasizes that such cooperation can be developed between core and periphery economies in a regional setting. In particular, clusters can develop across intraregional boundaries for at least certain sectors.

Summary and conclusions

Any analysis of rural-urban economic linkages has a rich theoretical literature to draw on. Unfortunately for industry targeting efforts, empirical studies in this vein only have generalized implications or are somewhat dated, limited in number, and in some regards limited in scope. Further applications of intraregional models as described here, or other applications with sufficient industry detail, are needed to fill this information gap and provide more specific recommendations in a greater variety of contexts. In particular, as highlighted earlier, industry targeting studies explicitly based on rural-urban linkages would inform the literature, enhance policy-making efforts, and increase the probability of rural-urban cooperation. Still, theoretical and empirical studies provide sufficient information for drawing some general inferences concerning industry targeted studies based on the situation at hand. Stated differently, the implications of rural-urban linkages for industry targeting analysis are based on the nature of the regional economy under study and the sectors to which the analysis is applied. For example, rural-urban linkages seem to be more important for industry targeting recommendations with respect to certain sectors, such as service sectors in rural areas.

Thinking about regional economies in terms of intraregional linkages provides a number of underexplored policy avenues. One major reason why such policy opportunities are not well explored is the lack of supporting analytical tools. That is, only a smattering of applied studies have been conducted that could be used to help point policy-makers in appropriate directions. Our challenge is to apply appropriate current core-periphery models in a variety of setting and develop new methods for examining interaction between rural and urban areas in a detailed manner. Specific needs include studies that rely on well-defined measures of commodity trade flows. The previous discussion concerning the potential for rural-urban interaction based on the demand for local foods that could be "missed" because of problems with commodity definitions is one example. Integrating commodity trade estimates that treat space as a continuum, probably through a gravity model approach, could also greatly advance our knowledge. Additional studies would also further test various hypotheses, including the stylized facts presented here.

Further research and application are needed both in the area of rural-urban linkages in general and in the influence that such linkages might have on industry targeting recommendations. In terms of the latter, a set of industry targeting studies for various types of regions that explicitly accounted for the role of rural-urban linkages along with other more traditional factors could prove to be especially informative. Studies that pushed back the frontiers of knowledge concerning rural-urban linkages in general, such as providing more reliable estimates of rural-urban trade, could also be used in shedding additional needed light on industry targeting recommendations. Such studies could also be used as a means for core and periphery leaders to find common ground and start thinking and acting from a regional perspective. Clusters can develop across intraregional boundaries in some cases, and quality of life can almost always be enhanced in selected ways if core and periphery policy-makers cooperate in their economic development efforts. Our challenge is to further the use of appropriate research tools, including industry targeting cluster analysis, that support and help define such policy efforts.

References

Albrecht, D.E. (1998) "The industrial transformation of farm communities: implications for family structure and socioeconomic conditions", *Rural Sociology*, 63: 51–64.

Alward, G., Siverts, E., Olsen, O., Wagner, J., Serif, O., and Lindall, S. (1989) *Micro IMPLAN Users Manual*, St. Paul: Department of Agriculture and Applied Economics, University of Minnesota.

Barkley, D., and Henry, M. (1997) "Rural industrial development: to cluster or not to cluster", *Review of Agricultural Economics*, 19(2): 308–25.

Brown, C. (2003) "Consumers' preferences for locally produced food: a study in southeast Missouri", *American Journal of Alternative Agriculture*, 18(1): 213–24

Christaller, W. (1966) *Central Places in Southern Germany*, trans. by C.W. Baskin, Englewood Cliffs, NJ: Prentice Hall.

Dumais, G., Ellison, G., and Glaeser, E. (2002) "Geographic concentration as a dynamic process", *The Review of Economics & Statistics*, 84(2): 193–204.

Glaeser, E., and Kohlhase, J. (2004) "Cities, regions and the decline of transport costs", *Papers in Regional Science*, 83: 197–228.

Hamilton, J.R., and Jensen, R.C. (1983) "Summary measures of interconnectedness for input-output models", *Environment and Planning A*, 15(1): 55–65.

Hamilton, J.R., Whittlesey, N.K., Robison, M.H., and Ellis, J. (1991) "Economic impacts, value added, and benefits in regional project analysis", *American Journal of Agricultural Economics*, 73(1): 334–44.

Harris, T.R., McArthuer, K., and Stoddard, S.W. (1996, May) "Effects of reduced public land grazing: urban and rural northern Nevada", in *Rural-urban Interdependence and Natural Resource Policy*, WRCD 42, Corvallis, OR: Western Rural Development Center.

Harrison, D.S. (1996, May) "Preface", in *Rural-urban Interdependence and Natural Resource Policy*, WRCD 42, Corvallis, OR: Western Rural Development Center.

Henry, M.S., Barkley, D.L., and Bao, S. (1997) "The hinterland's stake in metropolitan area growth", *Journal of Regional Science*, 37(3): 479–501.

Henry, M.S., Schmitt, B., and Piguet, V. (2001) "Spatial econometric models for simultaneous systems: application to rural community growth in France", *International Regional Science Review*, 24(2): 171–93.

Hirschman, A.O. (1958) *The Strategy of Economic Development*, New Haven: Yale University Press.

Holland, D.W., and Weber, B.A. (1996, May) "Strengthening economic linkages: a policy for urban and rural development", in *Rural-urban Interdependence and Natural Resource Policy*, WRCD 42, Corvallis, OR: Western Rural Development Center.

Holland, D.W., Weber, B.A., and Waters, E.C. (1996, May) "Modeling the economic linkage between core and periphery regions: the Portland, Oregon trade area", in *Rural-urban Interdependence and Natural Resource Policy*, WRCD 42, Corvallis, OR: Western Rural Development Center.

Hughes, D.W., and Holland, D.W. (1994) "Core-periphery economic linkage: a measure of spread and possible backwash effects for the Washington economy", *Land Economics*, 70(3): 364–77.

Hughes, D.W., and Litz, V.N. (1996a) "Rural-urban economic linkages for agriculture and food processing in the Monroe, Louisiana Functional Economic Area", *Journal of Agricultural and Applied Economics*, 28(2): 337–55.

Hughes, D.W., and Litz, V.N. (1996b) "Measuring rural-urban economic linkages in the Monroe, Louisiana, trading area through an interregional input-output model", Louisiana Agr. Exp. Sta. Bulletin Number 856, Baton Rouge: Louisiana State University.

Krugman, P. (1991) *Geography and Trade*, Cambridge: MIT Press.

McGranahan, D.A. (2002) "Local context and advanced technology use by small independent manufacturers in rural areas", *American Journal of Agricultural Economics*, 84(5): 1237–45.

Miller, R.E., and Blair, D. (1985) *Input-Output Analysis: Foundations and Extensions*, Englewood Cliffs, NJ: Prentice Hall.

Myrdal, G. (1957) *Economic Theory and Underdeveloped Regions*, London: Gerald Duckworth & Co. Ltd.

Parr, J.B. (1973) "Growth poles, regional development, and central place theory", *Papers of the Regional Science Association*, 31(1): 173–212.

——. (1987) "Interaction in an urban system: aspects of trade and commuting", *Economic Geography*, 63(3): 223–40.

Partridge, M., Bollman, R.D., Olfert, M.R., and Alasia, A. (2005) "Riding the wave of urban growth in the countryside: spread, backwash, or stagnation", paper Presented at the 2005 North American Regional Science Association International meetings in Las Vegas, Nevada.

Richardson, H.W. (1979) *Regional Economics*, Urbana: University of Illinois Press.

Stabler, J.C., and Olfert, M.R. (2002) *Saskatchewan's Communities in the 21st Century: From Places to Regions*. Regina, SK: Canadian Plains Research Center, University of Regina.

Waters, E.C., Holland, D.W., and Weber, B.A. (1994) "Interregional effects of reduced timber harvests: the impact of the Northern Spotted Owl", *Journal of Agricultural and Resource Economics*, 19(1): 141–60.

Weiler, S., Henderson, J., and Cervantes, K. (2006) "Innovative regional partnerships in the rural tenth district", *The Main Street Economist, Kansas City Federal Reserve, Center for the Study of Rural America*, 1(5): 1–5. Online. Available HTTP: <www.kc.frb.org/RegionalAffairs/Mainstreet/MSE_5_06.pdf>

12 Regional cluster analysis with interindustry benchmarks

Edward Feser, Henry Renski, and Jun Koo

Introduction

Industry cluster studies have become a very common type of applied regional economic analysis. Many involve detailed examination of the characteristics and competitive foundations of the local industrial base or investigation of formal and informal networks among local businesses. Others explore regional, national, and global linkages that manifest themselves through interindustry trade, management practices, and corporate governance of extended value chains. In practice, data limitations, differing views about the industry cluster concept and how it should be operationalized, and the sheer variety of planning and policy issues motivating applied studies have led to the development of multiple approaches to cluster analysis.

That is not a bad thing. Any notion that there must be a single best way to understand and define industry clusters and, consequently, an optimal technique for identifying and documenting their development is a red herring. Unlike techniques such as cost-benefit analysis, which are based on a systematic body of formal theory and related economic principles, industry cluster analysis aims to measure a concept that derives from a loose amalgamation of quite diverse and largely informal theories, a body of inductive case study research of widely varying quality, and comparatively few rigorously conducted quasi-experimental empirical studies (Feser and Luger 2003). In the absence of a formal and widely accepted "theory of clusters", there can be no optimal cluster analysis methodology. Instead, there are a variety of ways one might legitimately analyse industry clusters to inform development practice, provided one clarifies the specific planning or policy concerns at hand, narrows the operational definitions of industry clusters and clustering accordingly, uses measures and analytical techniques consistent with those definitions, and is forthright about what the given methodology is (and is not) capable of revealing about regional economic trends and opportunities.

In this chapter, we discuss a particular approach to regional industry cluster analysis – the use of *interindustry benchmarks* – and illustrate the use of *one* particular operationalization of that approach – the use of value chains derived from observed national interindustry trading patterns as a tool in an exploratory analysis of a region's economic base. We do not claim that the use of interindustry benchmarks is the universal standard bearer in analysis, or even that it is always the least flawed among a set of partially flawed approaches. We *do* claim that it is a good approach for some kinds of applications and policy contexts, and that there are superior techniques in other policy contexts. In the sections that follow, we discuss the benchmark approach in general, summarize briefly how the national value chains we use are derived, apply the value chains as benchmarks in an example analysis, and offer a short discussion of the strengths and weaknesses of the benchmarking approach to applied industry cluster studies.

What are interindustry benchmarks?

We define interindustry benchmarks as *classifications of interrelated industries* that have been developed from analyses of interindustry relationships undertaken for an appropriate reference region (or set of regions). The concept of interindustry benchmarks is perhaps best grasped by way of example. One of the earliest applications in the present context was a study by Bergman et al. (1996), who used factor analysis techniques applied to 1987 national input-output data to identify US manufacturing value chains, or groups of manufacturing industries trading directly and indirectly (see also Bergman and Feser 1999 and Feser and Bergman 2000). Initially, the purpose of the work was not industry cluster analysis as it is commonly understood today. It was to reveal empirically one set of pathways – trading linkages – through which manufacturing technology diffusion occurs. A state organization that wished to target scarce manufacturing technology assistance resources commissioned the project. The policy motivation was based on research that indicated that manufacturers upgrading their production technologies exert pressure on their upstream suppliers to do likewise, which implied that business assistance programmes aimed at end-market producers might yield more upgrading activity overall than if programmes are more or less untargeted.

Bergman and Feser's analysis does not classify detailed US manufacturing industries into groups according to similarities in their product, as they are under the Standard Industrial Classification (SIC) system, but rather by their patterns of direct and indirect interindustry trade. For example, for US motor vehicles production, auto assemblers are joined with tyre, glass, electronics, plastics, and other relevant industries in a vehicle value chain. The groups are non-mutually exclusive, since some value chains are highly interdependent, and the methodology provides a quantitative measure of the strength of the linkage between industries and the overall value chain.

Although the initial study was motivated by the question of technology diffusion, it became clear that a value chain classification of this kind can be a useful tool for a variety of exploratory analyses of the industrial mix and competitive advantage of specific regions, including a version of applied industry cluster analysis. Indeed, Feser and Bergman (2000: 2) describe the value chains as "national industry cluster templates" that, by identifying "relative specializations in the regional economy by exposing otherwise opaque extended product chains", are a "valuable analytic tool for the design of economic development strategies that seek to exploit or leverage direct and indirect interfirm linkages". They use the terminology "national cluster" to describe the chains following a distinction long established in the field of regional science that describes "clusters" as groups of trading industries and "industrial complexes" as specific places where those clusters are co-located (Feser et al. 2005). In essence, the national value chains are one *benchmark* against which an analyst can measure a region's economic mix and explore trends. Like any benchmarking standard, the chains have strengths and weaknesses and are useful for some kinds of applications and not others. Varying either the way industries are related (i.e., the type of industrial interdependence) or the geography used (e.g., the nation or the world) creates other benchmark classifications that are useful for different kinds of studies and development planning interventions. Trade flows are only one kind of interdependence; others are technology flows, informal networking, and shared labour pools. Also important are institutional and organizational forms of interdependence, or how relations between firms are governed, to use the terminology of the global value chains research paradigm (Gereffi et al. 2005).

Linkages and geography

Bergman and Feser's use of national input-output data was purposeful and helps illustrate an important point about the different ways geography might be handled in the creation of interindustry benchmarks that are intended for use in cluster studies and other kinds of economic analyses. Bergman and Feser used national rather than state-level input-output data because they sought to identify local gaps in national value chains with some presence in North Carolina, gaps that could potentially inhibit the diffusion of new technologies. Imagine that a North Carolina industry, such as truck manufacturing, comprises solely end-market assemblers and no suppliers. The state's truck producers cannot very well diffuse manufacturing technologies to in-state suppliers that do not exist. US interindustry data help reveal national value chains, which are then present to varying degrees and in differing subindustries in particular places. Reference to North Carolina input-output data would find that there is little trade between truck producers and other in-state manufacturing sectors, given the absence of trucking suppliers. However, without the *additional information on the structure of the broader value chain*, one would have no means of recognizing the lack of suppliers as meaning that North Carolina is capturing just one segment of the national truck manufacturing industry. In other words, one only knows one has a *gap* by reference to a relevant *whole*.

The nation is not necessarily the ideal reference area. The fragmentation and internationalization of production means that the relevant whole is increasingly the *global* value chain, not the national one. Bergman and Feser (1999: section 3.3.3) defended the use of US input-output (IO) data on the grounds that they are the best systematic source of trading information for the full range of industries: "Since there is no such thing as a global table, a national table (particularly in highly diverse economies such as the United States) constitutes a workable substitute".

An analysis of state or regional interindustry trading data could produce useful information, but it would be of a fundamentally different kind. For instance, we may suspect that some regional industries have value chains that are fundamentally unique. Indeed, industries may differ in their production technologies across regions simply because regions differ in the factor endowments and other locational characteristics that influence businesses' production technology options and choices (Moses 1958). Thus, a widget produced wholly in Los Angeles may have a value chain that looks quite different from the value chain for a widget produced wholly in Chicago. Documenting value chains using regional input-output data might help reveal unique local technologies, especially if used in conjunction with value chains derived from national or international data. Alternatively, studies that seek to identify clusters as groups of related industries concentrated in a particular region might use regional input-output data to identify local interindustry linkages. However, such studies are not equivalent to approaches using benchmarks. Again, what distinguishes the benchmark approach is that it uses a classification of linked industries derived for an appropriate reference economy, usually the nation as a whole.

The most widely known interindustry benchmarks used in economic development practice are the "clusters" developed by Michael Porter (Porter 2003, 2004). Porter began by segmenting 879 US SIC industries into three types: 241 that serve primarily *local* markets (e.g., retail, personal services), 48 that are *resource-dependent* (e.g., mining, logging, agricultural goods, etc.), and 590 that *trade* across regions and/or countries. He calculated Pearson correlation coefficients for each pair of traded industries using states as the unit of analysis and employment as the measure of industry size in each state. Arguing that a high correlation implies that the two industries in the given pair of industries are co-located, he then used the correlations to combine industries more or less by hand, "beginning with small groups of obviously related industries and then tracing correlation patterns to others" (2004: 4). Porter acknowledged a significant problem with this approach: that co-location among industries does not necessarily imply economic linkage – what can be called functional, as opposed to spatial, interdependence – among industries. Some industries are co-located for historical reasons, others by chance, others because they target similar large end-markets (e.g., major cities) or transportation infrastructure (e.g., ports), and still others because of their co-dependence on nearby natural resources. He addressed the problem by making adjustments in the composition of the groups using information from case studies of specific sectors and reference to national input-output data: "Through this sequence of steps, we eliminated those pairs of correlated industries where there was no apparent basis for linkages" (Porter 2004: 5). The result is 41 non-mutually exclusive groups of industries, or "traded clusters", comprising both manufacturing and nonmanufacturing industries.

Porter's classification is similar to Bergman and Feser's in that it groups US industries based on an analysis of interdependence. As in Bergman/Feser, that interdependence is also ultimately intended to be defined by functional economic linkage. In essence, Porter uses co-location only as an *initial indicator* of such linkages, making adjustments more or less in an ad hoc fashion when the spatial results prove implausible. In Bergman and Feser's case, interindustry linkages are measured directly by analysis of trade between industries without any reference to the subnational distribution of economic activity. Interestingly, Porter's 41 groups of industries are very close in number to the 45 found in the most recent update of the Bergman and Feser approach (Feser 2005). As might be expected, the two classifications differ given their underlying methodologies, but the overall categories of industries are very similar. Like Bergman and Feser, Porter views his classification as a cluster benchmarking tool: "Clusters, then, represent a different way of dividing the economy than is embodied in conventional industrial classification systems which are based primarily on product type and similarities in production" (Porter 2004: 6).

Subscribers to the Harvard Cluster Mapping Project website may access drop-down menus to investigate US state and metropolitan trends for industries aggregated into benchmark clusters according to the Porter classification. Or they may produce charts and graphs plotting employment by benchmark cluster for specific places. The implication is that if metropolitan area *A* has a high level of absolute and relative employment in, say, the industries Porter identifies as part of his automotive cluster, metropolitan area *A may* have a *regional* automotive cluster. Bergman and Feser's industry groupings are best understood as value chains, but their use as benchmarks in applied cluster studies is similar. If metropolitan area *A* has significant activity in the various industries that make up the US automotive value chain, Bergman and Feser argue that *A may* have a *regional* automotive cluster. The use of the term "may" in the two preceding sentences is quite intentional. Both industry classification schemes are derived using theories of economic interdependence. To the extent those theories are valid, they are useful tools. However, neither classification reveals anything about the actual behavior of companies at the regional or local scales (including trade, informal network, shared technology, etc.). Interindustry benchmarks are insufficient by themselves if the goal is to identify regional clusters defined as "geographically proximate group[s] of interconnected companies and associated institutions in a particular field, including product producers, service providers, suppliers, universities, and trade associations".[1] Interindustry benchmarks only suggest the *possible* presence of *actual* regional interconnections that are typically very difficult to measure.

The following example further illustrates the implications of the different ways Bergman/Feser and Porter handle geography in the derivation of their classification schemes. Imagine that US makers of automotive wiring harnesses are rarely co-located with automotive assemblers in the US. The Porter classification would exclude the wiring harness industry from the group of industries assigned to the automotive cluster, since it aims to reveal industries that are both linked *and* have a tendency to co-locate. A classification that indicates whether or not wiring harness makers are typically parts of localized agglomerations of automotive industry activity in the US is valuable knowledge for economic developers interested in supporting the growth of the motor vehicles industry.

In contrast, the Bergman/Feser classification would identify the wiring harness industry as part of the automotive value chain. That might be misleading to economic developers seeking to build regional clusters if they imagine that local gaps in chains are, *ipso facto*, good development targets. At the same time, knowledge of the entire (nonlocal) value chain can also be valuable for development practice because of the insight in can offer regarding local competitive strengths and weaknesses. With knowledge of the full extent of a given value chain, officials can ask *why* their region has developed some industries in a selected chain and not others. Sometimes the reasons are not subject to policy influence, such as when one segment of a chain must be nearby natural resources that a region does not possess. Frequently, however, the reasons are subject to public sector influence, such as when an industry's absence is a function of the region's inadequately trained labour force. Such exploratory work can be revealing. Feser and Bergman (2000) found, for example, that North Carolina specializes in labour-intensive, low-wage segments of most national manufacturing value chains, regardless of those chains' overall technology intensity, suggesting structural challenges in North Carolina related to workforce preparation and advanced infrastructure that are very much subject to policy influence.

As an important side note, acknowledging the role of international trade complicates matters significantly. In fact, the considerable share of the wiring harnesses used in cars, trucks, and other vehicles manufactured in the United States are produced just across the US-Mexico border in the *maquiladora* industry (Helper 1995). If the comparatively few *US-based* wiring harness makers are co-located with US-based assemblers, Porter's method applied to strictly US data would group the two industries together, whereas his method applied to global data would *not*. In contrast, Bergman and Feser's approach might not group the two industries in the same value chain because trade between US-based wire harness makers and US assemblers is modest. This problem illustrates an important limitation in the use of strictly US data to derive cluster benchmarks that afflicts both the Porter and Bergman/Feser classifications in slightly different ways.

The general insight is that there are two important dimensions of the industry cluster concept – *economic interdependence* and *geography* – that are necessarily handled in some fashion in any cluster analysis methodology. In the interindustry benchmarking context, different information is created by considering functional interdependence and spatial clustering jointly, as in Porter's classification, and distinctly, as in Bergman and Feser's classification.

Comprehensive versus focused benchmarks

We define *comprehensive* interindustry benchmarks as those that are based on a systematic analysis of interrelationships among many, if not all, industries in the economy. They are contrasted with *focused* interindustry benchmarks, which are derived only for selected industries. To ensure valid comparisons, comprehensive benchmarks require standard measurements for all industries, thus the reliance on input-output, occupational employment, simulated inter-industry patent flow, or regional employment data that may be assembled for the full industrial base. Because focused benchmarks are created for just one or a few industries, they may be based on a richer and more eclectic set of information. The development of focused benchmarks often relies heavily on primary data collection – a practical impossibility for comprehensive meth-odologies – as well as qualitative information about technologies, business management practices, and locational imperatives in specific industries.

Both the Bergman/Feser national value chain and Porter industry cluster classifications are comprehensive in their assessment of relationships among industries. The global value chains identified by Gereffi et al. (2007) provide examples of focused benchmarks. Claiming that "most industries today are globally organized and geographically fragmented", and that the "keys to economic development often depend on capturing or retaining the high-value activities in these industries", Gereffi et al. (2007: 1) use a combination of qualitative and quantitative information to map out global value chains for selected industries. They then analyse a regional economy's position within those chains.

For example, on a website entitled *North Carolina in a Global Economy*, maintained by Duke University's Center on Globalization, Governance and Competitiveness, users can examine establishment, employment, and wage trends in NAICS industries identified as components of one of seven global value chains; map industry activity by county; and produce tables listing the top employers in each industry. The methodology uses *focused* bench-marks in that each value chain – banking, furniture, hog farming, textiles and apparel, biotechnology, information technology, and tobacco, all industries of well-known strength in North Carolina – is the subject of considerable industry- and firm-specific research. Both quantitative and qualitative kinds of information are brought to bear to first chart or "map" the global value chains, and then to identify the specific North Carolina companies in those chains. Yet, like the Bergman/Feser and Porter approaches, the methodology is based fundamentally on a benchmarking logic: analysis of economic interdependence for a geographical baseline (in this case, worldwide production) beyond the locality in question (in this case, North Carolina) is used to gain insight into local economic trends, conditions, and opportunities. The incorporation of interindustry benchmarks into web tools and user-friendly software follows a broader trend, as illustrated by Porter's Cluster Mapping Project website, the Workforce and Innovation Technical Solution (WITS) system developed by the US Employment and Training Administration, and Economic Modeling Specialists, Inc.'s online database and analysis tools (called *Strategic Advantage*).

A common type of applied industry cluster analysis is work on local networks and linkages among the businesses located in a specific region. Such intraregional analysis of selected industries draws heavily on the theory of Marshallian industrial districts, which postulates that the determinants of competitive advantage are primarily local (see Humphrey and Schmitz 2002 for a discussion), such that linkages to companies, industries, and institutions outside the region may be de-emphasized or even ignored. The many case studies of industrial districts in Italy, Germany, and elsewhere are examples in the sense that they are focused on documenting ties among businesses located in specific places. Intraregional approaches are sometimes perceived as the *only* kind of regional industry cluster analysis but, as we have seen, that is an excessively narrow view of how the industry cluster concept is being used to inform economic development practice.

Table 12.1 distinguishes four common approaches to regional industry cluster analysis by whether they use *benchmark* or *intraregional* techniques and are *comprehensive* or *focused* in their treatment of industries. Note that the distinctions among study types are generally not as tightly drawn in practice, as it is very common for applied studies to use combinations of approaches. For example, cluster benchmarks might be used to scan the regional economy for an initial set of candidate industries for intraregional analysis of local company linkages.

One set of interindustry benchmarks: national value chains

We have argued that one way to operationalize the notion of a relationship between industries is through the concept of the industry value chain, which, in turn, can be useful as a benchmark in applied cluster studies. Any industry's value chain consists of that industry itself together with its supplier (upstream) and customer (downstream) industries, irrespective of where those industries are located (locally, nationally, or internationally). Although theoretically there is a distinct value chain for each industry, the level of overlap between value chains for highly detailed industries is often so high that we can justify combining some of them. We demonstrate the use of the reduced set of value chains as interindustry benchmarks in the last section of this chapter. In this section, we very briefly summarize Feser's (2005)

Table 12.1 Types of approaches to regional industry cluster analysis

Benchmark Analysis	Intraregional Analysis
Industry Coverage	
Comprehensive	*Comprehensive*
• Study applies industry groupings derived for a *relevant reference area* (e.g., nation or world) to regional data to identify potential regional clusters or to document regional specializations within broader national or global industries	• Study examines trends and linkages among firms and industries *within the study region* to identify local clusters (groups of related companies located in proximity)
• Groupings are developed from an analysis of interdependence among *all or most industries*, necessitating heavy reliance on secondary data sources (e.g., national input-output and other published economic series)	• *All or most industries* are included in the analysis, necessitating heavy reliance on secondary data sources (e.g., regional input-output and other published economic series)
• Example: McElroy et al. (2006)	• Example: Hill and Brennan (2000)
Focused	*Focused*
• Study applies industry groupings derived for a *relevant reference area* (e.g., nation or world) to regional data to identify potential clusters or to document regional specializations within national or global industries	• Study examines trends and linkages among firms and industries *within the study region* to identify local clusters (groups of related companies located in proximity)
• Groupings are identified for only *selected industries*, often those perceived as particularly important to the region, permitting use of labour-intensive qualitative methods and primary data collection	• Only *selected industries* are investigated, permitting use of labour-intensive qualitative methods and primary data collection techniques
• Example: Gereffi, et al. (2007)	• Example: RTS (2003)

approach to using national input-output data to identify value chains, which sought to address several technical and practical deficiencies in Bergman et al.'s (1996) methodology.

The approach begins by calculating measures of trading linkage between pairs of industries using two ratios calculated from a national interindustry transactions matrix, A:

$$x_{ij} = \frac{a_{ij}}{a_{+j}} \tag{1}$$

$$y_{ij} = \frac{a_{ij}}{a_{i+}} \tag{2}$$

The value x_{ij} is the ratio of purchases of industry j from industry i to total intermediate purchases by industry j. A vector of values of x, written x, is industry j's intermediate input purchasing pattern. The value y_{ij} is the ratio of sales of industry i to industry j to total intermediate sales by industry i, so that a vector of y values, written y, is i's intermediate selling pattern. Given x and y, sets S_i and B_i can be defined, where S_i is the set of industries supplying goods and services to industry i and B_i is the set of industries purchasing goods or services from industry i. At the extreme, S and B would contain, for industry i, all industries j for which x_{ij} and y_{ij} are, respectively, greater than zero. In practice, we might set a threshold, a, that x_{ij} and y_{ij} must exceed in order for sector j (i) to be included in sector i's (j's) set of key suppliers (or buyers).

The next step is to use the union and intersection of sets S and B in the calculation of four simple measures of interindustry linkage:

$$I_{ij}^{SS} = S_i \cap S_j, \ U_{ij}^{SS} = S_i \cup S_j$$

$$I_{ij}^{BB} = B_i \cap B_j, \ U_{ij}^{BB} = B_i \cup B_j$$

$$I_{ij}^{SB} = S_i \cap B_j, \ U_{ij}^{SB} = S_i \cup B_j \tag{3}$$

$$I_{ij}^{BS} = B_i \cap S_j, \ U_{ij}^{BS} = B_i \cup S_j$$

$$R_{ij}^{SS} = \frac{I_{ij}^{SS}}{U_{ij}^{SS}}, \ R_{ij}^{BB} = \frac{I_{ij}^{BB}}{U_{ij}^{BB}}, \ R_{ij}^{SB} = \frac{I_{ij}^{SB}}{U_{ij}^{SB}}, \ R_{ij}^{BS} = \frac{I_{ij}^{BS}}{U_{ij}^{BS}}, \tag{4}$$

The ratios in equation (4) are simple and intuitive measures of four kinds of relationships between industries i and j. The value R^{SS} is the number of supplier sectors that industries i and j have in common over the total number (or universe) of supplier sectors to both i and j. The higher is R^{SS}, the stronger is the value chain linkage between industries i and j as indicated by joint sourcing from the same suppliers. Similarly, R^{BB} is the share of common buyer sectors. R^{SB} and R^{BS} are measures of second-tier relationships between each pair of industries; they increase as one industry's suppliers are also the other industry's buyers. Statistical data reduction techniques can be applied to the measures in equation (4) to identify a set of value chains.

There are several steps in the data reduction process. First, the 489-sector US interindustry transactions matrix is reduced to a 463 dimension matrix by eliminating 26 local services (e.g., retail) and government industries; the aim is to focus on industries with export potential. Second, the measures in equation (4) are calculated setting a to a threshold level that is designed to capture the most important linkages since including all linkages – both strong and weak – will produce results that are too unwieldy to use in application. Third, a weight (<1.0) is applied to each of 55 producer services and transportation industries in the calculation of the R measures. The 55 industries may be viewed as "enabling industries" in the sense that they are linked to a very large number of other industries. Among them are banking, advertising, legal services, wholesaling, and warehousing and distribution. The weight discounts a linkage between industry *i* and a general enabling industry, which serves to emphasize linkages among more specialized industries in the identification of the value chains. Finally, the maximum of the four *R* measures is selected to produce a 463-dimension linkage matrix (R^{MAX}) that is subsequently analysed with statistical data reduction techniques.

Using the results of a Ward's hierarchical clustering algorithm applied to the matrix of linkages, Feser (2005) identified 45 mutually exclusive groups of related industries, or value chains. The concept of mutually exclusive value chains makes little sense, however, since most industries are linked to many different industries. In fact, value chains themselves are highly interrelated or "fuzzy". This inherent fuzziness among interindustry linkages is acknowledged by viewing the initial mutually exclusive results as defining a set of *core* value chains, each made up of "primary" members. Additional industries, called "secondary" members, are then added to the core chains. A nonprimary industry becomes a secondary member of a given value chain if the arithmetic average of its linkages with all primary members of the chain meets or exceeds a defined threshold.

We refer readers to Feser (2005) for additional details behind the selection of threshold values and weights and the Ward's clustering procedure. Here we wish to emphasize the interpretation of the results as interindustry benchmarks useful for applied regional cluster analyses. Table 12.2 reports the detailed make-up of several of the national chains, including primary and secondary members. The descriptor for each chain represents the predominant economic activity among the given group of industries, particularly those that are most tightly linked within the chain. Such summary descriptors should be interpreted carefully. None can adequately capture all of the relationships among industries in each chain. Again, the industries are grouped based on their economic interdependencies at the national scale, and therefore embed no information regarding subnational industrial location. Together, the industries included in the benchmarks constitute a significant fraction of US economic activity – roughly 65 per cent of total US employment in 2004. Not included among the national value chains, as noted above, are retail trade, government (including the US Postal Service), primary and secondary schools, and consumer and personal services industries.

Example application

To provide an overview of basic techniques, we briefly illustrate a version of cluster analysis for the state of Maine using the national value chains. Maine is a predominantly rural state with an industrial heritage rooted in natural resource extraction, agriculture, and manufacturing. Like other Northeastern states, Maine's economy slowed in the last decade of the 20th century, with job losses in its traditional industrial base. Although its health care and

Table 12.2 National value chains: Detail for selected chains

Value chain	NAICS	Industry	Category
Basic health services	6216	Home health care services	Primary
	6211–3	Offices of physicians, dentists, and other health practitioners	Primary
	6214–5 6219	Other ambulatory health care services	Primary
	5611	Office administrative services	Primary
	5612	Facilities support services	Primary
	5613	Employment services	Primary
	3254	Pharmaceutical and medicine mfg	Secondary
	334510	Electromedical apparatus mfg	Secondary
	339112	Surgical and medical instrument mfg	Secondary
	339113	Surgical appliance and supplies mfg	Secondary
	42	Wholesale trade	Secondary
	5411	Legal services	Secondary
	5412	Accounting and bookkeeping services	Secondary
	5413	Architectural and engineering services	Secondary
	54161	Management consulting services	Secondary
	54162–9	Environmental and other technical consulting services	Secondary
	5614	Business support services	Secondary
	5617	Services to buildings and dwellings	Secondary
Financial services & insurance	523	Securities, commodity contracts, investments	Primary
	5241	Insurance carriers	Primary
	5242	Insurance agencies, brokerages, and related	Primary
	525	Funds, trusts, and other financial vehicles	Primary
	492	Couriers and messengers	Secondary
	5222–3	Non-depository credit intermediation and related activities	Secondary
	521 5221	Monetary authorities and depository credit intermediation	Secondary
	5324	Machinery and equipment rental and leasing	Secondary
	533	Lessors of nonfinancial intangible assets	Secondary
	5411	Legal services	Secondary
	5412	Accounting and bookkeeping services	Secondary
	5413	Architectural and engineering services	Secondary

	54161	Management consulting services	Secondary
	5418	Advertising and related services	Secondary
	5613	Employment services	Secondary
	5614	Business support services	Secondary
Wood products & furniture	33711	Wood kitchen cabinet and countertop mfg	Primary
	337122	Non-upholstered wood household furniture mfg	Primary
	337124	Metal household furniture mfg	Primary
	337127	Institutional furniture mfg	Primary
	337125 337129	Other household and institutional furniture	Primary
	337211	Wood office furniture mfg	Primary
	337212	Custom architectural woodwork and millwork	Primary
	337214	Office furniture, except wood, mfg	Primary
	337215	Showcases, partitions, shelving, and lockers	Primary
	321911	Wood windows and door mfg	Secondary
	321999	Miscellaneous wood product mfg	Secondary
	337121	Upholstered household furniture mfg	Secondary
	339992	Musical instrument mfg	Secondary

Source: Feser (2005).

tourism sectors have flourished in recent years, the state has struggled to develop new industries that offer sustainable living wages. Driven by an overriding goal of expanding its economic base into growing higher wage sectors, Maine is seeking to concentrate its economic development resources on innovation-oriented industry clusters. To develop an initial picture of potential interindustry relationships and potential clusters in Maine, we examine the presence of national value chains in the state using data for two periods, 2000 and 2005.

The benchmarking approach is a kind of economic base analysis and, in that sense, is relatively straightforward to carry out. Six-digit level NAICS industries are matched to the national value chain classification and aggregated into the value chain groups to document overall trends. Then, the industry mix within each chain is examined in detail using data from the Quarterly Census of Employment and Wages (QCEW) provided by the Maine Labor Market Information Services. The classification of industries into value chains is repeated at the national level using publicly available national QCEW employment data from the US Bureau of Labor Statistics. We document the size, level of specialization (using location quotients), and growth of each value chain in Maine, as well as the industry mix or composition of selected chains.

Overall value chain trends

Table 12.3 reports employment, employment growth, specialization, and diversity for Maine for each of the 45 benchmark value chains. The largest value chain in the state is management, higher education and hospitals. It employs approximately 135,600 workers and accounts for 27.3 per cent of the state's private sector workforce. The next four largest chains – business services (17.0 per cent), basic health services (15.8 per cent), and hotels and transportation services (14.5 per cent) – also represent a sizable portion of the state's private sector economy. Maine also has a relatively large component of its workforce employed in the financial services and insurance, arts and media, and information services chains. The remaining value chains are considerably smaller. After information services, which accounts for 8.6 per cent of the state's 2005 employment, the next largest value chain is construction, which accounts for 2.5 per cent of employment.

Despite their significant absolute size, none of the eight largest chains are Maine specializations when their share of state private sector employment is compared against the share for the US economy as a whole. The share of Maine's employment in the management, higher education and hospitals value chain is nearly equal to the national share (2005 location quotient = 1.04), as is the share of employment in construction (location quotient = 1.01), but the remaining six of Maine's eight largest value chains are significantly underrepresented, with location quotients ranging from 0.88 to 0.76. That is not especially surprising given Maine's economic history, locational characteristics, and natural endowments, but it also highlights the continuing vulnerability of the state's economy given a general contraction in manufacturing and resource extraction industries nationwide.

Likewise, those benchmark value chains in which Maine specializes reflect the longstanding importance of natural resources in the state's economy. There are nine value chains in which Maine is specialized based on 2005 employment location quotients of 1.10 or higher, eight of which are the following (in descending order by total employment): wood processing, chemical-based products, plastics and rubber manufacturing, wood building products, wood products and furniture, paper, leather products, and dairy products. The ninth is aluminium and aluminium products, for which we cannot report the employment level or the exact location quotient because of confidentiality rules governing our use of Maine unsuppressed QCEW data. The four value chains with an especially pronounced relative presence in Maine – wood processing, chemical-based products, plastics and rubber manufacturing, and leather products – all declined in employment significantly nationwide between 2000 and 2005. In Maine, the rates of employment decline in those four chains were even higher.

Although the largest and most concentrated value chains in a given region often attract the bulk of policy attention as potential "clusters", it is chains that show signs of emerging in the state that are often more appropriate

Table 12.3 Maine's economic base by national value chain (sorted in descending order by 2005 employment)

Cluster	Estabs., 2005	Employment 2005	Employment Share	Employment Growth, 2000–05 Maine	Employment Growth, 2000–05 US	Specialization 2005	Specialization Change '00–'05
Management, higher education & hospitals	16,092	135,585	27.3%	5.9%	5.0%	1.04	0.02
Business services	17,573	84,703	17.0%	0.8%	1.5%	0.77	0.00
Basic health services	16,020	78,494	15.8%	3.3%	5.4%	0.79	-0.01
Hotels & transportation services	13,904	72,164	14.5%	-0.7%	0.9%	0.77	0.00
Financial services & insurance	8,870	51,973	10.5%	-2.3%	1.7%	0.75	-0.02
Arts and media	9,632	44,950	9.0%	1.1%	-1.0%	0.88	0.03
Information services	10,670	42,545	8.6%	0.4%	-3.4%	0.76	0.04
Construction	3,471	12,271	2.5%	-3.2%	5.5%	1.01	-0.08
Wood processing	1,363	9,500	1.9%	-16.6%	-9.7%	2.49	-0.18
Printing & publishing	2,044	9,211	1.9%	-7.6%	-7.0%	0.77	0.00
Non-residential building products	1,343	9,195	1.8%	-3.8%	-1.5%	0.88	-0.01
Chemical-based products	86	8,293	1.7%	-26.7%	-20.8%	4.07	-0.29
Plastics & rubber manufacturing	79	7,943	1.6%	-25.9%	-19.3%	2.84	-0.22
Packaged food products	383	6,307	1.3%	-14.2%	-5.6%	1.05	-0.09
Wood building products	415	5,177	1.0%	-17.9%	-4.8%	1.19	-0.18
Petroleum & gas	472	4,125	0.8%	-0.7%	-4.1%	0.67	0.03
Concrete, brick building products	279	3,905	0.8%	8.4%	-1.2%	0.96	0.09
Appliances	266	3,804	0.8%	1.9%	-8.8%	0.78	0.09
Machine tools	299	3,711	0.7%	-13.0%	-17.8%	0.77	0.05
Computer & electronic equipment	283	3,650	0.7%	-44.4%	-25.5%	0.59	-0.19
Wood products & furniture	391	3,191	0.6%	-37.5%	-16.2%	1.12	-0.37
Textiles & apparel	204	2,904	0.6%	-44.0%	-38.1%	0.80	-0.08
Paper	43	2,897	0.6%	-25.3%	-18.7%	1.19	-0.09
Non-durable industry machinery	332	2,693	0.5%	-12.4%	-18.1%	0.37	0.03
Feed products	680	2,528	0.5%	-23.0%	-4.0%	0.66	-0.15

(Continued overleaf)

Table 12.3 (continued)

Cluster	Estabs., 2005	Employment		Employment Growth, 2000–05		Specialization	
		2005	Share	Maine	US	2005	Change '00–'05
Leather products	102	2,506	0.5%	-55.8%	-30.6%	3.82	-2.13
Motor vehicles	165	2,389	0.5%	1.7%	-16.4%	0.43	0.08
Farming	622	2,287	0.5%	-2.6%	-2.0%	0.74	0.00
Plastics products	81	2,238	0.5%	-12.1%	-16.3%	0.63	0.04
Dairy products	188	1,949	0.4%	-14.1%	-1.6%	1.16	-0.16
Construction machinery & distribution equip	53	1,691	0.3%	-16.3%	-18.4%	0.60	0.02
Metalworking & fabricated metal products	119	1,657	0.3%	-23.6%	-13.7%	0.55	-0.07
Optical Equipment & Instruments	84	1,519	0.3%	-23.4%	-16.4%	0.77	-0.06
Breweries & distilleries	69	1,440	0.3%	6.2%	-8.1%	0.93	0.13
Pharmaceuticals	58	1,361	0.3%	3.6%	-4.1%	0.57	0.05
Rubber products	103	922	0.2%	-21.5%	-20.2%	0.40	0.00
Glass products	100	767	0.2%	-15.9%	-20.4%	0.49	0.03
Copper & copper products	78	687	0.1%	-26.2%	-22.8%	0.71	-0.03
Precision instruments	34	540	0.1%	-8.6%	-22.5%	0.30	0.05
Grain milling	21	237	0.0%	4.9%	-12.8%	0.62	0.11
Mining	48	115	0.0%	10.6%	9.2%	0.07	0.00
Steel milling	5	87	0.0%	2.4%	-23.1%	0.10	0.03
Aluminium & aluminium products	56	s	s	s	-20.4%	s	s
Aerospace	10	s	s	s	-8.2%	s	s

Source: Maine Labor Market Information Services, Quarterly Census of Employment and Wages (ES-202) series.

Note: The specialization rate is a location quotient: the share of Maine's total employment that is accounted for by chain i to the share of total national employment accounted for by chain i (values equal to or greater than 1.10 are shaded). "*s*" indicates data suppressed to protect company confidentiality. Chains are not mutually exclusive; share is share of total Maine private-sector employment.

targets for growth oriented development strategies. Detecting potential strengths and market opportunities is difficult using strictly historical data; the past is not necessarily a good barometer of what the future will bring. However, evidence of recent growth of related industries coupled with increasing regional specialization is one possible indicator of an emerging cluster. We define potential emerging value chain clusters in Maine as those posting employment growth of 3.0 per cent or more over the 2000–2005 period, a 0.05 point increase in the chain's location quotient between 2000 and 2005, and a 2005 location quotient of over 0.50 but below 1.0.

Application of those criteria singles out four chains: concrete and brick building products, breweries and distilleries, pharmaceuticals, and grain milling. The recent growth in the concrete and brick products chain is largely fueled by growing demand for residential building materials for new and second home construction. The possibility of an emergent pharmaceuticals cluster is clearly a promising sign for a state generally lagging in technology-related activity. Expansion of the industries in this value chain in Maine is not altogether surprising. The state has several anchor medicinal testing facilities such as Idexx and Jackson Laboratories, as well as a number of smaller testing facilities. The recent growth of the value chain can also be traced to the organic and botanicals niche market (e.g., Tom's of Maine). Growth in niche markets that play on Maine's image of an unspoiled environment and rugged individualism also explain the growth of the breweries and distilleries value chain. Out-of-state exports of Maine microbrews (e.g., by Shipyard Brewing Company, StoneCoast Brewing Company, and D.L. Geary Brewing Company, among others) and bottled spring water companies (e.g., Poland Springs) have been very strong in recent years.

Most of the benchmark value chains in Maine are small, shrinking, or both, though in many cases Maine's weak employment growth is not out of line with national trends. Only four value chains are growing in both US and Maine. They are, in descending order of their 2000–2005 US employment growth rate: mining (a tiny value chain cluster of just 48 establishments and 115 workers); basic health services; management, higher education and hospitals; and business services. Three of the four are underrepresented in Maine; the management, higher education, and hospitals chain is the exception with a 2005 location quotient of 1.04. The state did slightly outpace national employment growth rates in the mining and management, higher education and hospitals chains over the 2000–2005 period. The majority of value chains are declining in both the nation and the state, including all nine Maine specializations. Nine value chains are declining more slowly in Maine than the nation, whereas 19 are declining more rapidly.

Three value chains are growing at the national level but shrinking in Maine: hotels and transportation services, construction, and financial services and insurance. Nine value chains show employment gains in Maine and declines nationwide. Two of the nine – grain milling and steel milling – are a negligible presence in the state. The other seven, in descending order of employment size, are arts and media (with approximately 4,950 workers); information services; concrete, brick and building products; appliances; motor vehicles; breweries and distilleries; and pharmaceuticals.

Value chain composition: industry mix

Overall value chain totals provide only an initial picture of potential clusters in a given study region. The greatest value of any benchmark cluster analysis approach as an exploratory technique comes in examining the underlying industry mix of each interindustry benchmark category. Since there is considerable overlap in the composition of the value chains, the same large industries and companies may be driving trends in multiple value chains. In addition, examining industry mix reveals the segments of national value chains that a given study region has been able to capture. Two of Maine's largest value chains – management, higher education and hospitals, and arts and media – illustrate two important points about the benchmarks and their application.

First, as benchmarks, the US value chains help identify connections among industries at the national level that also manifest themselves to varying degrees at the regional scale. Maine's sizable hospitals (NAICS 622) and nursing and residential care facilities (NAICS 623) industries are well known to state policy-makers. Less well known are the linkages of those industries to other industries that are not directly involved in the provision of health care services. Figure 12.1 displays the distribution of employment in the management, higher education and hospitals value chain in Maine versus the US. Although many of the Maine businesses in this highly diverse chain are not in the health care industry *per se*, there may be important synergies – such as

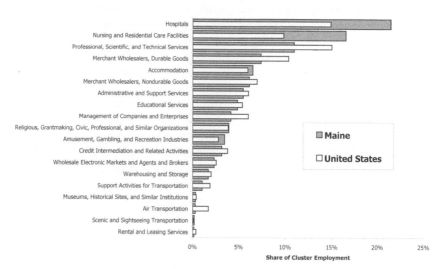

Figure 12.1 Value chain composition: management, higher ed., and hospitals.

utilization of labour pools or direct and indirect trade – that link their competitive success to the state's hospitals and nursing care industries and vice versa. The work of providing health care involves conducting testing and research, processing insurance claims, handling billing and accounting, and providing legal advice. Thus NAICS 622 and 623 are linked with NAICS 541 (professional, scientific and technical services, which accounts for 15 per cent of the value chain's overall employment in the state) and NAICS 561 (administrative and support services, accounting for 5 per cent of the chain's Maine employment). Health care facilities are also major institutional consumers of paper, plastics, medical devices, and many other durable and nondurable goods, purchased through durable or nondurable wholesalers (NAICS 423 and 424). Finally, many hospitals are centers for research and teaching, thus the linkages to educational services (NAICS 611).

Second, the largest industries in a given value chain are not necessarily those that serve that chain's primary end markets. For example, at the national level, the largest components of the arts and media value chain cluster are durable and nondurable goods merchant wholesalers, followed by professional, scientific, and technical services (see Figure 12.2). Amusement, gambling, recreation services, publishing, broadcasting, motion picture and sound recording, performing arts, telecommunications, Internet services, and data processing services are all much smaller industries in terms of employment. The durable goods wholesaling industry also accounts for a significant share of Maine's employment in the arts and media chain. Given that wholesaling is linked to a variety of industries, that could mean Maine is not especially strong in arts and media. On the other hand, the state has above-average shares of its employment in the amusement, gambling and recreation

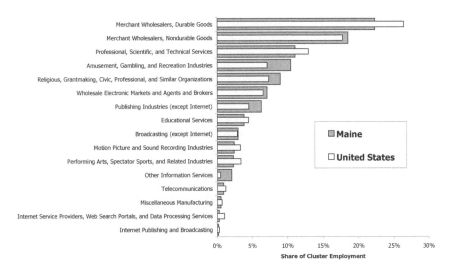

Figure 12.2 Value chain composition: arts and media.

industry and the publishing industry, and shares comparable to the national average in broadcasting, Internet broadcasting, and electronic wholesaling.

The issue of industry composition prompts the question: what do the interindustry benchmarks in general, and national value chains in particular, tell us that differs from what we would have learned by simply examining trends by individual industry? Table 12.4 reports basic trends for Maine and the US for each three-digit NAICS industry, excluding government, retail trade, the postal service, and personal services. To some extent, Table 12.4 tells a story very similar to that of Table 12.3. Indeed, some of the leading Maine industrial specializations revealed in Table 12.4 are forestry and logging, leather and allied products, wood products, and paper, all obviously part of value chains identified as specializations using the benchmarks. However, there are some important differences. Figure 12.3 lists those industries/chains from each table that are either indicated as Maine specializations or Maine growth industries relative to the US. Figure 12.3 also indicates where each NAICS industry falls within each identified value chain.

Some Maine industrial specializations identified in Table 12.4 – examples are textile mills, textile product mills, hospitals, nursing and residential care facilities, and accommodation – are not indicated as Maine specializations when the broader value chains in which those industries are primary members are considered, though most identified specializations are at least secondary members of other value chains with a significant presence in the state. For example, even though Maine has an above-average share of employment in two textile-related industries, the broader textiles and apparel value chain is underrepresented. That may be the result of perfectly logical locational dynamics in the US textiles and apparel industry vis-à-vis Maine as a production location, downward trends in the industry overall, or saturated markets. However, it may also hint at Maine strengths in selected textiles markets that might be the basis for economic advantage in industries with no presence in the state at present. One does not know without additional analysis, but finding out why Maine is overrepresented in some component industries and yet underrepresented in the overall value chains of which those industries are a part should reveal useful insights about the forces driving the state's growth.

Some of the value chains listed in Figure 12.3 are intriguing because they seem to have relatively few linkages to the dominant NAICS industries. Are such chains potential economic strengths for Maine that are not apparent in a scan of trends for isolated industries? In some cases, the answer is "no". For example, roughly 92 per cent of employment in the chemical-based products value chain is accounted for by two industries in Maine, paper mills and newsprint mills. In other cases, the answer is a qualified "yes". The pharmaceuticals value chain in Maine is small but growing robustly in some areas, with a distribution of activity across a number of related industries, including pharmaceutical preparations, in-vitro diagnostic substances, medicinals and botanicals, and professional, technical and research services.

Table 12.4 Maine's economic base by NAICS industry

Industry	NAICS	Empl., 2005	Employment Growth, '00 to '05 Maine	US	Specialization 2005	Change '00 to '05
Crop Production	111	1,518	-15.7%	-5.1%	0.62	-0.07
Animal Production	112	624	-17.6%	7.8%	0.65	-0.19
Forestry & Logging	113	2,705	0.6%	-13.9%	8.45	1.29
Fishing, Hunting & Trapping	114	379	45.2%	-19.1%	9.33	4.18
Support Activities for Agriculture & Forestry	115	430	-31.4%	-1.0%	0.30	-0.13
Mining (except Oil & Gas)	212	115	11.7%	-5.3%	0.12	0.02
Support Activities for Mining	213	0	-100.0%	34.5%	0.00	0.00
Utilities	221	1,903	-6.6%	-8.4%	0.77	0.02
Construction of Buildings	236	8,087	7.3%	10.4%	1.05	-0.02
Heavy & Civil Engineering Construction	237	3,341	-26.3%	-0.3%	0.80	-0.27
Specialty Trade Contractors	238	19,430	10.1%	11.0%	0.93	0.00
Food Mfg	311	6,353	-11.9%	-5.2%	0.96	-0.06
Beverage & Tobacco Product Mfg	312	1,040	-0.1%	-7.3%	1.20	0.10
Textile Mills	313	1,482	-40.8%	-42.7%	1.52	0.06
Textile Product Mills	314	1,141	-34.5%	-22.5%	1.50	-0.26
Apparel Mfg	315	265	-68.1%	-48.8%	0.23	-0.14
Leather & Allied Product Mfg	316	2,195	-57.3%	-43.3%	12.50	-3.95
Wood Product Mfg	321	6,656	-18.1%	-9.0%	2.65	-0.27
Paper Mfg	322	9,478	-26.2%	-20.1%	4.37	-0.31
Printing & Related Support Activities	323	2,510	-14.4%	-20.2%	0.87	0.07
Petroleum & Coal Products Mfg	324	400	14.0%	-9.1%	0.79	0.17
Chemical Mfg	325	1,555	-6.2%	-11.1%	0.40	0.02
Plastics & Rubber Products Mfg	326	2,295	-13.8%	-16.4%	0.64	0.03
Non-metallic Mineral Product Mfg	327	1,524	-16.4%	-9.6%	0.67	-0.05

(Continued overleaf)

Table 12.4 (continued)

Industry	NAICS	Empl., 2005	Employment Growth, '00 to '05 Maine	US	Specialization 2005	Change '00 to '05
Primary Metal Mfg	331	353	-18.5%	-25.4%	0.17	0.02
Fabricated Metal Product Mfg	332	4,683	-15.3%	-14.5%	0.69	0.00
Machinery Mfg	333	2,175	-24.3%	-20.5%	0.42	-0.02
Computer & Electronic Product Mfg	334	3,482	-48.9%	-27.6%	0.59	-0.24
Electrical Equip, Appliance & Component Mfg	335	871	-30.9%	-26.8%	0.45	-0.02
Transportation Equipment Mfg	336	9,311	-4.7%	-13.9%	1.17	0.12
Furniture & Related Product Mfg	337	1,565	-29.9%	-17.6%	0.62	-0.10
Miscellaneous Mfg	339	2,117	-2.3%	-12.5%	0.73	0.08
Merchant Wholesalers, Durable Goods	423	10,023	1.8%	-4.5%	0.74	0.05
Merchant Wholesalers, Nondurable Goods	424	8,312	-4.1%	0.4%	0.92	-0.03
Wholesale Electronic Markets, Agents, Brokers	425	3,198	27.7%	23.9%	0.96	0.04
Air Transportation	481	401	-31.8%	-18.0%	0.18	-0.03
Water Transportation	483	130	-18.2%	8.9%	0.49	-0.16
Truck Transportation	484	6,180	-3.7%	-1.7%	0.99	-0.01
Transit & Ground Passenger Transportation	485	1,453	6.7%	4.0%	0.84	0.03
Pipeline Transportation	486	74	2.8%	-16.2%	0.43	0.08
Scenic & Sightseeing Transportation	487	252	5.4%	-11.6%	2.03	0.34
Support Activities for Transportation	488	1,429	0.7%	3.2%	0.58	-0.01
Couriers & Messengers	492	1,886	-9.5%	-8.6%	0.75	0.00
Warehousing & Storage	493	2,318	-6.6%	13.3%	0.88	-0.18
Publishing Industries (except Internet)	511	3,589	-4.5%	-12.2%	0.88	0.08
Motion Picture & Sound Recording Industries	512	1,078	39.3%	-2.4%	0.64	0.20
Broadcasting (except Internet)	515	1,327	-19.4%	-3.8%	0.91	-0.17
Internet Publishing & Broadcasting	516	73	32.7%	-34.3%	0.52	0.26

	Code					
Telecommunications	517	3,087	−13.8%	−21.8%	0.69	0.07
ISPs, Web Search Portals, & Data Processing	518	1,112	−15.3%	−25.6%	0.65	0.08
Other Information Services	519	926	−17.0%	10.6%	4.12	−1.32
Monetary Authorities – Central Bank	521	0		−8.2%	0.00	0.00
Credit Intermediation & Related Activities	522	13,430	0.5%	13.0%	1.04	−0.12
Securities, Commodity Contracts & Other	523	1,508	1.9%	−2.0%	0.42	0.02
Insurance Carriers & Related Activities	524	10,870	−2.6%	2.3%	1.13	−0.05
Funds, Trusts, & Other Financial Vehicles	525	59	59.5%	3.4%	0.15	0.05
Real Estate	531	4,470	19.3%	10.4%	0.68	0.06
Rental & Leasing Services	532	2,733	−5.4%	−4.9%	0.95	0.00
Lessors of Non-financial Intangible Assets	533	5	−54.5%	−9.3%	0.04	−0.04
Professional, Scientific, & Technical Services	541	23,020	5.0%	3.7%	0.73	0.02
Management of Companies & Enterprises	551	5,617	−13.8%	−2.3%	0.72	−0.09
Administrative & Support Services	561	20,258	−5.3%	0.0%	0.58	−0.03
Waste Management & Remediation Services	562	1,692	3.0%	7.8%	1.11	−0.04
Educational Services	611	9,217	11.0%	18.7%	0.96	−0.06
Ambulatory Health Care Services	621	24,368	8.5%	18.4%	1.06	−0.09
Hospitals	622	29,037	19.0%	9.9%	1.50	0.13
Nursing & Residential Care Facilities	623	22,392	6.2%	10.2%	1.75	−0.05
Performing Arts, Spectator Sports & Related	711	1,035	8.5%	1.6%	0.61	0.04
Museums, Historical Sites, & Similar Institutions	712	437	18.1%	6.7%	0.82	0.09
Amusement, Gambling, & Recreation Industries	713	6,566	5.2%	1.4%	1.07	0.05
Accommodation	721	11,261	4.3%	−3.0%	1.38	0.11
Food Services & Drinking Places	722	40,039	5.1%	11.0%	0.98	−0.05
Religious, Grant-making, Civic, Prof & Similar	813	5,367	9.7%	4.5%	0.92	0.05

Source: Maine Labor Market Information Services, Quarterly Census of Employment and Wages (ES-202) series.

Note: The specialization rate is a location quotient: the share of Maine's total employment that is accounted for by chain i to the share of total national employment accounted for by chain i (values equal to or greater than 1.0 are shaded).

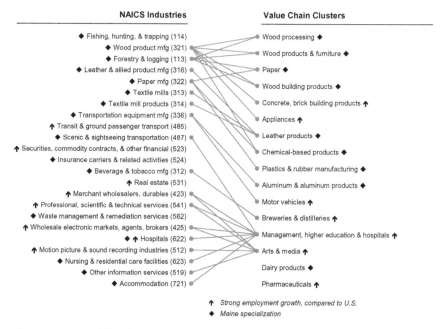

Figure 12.3 NAICS industry vs. national value chain trends: Maine.

Discussion

Interindustry benchmarks are groupings of industries – in essence, alternative industrial classifications to the standard SIC and NAICS systems – that are derived from analyses of industrial interdependence for relevant reference or baseline regions, usually the nation as a whole. They provide two major types of information when used in industry cluster studies for specific regions. First, they offer an initial indication of *potential* relationships among industries in a region. Second, they provide wholly different and conceptually useful frameworks for understanding and exploring regional competitive advantage. Value chains reveal how different industries work in concert to produce goods and services for specific domestic and international markets. Applied to regional data, they help uncover the economic niches a region has or might capture in a broader economy that is increasingly functionally and geographically fragmented.

We noted above that there are many potential kinds of benchmarks that might be usefully developed, since there are many forms of industrial interdependence. For instance, industries might be grouped based on their utilization of workers with similar skill sets. Used as benchmarks, such an industry classification would help identify those industries among which workers can reasonably transfer their skills, perhaps with varying levels of retraining (Koo 2005a). Or, industries might be grouped based on technology flows between them. Koo (2005b, 2006) has shown how technology flows, which do not necessarily follow value chain linkages or mimic mutual labour requirements, can be captured with matrices derived from patent citation records.

In applying interindustry benchmarks in regional cluster studies, analysts must be careful to avoid assuming that interindustry benchmarks are principally an instrument for *finding* local or regional clusters defined as spatial agglomerations of linked and competitive firms. Interindustry benchmarks, depending on their origins, may provide guidance on where to look for such regional clusters, but they provide no direct evidence of local interindustry ties (whether defined by trade, labour, technology, or otherwise). They are far more valuable as a flexible tool for better understanding the region's economic niches within a larger national and global economy, or as a starting point for more in-depth analysis of local linkages, than they are for identifying clusters as entities in a place.

Are we contradicting ourselves by advocating the use of interindustry benchmarks in regional cluster analysis but then cautioning against their use as a means of actually detecting competitive regional clusters? The answer is "no", because the best regional cluster studies are, thankfully, no longer just exercises in "cluster finding". Indeed, as the cluster concept has penetrated economic development practice, it has heightened awareness of the importance of understanding critical interdependencies among industries and businesses even as the ultimate value of targeting regional clusters has come to be questioned. Increasingly, regional cluster studies are focused on revealing sources of interindustry synergies – within a region and externally – and finding ways to leverage those synergies through a variety of local economic development interventions, from marketing and recruitment to workforce development and technology transfer. Deciding whether a given group of companies is or is not a "cluster" is much less valuable for policy purposes than understanding the markets those companies serve and the factors that influence the companies' individual and collective competitiveness. Interindustry benchmarks are a useful tool, among others, for helping analysts gain that understanding.

Note

1 The quote is from the Data Glossary page of the Harvard Cluster Mapping Project website, under the entry "cluster".

References

Bergman, E.M., and Feser, E.J. (1999) *Industrial and Regional Clusters: Concepts and Comparative Applications*, Morganton: Regional Research Institute, West Virginia University.

Bergman, E.M., Feser, E.J., and Sweeney, S.H. (1996) *Targeting North Carolina Manufacturing: Understanding the State's Economy through Industrial Cluster Analysis*, Chapel Hill: UNC Institute for Economic Development.

Feser, E.J. (2005) "Benchmark value chain industry clusters for applied regional research", Regional Economics Applications Laboratory, University of Illinois at Urbana-Champaign.

Feser, E.J., and Bergman, E.M. (2000) "National industry cluster templates: A framework for applied regional cluster analysis", *Regional Studies*, 34: 1–19.

Feser, E.J., and Luger, M. (2003) "Cluster analysis as a mode of inquiry: Its use in science and technology policymaking in North Carolina", *European Planning Studies*, 11: 11–24.

Feser, E.J., Sweeney, S.H., and Renski, H.C. (2005) "A descriptive analysis of discrete U.S. industrial complexes", *Journal of Regional Science*, 45: 395–419.

Gereffi, G., Denniston, R., and Hensen, M. (2007) "North Carolina in the global economy: A value chain perspective on the state's leading industries", *Journal of Textile and Apparel, Technology and Management*, 5: 1–2.

Gereffi, G., Humphrey J., and Sturgeon T. (2005) "The governance of global value chains", *Review of International Political Economy*, 12: 78–104.

Helper, S. (1995) "Can Maquilas be lean? The case of wiring harness production in Mexico", in S. Babson (ed.) *Lean Work: Empowerment and Exploitation in the Global Auto Industry*, 260–75, Detroit: Wayne State University Press.

Hill, E.W., and Brennan, J.F. (2000) "A methodology for identifying the drivers of industrial clusters: the foundation of regional competitive advantage", *Economic Development Quarterly*, 14: 65–96.

Humphrey, J., and Schmitz, H. (2002) "How does insertion in global value chains affect upgrading in industrial clusters?" *Regional Studies*, 36: 1017–27.

Koo, J. (2005a) "How to analyze the regional economy with occupation data", *Economic Development Quarterly*, 19: 356–72.

——. (2005b) "Knowledge-based industry clusters: evidenced by geographical patterns of patents in manufacturing", *Urban Studies*, 42: 1487–505.

——. (2006) "In search of new knowledge: its origins and destinations", *Economic Development Quarterly*, 20: 259–77.

McElroy, M., Olmedo, C., Feser E., and Poole, K.E. (2006) *Upper Rio Grande at Work: Upper Rio Grande Workforce Development Board Industry Cluster Analysis*, El Paso: Institute for Policy and Economic Development, University of Texas at El Paso.

Moses, L.N. (1958) "Location and the theory of production", *Quarterly Journal of Economics*, 78: 259–72.

Porter, M.E. (2003) "The economic performance of regions", *Regional Studies*, 37: 549–78.

——. (2004) *Methodological note based on an excerpt and adaptation of text from "The economic performance of regions"*, Cambridge, MA: Cluster Mapping Project, Harvard University.

RTS. (2003) *The Creative Enterprise Cluster*, Carrboro, NC: Regional Technology Strategies, Inc.

C. AHP and matching models

13 Targeting with the analytic hierarchy process

Thomas G. Johnson

Background

Despite repeated attempts to define and measure economic development, the concept remains largely subjective. As Partridge and Rickman (2003) point out, there are no agreed definitions of economic development. They conclude that, "the correct indicator of economic development, or combination of indicators, depends upon the characteristics of the region" (p. 35). In this chapter, we argue that at least part of the reason that there is no agreed indicator of economic development and that different regions require different combinations of indicators is that preferences for development differ from person to person and from place to place.

Each year, state and local governments in the US spend millions of dollars to stimulate economic development within their boundaries. Surprisingly, considering the vast amount of money being spent on economic development programmes, there is little research examining local residents' preferences for economic development outcomes, and even less evidence that preferences are considered as economic development programmes are planned and executed (see, for example, Harris et al., Chapter 14). Traditionally, the political process is the only means that residents have for expressing their preferences for the future of their communities.

These preferences, if known, could lead to much more proactive and cost-effective economic development programmes.[1] In the absence of articulated preferences, economic development is less likely to have clear objectives. In fact, most policies and programmes, if evaluated at all, are measured by numbers of jobs created, the easiest indicator available (Bartik 1991: 6). But what of other indicators such as the quality of jobs, the stability of the economy, the contributions to the local tax base, the environment, the social structure, and so on?

Community preferences should matter (Harris et al., Chapter 14; Deller et al., Chapter 17). Economic development outcomes, regardless of the programme or policy in question, are felt locally in a number of ways. For example, new or expanding firms create employment, generate incomes, add to the tax base, stimulate related businesses, generate demands on public infrastructure and services, create additional congestion, change property values, and generate both positive and negative externalities. Evaluating the desirability of these different outcomes depends on their relative magnitudes and residents' preferences. The result is a form of multi-attribute decision-making problem. The critical information in such a decision-making problem is the weights to attach to the different expected impacts.

This chapter describes a means of incorporating local preferences in industry targeting strategies and gives an example of its application. The approach involves three steps. Local residents are interviewed in the first step, and the analytical hierarchy process (AHP) is used to create cardinal weights for different local impacts of economic development outcomes. In the second step, the impacts of alternative economic sectors are identified and quantified. The third step involves applying the preference weights to the predicted impacts of each industry to derive a community-specific measure or score for each industry. This chapter focuses on the first step in this process.

Weighting community preferences

When development outcomes are multidimensional, a means of weighting these dimensions is needed to rank the events that cause the outcomes. If community preferences were known over the K dimensions (types of impacts) of an economic change, then scoring each of the $j = 1 \ldots J$ industries, on the basis of the set of impacts that it caused, would be straightforward:

$$S = IW^* \tag{1}$$

where S is a $Jx1$ vector of scores for the J industries, I is a JxK matrix of impacts of the jth industry on the kth, and W is a $Kx1$ vector of weights of the K impacts.

Previous economic evaluation systems have been limited by two typical characteristics. First, most attempts to evaluate alternative industries or firms rely on weights applied to the direct impact of the industry or firm – the number of jobs created, wages paid, among others. Few have tried to weight the final impact of the firm – changes in population, change in property values, environmental outcomes, as well as total employment and income effects. For example, Shaffer (1989) recommends use of a screening system in which a community assigns weights to the set of firm characteristics. Johnson et al. (1994) asked community members to assign weights to a list of screening criteria that were used to identify industries for targeting. These studies focus on the direct attributes of firms and sectors and do not examine the final impact on the regional economy.

The second major shortcoming of many studies is their reliance on ad hoc scoring methods that do not necessarily reflect the preferences of residents. Ad hoc scoring involves using equal weights or arbitrarily chosen weights with which to collapse several indicators into a score. This approach is simple, but will not, in general, lead to the same rankings that weights based on residents' preferences would. Alston et al. (1995) criticize scoring methods (in the context of agricultural research), showing that they frequently lack rigor, have no theoretical basis, and are fraught with inconsistencies in assigned weights. They conclude that "weights on objectives should reflect clients' value judgments about trade-offs among objectives" (p. 467).

Methods other than pairwise comparison as used in the AHP exist to obtain preferences from decision-makers. Ordinal rankings and fixed point scoring are two of the less rigorous methods available. Other preference elicitation methods include the Delphi technique, the multi-attribute utility procedure, and the Vickrey-Groves-Clarke voting procedure (Cohon 1978; Harker 1989; Romero and Rehman 1987; Tideman and Tullock 1976).[2]

The Delphi technique obtains preferences (weights) from decision-makers through anonymous questionnaires, controlled feedback, and statistical analysis of the results (Dalkey et al. 1972). Each person ranks the criteria using a scale of importance and explicitly states her underlying assumptions. The ranking is accomplished using a Likert-type scale (i.e., 1 = very important, 2 = moderately important, etc.). The assessments and assumptions of the group members are analysed, medians and quartiles are calculated, and the results are distributed to the group. Each member then has the opportunity to revise her earlier assessment, based on the results of the group. This process is repeated until a consensus has been reached (Hampton et al. 1973).

The multiple-attribute utility procedure requires the decision-maker to answer questions dealing with probabilities, usually in a lottery framework (Roberts 1979). Decision-makers are asked to predict the probability of a particular consequence (criterion). As the probabilities being elicited are usually subjective in nature, they "represent the 'degree of certainty' or 'degree of conviction' that the expert has that an event will occur" (Roberts 1979: 372). The outcomes derived from the probabilities represent the utility (weight) of each criterion.

The Vickrey-Groves-Clarke mechanism, or demand-revealing process, elicits preferences in a manner that rewards truthful representation of the intensity of the decision-maker's preferences (Auerbach and Feldstein 1987). In this procedure, each person is asked which of two or more options he or she prefers, and how much he or she would be willing to pay to have his or her preferred options rather than the others. The outcome is reached by summing the willingness-to-pay for each option. The amount is the most preferred. The mechanism ensures that all participants accurately revealed their preferences by levying a "tax" on participants based on their impacts on the outcome (Tideman and Tullock 1976).

The analytic hierarchy procedure

The AHP, developed by Saaty, is a means of weighting or prioritizing outcomes of a choice when several considerations are relevant. Through pairwise comparisons of several outcomes, the relative importance, or weights, of different factors can be measured; trade-offs between objectives are explicitly considered in these pairwise comparisons. The pairwise comparison process imposes rigour that is missing when directly assigning weights to a number of impacts, because possible inconsistencies (intransitivity and inconsistent weights) in the judgements can be calculated and reexamined. Even with subjective criteria, the weights obtained through the AHP are "ratio scale numbers and correspond to so-called hard numbers" (Saaty and Kearns 1985: 19). Thus, the derived priority weights are cardinal.

AHP has been applied to a variety of issues, including electric utility planning, portfolio management, conflict management, advertising, and resource allocation (for examples, see Dyer et al. 1992; Hämäläinen and Seppäläinen 1986; Lauro and Vepsalainen 1986; Saaty 1980; Saaty and Alexander 1989).

Structuring the problem

The first step in the AHP is to decompose the problem into a dominance hierarchy (Figure 13.1). The topmost level represents the goal or focus of the problem. Intermediate levels are the criteria on which lower levels depend, and the lowest level is the list of choices or alternatives (Saaty and Kearns 1985). As many levels as necessary can be used. The lower levels act as the criteria or factors contributing to the level immediately above (see Saaty and Kearns 1985 for applications of AHP). In the context of the economic development problem, the goal might be the overall enhancement of regional quality of life, and the criteria might be the industry impacts (such as total local jobs created or measured change in environmental quality following the industry location). The alternatives would be the firm or industry types.

Pairwise comparison

Once the problem is decomposed into a hierarchy, each element must be compared to other elements at that same level. The questions asked for the second level could take the form, "When comparing different criteria, which criterion is more important (in achieving the goal)?" Other kinds of questions that could be asked include: "When comparing A and B, 'Which is more

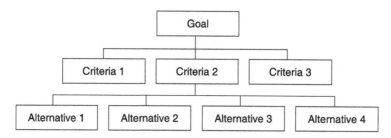

Figure 13.1 Generic decomposition of a problem into a dominance hierarchy.

important?' 'Which has a greater impact?' 'Which is more likely to happen?' and 'Which is more preferred?' " (Saaty and Kearns 1985). The nature of the question depends on the desired outcome and the level being compared.

Judgements from these pairwise comparisons are entered into a $K \times K$ square matrix P, with a column and a row for each criterion. The p_{ij} element is the numerical answer to the question "With respect to the goal, what is the importance of criterion i versus criterion j?" The matrix is reciprocal, with $K(K-1)/2$ pairwise comparisons, $p_{ij} = 1 / p_{ji}$, and $p_{ij} = 1$. If criterion i is more important than criterion j, the cardinal scale value representing the intensity is entered directly into the matrix position p_{ij}. However, if criterion j is more important than criterion i, the *reciprocal* of the scale value representing the intensity is entered into the matrix position p_{ij}.

If the actual utility weights of the criteria being compared were known, the p_{ij} would represent the ratio of the weights:

$$P = W, \tag{2}$$

Where $w_{ij} = w_i / w_j$ and w_i is the utility weight of the ith criterion (see equation 1). When the weights $(w_1, w_2, \ldots, w_K)$ are unknown, then the pairwise comparison is performed using subjective judgements estimated numerically from a scale of numbers. The scale recommended by Saaty (1977) has been validated for effectiveness in different applications (Table 13.1).

Solving for preference weights

Obtaining the relative weights would be simple if there were no errors or inconsistencies in comparisons. In such a case, W could be solved as an

Table 13.1 Scale of relative importance

Intensity of Relative Importance	Definition	Explanation
1	Equal importance.	Two activities contribute equally to the objective.
3	Moderate importance of one over another.	Experience and judgment slightly favor one activity over another.
5	Essential or strong importance.	Experience or judgment strongly favors one activity over another.
7	Demonstrated importance.	An activity is strongly favored and its dominance is demonstrated in practice.
9	Extreme importance.	The evidence favoring one activity over another is of the highest possible order of affirmation.

Source: Saaty and Kearns (1985).

eigenvector of P corresponding to an eigenvalue equal to K, which, in the perfectly consistent case, is also the matrix rank (Saaty 1980).

$$\mathbf{Pw} = \mathbf{Kw} \qquad (3)$$

where P is the comparison matrix, w is the eigenvector corresponding to K, and K is the number of rows and columns of P, or, in other words, the number of impacts being assigned weights.

In general, the P matrix will contain errors or inconsistencies. The inconsistencies can be attributed to the limitations put on the comparison by the scale being used. That is, each p_{ij} is based on subjective estimates, not on exact measurement. The judgement matrix is not an exact ratio of w_i / w_j, but rather, a ratio of integers used to scale preferences, which can lead to significant rounding error (Fichtner 1986).

Human error can also lead to inconsistency. The process of making pairwise comparisons can itself lead to changing estimation of one's preferences as more thought is given to the alternatives. Prior rankings of each pair of elements are difficult for people to consider as they compare new alternatives. This limitation is the primary reason for keeping the number of elements to be compared at each level of the hierarchy below nine (see Saaty 1980). Given the inevitability that there will be inconsistencies in the comparisons, the maximum eigenvalue is used in place of K to solve for w:

$$\mathbf{Pw} = \lambda_{max}\,\mathbf{w} \qquad (4)$$

where λ_{max} is the maximum eigenvalue of P, and w is the eigenvector corresponding to λ_{max}. Weights are calculated using the eigenvector corresponding to the largest eigenvalue, λ_{max}. The elements of **w** are normalized using:

$$w_i^* = w_i / \Sigma w_i \qquad (5)$$

These results (w_i^*) are the cardinal, or relative, values (weights) of the criteria. The vector of these weights W^* is used in equation 1.

A strength of the AHP is its ability to estimate preference weights even when there is some degree of intransitivity among criteria and inconsistency in the intensity with which judgements are expressed. The AHP provides a way for inconsistencies to be measured. It is desirable for judgements to fall under a given consistency threshold.

Applying AHP to targeted regional economic development: a case study

One of the earliest applications of the AHP to regional industrial targeting was Cox et al. (2000). The AHP was used to measure preferences by the development directors and other local leaders for alternative development outcomes in three Virginia counties.

The overall goal in the hierarchy was to maximize total quality of life in the locality. The second-level goals included the various types of impacts that a firm can have on a locality. Following a review of findings from other studies, and a survey of economic development directors in the state of Virginia (Bailey 1996), the following impacts were identified: number of jobs created, average wage or salary, average level of capital investment, average level of utility requirements, environmental impacts, effect on population growth, and impact on property values.[3]

The number of newly created jobs was often offered as an indication of success in economic development, but localities were also interested in job quality, and average wage or salary are indicators of job quality. Capital investment is important because it shows commitment to the community and increases the stream of property tax revenues.

In addition, the water and sewer requirements of new and expanding firms were included because of the potential for utility capacity constraints (Bailey 1996). Property values were important to the local government primarily because increased property values increase the tax base. The perceived cleanliness of industry was included to determine the importance of environmental considerations to decision-makers in these communities. Finally, the impact of population growth is a measure of several of the "costs" associated with economic development, such as congestion and increasing costs to local government.

AHP interview and results

The counties in this Cox et al. (2000) study were chosen because they were broadly representative of county types in rural Virginia. One county is heavily dependent on natural resource-based tourism. It also faces economic stagnation and contains a relatively high proportion of poor households. The second county is a mixed agricultural-manufacturing. The third county has grown rapidly in recent years and faces challenges of growth management.

Local government and business leaders were invited to participate in the industry ranking process as representatives of their county. Although it was recognized that the preferences of other county residents may vary from those invited to participate, local leaders' involvement in the community were thought to provide a broad, comprehensive view of the issues and constraints facing their county.

Participants were asked to consider every possible combination of two impacts: "When comparing impact A to impact B, how important was one over the other with respect to the attractiveness of an industry?" If there was immediate consensus, that judgement was entered into the matrix. If not, a discussion of the assumptions or considerations each individual used when making his or her value judgement ensued. At the end of the discussions, a person would be convinced enough to change his judgement or the group would agree on a compromise.

Calculation and re-evaluation of the comparison matrix

When the initial judgement matrix was filled, the priority outcomes were calculated as described above and the consistency ratio was calculated. If the consistency ratio (CR) was above the threshold of 0.2,[4] the judgement matrix was re-examined. Re-evaluation did not mean that respondents were forced to accept prioritization with which they disagreed; rather, reevaluation allowed respondents to review their choices and to ensure that no blatant inconsistency existed. For instance, if environmental quality is strongly favoured to number of jobs, and number of jobs is strongly favoured to capital investment, then environmental quality should also be strongly favoured to capital investment. Respondents discussed the inconsistencies and then identified which rankings or weights that did not make sense to them. This led the group to analyse their judgements and further discuss the assumptions behind the judgements. This process was repeated until the CR was lower than 0.2 and participants were satisfied that the ranking and weights adequately represented their preferences.

Results of AHP

Experience with the interviews varied by county, but the priority weightings and rankings were reasonably consistent across counties. For two out of the three counties, re-examining the pairwise comparisons was necessary because of initial inconsistencies in the judgement matrix. The rankings are shown in Table 13.2. Differences in rankings highlight the location-specificity of development preferences; different counties have different preferences.

Preferences for outcomes

Participants in all three counties had a strong preference for a clean environment. Environmental quality was ranked a strong first in two out of three of the counties and it finished second in the third (Table 13.2). County one's desire to maintain an attractive environment is probably due to the county's heavy reliance on tourism. County two, on the other hand, has aggressively recruited industry for more than a decade, and the high weight placed on industry cleanliness might be due to their experience with industries that were less than ideal in this regard. Decision-makers expressed the view that "smokestack chasing" was a strategy of the past. In both counties, environmental quality received more than double the weight of the next-preferred outcome.

In this study, the number of jobs associated with a development event was substantially less important than cleanliness of the firm and quality of jobs.

Table 13.2 Final ranking and weights by impact, three Virginia counties

	County One		County Two		County Three	
Rank	Impact	Final Weight (%)	Impact	Final Weight (%)	Impact	Final Weight (%)
1	Cleanliness of Industry	51	Cleanliness of Industry	49	Average Wage or Salary	35
2	Average Wage or Salary	16	Level of Capital Investment	23	Cleanliness of Industry	24
3	Impacts on Property Values	13	Average Wage or Salary	13	Level of Capital Investment	16
4	Number of Jobs	6	Number of Jobs	6	Number of Jobs	12
5	Level of Capital Investment	5	Impacts of Population Growth	5	Impacts of Population Growth	7
6	Level of Utility Requirements	5	Level of Utility Requirements	3	Impacts on Property Values	4
7	Impacts of Population Growth	4	Impacts on Property Values	2	Level of Utility Requirements	2
CR		.196		0.275		.142

This outcome was ranked only fourth most important in each county, with a weight ranging from 12 per cent to approximately 6 per cent. In all counties, number of jobs is an important consideration, but job quality and environmental quality rank higher. County one's respondents reasoned that although their unemployment rate was higher than the state average, the number of unemployed is small because of their small population. It is thus not essential to create large numbers of jobs locally.

Average wage or salary was the most important consideration for county three, with a priority weight of 35 per cent. Participants felt firms offering higher pay were more attractive because the county has an educated workforce, and decision-makers sought to increase the number of "head of household"-type jobs. Decision-makers in the other two counties ranked average wages highly and stated directly their belief that higher pay is associated with a higher quality job. Respondents in county two reasoned that the county had made great strides recently in increasing the number of jobs locally and that it was time to focus on job quality over quantity. Respondents in all counties valued the contribution of the development event to the local tax base. Capital investment is ranked second in county two (24 per cent) and third in county three (16 per cent). Participants considered tax revenues associated with higher capital investment to be important. Firms with large capital investments were also believed to be less likely to relocate in the future. In contrast, county one's respondents argued that the best way to effect increases in property tax revenues was by increasing local property values. They put a low weight on capital investment, reasoning that capital investment was associated with heavy industry, and such industry might damage the tourism base of the economy.

Respondents in two counties placed low weights on changes in property values. Impacts on utility requirements and population changes received low priority weights in all counties. In county one, utility requirements received a relatively low score because water, sewer, and electricity use are currently far below capacity. In the other counties, respondents decided that if a firm had desirable characteristics, the county would expand its sewer and water capacity to meet industry needs.

The impact of population growth was somewhat important to the respondents from county three (7 per cent), primarily because of the potential increase in traffic, and the resulting congestion occurring in the past several years. In two counties, respondents decided the schools, roads, and other facilities are more than adequate for the current population. In all counties, population increases were not viewed favourably, but in the latter two counties such increases were accorded small weights.

Scoring the impacts

The *level* of each type of impact associated with each industry was calculated for each county. Industry scores for all counties are found in Cox (1996).

Scored impacts were multiplied by the priority weights to calculate the adjusted score for each industry and the county-specific rankings of each industry. The scores are reported for one county in Table 13.3. Community preferences used as priority weights have a strong effect on the ranking of industries.

Environmental quality, as shown earlier, has a major effect on industry rankings. None of the top nine and only two of the top 20 industries in Table 13.3 had any adverse environmental impact. The top sectors are those with relatively low impacts on the environment and relatively high wages (Distilled Liquor, except Brandy; Federal Government, non-military). All of the top industries in Table 13.3 are highly linked to the local economy and have favourable overall impacts.

The most preferred industry for all counties is Pipelines, Excluding Natural Gas (Table 13.3). This industry had high average wages, represented the largest proportional capital investment, and had no adverse environmental impact.

Table 13.3 Overall ranking of top 20 sectors based on job, wage, and value-added impacts

Rank	Sector Name	Average Number of Jobs (per million output)	Average Wage or Salary ($/year)	Value-Added Effect (total VA/$ output)
1	Pipe Lines, Excluding Natural Gas	2	$58,113	0.9011
2	Railroads & Related Services	8	$61,152	0.7776
3	Communications, Except Radio & TV	6	$49,516	0.9074
4	Electric Services	3	$54,112	0.7027
5	Computing & Data Processing	13	$33,780	0.9108
6	New Government Facilities	10	$36,410	0.7366
7	Oil & Gas Wells Maintenance & Repair	27	$21,658	1.1702
8	Electronic Computers	6	$63,525	0.7947
9	Federal Government – Non-military	21	$47,933	1.1401
10	Distilled Liquor, Except Brandy	2	$57,072	0.9805
11	Research, Development & Testing	24	$27,336	0.9992
12	State & Local Electric Utilities	4	$44,098	0.7019
13	Wholesale Trade	13	$36,095	1.0206
14	Other Business Services	21	$16,709	0.9860
15	Arrangement Of Passenger Transportation	22	$20,393	0.9595
16	Transportation Services	13	$29,108	0.7744
17	State & Local Government, Non-education	32	$31,637	1.3026
18	Fluid Power Pumps & Motors	18	$46,088	1.1166
19	Residential Maintenance & Repair	13	$23,717	0.7337
20	U.S. Postal Service	18	$42,275	0.8909

Summary and conclusions

Traditional and even more novel industry targeting approaches answer such questions as the following: What types of firms and sectors will be most attracted to this region's assets, business climate, markets, labour force and policy regime? What impacts will typical firms in various sectors have on the economies of this region? What investments in infrastructure or human capital, or changes in policy, will make this region more attractive to firms in these sectors?

However, without some type of preference elicitation process, traditional targeting processes do not answer the question, How attractive are firms in these sectors (or more precisely, the impacts of firms in these sectors) to the residents of this region?

Economic development is rarely a controversial goal in general. However, as Partridge and Rickman (2003) demonstrate, diversity among regions and their residents lead to differences in preferences for these outcomes. These differences in preferences mean that policy-makers at local and state levels cannot assume that they know what the best economic development policies will be until they have explored these preferences with residents. Preference elicitation and the incorporation of these preferences regional economic development policy is a critical part of targeting. The AHP gives policy-makers a way to have residents communicate their preferences for economic, social, environmental, and other outcomes of economic development policy.

The diversity of preferences extends to different communities as well, ensuring that different policies will be appropriate in different communities. Cox et al. (2000) found different preferences and resulting differences in targeted industries among three rural communities in Virginia. People vote with their feet, which, over time, can lead to quite different community-level preferences.

Of course, in order to take advantage of the weights determined with this approach, policy-makers must have information on the differential impacts of firms or industries in terms of the dimensions identified in the AHP process. These issues are addressed elsewhere in this volume.

Overall, including community preferences through the AHP promises to be a valuable tool for targeting regional economic development efforts. It accommodates the diversity of values among people and of the resulting differences among communities. AHP provides a means of choosing among multiple alternatives while accommodating multiple objectives and multiple decision-makers.

Notes

1   Interestingly, Arrow's Impossibility Theorem (1950) shows that when there are two or more stakeholders and three or more alternatives, it is impossible to find a decision-making system that does not violate at least one of four basic principles. More recent work (Saaty 1997) shows that when preferences are cardinal rather

than ordinal, Arrow's principles are not violated, although this introduces rather strong assumptions about preferences and interpersonal comparisons.

2   For a more detailed description of these and other methods used to support multicriteria decision-making, see Romero and Rehman (1987), Hampton, Moore, and Thomas (1973), and Roberts (1979). For an evaluation of group decision-making methods, see *Srisoepardani* (1999).

3   Bailey surveyed economic development directors to understand which firm attributes made the firm likely to receive an incentive package. Bailey's results were used to define the universe of plausible firm impacts on the community and are not assumed to reflect "community values".

4   The developers of the Expert Choice, the AHP software used in this study, recommend that users continue to refine their pairwise assessment until their consistency ratio falls below 0.1. This threshold is arbitrary and is often very difficult to attain. Tests with the process convinced us to accept the higher threshold of 0.2 for expediency's sake, recognizing that this may lead to inaccuracies in the resulting weights.

References

Alston, J.M., Norton, G.W., and Pardey, P.G. (1995) *Science Under Scarcity: Principles and Practice for Agricultural Research Evaluation and Priority Setting.* Ithaca: Cornell University Press.

Arrow, K.J. (1950) "A difficulty in the concept of social welfare", *Journal of Political Economy*, 58(4): 328–46.

Auerbach, A.J., and Feldstein, M. (1987) *Handbook of Public Economics, Volume II.* The Netherlands: Elsevier Science Publishers B.V.

Bailey, T.M. (1996) "Analysis of firm desirability among Virginia's economic development directors", unpublished MS Thesis, Blacksburg, VA: Department of Agricultural and Applied Economics, Virginia Tech.

Bartik, T.J. (1991) *Who Benefits from State and Local Economic Development Policies?* Kalamazoo, MI: W.E. Upjohn Institute.

Cohon, J.L. (1978) *Multiobjective Programming and Planning*, New York: Academic Press.

Cox, A.M. (1996) "Proactive industrial targeting: an application of the analytical hierarchy process", unpublished MS Thesis, Department of Agricultural and Applied Economics, Virginia Tech.

Cox, A.M., Alwang, J., and Johnson, T.G. (2000) "Local preferences for economic development outcomes: an application of the analytical hierarchy procedure", *Growth and Change* 31(3): 341–66.

Dalkey, N.C., Rourke, D.L., Lewis, R., and Snyder, D. (1972) *Studies in the Quality of Life: Delphi and Decision-Making.* Lexington, MA: Lexington Books.

Dyer, R.F., Forman, E.H., and Mustafa, M.A. (1992) "Decision support for media selection using the analytical hierarchy process", *Journal of Advertising*, 21(1): 59–72.

Fichtner, J. (1986) "On deriving priority vectors from matrices of pairwise comparisons", *Socio-Economic Planning Sciences*, 20(6): 341–45.

Hämäläinen, R.L., and Seppäläinen, T.O. (1986) "The analytical network process in energy policy planning", *Socio-Economic Planning Sciences*, 20(6): 399–405.

Hampton, J.M., Moore, P.G., and Thomas, H. (1973) "Subjective probability and its measurement", *Journal of the Royal Statistical Society, Series A*, 136(1): 21–42.

Harker, P.T. (1989) "The art and science of decision-making: the analytical hierarchy process", in B.L. Golden, E.A. Wasil, and P.T. Harker (eds), *The Analytical Hierarchy Process*, Heidelberg: Springer.

Johnson, T.G., Wade, E.W., and Archambault, R. (1994) *An Economic Opportunities Analysis for the New River Valley*. Blacksburg: Department of Agricultural and Applied Economics, Virginia Tech.

Lauro, G.L., and Vepsalainen, A.P.J. (1986) "Assessing technology portfolios for contract competition: an analytic hierarchy process approach", *Socio-Economic Planning Sciences*, 20(6): 407–15.

Partridge, M.D., and Rickman, D.S. (2003) "Do we know economic development when we see it?" *Review of Regional Studies*, 33910: 17–39.

Roberts, F.S. (1979) *Measurement Theory with Applications to Decisionmaking, Utility, and the Social Sciences*. Reading, MA: Addison-Wesley.

Romero, C., and Rehman, T. (1987) "Natural resource management and the use of multiple criteria decision-making techniques: a review", *European Review of Agricultural Economics*, 14: 60–89.

Saaty, T.L. (1977) "A scaling method for priorities in hierarchical structures", *Journal of Mathematical Psychology*, 15: 234–81.

——. (1980) *The Analytic Hierarchy Process*. New York: McGraw-Hill.

——. (1997) "That is not the analytic hierarchy process: what the AHP is and what it is not", *Journal of Multi-Criterion Decision Analysis*, 6: 320–39

Saaty, T.L., and Alexander, J.M. (1989) *Conflict Resolution: The Analytical Hierarchy Approach*. New York: Praeger.

Saaty, T.L., and Kearns, K.P. (1985) *Analytical Planning: The Organization of Systems*. Oxford: Pergamon.

Shaffer, R. (1989) *Community Economics: Economic Structure and Change in Smaller Communities*. Ames: Iowa State University Press.

Srisoepardani, K.P. (1999) "Evaluation of group decision-making methods", Expert Choice, Inc. Online. Available HTTP: <http://www.expertchoice.com/support/ahp-compare/chapter6.htm>

Tideman, T.N., and Tullock, G. (1976) "A new and superior process for making social choices", *The Journal of Political Economy*, 84(6): 1145–59.

14 The community business matching model

Combining community and business goals and assets to target rural economic development

Linda J. Cox, Jonathan E. Alevy,
Thomas R. Harris, Barbara Andreozzi,
Joan Wright, and George "Buddy" Borden

Introduction

Regional economic development programmes have traditionally concentrated on attracting export-oriented, goods-producing industries, such as manufacturing. Local economic development professionals pursue such programmes because export industries generate local expenditures for existing economic sectors, a result of the additive development effect. Moreover, success in attracting a manufacturing firm is highly visible with abundant opportunities for media coverage (Eisinger 1995), in addition to the directly measurable effects on employment and income.

Recruitment programmes aimed at export-oriented, goods-producing industries, however, are relatively expensive with a high degree of risk, which can result in low net returns for smaller communities with limited resources. Hansen (1970) found that many communities may have limited success at targeting these industries when they lack the assets the businesses desire. In order to assist, tax concessions may be granted to new or relocating firms, limiting the opportunities for local fiscal gains. The use of tax concessions can increase the local tax burden because the cost of increased services for the new business may not be necessarily offset by an expansion in the tax base (Tweeten and Brinkman 1976). Moreover, firms that are attracted to a community if offered sufficient incentives are also likely to leave if better offers are found elsewhere (Winder 1969; Kilkenny and Melkonyan 2002). McNamara and Green (1988) concluded that planning commissions continue to emphasize the recruitment of export-oriented industries. However, as planners become more educated about the possibilities for import substitution, the pursuit of alternative economic development strategies, such as local services and retail sector development, becomes more common (Deller, Chapter 4).

Economic development planners and practitioners have often felt the need to act quickly and so have recruited industries with little or no input from community residents. Without the support of local residents, the sustainability of these efforts is questionable (Blakely 1994; Ayres 1996). Incorporating community preferences adds complexity to development strategies and to the decision-making processes needed to formulate them. When citizen input is solicited, environmental and social goals must be addressed alongside objectives for economic development (see, e.g., Mountain Association for Community Development 1997). Development strategies become more complex since tradeoffs between economic, environmental, and social goals are inevitable. Strategies that ignore these interactions run the risk of unintended long-term consequences, such as sprawl at the expense of environmental quality. Decision-making that incorporates community preferences can be difficult since the issues under consideration can be hard to quantify. Further, if, as is likely, a diversity of views exits within a community, unanimity regarding the weights that should be given to different goals cannot be achieved.

The Community Business Matching (CBM) model provides a framework for addressing the complexities that arise when community preferences are elicited and economic development opportunities must be weighted alongside environmental and social goals. The objective of CBM is to assist communities in identifying (i) their goals for targeted economic development, (ii) the assets that will help them achieve those goals, and (iii) the types of businesses that will be most compatible with these goals and assets. CBM is a transparent and replicable process for measuring community goals and assets relative to economic development and a systematic procedure for matching these goals with the characteristics and requirements of businesses. Importantly, CBM can reveal differences in preferences within a community and therefore provide a foundation for discussion and reevaluation of priorities.

CBM was piloted in 1995 in Richmond, Vermont (Buescher et al. 2001) using a business data set that included only the agricultural sector. The researchers concluded that CBM shows promise as an economic development tool. They cautioned, however, that the business data would need to be appropriate for the purpose. In 2002, a group of community development professionals from Montana State University, the University of Nevada, and the University of Hawaii became interested in the Buescher et al. (2001) model and began to adapt it for use in the western United States. As described in more detail below, several aspects of the model were refined and surveys were prepared to collect both business- and community-level data. CBM was piloted in the town of Anaconda, Montana, and results of the pilot have been used to target Anaconda's economic development efforts and enhance community assets in order to attract the desired businesses.

Interestingly, the community used the process in a way that differed somewhat from what was initially expected. Rather than restricting their focus to targeting and recruiting new businesses, the community identified opportunities for collaboration and expansion within the existing construction industry. This activity suggests that the community took advantage of the CBM results to build on existing strengths, pursuing activities consistent with clustering approaches (Gabe, Chapter 6). Further, it confirms that communities can more finely hone their economic development strategies by engaging in the CBM process.

Review of literature

Industrial targeting is the process of focusing industrial development programmes and efforts at specific industries or clusters of related industries. The principal objectives of an industry targeting programme are to identify (1) industries that have high potential for locating in the area and (2) industries that provide attractive local economic development impacts in terms of long-term and sustainable future employment growth, employee compensation, and contributions to the local tax base (Barkley and Henry 1997). By targeting development efforts, communities can focus their recruitment, retention, and expansion efforts, rather than attempting to provide assistance for many different industry types.

Targeted development strategies can help a community distinguish itself from other communities with less focused strategies (Blakely 1994). Evidence suggests that targeted strategies are more effective at attracting business investment than broader strategies such as unsolicited mailing to all manufacturing industry headquarters (Phillips 1990). However, communities are notoriously unskilled at selecting sectors to target, whether the goal is to recruit new businesses or to further develop existing sectors and the linkages among them (Courant 1995).

A wide range of strategies can be used to identify sectors to target. Location quotients, shift-share analysis, input-output, and location models all provide significant data about the economic structure of a particular region, and can be used to examine the strengths and weaknesses of local economies (Blair 1990; Part III of this volume). Importantly, all of these methods are positive, rather than normative, and do not reflect the values of local residents (Johnson and Cox, Chapter 13). Their objective is to describe the economic structure of a community or region, rather than to discuss what the economic structure *should* be in order for the community to move itself toward a vision consistent with their own values. Thus, while they are based on accurate information and analysis, these methods may recommend targeted strategies that bear little resemblance to local residents' visions for their community. However, an assessment of community goals without an understanding of the underlying economic realities is also likely to flounder. What is required, then, is a development strategy that combines both the positive and normative elements in a way that is accessible and educational to stakeholders in the community (see Deller et al., Chapter 17)

The recognition that community participation is vital to sustainable economic development decision-making has led to the creation of several models that allow communities to discuss their development goals (Mountain Association for Community Economic Development 1997; North Central Regional Center for Rural Development 1997; Community Development Academy 1996). These models also acknowledge the interaction between economic, social, and environmental impacts of development. However, these models lack concrete procedures to determine the community's best opportunities for realizing their goals in the context of the tradeoffs among them. CBM and other new approaches such as the one developed by Deller et al. (Chapter 17) attempt address these deficiencies.

Cox (1996) and Cox, Johnson, and Alwang (1997) also attempt to bridge this gap. In their work, leaders in three Virginia counties were asked to formulate economic development goals using seven indicators of economic, environmental, and social impact. The Analytical Hierarchy Process (AHP) (Saaty 1990) was used to determine the relative importance of each goal to the community. The CBM as it is currently structured builds on this work by using the AHP as the foundation for the elicitation of community preferences. CBM adds a further dimension by surveying businesses on the likelihood of relocation or expansion, and by cataloguing community assets that are valuable to businesses. These new elements are combined with the elicited community preferences to provide indices of the match between communities and businesses.

CBM, therefore, combines positive and normative approaches by merging elements of industrial location models with quantified community preferences (Buescher et al. 2001).[1] The participation of local residents is critical to CBM, but their participation does not mean that economic details are ignored. Community organizers have repeatedly shown that "average" citizens are capable of understanding the economic structure of their communities (Highlander Research and Education Center 1997). With this in mind, CBM combines the rigour of traditional economic models with the local participation and emphasis on the interconnectedness of economic, environmental, and social concerns. CBM adds a quantitative focus on the tradeoffs between economic, environmental, and social concerns, by requiring community members to systematically define and prioritize their goals. In addition, the CBM model incorporates information on the location decisions of small businesses. Results from the CBM model not only pinpoint industries that could be targeted for local economic development, but also identify deficiencies in community assets that could be addressed in order to facilitate the targeting process. As such, this approach adds an important "firm supply" dimension to that of the firms' demand elaborated, for example, in the work of Gabe (Chapter 6) and Leatherman and Kastens (Chapter 7) and elsewhere.

Conceptual model

The overall objective of the CBM model is to assist communities in targeted economic development. First, the community must quantify their goals and assets and then determine whether any businesses are likely to both meet the community's goals for economic development and find the community an attractive place to locate or expand. The best "matches" occur when the goals of the community correspond to the benefits provided by a business, and when the assets of the community correspond with the demands of the business. The CBM process also provides an opportunity for the community to refine its economic development strategies, using the knowledge they gain to evaluate the possible matches identified by the model. The community's engagement allows them to educate themselves in a manner that empowers rather than threatens since the CBM model provides an objective quantitative analysis based on community and business input.

The two dimensions of the CBM model are captured in desirability and compatibility indices that rank potential matches. The desirability index makes use of objective measures of a new or expanded business's impacts on a community along dimensions such as job growth, environmental impacts, fiscal impact, and quality of life issues. A catalogue of the impacts that are currently measured is presented in Table 14.1, below. The desirability of a firm or sector is determined by incorporating community weights on the importance of each of these impacts.

As Cox (1996) and Cox et al. (1997) recognized, identifying businesses that are desirable from the community's point of view fulfils only half of the targeted economic development effort. The businesses also examine the community to see if the community's assets match the business's requirements (Johnson, Chapter 13). To capture this second dimension, the CBM compatibility index measures how well the assets of the community match the requirements of the business. Businesses will be more likely to locate in a community whose assets match their needs for infrastructure, space, labour, and other critical factors. The compatibility index is derived from factors that the businesses indicate are important to them in making location decisions. A significant amount of research has been done on business location decisions (King 1997; McNamara et al. 1995; Blakely 1994; Glaser and Bardo 1991; Goetz 1995, 1997; as well as Chapters 7 to 14 in this volume), which guide data collection for the business database in the CBM model, which along with community assets constitute the building blocks of the compatibility index.

The best matches for a community are businesses that most closely meet the community's economic development goals, indicated by a high desirability value, and which are simultaneously best served by the existing assets of the community, indicated by a high compatibility value. While the compatibility index can focus on assets such as infrastructure and education, it can also be extended to examine the extent to which businesses value existing firms either within a value chain or within their own sector. Thus, the compatibility index can identify firms or sectors whose location and expansion decisions are determined at least in part by clustering and agglomeration externalities. Tables 14.1 and 14.2 identify the indicators used in the pilot study and are discussed in the accompanying text. Potential additions and alterations are considered below in the section on directions for future research.

Despite the quantitative nature of CBM and other development tools, economic development is not an exact science. CBM cannot conclusively identify the "best" sectors for a particular community to target, because many subjective factors such as management style will have a strong impact on the business's appropriateness to a community. For this reason, non-quantitative regional targeting methods such as that outlined by Johnson (Chapter 13) can provide useful inputs through a consensus-building approach. In our view, however, the CBM approach need not exclude this possibility. The use of quantitative measures of preferences can identify differences that exist within the community and provide a solid foundation for discussions leading to consensus. By engaging in the CBM process, community members also gain more technical skills, enabling them to make more informed decisions and rely less on outside consultants for technical assistance. The CBM framework therefore in its use of both positive and normative methods contains the key elements of a community educational programme for targeted development as discussed by Deller et al. (Chapter 17). Information provided by a research team serves both as an input to inform the community about their asset base and as a complement to community preferences, allowing an evaluation of the impacts of businesses on community priorities.

Measuring desirability

Calculation of the desirability index closely follows procedures outlined by Buescher et al. (2001). Four primary goals are identified that include Economic Efficiency, Employment Opportunities, Protection of the Environment, and Existence Quality of Life for local residents. Economic Efficiency measures the potential for business and worker revenues to remain in the local economy. Employment Opportunities measures both the quantity and the quality of jobs offered by a business. Environmental Protection measures a business's stewardship of natural resources, including air and water quality. Existence Quality of Life describes the impact of available jobs on the well-being of the community. Quantifiable indicators are used to identify the underlying characteristics of each goal. Table 14.1 presents the indicators used in the pilot CBM study for each of the four goals.

The category Employment Opportunities, for example, includes the number of jobs available to local residents, the average wage, the level of benefits, and the amount of training provided to employees. Communities identify their priorities among these four indicators, as well as the overall goal of employment opportunity among the other three goals. The CBM model quantifies these contributions by the private sector as business benefits. Desirability is a measure of the strength of the match between the priority ordering of community goals and the ranked contribution of business benefits.

The strength of a match for a particular business *j* depends on the benefits that business *j* would provide to the community and the particular goals of the community. The general form of the Desirability function is given in equation 1:

Desirability of Business$_j$ = D_j (Efficiency, Employment, Environment, Quality of Life)   (1)

The calculation used to create the desirability index follows Bueschler et al. (2001) and Zheng (2000) in its general form, but includes a modification that provides more interpretable measures of the contribution that a business makes to each of the indicators identified in Table 14.1. In addition, the calculation introduced below avoids the possibility that elements of the index cannot be calculated due to division by zero (Burkey 2006). The desirability index of business *j* is given by:

$$D_j \equiv \prod_{i=1}^{I} \left[\prod_{k=1}^{K} (x_{ijk})^{\beta_{ik}} \right]^{\beta_i}$$ (2)

where $i = 1, \ldots, I$ represent the community goals and $k = 1, \ldots, K$ the indicators (or subgoals). The β_i and β_{ik} are respectively, the importance weights placed by the community on the goals and indicators. The weights are derived using the analytical hierarchy process (AHP), which is discussed in greater detail below (see also Johnson, Chapter 13).

The specification of the x_{ijk} term is novel in our application. Following Burkey (2006), we calculate:

$$x_{ijk} = 1 - \frac{|CT_{ik} - BI_{ijk}|}{2R_{ijk}}$$ (3)

where CT_{ik} is the *community target* or the change desired by the community for the *k*th indicator to the *i*th goal. That is, it is the difference between the community's target for the indicator and the existing baseline measure. Importantly, the CT_{ik} measure is independent of the business under consideration. BI_{ijk} is a measure of the impact of the *j*th business on the *k*th indicator of the *i*th goal. It is a measure of the change in the indicator that is expected from the introduction of the new business, and is independent of the community. The R_{ijk} value is the range over which the *k*th indicator for the *i*th goal can vary. The x_{ijk} term, therefore, can range from a value of zero (worst) to 1 (best). The index is zero when the business impact is of the same magnitude

Table 14.1 CBM community goals and indicators

Indicator

I. Economic Efficiency
Every new job generates additional jobs in the community
New businesses return capital to the local economy
New businesses use locally available resources
New businesses increase the local economy

II. Employment Opportunity
New jobs pay at or above liveable wage
New jobs are full-time and permanent
New jobs offer benefits
New jobs provide training programs to increase worker skills

III. Environmental Protection
New businesses make only EPA compliant discharges to water
New businesses report all toxic releases
New businesses are in compliance with hazardous waste management
New businesses are not listed as participants in an active or archived superfund report
New businesses have not been reported for non-compliant air releases

IV. Existence Quality of Life
New businesses effectively increase the average local wage
New businesses increase the local tax base
New businesses are committed to the community as a whole how is this measured

---

but of the opposite sign of the community target. The index is 1 when the business impact completely achieves the community's objectives.

Measuring compatibility

The compatibility index measures the fit between a community's assets and an industry's need for those assets. For example, one industry might be best served by sites near a major airport, whereas another might demand a highly skilled labour force. Communities that lack these assets will likely face challenges in targeting these industries and may decide to develop these assets to assist in their targeting efforts. At the same time, businesses location decisions are complicated and often based on a range of criteria (Goetz 1997; Reum and Harris 2006). These criteria include available land and buildings, access to transportation, utility and telecommunications infrastructure, labour skills and costs, and quality of life (Leatherman and Kastens, Chapter 7; McNamara et al. 1995; Glaser and Bardo 1991). These business demands are matched with community assets, which quantify the availability of these resources at the chosen site.

The CBM model follows the existing literature by incorporating the community assets that have been found to have the most influence on business location decisions into the compatibility index (McNamara et al. 1995; Blakely 1994; Moore et al. 1991). These assets can be grouped roughly into the categories of (i) physical infrastructure and business development resources, (ii) business costs such as wage and tax rates, and (iii) quality of life, which incorporates economic, social, and environmental dimensions. The degree to which a community's stock of a particular asset corresponds with the business's need for that asset determines the compatibility of that business with the community.

The general form of the Compatibility function is given in equation (4):

Compatibility of Business j = C_j (Acreage & Space, Physical Infrastructure, Economic Infrastructure, Quality of Life) (4)

Each of these categories is measured by a number of specific indicators that are presented in Table 14.2.

The functional form of the compatibility index is:

$$C_j \equiv a_j \sum_{m=1}^{M} y_M^{\delta_{mj}}$$ (6)

where $m = 1, \ldots, M$ are the community assets, C_j is the Compatibility index for business j, and $a_j \in [0,1]$ is the business acreage and space coefficient, which is a measure of the proportion of business needs that are met by local resources. The δ_{mj} exponent measures how important asset m is to business j, and the y_m indicator measures how community assets compare to relevant competitors or to objective benchmarks. The calculation for y_m is:

$$y_m = 1 - \left(\frac{Best_m - Com_m}{Best_m - Worst_m} \right)$$

Where:

$Best_m$ is the best case value for asset m,
$Worst_m$ is the worst case value for asset m,
Com_m is the community's value for asset m.

Thus, $y_m \in [0,1]$ and equals 1 when the community has the best value for asset m across all relevant comparisons and zero when it has the worst.

Method

Five main blocks of data form the basis of CBM. The data include (1) a community profile, quantifying the community's goals for economic development, (2) the assets individual communities offer businesses, (3) a database of business survey responses quantifying the ranked preferences for assets and goals, (4) purchased data from Harris Info specific to the businesses included

Table 14.2 Indicators of community assets

I. Environmental Protection
Local Wastewater Remediation Costs
Local Toxic Release Cleanup Costs
Hazardous Wastes Remediation Costs
Superfund Redevelopment Costs
EPA Air Quality Remediation Costs

II. Quality of Life
Average Wage Jobs
Living Wage Jobs
Employee Benefits
Local Tax Base
Income Distribution
Proprietor Income

III. Available Land and Building Space
Available Undeveloped Land
Available Undeveloped Land with Infrastructure
Available Undeveloped Land with Partial Infrastructure
Available Undeveloped Land near Infrastructure
Available Warehouse Space
Available Manufacturing/Operations Space
Available Office Space
Available Retail Space

IV. Infrastructure and Business Development Resource Availability
3-Phase Electric Power
Natural Gas Pipeline
Internet/High Speed Telecommunications
High-Volume Water Supply
High-Volume Wastewater Supply
High-Volume Solid Waste Disposal
Access to Ponds and Streams
Available Commercial Sites with Room for Future Expansion
Mass Transportation for Workers
Community Job Training Programs
Local Development Assistant
State Development Assistance
Competitive Commercial Real Estate Sales Market
Competitive Commercial Real Estate Leasing Market
Community College
Quality Health Care

V. Business Costs, Resources, and Other Indices
Local Labour Costs
Local Business Tax Rate
Average Worker's Compensation Tax Rate
Local Commercial Loan Rate
Cost of Living Index
Retail Shopping Expenditure
Local Crime Rate

in the surveys, and (5) third-party information such as IMPLAN analyses and the Censtats databases containing county-level characteristics provided by the US Census Bureau. Other third-party data sources include state and county annual reports, BLS and BEA data on labour and employment, County Business Patterns, and EPA data on environmental quality. Together, these allow analytical inferences to be drawn regarding the benefits and impacts these businesses bring to communities. Desirability and Compatibility are calculated directly from this information.

Community goals

The community goals are determined by means of a community goals survey. The community goal elicitation is fundamental to the CBM process for two reasons. First, goals prescribed by elected or other designated decision-makers in a community have limited ownership by citizens as a whole. Focus groups that include representatives of different stakeholder groups ensure that priorities relevant to their interests are identified. The process also signals to the community that the process is inclusive of diverse community voices. Second, research into multicriterion decision-making repeatedly finds the same result: priorities and preferences of the group are more intelligent and consistent (an internal logic metric) than priorities and preferences of individuals (Saaty 2000). The goal survey is then conducted using representative focus groups or randomized from the community as a whole. Whichever method is used, care must be taken to avoid bias in the sample: in other words, it is important to include representative interests, age groups, and genders.

Goals are evaluated using the AHP algorithm designed by Saaty (1986). In parallel to the calculation of the desirability index, the task of determining community objectives is broken into component criteria (goals) and the goals are further broken into component indicators. The literature of decision psychology (Bazerman et al. 1999; see also Dehaene 1997 for an overview) affirms that individuals are generally less skilled at ranking lists of ideas, but more skilled at choosing their preference between two ideas presented as a pairwise comparison. In the case of the CBM, the multiple criteria are the goals of Economic Efficiency, Employment Opportunity, Environmental Protection, and Existence Quality of Life (Table 14.1). Individuals in the focus groups are introduced to the idea of the pairwise comparison (Table 14.3a) in which they choose which of two indicators of the goal is more important to them, and then how much more important is that preferred indicator. Each indicator within a goal is compared in this way with the others. After evaluating the indicators, individuals are asked to make pairwise comparisons across the broader goals. Table 14.3a contains the cover sheet, which introduces the respondents to the survey format. The balance of the survey contains similar questions for each goal so that pairwise comparisons for all the indicators within each goal are made. The final page, presented as Table 14.3b, asks the respondents to make the comparisons at the level of the goals.[2]

The survey in this format was used in the Anaconda, Montana pilot that is discussed in more detail below. In this application, individuals in the focus group completed their surveys independently. The AHP is also suited to generating consensus values. This can be done either in an initial survey (Saaty 2000) or after using the individual surveys to provide background information on the diversity of views.

The comparison scale (1 to 9 – see Tables 14.3a and 14.3b) has been shown to perform well in measuring strength of preferences (Dehaene 1997; Saaty 1977). Preference weights are derived using the procedures of Saaty and Vargas (1979 and 1984b). The weights prioritize both goals (criteria) and indicators in discrete calculations.

Tables 14.3a and 14.3b demonstrate that each indicator and each goal is pairwise compared with all of the others. Preferences across each pair are measured on a scale from 1 to 9. If each indicator (or goal) of the pairwise choice is valued equally, the scale ranking is 1. Alternatively, if one is preferred, the extent to which it is preferred is indicated by an integer in the interval [2, 9]. The extent to which this preference represents an intensity weighting on the difference between the two goals is a matter of some discussion in the literature (Saaty and Ozdemir 2003). Investigation and testing of the various claims is the subject of subsequent work by these authors. In our discussion of future research we consider an alternative approach that can robustly determine magnitudes of differences in pairwise comparisons, based on the economic concept of willingness to pay.

A benefit of the Saaty methodology is that it incorporates a check on the logical consistency of responses (Saaty and Vargas 1984a). Inconsistencies can enter the AHP process in two ways. First, intransitivities across items can occur. Referring to Table 14.3b, consider the following example. Suppose in Row 1 that the left choice "Economic Efficiency" is indicated as preferred to "Employment Opportunity", and in Row 2 "Environmental Protection" is preferred to "Economic Efficiency". If in Row 4, "Employment Opportunity" is preferred to "Environmental Protection" and intransitivity is observed. In addition inconsistencies with regard to the intensity weightings can arise. If "Economic Efficiency" is preferred to "Employment Opportunity" by 3 (moderately more important), and "Employment Opportunity" is preferred to "Quality of Life" by 2, then "Economic Efficiency" should be preferred to "Quality of Life" by 8; however, respondents do not always make this choice. When a significant number of individuals give inconsistent responses, the indicators and goals should be considered suspect and it is advisable to develop more clearly distinguishable comparisons. In the pilot study, individuals with more than 10 per cent inconsistent responses were omitted from the analysis.

The results of the Anaconda, Montana data are consistent with the existing literature from the Saaty school. They demonstrate that the internal consistency of the summarized data (the single vector of weights calculated for the group) is very high, independently of the inconsistency of select

Table 14.3a Community goals questionnaire

Survey of Community Priorities for Economic Development

This survey asks you to compare several specific goals and sub-goals of a local economy. Every item is compared in a pair wise manner, meaning, for each pair, you need to answer

1. which of these two things is most important to me, and
2. how much more important is the goal I circled than the other goal?

Keep in mind the relative importance of each goal-pair and how it ranks in your mind within the whole group.

The example below shows you what we are expecting in the way of your participation.

Which is more important? (Circle one)		Equal	Moderately more important		Strongly more important		Very strongly more important		Extremely more important
every new job generates additional jobs in the community or	the new business returns capital to the local economy	1	2	3	④	5	6	7	8	9

In the example above, the answers mean the survey-taker felt having more jobs created locally for each new job was four times more important than having the new business get its supplies locally.

You will compare five pages of choices. The first four pages compare economic sub-goals in the goal categories of "Economic Efficiency," "Employment Opportunities," "Environmental Protection," and "Quality of Life." The fifth page asks you to then rank the each goal category. A glossary of terms used in this survey can be found on the last page.

Thank you for your participation!

Table 14.3b Community goals questionnaire

Category Comparisons

Now that you have considered thoughtfully some components of each category of economic well-being, please compare the categories themselves. Keep in mind the relative importance of each goal-pair and how it ranks in your mind within the whole group.

Which is more important? (Circle one)		Equal	Moderately more important		Strongly more important		Very strongly more important		Extremely more important
Economic Efficiency	or Employment Opportunity	1	2	3	4	5	6	7	8	9
Economic Efficiency	or Environmental Protection	1	2	3	4	5	6	7	8	9
Economic Efficiency	or Quality of Life	1	2	3	4	5	6	7	8	9
Employment Opportunity	or Environmental Protection	1	2	3	4	5	6	7	8	9
Employment Opportunity	or Quality of Life	1	2	3	4	5	6	7	8	9
Environmental Protection	or Quality of Life	1	2	3	4	5	6	7	8	9

individuals. Future analyses will test the degree of influence inconsistent individuals have on synthesized rankings. Inconsistency values for indicators within goals, for all indicators, and for the goals are reported in the section below on the Anaconda pilot. All incomplete surveys were omitted from analyses.

Community assets

The community assets that enter the compatibility calculation are listed in Table 14.2. The values of these assets are identified either by the community steering committee or from other sources. Economic data such as that related to employment multipliers comes from IMPLAN (see Deller, Chapter 19, for a more detailed discussion of IMPLAN). For the environmental assessment data, local government officials have access to EPA databases to which researchers outside of local government do not have access. In addition, CenStats and Community Business Patterns data may be used to complete the data required for the analyses. In some cases, experts may have to inventory their local resources. However, communities that have completed the data gathering process for CBM have without exception and repeatedly reported that the data gathered for CBM have been useful.

Business profiles

Primary business survey data were collected during 2003 and 2006 as part of a joint effort between the University of Hawaii, Manoa, University of Montana, and University of Nevada. Data for a sample of 2,129 firms were purchased from Dun and Bradstreet in 2003, and a sample of 2,700 firms in 2006, that contained a general description of US firms including size, revenue, contact information, and CEO's or manager's name. Researchers selected the initial group of businesses to survey from a sample of the fastest growing national industry sectors that pay above-average wages. A stratified sample that included firms from each NAICS sector was created. Within each NAICS sector, 10 individual firms were chosen at random.

To supplement the survey, Harris Info Source data was purchased for the selected firms to integrate with the community asset information. Community Business Patterns and Censtats data also supplemented the database of business characteristics and economic influence on communities.

In the first survey (2003), after the sample had been selected, the survey questionnaire was sent to the manager or the CEO of each firm. Following this first round of surveys, reminder cards were sent to those firms that had not returned their survey after two weeks. Because of the limited response from the mail survey, telephone surveys were conducted from sample groups until an adequate sample had been obtained. In 2006, all surveys were conducted by telephone. The total number of completed questionnaires was 213 of 2,129 for the 2003 data and 1,064 of 2,700 for the 2006 data, constituting a total response rate of 26.4 per cent (1,277 of 4,829 firms) with a 10 per cent rate using the mail survey (2003) and 39 per cent for the phone survey (2006).

The response rate was larger for the 2006 survey for a number of reasons. The 2003 mail survey often did not end up in the hands of the appropriate person. As the interviewers became more skilled at the process, they discovered that a telephone survey allowed them to connect with the right person more quickly. The 2006 data set did not include all subsidiaries and branch offices that were found in the 2003 data set, which allowed more small firms to be represented and therefore drawn in the sample. Small firms were more willing to participate, although this type of clarity is costly given the challenges of identifying the motivations behind expansion and relocation decisions. In the Vermont CBM analysis, the response rate to the business questionnaire was 19.4 per cent (Buescher et al. 2001). The response rate to this study compares favourably with the response rates to similar studies by Buescher et al. (2001) and Moore et al. (1991).

The business questionnaire contained four sections. The first section asked questions about the general status of the firm, including the firm's NAICS code, contact information, size, revenue, and other internal information, ending with the question, how likely is the firm to move or relocate in the next five years?

The second section elicited the self-explicated importance rating for a series of factors. Details on the factors are reported in the Appendix. Topics such as location, transportation, proximity to the market, natural resource supply, technology support, natural environment amenities, location size capacity, labour supply potentials, local tax benefit, employees' compensation plan and recreational opportunity, local residence security, and public service support are covered. The factors in this section were selected based on the literature review introduced previously and incorporated elements of various established firm location theories as well as newly emerging practices. For example, these factors incorporate concerns raised from the purely economic perspective such as proximity to the market. They also contain factors that cannot be adjusted by the firms directly, such as natural environmental amenities, as well as institutional factors such as local tax benefits and public service support.

The third section contained the decision variables. The first question asked firms to reveal whether they had moved in the past five years. This is commonly known in other studies as the revealed choice (Guimarães et al. 1998). The second question asked firms to indicate how likely they were to move or expand in the next five years. Respondents rated their firms' propensity to relocate on a scale from 1 to 4, where 1 represented very unlikely and 4 stood for very likely. This type of responses is often known as stated choice or stated preference (Bateman et al. 2004). Therefore, for each firm the data contain two types of decisions: a binary response for the past relocation activity and an ordered response for future relocation decisions.

The last section of the survey contained questions pertaining to a firm's preference for a relocation site. Those firms that did not indicate any propensity to relocate were not queried, since participants were often impatient or non-responsive when asked about activities they that they have no interest in. In the future, more effort will be directed toward these non-respondents in order to ensure that the business database is not biased.

Results from the Anaconda pilot

The community of Anaconda, Montana faced many challenges when the copper smelter closed in 1980. Community leaders were interested in the CBM model because they felt that the programmes to address the development of entrepreneurs and business retention and expansion were already in place. Although these programmes were effective, community leaders felt that business recruitment should be investigated as a means of economic development. The experiences and outcomes from a pilot study in Anaconda, Montana are presented here to highlight what a community could expect in making the decision to engage in CBM.

Sustainable development efforts require that all interested members of the community be involved in the decision-making (Deller et al., Chapter 17). With CBM, a community profile is developed through meetings with and research by interested local residents. The timeline in Table 14.4 outlines the community meetings that are needed to engage in CBM. In contrast to Buescher et al. (2001), the community committee met more than twice and was structured in two tiers. The first tier was a small group of three that involved a community facilitator, an economic development professional who was head of the Anaconda Community Development organization, and a small-business owner who was knowledgeable and committed to the project and to the community at large. The community facilitator was an extension agent, who provided an interface between the community and the researchers running the CBM model. The larger group had 15 members and included additional community and business leaders. The small steering community worked on CBM-related issues on a bi-weekly basis and ensured the meetings that involved the second tier were as productive as possible.

While the pilot took longer than one year, the group basically engaged in a series of meetings as described in Table 14.4. In future applications, these meeting would likely take nine months. After these meetings are completed, the group should expect to meet for about three more months to develop a follow-up strategy.

The follow-up strategy will vary depending on the community. For example, one community might decide they need an asset such as a better rail line in order to raise their compatibility score for a target industry. This would mean that some effort would need to be put into grants writing or other activities that would raise the funds needed to enhance the asset. The CBM results could serve as justification for this effort. Another community might approach members of the targeted industry that was identified as desirable and compatible.

Table 14.4 Timeline for CBM meetings

Month	To Do
1	Provide CBM overview
2	Organize CBM steering committee. Steering committee is 15–25 people from across the community that is interested in economic development. Should include 2–3 people for the executive team. Executive team has more commitment and understanding of process.
3	More in-depth CBM discussion. Complete goal rankings.
4	Review goal rankings. Begin asset assessment.
5	Continue asset assessment.
6	Examine initial CBM results
7	Look at individual business profiles based on CBM results.
8	Select two or three business types and begin to brainstorm how to approach them.
9	Continue working on the business approach.

The CBM steering committee in Anaconda decided that opportunities existed for the county in the construction sector. While committee members were interested in recruiting members of this industry, they also met with local construction firms to assess the possibilities for growth. The group quickly recognized that a critical mass of available construction projects did not exist in the county, but they did exist in nearby counties. They formed a construction business association that developed into a builders association. After pooling their resources, co-op agreements that included subcontractor templates were initiated, a "plan exchange" was formulated, and a blueprint copy service was set up at the Anaconda Local Development Corporation (ALDC). The plan exchange gave greater access to local contractors to bid on projects outside the area. The association also put together a marketing campaign aimed at general contractors to position themselves as major subcontractors. Web sites, DVD demo, and brochures aimed at new residents interested in building custom homes were developed. Traditionally, builders located in larger communities in which architects reside have won these contracts. Since the CBM effort was initiated, Anaconda's construction businesses have grown and are working in other communities. Some have been competitive with larger, local contractors and have won multi-million-dollar contracts.

The benefits associated with the CBM process can be contrasted with those from a business retention and expansion programme that had previously been conducted in the community. A critical difference between the two efforts was the sector specificity of the CBM application. After identifying the construction sector as a target, the community spent considerable time examining industries that supply inputs and purchase the outputs of the construction industry. Thus, the cluster of activities associated with construction and the positive agglomeration externalities within the industry were explicitly considered. The benefits derived from this activity support the arguments that have been stressed by Porter and others on the importance of these effects. In particular, the community was more able to understand the economies of scale associated with industry clusters because the CBM model organizes the analysis based on industries rather than individual businesses and stresses the importance of various assets to an industry.

Another outcome of the CBM effort is the ALDC's recruitment of firms that supply the inputs needed by the construction industry or firms that need construction services. As a result, three such firms have come to the area, including two manufactured housing plants and one supplier of insulation products to major west coast distributors. While both of these businesses are small, employing fewer than 14 employees, the community hopes they will grow to firms of 25–50 employees.

The Steering Committee feels that they now have much insight into what businesses need and can pool resources for growth. The goals helped the community understand what is important, what to focus on, and how to partner with the larger Butte-Silverbrow County to successfully attract new business. Their success led to a six-county regional CBM project.

Areas for future research

The success of the Anaconda pilot suggests that the CBM can help communities identify and achieve development goals. Lessons learned in Anaconda and in pilots currently underway, however, suggest that the implementation of the CBM model can be improved. Further research is warranted in several areas. First, variants of, or alternatives to, the existing method for eliciting community preferences should be developed and tested. Since community input is at the heart of the CBM method, improvements in this area are a high priority. A particular concern is the high number of individuals who give inconsistent responses. Other areas to ripe for refinement include methods of (i) aggregating preferences, (ii) clarifying question content, and (iii) strengthening the data underlying the index calculations.

The earlier discussion noted that the current methodology of eliciting community preferences makes it easy to identify individuals who make inconsistent responses. An important priority, however, is to improve the questionnaire to minimize the inconsistencies. Debriefing sessions in pilots currently underway suggest that while the pairwise comparison is a viable question style, exhaustive pairwise comparisons may confuse and frustrate respondents, especially when they realize that the question style makes these inconsistencies likely. Confusion among respondents can also arise when the content of questions is vague. Comparing job gains to fiscal gains, for example, is difficult when there are no magnitudes associated with these benefits. Improvements in the questionnaire, then, are possible with regard to both question format and question content.

With regard to format, three alternatives in the literature warrant consideration. One possibility is to ask directly about a specific goal or indicator, rating its importance on an ordered Likert scale. This is a cognitively much simpler process than the pairwise comparisons, and this method allows weights to be calculated as in the AHP. A drawback of this methodology is that since no direct comparison between goals in the direct rating question style is made, it is not clear what kind of internal comparison the respondent is making when determining each individual rating. The stability of responses in this type of format relative to pairwise comparisons is a research question of some interest in the literature on non-market valuation. It appears that results are sensitive to the characteristics of the goal under consideration (Alevy, List, and Adamowicz 2006). Whether this question style will be an improvement over the pairwise comparisons remains an open question.

A second approach would be to retain pairwise comparisons but structure the questions so that each goal was compared with only one other. This would simplify the question style that is presented in Table 14.3b. Eliminating the repetition of questions about a specific goal imposes consistent responses. Relatively simple tests can be conducted to determine the effectiveness of this approach.

A final survey variant would utilize pairwise comparisons, but import techniques from the non-market valuation and marketing literatures to provide more nuanced information on preferences and be interpretable with traditional economic theory. This elicitation mechanism requires that the magnitude of goals vary across questions. Varying the magnitudes allows the researcher to identify marginal values for tradeoffs across goals, providing detail otherwise unavailable.

A further concern regarding the elicitation of community preferences is how to ensure that the results truly represent the community's views. The most common way of ensuring representativeness is to sample randomly from the population. In the CBM context, it is likely that budgetary and logistical issues will often make this approach unfeasible. An alternative would be to collect additional information about those who do respond. Econometric modelling that compares the characteristics of responders to those of the broader community would shed light on whether and how the responses should be weighted to better reflect the makeup of the community. A benefit of explicitly accounting for the heterogeneity in the community is that it will remind researchers and community leaders that aggregating preferences into a single number can obscure a diversity of interests across different segments of the population. This diversity may be relevant for decision-making since equity associated with the economic development effort may affect sustainability.

Additional efforts to improve measures of community assets and of business impacts could strengthen the CBM methodology. All asset values that can be taken from standardized government surveys should be integrated into the compatibility calculation. In some instances, more subjective measures have been used, and the robustness and defensibility of the results would be strengthened if this practice were minimized. For example the quality of education and of health care has relied on subjective measures, when Census and other data are available to make meaningful comparisons between communities. Using the Census data would strengthen the compatibility index, but the subjective assessments could still be collected to provide insight on the extent to which communities made realistic evaluation of their assets. Similar work on business impacts would strengthen the calculation of the desirability index, for example by generating indices of environmental impacts from EPA databases. Standardizing the underlying data would foster research across communities, if the CBM methodology were widely applied.

A long-term CBM agenda would require a time series of business survey responses. A subset of this data should include a panel in which the same institutions are surveyed over time. This will facilitate applied research on the factors driving firm expansion and relocation decisions. At the same time, a more robust business database is needed since non-respondent bias is a concern. Not all industries were included in the survey, and a long-term strategy for sampling across all industries is needed. Communities may also engage in the CBM process more than once, and therefore an up-to-date business database would be required.

Finally, monitoring and evaluation of outcomes of the CBM process would be beneficial. Communities face different resource constraints and may have different goals. A thorough understanding of the benefits and challenges encountered by communities would prove very useful in refining the CBM model. This information will also prove useful as researchers continue to examine the merits of industry targeting.

Conclusions

To ensure that industrial targeting has the highest possibility of success, input from residents is needed (Johnson, Chapter 13). Without citizen input, the community may not attempt to actively attract and retain the new businesses. The Community Business Matching process takes the goals of the community and demands of business to determine which industries are desirable based on the community's goals and compatible based on the community's assets. The CBM model derives a list of industries that may locate in an area, and therefore a more targeted and efficient local industrial targeting programme can evolve.

The CBM process also provides local decision-makers with information about local resource deficiencies that arise for a given industry that they want to recruit. If this local resource can be improved upon or expanded by public investment or policies to increase probability of success for targeted industries and industry clusters, a more efficient and effective public investment and policy can evolve (Gabe, Chapter 6; Woodward and Guimarães, Chapter 5). At the same time, community involvement in the process of identifying target industries allows the community to learn more about what it really takes to attract an industry. This allows the community to educate themselves and become more technically empowered to help themselves, which is likely to provide more sustainable economic development in the long run (Deller et al., Chapter 17).

Notes

1   A two-dimensional matching process has been developed by Hunker (1974) and Shaffer (1989).
2   The full survey is available on request.

References

Alevy, J.E., Adamowicz, W., and List, J.A. (2006) " 'More is less': preference reversals and non-market valuation", University of Maryland Working Paper.

Ayres, J. (1996) "Essential elements of strategic visioning", in N. Walzer (Ed.) *Community Strategic Visioning Programs*, Westport, CT: Praeger.

Barkley, D., and Henry, M. (1997) "Rural development: to cluster or not to cluster?" *Review of Agricultural Economics*, 19(2): 308–25.

Bateman, I., et al. (2002) *Economic Valuation with Stated Preference Techniques: A Manual*, Cheltenham, UK: Edward Elgar.

Bazerman, M.H., Moore, D.A., Tenbrunsel, A.E., Wade-Benzoni, K.A., and Blount, S. (1999) "Explaining how preferences change across joint versus separate evaluation", *Journal of Economic Behavior and Organization*, 39: 41–58.

Blair, J. (1990) *Urban and Regional Economics*, Homewood, IL: Richard D. Irwin.

Blakely, E. (1994) *Planning Local Economic Development: Theory and Practice* (2nd edn), Thousand Oaks, CA: Sage.

Bonnett, T.W. (1993) *Strategies for Rural Competitiveness: Policy Options for State Governments*, Washington, DC: Council of Governors' Policy Advisors.

Buescher, M., Sullivan, P., Halbrendt, C., and Lucas, M. (2001) "The Community Business Matching project: new tool for rural development", *Journal of Sustainable Agriculture*, 17(4): 57–74.

Burkey, J. (2006) "CBM project analysis and design", unpublished, University Center for Economic Development, University of Nevada-Reno.

Community Development Academy. (1996) *Building Communities from the Grassroots*, St Louis: University of Missouri Press.

Courant, P. (1995) "How would you know a good economic development strategy if you tripped over one? Hint: don't just count jobs", *National Tax Journal*, 47(4): 863–81.

Cox, A. (1996) "Proactive industrial targeting: an application of the analytical hierarchy process", Master's Thesis, Virginia Technical University.

Cox, A., Alwang, J., and Johnson, T. (1997) "Local Preferences for Economic Development Outcomes", Unpublished work in the Department of Agricultural and Applied Economics, Virginia Polytechnic Institute and State University.

Eisinger, P. (1995) "State economic development in the 1990s: politics and policy learning", *Economic Development Quarterly*, 9: 146–58

Dehaene, S. (1997) *The Number Sense: How the Mind Creates Mathematics*, New York: Oxford University Press.

Galston, W., and Baehler, K. (1995) *Rural Development in the United States: Connecting Theory, Practice, and Possibilities*, Washington, DC: Island Press.

Glaser, M., and Bardo, J. (1991) "The impact of quality of life on recruitment and retention of key personnel", *American Review of Public Administration*, 21(1): 57–72.

Goetz, S. (1997) "State- and county-level determinants of food manufacturing establishment growth: 1987–93", *American Journal of Agricultural Economics*, 79: 838–50.

Guimarães P., Rolfe, R., and Woodward, D. (1998) "Regional incentives and industrial location in Puerto Rico", *International Regional Science Review*, 21(2): 119–38.

Hansen, N.M. (1970) *Rural Poverty and the Urban Crisis*, Bloomington, IN: Indiana University Press.

Highlander Research and Education Center. (1997) *A Very Popular Economic Education Sampler*, New Market, TN: Author.

Hunker, H. (1974) *Industrial Development: Concepts and Principles*, Lexington, MA: D.C. Heath.

Kilkenny, M., and Melkonyan, T. 2002 "Local fiscal strategy to retain heterogeneous firms", *Journal of Regional Science*, 42(4): 753–71.

King, L. (1997) "Assets and Constraints of Small Business Manufacturers in Vermont". Unpublished Honours Thesis, Department of Community Development and Applied Economics, University of Vermont.

McCoy, M., and Filson, G. (1996) "Working off the farm: impact on quality of life", *Social Indicators Research*, 37: 149–63.

McNamara, K., and Green, G. (1988) "Local and regional economic development practitioners", *Journal of the Community Development Society*, 19: 42–55.

McNamara, K., Kriesel, W., and Rainey, D. (1995) "Manufacturing recruitment as a rural development strategy", in D. Sears and N. Reed (eds), *Rural Development Strategies*, Chicago: Nelson-Hall.

Moore, B., Tyler, P., and Elliot, D. (1991) "The influence of regional development incentives and infrastructure on the location of small and medium sized companies in Europe", *Urban Studies*, 28(6): 1001–26.

Mountain Association for Community Economic Development. (1997) *Communities by Choice: An Introduction to Sustainable Community Development*, Berea, KY: Author.

North Central Regional Center for Rural Development. (1997) *Working Toward Community Goals: Helping Communities Succeed*, Ames, IA: Author.

Phillips, P.D. (1990) *Economic Development for Small Communities and Rural Areas*, Urbana-Champaign, IL: University of Illinois Press.

Reum, A., and Harris, T. (2006) "Exploring firm location beyond simple growth models: a double hurdle application", *The Journal of Regional Analysis and Policy*, 36: 45–67.

Saaty, T.L. (1977) "A scaling method for priorities in hierarchical structures", *Journal of Mathematical Psychology*, 15(3): 234–81.

——. (1986) "Axiomatic foundations of the Analytic Hierarchy and Network Processes (AHP/ANP)", *Management Science*, 32(7): 843–55.

——. (1990) *Multicriteria Decision-making: The Analytic Hierarchy Process*, Pittsburgh: RWS Publications.

——. (2000) *Fundamentals of Decision-making and Priority Theory*, Vol IV, AHP Series, Pittsburgh: RWS Publications.

Saaty T.L., and Ozdemir, M. (2003) "Why the magic number seven plus or minus two", *Mathematical and Computer Modeling*, 38(3–4): 233–44.

Saaty, T.L., and Vargas, L.G. (1979) "Estimating technological coefficients by the Analytic Hierarchy Process", *Socio-Economic Planning Services*, 13(6): 333–6.

——. (1984a) "Inconsistency and rank preservation", *Journal of Mathematical Psychology*, 29(2): 205–14

——. (1984b) "Comparison of eigenvalue, logarithmic least squares and least squares methods in estimating ratios", *Mathematical Modeling*, 5(5): 309–24.

Shaffer, R. (1989) *Community Economics: Economic Structure and Change in Smaller Communities*, Ames: Iowa State University Press.

Tweeten, L., and Brinkman, G.L. (1976) *Micropolitan Development: Theory and Practice of Greater Rural Economic Development*, Ames: Iowa State University Press.

Winder, R. (1969) "Economic development and social change", in *Proceedings of Government Relations and Planning Conference*, Washington DC: American Institute of Planners.

Zheng, Y. (2000) "An Application of the Community Business Matching Model in Enosburg Falls, Vermont". Unpublished Master's Thesis, University of Vermont.

Part III

Applications and case studies

15 Identifying food industry clusters

A comparison of analytical tools

Stephan J. Goetz, Martin Shields, and Qiuyan Wang

Introduction

Other chapters in this volume apply particular analytical tools and methods to specific communities or industries with the goal of identifying opportunities for targeted regional economic development. This chapter takes a different approach by examining how alternative analytical tools rank specific food sector clusters in counties of Pennsylvania or the Northeast US for potential support by public policy-makers. In particular, we apply several analytical tools to empirically identify industry clusters within the food and agriculture industry: local employment analysis, location quotients, shift-share analysis, analysis of wages, bubble charts, local Moran statistics, locational correlations, and input-output analysis. These analytical tools are not meant to be exhaustive or necessarily conclusive. However, they do generate substantial information that can help us better understand the competitive advantage of particular food and agriculture industries. In turn, this can be useful for identifying targeted investment and workforce and economic development strategies.

The analysis is based on data from the County Business Patterns, the Census of Agriculture, and the IMPLAN (Impact Planning for Analysis, from the Minnesota IMPLAN Group) database for the food and agriculture industry in Northeast US counties, with a special focus on Pennsylvania. By clarifying local employment concentrations and trends in wages and establishments, industry cluster analysis can provide a solid foundation and effective tool around which planning, policy-making and service delivery activities can be focused (Herr 2003: iii). This study aims to identify areas of local competitive advantage in the food and agriculture industry that will likely provide for future employment growth. Ideally, the results will help to focus public sector investments to those areas with the highest potential for economic growth.

The primary dataset used in this analysis is the 1998 and 2001 County Business Patterns (CBP) data (US Bureau of Census), covering establishments, employment, and wages by county at the six-digit NAICS (North American Industry Classification System) level. Since CBP data do not include agriculture, we use 2002 Census of Agriculture data to identify farm clusters in the region (US Department of Agriculture 2002). For the input-output analysis (Pennsylvania only), we use the 2000 and 2001 IMPLAN databases.

The chapter is organized into three sections. The first section reviews the concept of industry clusters as a framework for identifying the Northeast region's key food and related agricultural industries. The second section presents results of our analysis, while the third provides a summary and conclusions. Our main objective is to show that different analytical tools identify different combinations and sets of food and agricultural clusters. Thus, readers should use caution when comparing the results obtained from different methods.

The concept of industry clusters

Numerous definitions can be found in the literature for industry clusters (see also Shields et al., Chapter 3, and Woodward and Guimarães, Chapter 5), as discussed in other chapters of this volume. Gibbs and Bernat (1997: 18) suggest that this variety of definitions is due to the different types of clustering that exist, and to the difficulty of precisely measuring cluster features. The Colorado Department of Labor and Employment (2003: 1) describes industry clusters as follows:

> An industry cluster can be a group of interrelated industries that drive wealth creation within a region, primarily through the export of goods and services. An industry cluster may consist of industries that share the same or similar workforce, factors of production or infrastructure. It may also be defined by the production of similar outputs, complementary output or other interdependent relations. Unlike the traditional Standard Industrial Classification (SIC) System or the North American Industry Classification System (NAICS), industry clusters can represent the entire value chain of a broadly defined industry from shared suppliers to end products, including supporting services and specialized infrastructure. Analyses of industry clusters therefore, help in defining economic drivers (key industries) within a geographic region, and facilitate a better understanding of regional economies and how they evolve over time.

The emphasis on exports is important. Regional economists for many years have distinguished between basic and non-basic activity in a given region. For the most part, basic activity involves *exports* from the region, that is, the activity brings new income and wealth into the local economy. Regional exports vary greatly (e.g., cars, chocolates or legal services), and they are usually driven by competitive advantage. A key distinction is that the non-basic sectors do not in and of themselves generate new income or wealth, although our thinking around this is also changing – see, e.g., Markusen (2007). Instead, they serve to make the basic economy function. Examples include grocery stores, retailers such as Wal-Mart, or hairdressers. While non-basic sectors are important, their contribution to local prosperity usually depends closely on the prosperity of the basic sector. In other words, they are not themselves direct generators of new growth or economic activity. This, along with the fact that manufacturers also tend to pay higher wages, explains why industrial recruiters generally pursue manufacturing facilities that export goods outside the region, rather than retailers. It also explains why the loss of a manufacturer, as opposed to a retailer, is usually seen as a significant loss to a community.

In terms of data, establishment counts, earnings, or employment numbers are typically used in the types of analyses presented here. We maintain that establishments are the best unit of analysis, where applicable, because establishments are most closely aligned with the concept of a cluster. After all, clusters are about *firms* competing cooperatively, or cooperating competitively with one another (Porter 2003). Thus, it is the number of establishments or firms that matters most in identifying clusters, rather than the size of the workforce. Another important advantage of using establishment counts is that they are never suppressed because of disclosure rules, whereas employment data may be, especially in rural areas. Nevertheless, because jobs are of primary interest to decision-makers, we present results using both employment and establishment data (employment data are imputed where necessary).

Analytical tools

To identify the Northeast region's food and agriculture industry clusters, we compare the following analytical tools (see also Munnich 1999 and Smith 2003: 5). A number of these are also discussed by other authors in this book. These tools are neither complete nor do they necessarily provide conclusive results. They are simply means of helping us better understand the *potential* competitive advantage of particular food and agricultural industries. Although some of the tools described require specialized software, much of the analysis can be completed in a spreadsheet.

To allow for a general discussion and following the notation in Ellison and Glaeser (1997), we use $i = 1, 2, \ldots, I$ to index counties. Furthermore, we have $m = 1, 2, \ldots, M$ different industries and let $X_{1m}, X_{2m}, \ldots, X_{Im}$ denote employment in industry m in a given county. In our specific application, we have 300 counties in the Northeast US, and we analyse data on establishments in the food industry, a subset of which are candidates for clusters, and we have subindustry data such as beverages and canning establishments as well as employment numbers by industry at the county level (X_{im}), as well as establishment-level employment data (the latter are not required for most of the analyses presented here).

Local employment analysis

In local employment analysis (LEA), the percentage of local employment in a particular industry or sector is calculated to identify the relative importance of that industry to the local economy: $LE\%_i = X_{im}/X_i \times 100$, where X_{im} is employment in industry m and $X_i = \Sigma_m X_{im}$ refers to total employment (across all industries) in the county or community. As an additional step, changes over time in the employment shares can be calculated and analysed to identify potential threats to, and opportunities for, the local employment base. It should be noted that "high concentrations of employment do not specifically correlate into competitive advantages" (Smith 2003: 5). Often this information is supplemented with recent employment growth rates in the different sectors ($[X_{b+t,im}/X_{b,im} - 1] \times 100$), where b refers to the base year and $b + t$ refers to a subsequent period (e.g., five or 10 years later).

Location quotients

The location quotient (LQ) extends LEA and is, perhaps, the most widely used tool in industry cluster analysis. The LQ is calculated as the share (per cent) of employment or earnings in a given local industry divided by the share of employment in that industry nationally: $LQ_{im} = (X_{im}/X_i)/(X_{um}/X_u)$ where the subscript u refers to national employment numbers (US). Basically, the LQ compares the relative importance of the sector locally with that sector's relative importance nationally. For example, if 30 per cent of all jobs in a community are in manufacturing while nationally 15 per cent of all jobs are in that sector, then the LQ is (30%/15%) = 2.0. In this case, manufacturing is "relatively more important" to the local economy than it is nationally. The opposite would be true if the local share were only 10 per cent, in which case the LQ = (10%/15%) = 0.66. Thus, the LQ goes beyond the LEA coefficient by comparing the local economy to the national or state economy (depending on the objective). The LQ is used to identify a region's "defining industries" (Wilkerson and Williams 2007). Several important assumptions underlie this measure, however, which are often ignored (for a discussion of these assumptions and their ramifications, see Shaffer et al. 2004 as well as other chapters in this volume).

In terms of interpreting the LQ, a coefficient for an industry that is greater than 1.0 (or for more certainty 1.25) suggests that the local economy is exporting goods from that particular industry, while a coefficient of less than 1.0 implies that the economy imports goods in that industry from elsewhere in the nation. A coefficient near 1.0 implies the economy is self-sufficient. It is important to note that the more detailed the industry code (i.e., the larger the number of NAICS digits), the greater the likelihood of a large LQ. For example, Cortland, New York for many years was the last place in the US to manufacture typewriters (Smith Corona). Thus, the LQ for that industry in that county was potentially infinite, since the US share of employment in typewriter manufacturing was very small or negligible, and dividing a relatively large number by a very small number yields a large number.

There are, however, significant limitations of the LQ in identifying viable clusters, which also are highlighted in other chapters within this volume. For example, while Cortland had a high typewriter industry LQ, the industry closed down completely in the late 1990s. Thus, the large LQ did not guarantee perpetual competitiveness.

Further, in industry cluster analysis, all industries are of potential interest. Those that are already exporting could be enhanced to expand and export even more goods, bringing in more money into the community. In contrast, those with location quotients of less than 1.0 represent potential opportunities for import substitution, whereby goods that were previously imported are now produced locally. Thus, a focus only on high LQs can mean that potentially important opportunities are overlooked.

Shift-share analysis

In shift-share analysis, the change in local employment in different industries is decomposed into three components:

1   National: the county's job base is growing simply because the nation is growing. Adding together these three components yields the actual change in employment in a county, which can be negative, zero, or positive.
2   Mix: the county has a portfolio of industries that are growing more rapidly nationally, and as a result the county has more favourable growth (faster than the national average).
3   Competitive share: local job growth due to the fact that the county is, in a sense, drawing away jobs from other places in the nation. The county offers more competitive conditions than other communities, and so firms and jobs are relocating into the county.

Each of these components is calculated as follows. First, the national growth component [NG] is:

$$NG = \sum_{m} X_{mb} \bar{g}^{u}$$

where we have dropped the county subscript i, X measures employment as above, m refers to the industry, b is the base year which is compared with a later year representing the period over which the growth has occurred (such as five or 10 years), and $\bar{g}^{u}$ is the national average employment growth rate calculated over *all* sectors. Essentially, *NG* represents local growth in jobs that is due to national economic trends. If the actual total job growth in the community exceeds the national growth rate (i.e., it is faster than would be predicted based on national trends), then the community is obviously performing better than the nation.

The industrial mix component [*IM*] is calculated as follows, where g_m^u refers to the national average growth rate in industry *m*:

$$IM = \sum_m X_{mb} \, (g_m^u - \bar{g}^u)$$

If *IM* is positive, the implication is that most of the local employment is in sectors that are growing more rapidly than total national employment, and vice versa for

$$IM < 0.$$

The third component [*CS*] compares the *local* growth rate (g_m^i) in a given sector and with the national growth rate in that same sector:

$$CS = \sum_m X_{mb} \, (g_m^i - \bar{g}_m^n)$$

This component measures the local community's ability to capture or draw away an increasing share of a particular sector's growth from the national economy. This happens if the local economy is more competitive than the nation's, and vice versa.

Shift-share analysis is a descriptive rather than a diagnostic tool because it does not explain why the trends are occurring, that is, whether the differences in competitiveness are due to varying managerial ability, technology, or labour productivity. As a check to see if the calculations are correct, the total change in employment over the period of observation should sum to *NG* + *IM* + *CS*. For further discussion, see Shields (2003).

Wage analysis

Wages are potentially important in cluster analysis, as they tend to reflect worker productivity and competitiveness at a point in time. They are also important to economic developers because they affect standards of living and economic well-being. At the same time, high LQs do not necessarily imply high wages, or vice versa (San Diego Association of Governments: 7; Smith 2003: 5), but evidence suggests that successful clusters do pay higher wages (e.g., Gibbs and Bernat 1997). Wages can be analysed simply by ranking wage levels by industry and by comparing them over time and space.

Bubble charts

So-called bubble charts are widely used to identify and compare clusters within a region. One reason for their popularity is that they do "not require assigning degrees of importance to measures" (National Governors Association 2002: 18). Usually, "[t]wo variables are chosen for the '*x*' axis and '*y*' axis, which might be growth rates and wages. A third variable is represented by the size (radius) of a circle around the point on the graph. A fourth variable can be represented by the degree of shading in the circles" (National Governors Association 2002: 19).

Local Moran statistic

In their pioneering work, Gibbs and Bernat (1997) write that they seek to identify clusters in different industries by separating counties into four distinct groups, as follows (p. 19):

1   counties that have no establishments in a given industry;
2   counties with establishments that are not clustered;,
3   counties that are peripheral to cluster core counties; and
4   core or central counties that are clustered, having the greatest concentration of establishments in an industry compared with their neighbours.

They calculate a local Moran statistic for each county to identify those counties which have a number of firms in an industry or sector that is greater or smaller than would be expected based purely on chance (p. 20).

Calculating the local Moran statistic (LM) requires a spatial weights matrix to capture the distance between counties, or whether or not they are contiguous. LM_i is calculated for each county as follows, using data on the number of establishments (e_{mi}) in a specific industry, m, in county, i or j, and spatial weights matrix, w_{ij}:

$$LM_i = n(e_{mi} - \bar{e}_m) \sum_j w_{ij} (e_{mj} - \bar{e}_m)$$

The quantity $\bar{e}_m$ is the average number of establishments in the given industry, calculated across all counties, and n is the sample size. The weights matrix used in our example below represents "queen contiguity", so that a county is considered to be adjacent to another county if both counties have the same border. An alternative specification is that of "Bishop" contiguity, in which case only counties immediate to the east, north, west, and south are considered contiguous. Because we are looking only at counties in the North-east, where county sizes are roughly comparable, we are less concerned about distances between county centroids than we would be in the US West, for example. For further reading on spatial statistics, see Rogerson (2006).

Intuitively, this procedure captures whether or not a county has a high or low number of establishments in the given industry, and then also factors in whether the concentration of establishments in adjacent counties is high. County groups that have a higher number of establishments than would be expected based on chance alone and that are co-located (i.e., adjacent to one another) are designated under category (4) above. The cut-off or threshold as to what constitutes a higher number than expected varies from one industry to the next. Counties that have a higher than expected number of establishments but are not adjacent to other counties with a similarly high number are give the code (2) above.

An important feature of this measure is that, unlike the LQ that is limited to a particular geography (e.g., county), the Moran statistic picks up relationships over space and across county or community borders. Moreover, it can be used to identify industry clusters that straddle one or more state borders (see Gibbs and Bernat 1997). Carroll et al. (2008) compare location quotients and the Getis-Ord spatial statistic (which also uses a spatial weights matrix) as alternative tools for identifying potential clusters, and highlight strengths and weaknesses of each.

Locational correlation

Locational correlation (LC) is another spatially explicit measure of clustering, although by itself if does not capture relationships across county lines. Porter (2003: 562) notes that spillovers (or externalities) across industries can be uncovered by using the LC based on employment (or other) data, and boundaries of clusters can also be identified using this statistic. Porter gives the example of hardware and software industries and points out that if these industries are co-located in the same county then that would be an indicator of externalities or industry spillovers, and clustering. The simple (Pearson's) coefficient of correlation, r, of co-location of two industries 1 and 2, is calculated as:

$$r = \frac{\sum_{i=1}^{N} (X_{1i} - \bar{X}_1)(X_{2i} - \bar{X}_2)}{(N-1)\, s_{X1}\, s_{X2}}$$

where s refers to the standard deviation of variables X, which may measure the number of establishments in different industries (X_1 and X_2), and the bar denotes a mean value for the number of establishments.

Note that this method, unlike the local Moran statistic, does not capture whether the industries are located in adjacent counties. Nevertheless, this is an interesting supplement to the spatial results obtained using the local Moran statistic. Locational correlation captures clustering propensities across rather than within industries. And, although it takes into account spatial relationships (i.e., co-location), it does not capture spillovers across county or state lines. In our application below, we define clusters as those industries that have a locational correlation of at least 0.80 across any two pair of industries. See Porter (2003) for further discussion of this approach.

Another increasingly popular measure is the so-called Ellison-Glaeser (EG) index of industry co-agglomeration (Ellison and Glaeser 1997). Although we do not apply it in this chapter, we briefly present it for the sake of completeness. In addition to the variable already defined above, we define some other measure of each county's size, Z_1, Z_2, ... Z_I, such as the share of total population or employment of all counties found in the county. The EG index of industry co-agglomeration is then defined as:

$$\gamma \equiv \frac{G_m /(1 - \sum_i Z_i^2) - H_m}{1 - H_m}$$

where G_m is industry m's raw index of spatial concentration, calculated as:

$$G_m = \sum_{i=1}^{I} (X_{im} - Z_i)^2$$

and H_m is the m-th industry's Herfindahl employment index, calculated at the establishment level: $H_m = \sum_j^{N_m} k_{jm}^2$ where $k = 1, 2, \ldots N_i$ is an index for each establishment in the m-th industry and k denotes the number of jobs at the j-th establishment as a proportion of industry m's total employment.

In a subsequent paper, Ellison et al. (2007) show, in the case where only two industries are being compared, that the above definition can be simplified to:

$$\gamma^c = \frac{\sum_{i=1}^{I} (X_{i1} - Z_i)(X_{i2} - Z_i)}{1 - \sum_{i=1}^{I} Z_i^2}$$

so that, in essence, the EG index reflects the covariance between the employment shares of the two industries measured across the counties (Ellison et al. 2007: 5). Ellison et al. go on to disentangle the relative importance of labour pooling, knowledge spillovers, and transportation cost savings on industry co-agglomeration. To measure the latter factor, they employ input-output analysis, which we discuss next as a tool for identifying clusters.

Input-output analysis

Input-output (IO, also known as make-and-use) models track flows of goods and services among industries of an economy. Early in the 20th century, Russian planner Wassily Leontief devised this mathematical tool to describe the Soviet economy; his goal was to improve the functioning of the economy by better understanding and modelling the flows of inputs and outputs across its various sectors. IO analysis can be used to measure the relative importance of different industries or sectors within the economy (Sporleder 2003: 2 and other chapters in this volume) and also to calculate so-called economic multipliers. For example, it can be used to address the question, if a given manufacturing facility expands production, by how much do jobs, earnings, and output increase in the overall local economy beyond the direct effects that occur at the facility.

For this analysis, we use the IMPLAN software and data for Pennsylvania to carry out the input-output analysis following Sporleder's (2003) work in Ohio. In essence, the approach allows us to identify the horizontal and vertical linkages and interrelationships among agricultural producers and food manufacturers in a given county. Again, this procedure involves a number of important assumptions, as described in greater detail in Shaffer et al. (2004). Following Sporleder, we define five components to delineate the cluster: (1) farm inputs and machinery, (2) on-farm production, (3) food and forestry products processing, (4) food and forestry products wholesale and retail, and (5) food services. Readers are cautioned that including food services is a potential concern, because the sector traditionally is not normally considered part of the economic (or export) base.

IMPLAN provides estimates of total jobs, earnings, output, and value-added in each sector of the local economy, in addition to economic multipliers for the sectors of interest. These numbers can then in turn be used to identify the top 25 clusters in a county, following the approach in Muench and Deller (2001) and Deller in Chapter 19 of this volume. The information generated can then be used to identify opportunities for import substitution, by focusing on those goods and services that are used locally but imported into the state. Further, we search for gaps or disconnects by singling out industries with specific commodities that are purchased by local businesses that are not produced in Pennsylvania. Also, the local purchasing patterns (or the local purchase coefficient) are scrutinized by verifying the amount of goods and services that are imported from outside the state.

Analytical results

We present the results of our study in the same order as the sequence of analytical tools listed above. Our study area is the Northeast region, as defined by the US Department of Agriculture, and includes Connecticut, Delaware, Massachusetts, Maryland, Maine, New Hampshire, New Jersey, New York, Rhode Island, Pennsylvania, Vermont, and West Virginia. A key purpose of this work is to show that different analytical tools identify different combinations and sets of food and agricultural clusters. Thus, caution is needed when comparing the results obtained from different methods. Table 15.1 shows the six-digit food industries from the 2001 County Business Patterns that are included in this study.

Local employment analysis

Table 15.2 shows food industry employment in 2001, the per cent of total cluster employment, and employment growth rates between 1998 and 2001 for the entire Northeast US. The employment data are based on the number of employees for the week including March 12 and represent the sum of each Northeast state's employment. Due to data suppression, employment data had to be imputed using the mid-point of categorical data in a number of cases.

The industries are sorted in descending order of 2001 employment. The most significant industries by employment are commercial bakeries, poultry processing, retail bakeries, soft drink manufacturing, meat processed from carcasses, and fluid milk manufacturing. However, employment rank does not predict employment growth well. With the exception of commercial bakeries, the other top employment rank industry clusters all have negative employment growth rates between 1998 and 2001. This also points to the problem that a small growth in employment can represent a large percentage increase if the industry is small, and vice versa.

One question that is raised by this analysis is whether or not commercial bakeries are important clusters that represent potential regional economic growth engines. If the products of these bakeries are exported outside the region of interest, then they would potentially qualify. However, if the bakeries are not part of the economic base but are important only because the Northeast has large population centres, then they would likely not qualify as a potential cluster.

Location quotient

We calculate six-digit food industry LQs for each Northeast state using imputed employment data for 2001 and 1998, but report results only for Pennsylvania due to space constraints.[1] Also, we list the industries with a 1998 location quotient of greater than 1.25 in Table 15.3, along with the

Table 15.1 NAICS food industries and subsectors

NAICS	Industry Title	NAICS	Industry Title
311111	Dog & cat food manufacturing	311615	Poultry processing
311119	Other animal food manufacturing	311711	Seafood canning
311211	Flour milling	311712	Fresh & frozen seafood processing
311213	Malt manufacturing	311811	Retail bakeries
311221	Wet corn milling	311812	Commercial bakeries
311222	Soya bean processing	311813	Frozen cakes, pies & other pastries manufacturing
311223	Other oilseed processing	311821	Cookie & cracker manufacturing
311225	Fats & oils refining & blending	311822	Flour mixes & dough manuf. from purchased flour
311230	Breakfast cereal manufacturing	311823	Dry pasta manufacturing
311311	Sugarcane mills	311830	Tortilla manufacturing
311312	Cane sugar refining	311911	Roasted nuts & peanut butter manufacturing
311313	Beet sugar manufacturing	311919	Other snack food manufacturing
311320	Chocolate & confectionery manufacturing from cacao beans	311920	Coffee & tea manufacturing
311330	Confectionery manufacturing from purchased chocolate	311930	Flavouring syrup & concentrate manufacturing
311340	Non-chocolate confectionery manufacturing	311941	Mayonnaise, dressing & other prepared sauce manufacturing
311411	Frozen fruit, juice & vegetable manufacturing	311942	Spice & extract manufacturing
311412	Frozen specialty food manufacturing	311991	Perishable prepared food manufacturing
311421	Fruit & vegetable canning	311999	All other miscellaneous food manufacturing
311422	Specialty canning	312111	Soft drink manufacturing
311423	Dried & dehydrated food manufacturing	312112	Bottled water manufacturing
311511	Fluid milk manufacturing	312113	Ice manufacturing
311512	Creamery butter manufacturing	312120	Breweries
311513	Cheese manufacturing	312130	Wineries
311514	Dry, condensed, evaporated dairy product manufacturing	312140	Distilleries
311520	Ice cream & frozen dessert manufacturing	312210	Tobacco stemming & redrying
311611	Animal (except poultry) slaughtering	312221	Cigarette manufacturing
311612	Meat processed from carcasses	312229	Other tobacco product manufacturing
311613	Rendering & meat by-product processing		

Table 15.2 Industry employment and growth (top and bottom five by employment)

NAICS	Industry Title	2001 Employment	% of Total Employment	Employment Growth 98–01 (%)
311812	Commercial bakeries	36983	14.14	3.15
311615	Poultry processing	19629	7.51	−10.35
311811	Retail bakeries	18409	7.04	−8.23
312111	Soft drink manufacturing	14723	5.63	−1.21
311612	Meat processed from carcasses	13110	5.01	−6.44
311223	Other oilseed processing	120	0.05	100.00
311313	Beet sugar manufacturing	70	0.03	16.67
312210	Tobacco stemming & redrying	70	0.03	−41.67
312221	Cigarette manufacturing	70	0.03	0.00
311311	Sugarcane mills	30	0.01	50.00

Table 15.3 Selected industries by 2001 and 1998 location quotients, Pennsylvania

NAICS	Industry Cluster Title	LQ01	LQ98
311320	Choc & confectionery manufacturing from cacao beans	7.92	7.81
312229	Other tobacco product manufacturing	5.27	2.22
311919	Other snack food manufacturing	3.91	3.34
311330	Confectionery manufacturing from purchased chocolate	3.32	3.83
311422	Specialty canning	3.12	2.18
311813	Frozen cakes, pies & other pastries manufacturing	2.53	3.16
311821	Cookie & cracker manufacturing	1.95	1.75
311340	Non-chocolate confectionery manufacturing	1.82	1.63
311111	Dog & cat food manufacturing	1.80	1.71
311511	Fluid milk manufacturing	1.33	1.32
311823	Dry pasta manufacturing	1.29	1.34
311421	Fruit & vegetable canning	0.69	1.42

2001 LQ. This cut-off point is arbitrary, but preferred by some analysts. Also, as noted earlier, some key assumptions are necessary in using this measure, including that consumers everywhere have similar tastes and preferences.

The industry clusters are sorted in descending order by 2001 LQ. The interpretation of the results is that a larger LQ points to a potential industry cluster. Again, however, the results have to be viewed with caution. For example, if consumers in Connecticut have disproportionately stronger preferences for products manufactured by retail bakeries, then the high LQ of 3.65 (not shown in Table 15.3) would not be unexpected. However, if

Connecticut residents are like other Americans in terms of their consumption of bakery products, then the high LQ could indicate a clustered industry that has a strong export focus (perhaps supplying cafeterias in New York City or Boston). Of course, the LQ is calculated here using employment numbers; to determine if the industry is also potentially competitive, it would be important to see how many firms are in fact located in that state.

It is interesting to examine changes in the LQ over time. Sometimes LQs increase noticeably and in other cases they decline, likely in response to dynamically changing competitive positions of the industries in the different states – relative both to other states in the Northeast and to other states outside the region. In some cases, changing LQs appear to reflect firms relocating from one state in the Northeast to another. For example, Connecticut's LQ for confectionary manufacturing from purchased chocolate declined from 3.46 to 2.03 between 1998 and 2001, while Massachusetts's LQ increased from 2.51 to 3.65. This change in LQs may reflect a relocation of firms in this NAICS code from Massachusetts to bordering Connecticut. That state also experienced a significant increase in coffee and tea manufacturing.

Delaware increased its employment concentration in seafood canning (with the LQ rising from 10.73 to 14.01), but lost considerable activity in fruit and vegetable canning (with the LQ slipping from 2.07 to 0.55). In New York, the LQ for seafood canning slipped slightly, from 1.27 to 1.14. It is important to reiterate that the LQ is a relative concept, and that in Delaware total employment in fruit and vegetable canning may still exceed total employment in seafood canning, even after the apparent loss of competitive advantage.

Chocolate and confectionery manufacturing from cacao beans (PA), coffee and tea manufacturing (CT), seafood canning (DE), ice cream and frozen dessert manufacturing (MA), spice and extract manufacturing (MD), breweries (NH), cane sugar refining (NY), and other tobacco product manufacturing (WV) are the top industry clusters, based on 2001 location quotients, in the Northeast states.

Shift-share analysis

With shift-share analysis, we can decompose total employment change in any given industry into three components of change: one due to national growth, one due to a favourable or non-favourable mix of existing jobs, and one due to the fact that the state's economy is more or less competitive than that of other states in the Northeast. Adding up these three components yields the total change in the number of jobs over time. Industries with growth due to positive competitive advantage (in a sense, the ability to draw jobs away from other states because of favourable local conditions – note that this does not have to mean that growth in one state comes only at the expense of another) are listed in Table 15.4. The industries are sorted according to declining

Table 15.4 Shift-share analysis of food industry, Pennsylvania (top and bottom five competitive)

NAICS	Industry Cluster Title	National	Competitive	Mix
312229	Other tobacco product manufacturing	1.44	995.36	3.20
311422	Specialty canning	3.36	738.20	103.45
311919	Other snack food manufacturing	11.48	688.59	−1165.06
311119	Other animal food manufacturing	2.75	654.03	27.23
311812	Commercial bakeries	15.28	409.70	139.02
311830	Tortilla manufacturing	0.09	10.38	4.53
311711	Seafood canning	0.12	9.72	−9.84
311230	Breakfast cereal manufacturing	1.44	9.66	−11.10
311613	Rendering & meat by-product processing	0.62	2.16	−21.77
311211	Flour milling	0.72	1.52	−2.24

competitive advantage for each state, as measured by the total number of jobs generated because the state was more competitive in that industry than the nation (or other states). The national component is small in most places because not much growth occurred in this industry nationally over the period studied. This is in large part likely to be due to plant-level increases in labour productivity.

The results of the shift-share analysis suggest that coffee and tea manufacturing (CT), other tobacco product manufacturing (PA), retail bakeries (DE, MD), fresh and frozen seafood processing (MA), commercial bakeries (ME, NJ), soft drink manufacturing (NH), fruit and vegetable canning (NY), chocolate and confectionery manufacturing from cacao beans (VT), all other miscellaneous foods and ice manufacturing (RI), and ice cream and frozen dessert manufacturing (WV) are the most competitive industries in the Northeast states.

This shows, again, that these results have to be interpreted with great care. For example, Maine is highly competitive according to the shift-share analysis in commercial bakeries (according to these results), but that sector does not show up prominently in the location quotient results.

Wages

Wages are another important aspect of cluster activity. In this study, wage data are calculated by aggregated annual payroll divided by employees for the Northeast. Due to data suppression, some industry clusters have no payroll data in the County Business Patterns file. The results are provided in Table 15.5. It is apparent that the ranking by average annual wages does not follow the order of the employment ranking.

Spice and extract manufacturing had the highest average annual wages

Table 15.5 Average wages and wage growth (top and bottom five)

NAICS	Industry Cluster Title	2001 Average Wages	1998 Average Wages	Wage Growth 98–01 (%)
311942	Spice & extract manufacturing	45251	42557	6.33
311821	Cookie & cracker manufacturing	37566	33444	12.32
311930	Flavoring syrup & concentrate manufacturing	35125	27846	26.14
311320	Chocolate & confectionery manuf. from cacao beans	32380	28677	12.91
312111	Soft drink manufacturing	31636	20512	54.23
311411	Frozen fruit, juice & vegetable manufacturing	8179	11562	−29.26
311823	Dry pasta manufacturing	7919	8655	−8.50
311421	Fruit & vegetable canning	6213	26586	−76.63
311211	Flour milling	5350	5065	5.63
312113	Ice manufacturing	1794	12337	−85.46

($45,251) in 2001. Cookie and cracker manufacturing followed with a wage of $37,566. A gradual decline in wages is observed for each subsequent cluster, until we reach fresh and frozen seafood processing, where the drop is more significant. The overall average wage range ranges from a low of $1,794 to a high of $45,251. There is clearly some concern about the reliability of these low wage numbers, which like represent seasonal employment and other statistical problems related to the data suppression used, and they need to be interpreted with extreme caution.

Bubble charts

To illustrate employment, employment growth, wages, and location quotients in one chart for different industries, we created bubble charts to help visualize clusters in each state. In the bubble chart, 1998 wages are plotted along the *x*-axis, while the *y*-axis measures job growth between 1998 and 2001. The size (radius) of the circle reflects the number of employees in 1998, while the shading or color of the bubble represents location quotients. The darkest shading represents location quotient greater than 2.5, the lighter shading (lines) greater than 1.5 but equal to or less than 2.5, and the white circles represent location quotient less than or equal to 1.5. Results for Pennsylvania are shown in Figure 15.1.

Figure 15.1 reveals that in Pennsylvania, ice cream and frozen dessert manufacturing had high job growth during 1998 and 2001 and relatively high average wages in 1998. The sector also had a competitive advantage as revealed by its location quotient of greater than 1.5.

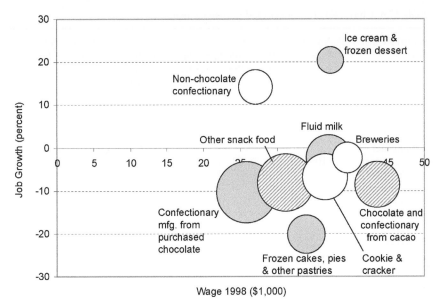

Figure 15.1 Pennsylvania's food industry clusters (selected).

Local Moran statistic

Following Gibbs and Bernat (1997) in using the local Moran's *I* statistic and county-level establishment data, we identified four groups of counties: central cluster counties, counties peripheral to the clusters, counties that have establishments from the industry in question but that do not meet the clustering criterion, and counties without any establishment for the given industry. In addition to using establishment data for food industries from the County Business Patterns, we also included farm production data from the 2002 Census of Agriculture. Table 15.6 presents summary statistics for 10 illustrative food and agricultural industry clusters. Examples of the spatial distributions of industry clusters for the Northeast are shown in the three Maps (Figure 15.2a, b, c).

From Figure 15.2a, b, & c it is clear that some industry clusters are more concentrated than others. For example, vegetable and melon farming operations are highly concentrated in Maine, western New York State and parts of Pennsylvania and New Jersey. Some industries are clustered across state borders. For example, oil seeds and grain farming are clustered across the Pennsylvania and Maryland/New Jersey borders. The mapping of industry clusters in the entire study area helps us better understand the geographic distribution of food and agriculture industry clusters in the Northeast. It also shows where the potential exists for agglomeration economies among firms and where it does not.

Table 15.6 Characteristics of selected industry clusters

Industry Cluster Title	No. of Counties with Establishments	No. of Counties with Above Average Establishments	No. of Counties with Sig. High-high Local Moran's I	Central Clusters	Peripheral Clusters
Breakfast cereal manufact.	8	1	1	0	0
Confectionery mfg, prchsd choc.	110	33	26	9	23
Fluid milk mfg	96	34	19	10	16
Poultry processing	41	15	14	7	9
Breweries	80	21	11	8	9
Wineries	75	22	7	6	8
Logging	245	74	17	17	15
Forestry support activities	111	43	10	10	47
Oilseed and grain farming	264	100	42	41	41
Vegetable and melon farming	280	109	19	19	29
Poultry and egg production	264	51	19	19	18

Locational correlation

The locational correlation method potentially points us to geographic clustering of "linked industries" within individual counties. We again use the same broad definition of food and agricultural industries in our locational correlation analysis as was used above. The industry starts with the growing of food crops, including grains and livestock, and ends with wholesaling and retailing functions for these products. The cluster also includes supporting industries such as refrigerated storage and fertilizer production. Most of these food and agriculture industry clusters overlap with industry clusters examined in the report *Pennsylvania's Targeted Industry Clusters: Agriculture and Food Production* (Center for Workforce Information and Analysis 2004).

The list of industry clusters with locational correlation coefficients above 0.75 or 75 per cent is provided in Table 15.7. The first coefficient's value of 0.77, for example, shows that there is a 77 per cent correlation between hog and pig farming and other animal food farming firms within counties in the Northeast; in other words, these firms are very likely to be (co-)located in the same county (77 per cent of the time). This correlation is even higher for retail bakeries and general line grocery wholesalers (0.94). Thus, this analysis

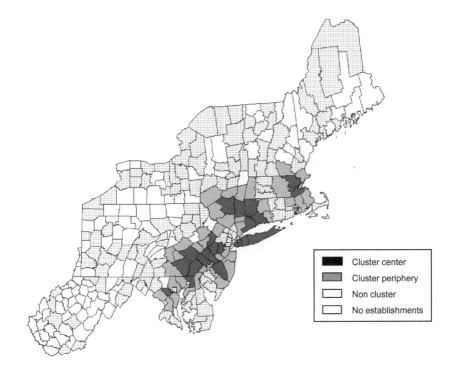

Figure 15.2a Animal production support activity clusters in the Northeast.

goes beyond the single-industry focus of a cluster, to begin to understand which firms from different industries may be more (or less) likely to associate with one another by locating in the same county. Of course, especially for wholesalers and retailers, much of this co-location is likely being driven by a third factor – namely, population concentrations.

This analysis can begin to shed light on vertical linkages within the industry complex (as opposed only to horizontal, competing linkages). It identifies not only how many firms from a given industry need to cluster to develop agglomeration economies, but also which complementary or supporting industries need to be present in order to make a cluster competitive.

Input-output analysis

Using the IMPLAN input-output software and Sporleder's (2003) sector definitions, we develop total output, value added, income, and employment statistics for Pennsylvania's food and related agricultural sector in 2000 (Table 15.8). The sector's total output was $83.8 billion, distributed across the food and agricultural cluster (five components). Processed food and forestry products make up the largest component ($41.5 billion of the output, or about 49.5 per cent of the total). This $41.5 billion is in turn made

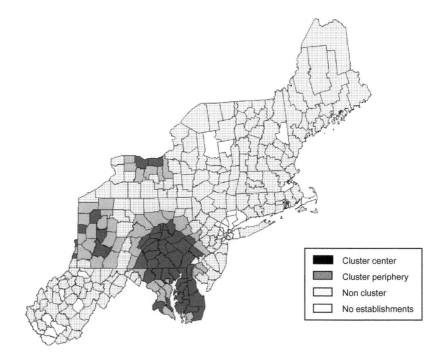

Figure 15.2b Oil seeds and grain farming clusters in the Northeast.

up of food processing ($25.4 billion) and forestry processing ($16.1 billion), including manufacturing of paper, wood processing, and wood furniture.

Food processing makes up approximately 61 cents of every dollar of output from food and forestry processing overall. In Pennsylvania, agricultural production adds close to $5.7 billion or about 7 per cent of the total output of the state's economy. Within the agricultural sector, the nursery and horticultural industries contribute largest shares, of approximately $2.1 billion in output. Dairy farms account for more than $1.5 billion in sector output.

In 2000, the total value added to Pennsylvania's economy by the food and agricultural cluster was $36 billion. Total value added takes into account the amount of output of a state's economy that is produced elsewhere but is imported into the state. It is an important and useful measure for comparing the net relative importance of the sectors of an economy. Of this $36 billion, 35.6 per cent is attributable to the total food and forestry-processing sector. Wholesaling and retailing in food and forestry make up another 34 per cent of the entire total value added by the food and related agricultural cluster ($12.3 billion). Food service contributes $6.7 billion, while farming and farm inputs and machinery account for 2 and 9.5 per cent, respectively, of all value added.

Close to $22.4 billion of total earned income is generated in the food and related agricultural cluster. Roughly one-third of this output ($7.46 billion)

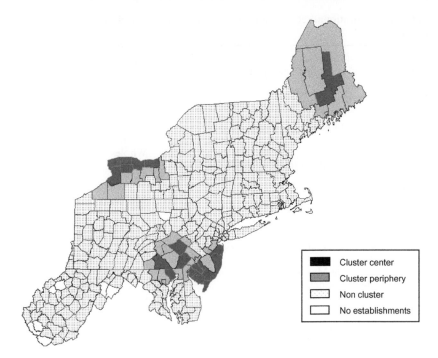

Figure 15.2c Vegetable and melon farming clusters in the Northeast.

is contributed by the food and forestry product processing sector, which is virtually tied with food and forestry products wholesaling and retailing at $7.5 billion. Farm production income is was $563 million in 2000.

More than 861,000 jobs existed in Pennsylvania in 2000 in the food and agricultural sector. Two-thirds of these jobs were in wholesaling and retailing and food services (for approximately 638,000 total jobs). The food and forestry processing sectors accounted for nearly 178,000 jobs (21 per cent of the cluster's employment), while farm production provided 24,000 jobs (about 3 per cent of the total).

We next report Type II economic multipliers, which capture the direct, indirect, and induced effects of a shift in final demand for the products of a sector on total output, employment, value added, or earnings in an economy. More specifically, the output multiplier shows the total change in output that would result from a $1.00 change in the final demand for a sector's output. Analogous multipliers exist for income, employment, and value added. In particular, a $1.00 change in the final demand for the output of dairy farms leads to a total economy increase in income of $1.892, after the multiplier effect has taken its course (Table 15.9). In that table, high employment and income multipliers are evident for the dairy sector in Pennsylvania.

Following the work of Muench and Deller (2001) and Deller et al.'s Chapter 17 in this volume, we identify the top 25 food industry clusters as

Table 15.7 Locational correlation of industry clusters (selected – equal to or above 0.80)

	Retail Bakeries
Supermarkets and Other Grocery Stores	0.96
Baked Goods Stores	0.96
Commercial bakeries	0.95
General Line Grocery Wholesalers	0.94
Other Grocery and Related Products Wholesalers	0.94
	Fresh Fruit and Vegetable Wholesalers
Supermarkets and Other Grocery Stores	0.85
Retail bakeries	0.82
Meat Markets	0.81
General Line Grocery Wholesalers	0.80
Meat and Meat Product Wholesalers	0.80
	Meat Markets
Supermarkets and Other Grocery Stores	0.97
Retail bakeries	0.94
Fruit and Vegetable Markets	0.93
Meat and Meat Product Wholesalers	0.91
Fish and Seafood Markets	0.91
Other Grocery and Related Products Wholesalers	0.90
Dairy Product(except Dried or Canned)Wholesalers	0.89
All Other Specialty Food Stores	0.88
General Line Grocery Wholesalers	0.86
Packaged Frozen Food Wholesalers	0.82
Fresh Fruit and Vegetable Wholesalers	0.81
	Finfish Fishing
Shellfish fishing	0.84
	Dairy Cattle and Milk Production
Hog and pig farming	0.82

measured by total output, employment, total value added and total output per employee, total value added per employee for Pennsylvania food and agricultural sectors. These food and agricultural sectors are calculated using the IMPLAN software and 2001 Pennsylvania data, with results shown in Tables 15.10 to 15.14.

Confectionery manufacturing from cacao beans is the sector with largest total industry output, of nearly $2.7 billion (Table 15.10). The top 10 industries account for $18.8 billion, or 57 per cent of Pennsylvania's total output in this industry. Looking at the sum of the top 25 industries, we find that they account for 87 per cent ($28.5 billion) of all industry output.

Cattle ranching and farming establishments in Pennsylvania – which include dairy farms – are by far the single largest employer in the food and agricultural sector, accounting for 40,417 jobs, or about 21.4 per cent of all sector employment (Table 15.11). This is followed by bread and bakery manufacturing product (except frozen) with 16,667 jobs and all other crop farming

Table 15.8 Pennsylvania food & related agricultural cluster output, value added, income, and employment, 2000

Food & Related Agricultural Cluster	Total Output ($ Millions)	Total Value Added ($ Millions)	Income ($ Millions)	Employment (Person Years)
Farm Inputs & Machinery	**7,496.3**	**3,432.9**	**2,123.8**	**21,455**
Farming	**5,658.6**	**729.8**	**563.6**	**23,603**
Dairy Farms	1,520.4	458.6	403.6	10,189
Poultry & Eggs	647.3	102.1	76.4	3,168
Cattle Feeding	145.4	34.8	28.0	794
Swine	155.1	24.6	18.1	2,089
Miscellaneous Livestock	79.8	22.0	17.4	3,704
Food Grains	23.2	7.9	3.8	695
Feed Grains	282.2	106.5	55.5	5,161
Nursery & Horticulture	2,125.5	1,220.2	766.8	48,093
Fruits & Vegetables	222.6	87.9	66.0	3,211
Oil Bearing Crops	65.8	28.2	15.9	1,603
Misc Crops/Hay/Sugar/ Tobacco/Nuts	12.9	3.3	1.6	247
Forestry, Fishing, Ag Services	378.5	271.2	160.1	13,414
Processing	**41,545.0**	**12,831.3**	**7,457.6**	**177,732**
Food Processing	25,444.0	7,277.0	3,780.0	87,589
Processed Meat, Fish & Eggs	3,983.7	703.6	562.6	15,681
Dairy Processing	2,669.4	502.8	306.3	7,258
Processed Food & Kindred Products	15,162.7	5,048.5	2,417.2	54,782
Grain Milling & Flour	779.5	167.3	100.5	1,586
Fats & Oils	138.6	34.6	18.2	415
Beverage Processing	2,710.1	820.2	375.2	7,867
Wood/Paper/Furniture Manufacturing	16,100.9	5,554.3	3,677.6	90,143
Food & Forestry Wholesaling/ Retailing	**16,439.1**	**12,286.4**	**7,525.0**	**291,656**
Food Services	**12,666.5**	**6,740.7**	**4,770.6**	**346,735**
Total Food & Related Agricultural Cluster	**83,805.5**	**36,021.1**	**22,440.6**	**861,181**

Note: Each sector's output, value added, income and employment are provided through IMPLAN Industries Input-Output Model (Sporleder 2003). The wholesaling and retailing sector is treated as one sector for purposes of the input-output model definition. Similar to Sporleder (2003), the percentage of payroll (23.9%) is used to estimate the proportion of food- and agriculture-related output, valued-added, and income. The percentage of employment (28.5%) is used to allocate employment in a similar fashion.

with 13,175 jobs. These top three employment sectors account for 70,259 jobs or 37.2 per cent of total employment. The top 25 employment sectors account for 170,947 jobs, or 90.5 per cent of all food and agriculture cluster employment. It should be noted that these employment figures include

Table 15.9 Pennsylvania food & related agricultural cluster multipliers: output, value-added, income, and employment, 2000

Food & Related Agricultural Cluster	Total Output	Value Added	Income	Employment
Farm Inputs & Machinery	**1.806**	**2.049**	**2.020**	**3.008**
Farming				
Dairy Farms	1.674	2.297	1.892	2.346
Poultry & Eggs	1.572	2.999	2.656	2.360
Cattle Feeding	1.657	2.554	2.161	2.471
Swine	1.684	3.304	2.880	1.647
Miscellaneous Livestock	1.683	2.343	2.003	1.137
Food Grains	1.916	2.508	2.732	1.265
Feed Grains	1.805	2.225	2.374	1.447
Nursery & Horticulture	1.855	1.922	1.905	1.457
Fruits & Vegetables	1.904	2.308	2.074	1.700
Oil Bearing Crops	1.821	2.144	2.156	1.346
Misc Crops/Hay/Sugar/Tobacco/Nuts	1.859	2.747	3.445	1.405
Forestry, Fishing, Ag Services	1.724	1.530	1.470	1.186
Processing				
Food Processing				
Processed Meat, Fish & Eggs	1.835	2.789	2.440	2.683
Dairy Processing	2.124	3.702	4.326	4.880
Processed Food & Kindred Products	1.842	2.398	2.839	2.901
Grain Milling & Flour	1.846	3.136	3.629	4.819
Fats & Oils	1.705	3.742	3.904	4.730
Beverage Processing	1.721	2.075	3.175	3.079
Wood/Paper/Furniture Manufacturing	1.897	2.334	2.168	2.185
Food & Forestry Wholesaling/Retailing	**2.054**	**1.852**	**1.854**	**1.691**
Food Services	**1.913**	**2.000**	**1.880**	**1.354**

Source: Computed based on IMPLAN Pro 2000.

Table 15.10 Top 10 industries total industry output, Pennsylvania, 2001

Industry Cluster Title	Total Industry Output
Confectionery manufacturing from cacao beans	$2,669,563,000
Bread and bakery product, except frozen, manufacturing	2,229,239,000
Cattle ranching and farming	2,211,838,000
Soft drink and ice manufacturing	2,111,722,000
Animal, except poultry, slaughtering	2,059,514,000
Fruit and vegetable canning and drying	1,948,240,000
Other snack food manufacturing	1,732,727,000
Fluid milk manufacturing	1,497,860,000
Meat processed from carcasses	1,201,946,000
Confectionery manufacturing from purchased chocolate	1,184,536,000

Source: IMPLAN 2001.

Note: Top 10 out of a possible 64 food and agricultural sectors.

Table 15.11 Top 10 industries employment, Pennsylvania, 2001

Industry Cluster Title	Employment
Cattle ranching and farming	40,417
Bread and bakery product, except frozen, manufacturing	16,667
All other crop farming	13,175
Agriculture and forestry support activities	11,335
Grain farming	9,264
Animal production, except cattle and poultry	6,870
Soft drink and ice manufacturing	6,723
Fruit and vegetable canning and drying	6,380
Confectionery manufacturing from purchased chocolate	5,805
Other snack food manufacturing	5,747

Source: IMPLAN 2001.

Note: Top 10 out of a possible 64 food and agricultural sectors.

Table 15.12 Top 10 industries total value added, Pennsylvania, 2001

Industry Cluster Title	Total Value Added
Bread and bakery product, except frozen, manufacturing	$1,098,634,000
Confectionery manufacturing from cacao beans	815,977,000
Other snack food manufacturing	673,011,000
Fruit and vegetable canning and drying	624,757,000
Soft drink and ice manufacturing	606,268,000
Confectionery manufacturing from purchased chocolate	530,357,000
Other tobacco product manufacturing	363,470,000
Frozen food manufacturing	330,761,000
All other crop farming	319,310,000
Breweries	300,671,000

Source: IMPLAN 2001.

Note: Top 10 out of a possible 64 food and agricultural sectors.

part-time and full-time jobs. Therefore, caution is needed in using these results. IMPLAN production agriculture data are notoriously (and admittedly) of questionable quality (Lindall 1998).

The bread and bakery manufacturing product (except frozen) sector contributes the largest amount of total value added, at $1.1 billion (Table 15.12), followed by confectionery manufacturing from cacao beans sector and other snack food manufacturing sector. The top three sectors account for 25.5 per cent of the food and agricultural cluster's total value added.

Industry output per employee (Table 15.13) and total value added per employee (Table 15.14) are other important measures for assessing the productivity and potential competitiveness of a sector. The measure is interesting because it can account for differences across firms with varying scales of operation. The tables report statistics for the top 10 industries in the state.

Table 15.13 Top 10 industries based on industry output per employee, Pennsylvania, 2001

Industry Cluster Title	Total Output per Employee	Jobs
Cigarette manufacturing	$13,361,000	4
Fats and oils refining and blending	1,063,551	49
Creamery butter manufacturing	983,289	76
Soya bean processing	945,667	3
Breakfast cereal manufacturing	794,837	815
Wet corn milling	784,667	3
Cheese manufacturing	578,219	1,098
Dry, condensed, and evaporated dairy products	578,135	913
Tobacco stemming and redrying	527,767	120
Confectionery manufacturing from cacao beans	497,125	5,370

Source: IMPLAN 2001.

Note: Top 10 out of a possible 64 food and agricultural sectors.

Table 15.14 Top 10 industries based on total value added (TVA) per employee, Pennsylvania, 2001

Industry Cluster Title	TVA Per Employee	Employment
Cigarette manufacturing	$7,794,750	4
Flavouring syrup and concentrate manufacturing	255,798	397
Other tobacco product manufacturing	237,252	1,532
Distilleries	234,411	190
Breweries	231,642	1,298
Wet corn milling	193,333	3
Dry, condensed, and evaporated dairy products	184,301	913
Frozen food manufacturing	157,281	2,103
Breakfast cereal manufacturing	153,590	815
Confectionery manufacturing from cacao beans	151,951	5,370

Source: IMPLAN 2001.

Note: Top 10 out of a possible 64 food and agricultural sectors.

By far the greatest amount of total output and value added per employee in Pennsylvania's food and agricultural industry are produced in cigarette manufacturing, which contributes $13.4 million to total output and $7.8 million to total value added per employee. However, only four workers are employed in cigarette manufacturing, which skews and raises questions about the validity of these numbers. These four employees compare with 11 workers in 2000. After cigarette manufacturing, the second largest food and agricultural industry in terms of total output per employee is fats and oils refining and blending industry, accounting for nearly $1.1 million total output per worker. The second largest food and agriculture industry in terms of total value added per employee is flavored syrup and concentrate manufacturing, which accounts for $255,798.

Input-output analysis applied to targeted industry cluster analysis also provides information on the size and of linkages among a state economy's sectors, as well as the importance of imports from and exports to various sectors. This information is useful for identifying potential "gaps" or "disconnects". In particular, Muench and Deller (2001: 16) argue that this information can be used to launch economic development plans and strategies.

Table 15.15 presents findings of this "absolute gaps" analysis that identifies the four local industries that buy goods that are not manufactured in the state. The largest gap in monetary terms occurs with sugar manufacturing, where total imports exceed $400.6 million, followed by the fishing industry with total imports of $277.8 million. Other gaps, although significantly smaller, include imports of products from cotton farming, as well as sugarcane and sugar beet farming. Obviously, climatic and other geographic constraints will limited the feasible set of commodities that can be grown in any given state, and they need to be considered in this kind of analysis.

Locally available goods may be imported from outside the state as a result of a "disconnect" or for reasons "such as product specifications, pricing, or national contracts that supercede local contracts" (Muench and Deller 2001: 17 or Deller, Chapter 19). Table 15.16 presents potential disconnects as identified by our input-output analysis. For example, the cigarette manufacturing industry imports $1.9 billion worth of goods, many of which are also available locally. In turn, Pennsylvania's cigarette manufacturers export $2.6 million worth of product.

Another example of a potential disconnect involves soft drink and ice manufacturing, which imports $1.3 billion worth of product but exports $1.8 billion. While this appears to be a significant disconnect, it might be readily explained by the types of soft drinks produced locally and needed by local demand, by pricing, by transshipment, or by the fact that the industry category is too highly aggregated (e.g., soft drinks are imported whereas ice is exported).

A comparison of the levels of local industry output along exports and imports can serve to identify gaps, disconnects, and opportunities for import

Table 15.15 Imported commodities not available locally, Pennsylvania, 2001

Importing Industry	Total Imports ($ millions)
Sugar manufacturing	400.635
Fishing	277.761
Cotton farming	17.962
Sugarcane and sugar beet farming	7.010

Source: IMPLAN 2001.

Table 15.16 Industry "disconnect" and "gaps", Pennsylvania, 2001 (top 10 by imports)

Industry Cluster Title	Total Imports	Total Exports
Cigarette manufacturing	$1,975,136,840	$2,601,280
Soft drink and ice manufacturing	1,352,210,210	1,858,147,850
Fruit and vegetable canning and drying	1,348,130,490	1,854,772,410
Frozen food manufacturing	962,487,610	659,847,490
Grain farming	872,694,030	262,414,630
Poultry processing	771,751,950	51,940,720
Animal- except poultry- slaughtering	762,153,380	262,292,510
Breweries	750,262,080	432,950,700
Vegetable and melon farming	737,588,810	12,437,070
Fruit farming	593,337,460	25,700,490

Source: IMPLAN 2001.

substitution in a state's economy. Local industries with high production levels occurring at the same time as high levels of imports may suggest a potential disconnect. Conversely, large quantities of imports of goods and services that are not produced locally may point to gaps ripe for exploitation (Muench and Deller 2001: 23). Tables 15.15 and 15.16 provide basic results needed to identify potential gaps or disconnects that may warrant further analysis and attention.

Summary and conclusions

We use County Business Patterns data, Census of Agriculture data, and the IMPLAN database to identify industry clusters on food and agriculture in the Northeast region of the United States. We adopt several analytical tools to identify industry clusters in the food and agriculture industry: local employment analysis, location quotient, shift-share analysis, wage analysis, bubble chart, local Moran's I, locational correlation, and input-output analysis. These analytical tools help us better understand the competitive advantage of particular food and agriculture industry through cluster analysis.

Our results show that different analytical tools produce different results in terms of which sectors are the most important as potential industry clusters that warrant further attention. Even so, certain sectors do tend to rise to the top when different methods are used. In a certain sense this kind of analysis may be viewed as being more art than science. However, we also submit that until more comparative analyses, such as the ones presented here are carried out, this will not change. We hope that the review of methods described here is a first step in the right direction. We also believe that using a combination of methods, such as the local Moran statistic in conjunction with an LQ or shift-share analysis, will yield stronger results.

Note

1   Complete results are available at: http://nercrd.psu.edu/Publications/rdppapers/
rdp26BW.pdf.

References

Carroll, M.C., Reid, N., and Smith, B.W. (2008) "Location quotients versus spatial
autocorrelation in identifying potential cluster regions", *Annals of Regional
Science*, 42: 449–63.

Center for Workforce Information and Analysis, Pennsylvania Department of Labor
and Industry. (2004) "Pennsylvania targeted industry clusters", report, April
2004. Online. Available HTTP: <http://www.dli.state.pa.us/landi/cwp/view.asp?a=
140&Q=210325&PM=1&pp=3> (retrieved July 21, 2004).

Colorado Department of Labor & Employment. (2003) "Industry clusters for the State
of Colorado", Workforce Research & Analysis, Labor Market Information,
Colorado Department of Labor & Employment. Online. Available HTTP: <http://
www.coworkforce.com/lmi/WRA/ClusterReport-Final.pdf>(retrieved July 21, 2004)

Ellison, G., and Glaeser, E.L. (1997) "Geographic concentration in US manufacturing
industries: a dartboard approach", *Journal of Political Economy*, 105: 889–927.

Ellison, G., Glaeser, E.L., and Kerr, W. (2007) "What causes industry agglomeration?
evidence from coagglomeration patterns", NBER Working Paper 13068.

Gibbs, R.M., and Bernat, G.A. (1997) "Rural industry clusters raise local earnings",
Rural Development Perspectives, 12(3): 18–25. Online. Available HTTP: <http://
www.ers.usda.gov/publications/rdp/rdp697/rdp697d.pdf> (retrieved July 21, 2004).

Herr, A. (2003) "Industry cluster analysis of Westmoreland and Fayette counties
addressing workforce development needs", prepared for the Westmoreland-
Fayette Workforce Investment Board. Online. Available HTTP: <http://www.pitts
burghregion.org/public/cfm/library/reports/Westmorelandfayettecluster.pdf>
(retrieved July 1, 2004).

Lindall S. (1998) "How does MIG estimate that pesky agricultural data anyway?"
Stillwater, MN: Minnesota IMPLAN Group, Inc.

Markusen, A. (2007) "A consumption base theory of development: an application
to the rural cultural economy", *Agricultural and Resource Economics Review*, 36(1):
9–23.

Minnesota IMPLAN Group, Inc. IMPLAN Professional Software Version 2.0. http://
www.implan.com/index.html

Muench, D., and Deller, S.C. (2001, September) "The economic structure of the Fox
Valley: a study of economic opportunity," Department of Agricultural and Applied
Economics Staff Paper No. 444, University of Wisconsin-Madison/Extension.
Online. Available HTTP: <http://www.aae.wisc.edu/pubs/sps/pdf/stpap444.pdf>.

Munnich, L.W. (1999, January) "Industry clusters: an economic development strategy
for Minnesota", preliminary report. Online. Available HTTP: <http://www.
hhh.umn.edu/centers/slp/projects/edweb/ic-rep.htm> (retrieved July 1, 2004).

National Governors Association. (2002) "A governor's guide to cluster-based economic development", Washington, DC: National Governor's Association. Online.
Available   HTTP: <http://www.eda.gov/ImageCache/EDAPublic/documents/
pdfdocs/nga_5fclusters_2epdf/v1/nga_5fclusters.pdf> (retrieved July 1, 2004).

Porter, M. (1990) *The Competitive Advantage of Nations*. New York: Basic Books.

—— . (2003) "The economic performance of regions", *Regional Studies* 37(6&7): 549–78.

San Diego Association of Governments. "Understanding cluster analysis". Online. Available HTTP: <http://www.sandag.cog.ca.us/rta/transfer/cluster_analysis.pdf> (retrieved July 1, 2004).

Shields, M. (2003) "Tool 4: shift-share analysis helps to identify local growth engines", *Understanding Economic Change in Your Community*, Penn State University. Available HTTP: <http://www.cdtoolbox.net/economic_development/000201.html>.

Smith, R.V. (2003) "Industry clusters analysis: inspiring a common strategy for community development", Central Pennsylvania Workforce Development Corporation, Lewisburg, PA. Online. Available HTTP: <http://www.extension.psu.edu/workforce/Briefs/INDclustAnal.pdf> (retrieved July 1, 2004).

Sporleder, T.L. (2003, June) "OHFOOD: an Ohio food industries input-output model, version 6", AED Economics Report AEDE-RP-0033-03, Columbus, OH: The Ohio State University.

US Census Bureau. (2001) "Frequently asked county business patterns (CBP) questions", last revised May 18, 2001, 08:36:12 EDT. Online. Available HTTP: <http://www.census.gov/epcd/cbp/view/cbpfaq.html#Q4> (retrieved July 21, 2004).

—— . *County business patterns*. Last revised April 10, 2003, 11:30:48 EDT. Online. Available HTTP: <http://www.census.gov/epcd/cbp/download/cbpdownload.html> (retrieved July 1, 2004).

US Department of Agriculture, National Agricultural Statistics Service. (2002) *Census of agriculture*. Online. Available HTTP: <http://www.nass.usda.gov/census/> (retrieved July 1, 2004).

Wilkerson, C., and Williams, M. (2007) "The tenth district's defining industries: how are they changing?" *Economic Review*, 3rd quarter, 59–81.

16 Targeted industry analysis in a "comprehensive" economic development extension programme

James R. Nelson, Michael D. Woods,
La Dee Homm, and Gerald A. Doeksen

Introduction

Extension economic development professionals have noted several challenges they commonly encounter when using targeted industry lists, or for that matter other common tools, with community economic development teams (Homm et al. 2003). These include:

- lack of community support;
- preconceived team member notions about community priorities;
- unrealistic community expectations;
- inability of the community team to build and implement a plan; and
- competition from other communities.

Often an effective way to deal with such challenges is to present community teams with comprehensive economic development programmes that educate and inform them about a few tools that they need, but also about the conceptual bases, rationales, interdependencies, and limitations of available tools.

This chapter describes common components of comprehensive economic development extension programmes and attempts to indicate how targeted industry analysis fits into extension economic development programmes. Then, in the final section, we make some suggestions about how targeted industry analysis might be used more effectively than is currently the case, given the resource limitations that constrain most rural community economic development efforts.

Common extension economic development programme components are presented below in an order that matches with how they are often used in extension programmes:

- general economic information about community and area economies;
- information on the dynamics of economic development;
- a planning process to help community leaders understand the strengths

and weaknesses of their communities, and to help them develop community visions;

- ideas and tools to address community service and infrastructure deficiencies in communities (water, fire protection, emergency medical, rural health clinics, etc.);
- ideas and tools directed toward the use of industry targeting to accomplish community goals and objectives; and
- ideas and tools directed toward helping entrepreneurs and business managers make good decisions about strengthening existing business operations, expanding business operations, and establishing new firms.

General economic information about community and area economies

A great deal of secondary data are available about state, county, and community economies. Much of these data originate with the US Department of Commerce. Such data are commonly supplemented and organized by state departments of commerce and by commercial entities (such as ePodunk, Inc., Pacific Northwest Regional Economic Analysis Project) into state, county, and community profiles. Community profile information can be very useful to local citizens working on economic development as they strive to understand their local economies. They can see changes and trends in socioeconomic variables, including population, income, employment, poverty, and local taxes, to name a few. Also, they can get a sense for the economic importance of various industries in their economy and how this has changed over time by reviewing employment numbers by industry. From profile data, they can also learn about many other issues in their state, county, or community, including housing, crime, age distribution of the population, education of the population, commuting patterns, and land use. Finally, they can identify, at least tentatively, potential opportunities for further economic growth and development.

Numerous extension programmes throughout the nation have example community, county, and/or area socioeconomic profiles. Community reports available through the Oklahoma State University Extension Web site cover three areas: socioeconomic data and trend analysis, retail trends and gap analysis, and more complex economic and fiscal impact analysis. These extension reports, like others in the nation, are generally provided to community groups to enhance understanding of international, national, state, and local socioeconomic trends. Theses reports stand alone as an educational programme and are also used as the introduction to a broader comprehensive economic development effort. Typically, the report, along with a PowerPoint presentation, is provided to Extension field staff who are trained to work with local community groups to analyse the data contained in the reports.

How does the local economy work?

Sharing and presenting socioeconomic data can be useful to assist local citizens working on economic development to better understand their problems, as well as the strengths of their local economy. However, seeing local socioeconomic data generally does not contribute to helping people realize what opportunities or problems exist in their community, much less how to address these opportunities or problems. To begin to get a sense for how opportunities or problems might be addressed, local citizens need to know how dollars, goods and services, and labour flow within an economy. A simple flow chart (Figure 16.1) can be useful in explaining these concepts.

Figure 16.1 illustrates the major linkages between components of an economic system:

1   A household earns a paycheck through employment in one of the basic industries. Basic industries are those which produce goods or services for sale outside the community.
2   The household then uses its income to purchase goods and services in the local economy.
3   Basic industry may also purchase goods and services from local businesses, or vice versa.

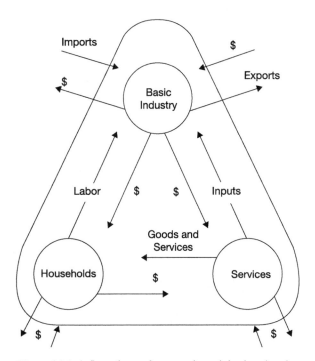

Figure 16.1 A flow chart of economic activity in a local economy.

4 Households may seek employment outside the community. Households may also choose to purchase goods and services outside the community. Consumers may have many motives for these decisions, including availability, selection, or price.
5 Local businesses also purchase items outside the community. When a community has a strong retail sector, it may actually draw consumer purchases from a larger area.
6 Basic industry purchases production inputs outside the community. Production inputs may include raw materials, labour, or specialized services. Industries sell their production outside the community and thus bring money into the community.

By understanding how a community works, it is possible to develop a consistent, beneficial community development plan and reach your economic goals.

Planning process for community economic development

Once communities understand the basic concepts of economic development, they must address the questions, "What does our community want to be? What is our community vision?" At this stage, it is time for communities to develop an economic development plan that encompasses the economic development cycle. Figure 16.2 shows the community development cycle or planning process (Peterson, 1996).

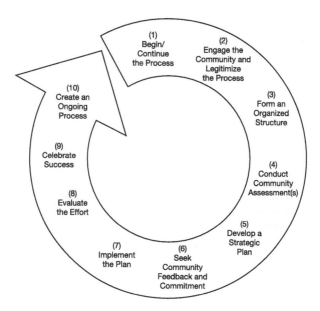

Figure 16.2 The community development cycle.

The following 10-step process describes the efforts involved in local community development planning. The steps are interrelated and may not always occur in exactly this sequence. However, the cycle presents a useful overview of the process.

1   **Begin/continue the process:** someone or some group must make the initial decision to build a community strategy. At this point, the community decides if the benefits of such a process are worth the effort. This is often the time when the community contacts a resource provider such as the Oklahoma Cooperative Extension Service to assist in the planning effort.

2   **Engage the community:** plans are not successful if only a few individuals are involved. Broad community support is critical. Therefore, the wider the range of participants, the greater the pool of talents available to help a targeted industry plan. Public-sector groups, private-sector representatives, and volunteer organizations should all be encouraged to participate.

3   **Form an organized structure:** use an existing organization or form a new one. Someone or some group needs to be responsible for the effort. If a new group is formed, a more formalized structure with byelaws may be desired as the process continues.

4   **Conduct community assessment(s):** data and information provide useful perspectives for planning. Communities should assess local assets and determine what resources are available to move forward. There are many tools available to assist in assessing community resources, including targeted industry analysis, as described in this chapter. Other assessment tools include community surveys, data and trends analysis, economic impact analysis, and sales gap (retail) analysis.

5   **Develop a strategic plan:** communities should identify goals and measurable objectives. Often a common language is useful. Communities needing assistance in developing a strategic plan could review the extension fact sheet by Woods et al. (1999).

6   **Seek community feedback and commitment:** share the initial draft of community goals and objectives. Involve the local media and let local residents know of the effort. Be prepared for new ideas and be receptive to additional suggestions.

7   **Implement the plan:** hopefully, adequate resources and volunteers have been identified to follow through and successfully implement the planned objectives. This is the stage where most plans falter and end up "sitting on the shelf". Lack of adequate resources will probably ensure failure and disappointment.

8   **Evaluate the effort:** continue to monitor and evaluate to determine when you are successful. If you set benchmarks to measure achievement, then you will be able to document success.

9   **Celebrate success:** reward yourself and the entire community when objectives and tasks are accomplished. One way to ensure continued

interest and excitement is to organize a community-wide celebration to acknowledge both short-term and long-term achievements.

10   **Create an ongoing process:** the effort does not end but is to be continued and evaluated annually. Each year or two, you need to reevaluate and possibly modify or add to the plan. Of course, you will be removing goals and objectives that are accomplished.

Targeted industry analysis may be an important part of this process. As we indicated earlier, it can be used in the community assessment stage of the process. However, targeted industry analysis can have a broader role and may be consulted and utilized throughout the community development cycle.

Targeted industry analysis and economic development

In general, there are four approaches to economic development:

Creation
Attraction
Retention
Expansion

1   **Creation** – new businesses develop in the community through entrepreneurial activities.
2   **Attraction** – new industries come into the community, through either the relocation of existing plants or the establishment of new branch plants.
3   **Retention** – companies that are already established in the community remain in the community and do not shut their doors or move elsewhere.
4   **Expansion** – existing business establishments expand and increase their production or services offered. This leads to enlarging the physical plant size, hiring new employees, and purchasing additional raw materials and supplies.

All four of these activities are vital to the economic development process and valid in their own right. Together, they promote the idea that to be successful in development efforts, you must CARE for your community. The data generated here by targeted industry analysis can be beneficial in accomplishing all four activities.

Targeted industry analysis is a potentially powerful tool to enhance and focus the economic development activities. However, the list is sometimes not used to its potential.

> **The primary objective of targeted industry analysis is to develop a list of industries, that have a moderate-to-strong likelihood of containing companies that might be interested in locating or expanding in the community under study.**

The developer can use the list to identify business contacts. Ideally, this will result in an increase in the cost-effectiveness of direct mailings and prospecting trips. The developer can also use the list to identify trade publications for the placement of advertisements and to determine which trade shows to attend. Additionally, the developer can use the list to prepare promotional materials and advertisements with particular industries in mind. If an industry tends to have certain locational requirements, the brochure or the advertisement can emphasize how the community meets these industrial needs. Thus, targeted industry analysis enables economic development professionals to focus their business recruiting resources.

Targeted industry analysis can also help to understand the limitations of the community as an industrial location. Communities can then address these weaknesses. This is an important by-product of the process. Targeted industry analysis is just the beginning of economic development, not the answer to all problems!

Data and methods

The data used in this analysis are from IMPLAN Professional, an economic impact assessment modelling system. IMPLAN has the ability to build economic models that will estimate the impacts of economic changes in states, counties, or communities. With this feature, the multicounty region can be built and analysed.

The three-step analysis used in this project produced two lists; one contains the top 50 community exports and the other the top 50 community imports. This initial sorting is based on the concepts of export enhancement and import substitution (see Figure 16.3).

Second, targeted industry analysis considered how communities might refine the list by considering desirability factors. This is accomplished on the basis of the total employment, total employee compensation, and direct compensation per employee of the region, as well as the employment growth rate by industry. For this analysis, employment growth rates were used.

The third feature of this data set is the ability to weight each of the desirability factors and establish rankings specific to the community's needs.

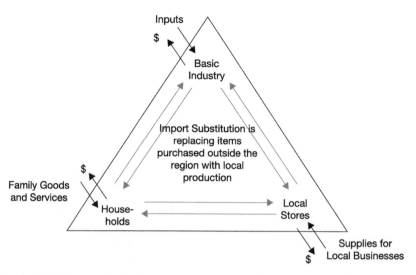

Figure 16.3 Import substitution.

Step one: community export enhancement vs. community import substitution

Community export enhancement

Export enhancement (Figure 16.4) is expanding the volume of goods and services the region sells to the rest of the world. To examine export enhancement opportunities, total exports, including domestic and foreign exports, were calculated.

The export base of a regional economy consists of goods and service sectors that sell a large portion of their products outside the region. The expansion of an export base industry leads to expansion of local non-basic industries through the "multiplier" or ripple effect.

Community import substitution

Import substitution is replacing items purchased outside the region with local production. To examine import substitution opportunities, the region's total imports were calculated by taking commodity demand minus commodity supply.

Commodities produced in one region often use goods and services (inputs) imported from outside the region. When import substitution can occur, economic leakages are plugged and the ripple effects from a given export base are strengthened.

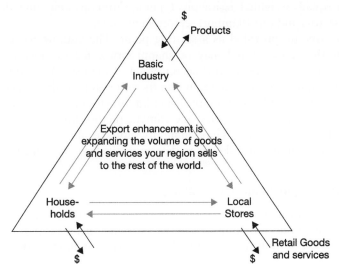

Figure 16.4 Export enhancement.

Step two: desirability criterion

The four desirability criteria were designed to give the community additional information about economic activity. The criteria chosen are total employment, total employee compensation, direct employee compensation per employee, and employment growth rate. By incorporating these criteria into the model, the community can consider "quality" features of each industry.

Step three: weighting system

Each of the four desirability criteria can be weighted on the basis of the needs of the community. The weighted rank is produced by multiplying the rank by a user-defined weight factor. To assign or change the weight given to a specific factor, change the weight factor in the corresponding column. The authors have provided a computer database (in Microsoft Access) that allows variations in the weighting factors.

Results of targeted industry analysis

Several regional reports were generated as a result of a study funded by Oklahoma Service Company by Oklahoma. These reports contain the top 50 sectors for a specified region ranked by both level of exports and level of imports.

Through the above process, the data were divided into two basic lists of import sectors and export sectors. Each list was then sorted on the basis of the four equally weighted desirability criteria. From this weighting, the top 10 export sectors and top 10 import sectors were listed.

These lists are provided as a starting point. The authors recognize that some of the sectors listed may be inappropriate for the region, and no attempt has been made for further screening of the lists. An example of an industry that most likely will not fit into the community is the tobacco industry. This sector could appear on the list of imports for many regions; however, because of economic, regulatory, and climatic factors, tobacco production is not feasible for Oklahoma. The community should evaluate and refine the list on the basis of research and logic to determine the feasibility of each sector.

Using the targeted industry database

It is up to local decision-makers to determine how this information will be used to benefit the community. Factors to consider include the strengths and weaknesses of both the industries under consideration and the community as a whole.

As we mentioned earlier, the targeted industry analysis is not always used to its full potential. It would be beneficial for communities to explore the many applications of this data in business recruitment and retention efforts.

Refining targeted industry list

Once the community begins to consider the targeted industry analysis list, it should establish a process for considering each industry on the list. Some industries will easily drop out of the list, as they are not feasible for the region. Others will require more research before making a decision. This section will outline some potential methods of considering the targeted industry analysis list.

One tool for helping in this process is the weighting system. As we discussed previously, the weighting system is a feature built into the database to consider the value judgements of the community. The development group can assign a weight to each factor: total employment, total employee compensation, direct compensation per employee, and employment growth rate based on the community's needs.

There are numerous ways to arrive at the values you will use as weight factors. One method is to allow everyone to discuss the merits of each criterion and vote once for the criterion that each person feels is the most important. The database can then be assigned values according to the relative importance to each factor.

Once the weights are assigned and changed in the database, the "Top Exports" and "Top Imports" reports can be printed. This will show the sectors that have the most data support of the desirability criterion based on economic activity in the region and the weight factors set by the community

As the community continues the process of refining the list, it becomes vital to research the merits of each industry. Other factors, not included in the database, may be very important in considering the target list, such as environmental impact, property values, and changes in population. This type of evaluation closely follows the community business matching model procedures.

Before embarking on costly recruiting efforts, the community must realistically assess its own strengths and weaknesses, a process that will create a more efficient economic development plan.

Community service assessment

It would be a rare situation indeed for a community economic development planning process to not point out at least a few significant deficiencies of community services and infrastructure that constrain economic development. Extension has a long history of programmes addressing such constraints.

In general, these programmes involve using community service budgets to estimate needs, costs, and revenues. A budget-based methodology for evaluating alternative community services provision options must include the following:

- definition of constituent needs and desires for particular services;
- designation of alternative systems for the provision of these services; and
- costs and revenues associated with alternative systems and financing options.

In many instances, decision-makers are interested in evaluating alternatives to existing community service systems.

A brief example will clarify the budget methodology. Community leaders in Fairfax, Oklahoma recently wanted to evaluate how to provide emergency medical services (EMS). The constituent needs were evident as the community was more than 20 miles from the nearest emergency medical services. On the basis of data gathered from the existing EMS operation, the community could expect more than 400 EMS calls per year. The alternative systems they chose to evaluate were a basic EMS system and a paramedic system. In addition, the leaders wanted to consider part-paid and on-call staffing versus a fully paid system for each level of service. Thus, costs and revenue for the four alternatives had to be estimated. Costs included all capital costs (ambulance, equipment, building, and all operating costs). Revenue options included fee per call, sales tax, and special EMS districts. From the alternative budgets, decision-makers could evaluate tradeoffs between costs of service and level of service.

Methodologies have been developed and tested for analysis of alternative budgets for many types of services. Some examples include fire (St Clair et al. 2001); emergency medical services (St Clair et al. 2003); rural clinics (Barnes and Doeksen 2004); and solid waste (Eilrich et al. 2002). Numerous land grant extension programmes have materials on their Web sites to evaluate local community services.

Assistance to local entrepreneurs

An important aspect of a "comprehensive" economic development extension programme is decision-making assistance for entrepreneurs and firms. This is especially true in rural communities where most businesses (existing or new) are small. Small businesses face high risks: one-third of small business start-ups survive for less than two years, and half survive for less than four years (US Small Business Administration n.d.).

A high proportion of new business failures occur because potential costs, profitability, cash flow, and risk and uncertainty associated with new enterprises are not given thorough pro forma consideration. These issues can also be critical for existing firms that expand with new enterprises or new markets.

To address these issues, new and changing small businesses need help with economic feasibility analyses and business plans. So it is appropriate, and often very important, that extension economic development programmes include such assistance.

Economic feasibility analyses are conceptually rather simple. They involve estimating investment costs, annual operating costs, net revenues, and cash flows. However, it can be quite problematic to actually conduct such an analysis for a planned business venture for which some of the costs (especially some of the operating costs) may not be easy to predict, and for which markets for products, market prices for products, and quantities of products to be sold are almost certainly difficult to predict. A generalized small business feasibility model such as the one developed by Widner and Nelson (2004) can be very useful for this purpose.

Once it has been determined that a new business or a potential expansion or relocation of an existing business may be economically feasible, it is important, even critical, that a thorough business plan be developed for the planned business venture. This is important because a business plan facilitates consideration of business issues that go far beyond the cost and revenue estimates of a feasibility study. A thorough business plan addresses issues of entrepreneur and family goals related to the business; entrepreneurial and business skills needed to run the business; specific plans for financing the business; and in-depth consideration of competition, markets, marketing issues, and labour force issues.

Completing a thorough business plan is not a short-term process. To do it well takes several months of research, contemplation, writing, and rewriting. A good way to approach a business plan is in a structured course. Such courses are commonly taught for academic credit and as outreach or extension courses at many universities, colleges, and community colleges.

It is important for extension professionals and others working with firms and entrepreneurs on issues of business creation, attraction, retention, and expansion to recognize that developing a business plan requires a great deal of research, thought, and decision-making on the part of the entrepreneur or business owner-manager who needs it. Developing business plans for entre- preneurs and small business owner-managers is not usually a very productive process. Helping them develop business plans for themselves is generally much more likely to benefit them and their planned businesses. Many good references are available on developing business plans (National Home-Based and Micro Business Design Team 2003; Sumner 1999; Wold et al. 2000).

Many entrepreneurs and owner-managers are not willing to devote the necessary time and effort to develop thorough business plans. These indi- viduals should be reminded that it may be worth several months of intensive effort on their part to avoid losing their life savings, forfeiting their children's college educations, and maybe destroying their marriages.

Most new small businesses fail. The payoffs for small business success can be high in terms of profits and personal satisfaction, but the risks of failure are also high, especially if thorough and realistic business planning is not carried out.

Conclusions and implications

Clearly, targeted industry analysis can play an important role in extension economic development programmes. At a minimum, the conceptual frame- work of industry targeting contributes greatly to the rationale of community economic development. Simply knowing about the imports and exports of existing local firms provides a solid basis for an important set of local economic scenarios.

However, given typical resource constraints, it probably does not make sense to apply the full arsenal of industrial targeting tools directly and fully to every local rural community economic development need. An effective scheme for allocating resources efficiently might be to apply a fairly com- prehensive set of industrial targeting tools at the level of regional economies (perhaps at the state level). Then results of such regional analyses along with specific local information about economic development opportunities (per- haps derived from primary data collection) can be used effectively to develop local economic development programmes that are consistent with the realities of regional economies.

If the approach discussed above is a reasonable one for incorporating the full range of industrial targeting tools into specific local programmes, then there is a need for applied research and extension personnel (with appropriate expertise) to identify those industrial targeting tools that are most appropri- ate for use at the level of regional economies and those that are most readily applicable at the local level. Research and extension economic development professionals should develop guidelines concerning when and where to use what tools.

324 *Applications and case studies*

References

Barnes, J., and Doeksen, G.A. (2004) *A Guide to Establishing a Rural Health Clinic*, Stillwater: Oklahoma State University Extension Service.

Eilrich, F., et al. (2002) *A Guidebook for Solid Waste Services*, Stillwater: Department of Agricultural Economics, Oklahoma State University.

Homm, L., Woods, M.D., and Barta, S. (2003) "Rebuilding after natural disaster: a targeted economic development approach", *Journal of the Community Development Society*, 34(1): 107–24.

National Home-Based and Micro Business Design Team. (2003) *Cashing in on Business Opportunities*, SRDC #210, Starkville: Mississippi State University Extension Service and Southern Rural Development Center.

Peterson, M. (1996) "Harnessing the Power of Vision: Ten Steps to Creating a Strategic Vision and Action Plan For Your Community", Cooperative Extension Service, University of Arkansas.

St Clair, C., et al. (2001) *A Guidebook for Rural Fire Protection*, Prepared for the Oklahoma Sub-State Rural Fire Coordinator.

—— . (2003) *A System Development Guide for Emergency Medical Services*, Report prepared as part of Mississippi Delta Project (www.ruralhealthworks.org).

Sumner, H. (1999) *Tilling the Soil of Opportunity, NxLevel176 Guide for Agricultural Entrepreneurs*, Denver, CO: University of Nebraska and US West Foundation.

US Small Business Administration. (n.d.) *General Small Business Frequently Asked Questions*. Online. Available HTTP: <http://app1.sba.gov/faqs/faqIndexAll.cfm?areaid=24>.

Widner, L., and Nelson, J. (2004, December) *A Generalized Model for Feasibility Analysis of Small Businesses*, Moscow: Department of Agricultural Economics and Rural Sociology, University of Idaho.

Wold, D., et al. (2000). *NxLevel176 Guide for Entrepreneurs*, Denver: Nxlevel Education Foundation.

Woods, M., Frye, J., and Ralstin, S. (1999) *Blueprints for Your Community's Future: Creating a Strategic Plan for Local Economic Development*, WF-916, Stillwater: Oklahoma Cooperative Extension Service, Oklahoma State University.

Woods, M., Nelson, J.R., Peterson, S., Wittman, P., Frye, V.J., and Ralstin, S. (2004) *Care for Your Local Economy – Strategies for Local Economic Development*. Southern Rural Development Center. Online. Available HTTP: <http://srdc.msstate.edu/care/>

17 TRED as an educational tool

*Steven Deller, John Leatherman, and
Martin Shields*

Introduction[1]

Numerous other chapters in this volume note that communities are facing increasing pressure to be proactive in the promotion of economic growth and development. As community leaders and concerned citizens attempt to accomplish this, they face difficult questions about how to proceed. In addition, the range of sophistication across communities varies greatly, with some having a professional staff of economic development practitioners while others rely on citizen ad hoc committees made up of well-meaning, but inexperienced volunteers. Johnson (Chapter 13) and Cox et al. (Chapter 14) note that often local preferences are not considered and policies reflect the desires of a small set of people within the community. Finally, the increasingly wide use of the Porter approach to think about and identify clusters at the state level has spurred significant interest at the local level for comparable analysis.

One limitation of many industry targeting studies – of which Porter's are but one example – is that they are often technical consultant reports. One consequence is a lack of local ownership in the analysis by economic development decision-makers and other community members. As outlined in Shaffer, Deller, and Marcouiller (2004) and reinforced by Nelson et al. (Chapter 16), for community economic development to be effective and sustainable, communities must not only feel that they own the process and the policy recommendations but they also must understand, believe, and buy into the analysis that leads to the policy recommendations. Because so many cluster studies are best described as consultant reports, the effectiveness and sustainability of such efforts come into question.

Ayres (1996) explains that the transition from a top-down to a bottom-up approach in local economic development efforts creates an environment that is both more innovative and sustainable. As opposed to an outside consultant or expert providing "*the* answer" to economic development needs, communities are turning to economic development practitioners who act as facilitators of strategic planning processes. As Ayres (1996: 23) notes, "there is a shift from 'let the expert do it' to the 'we know the community best and we can do it' ". One key outcome of locally driven strategic visioning or planning efforts is the building of social capital. A central concept here is that no one individual, agency, or organization has the authority, resources, or knowledge necessary to solve issues unilaterally. A parallel principal is that local residents should determine the future course of their communities (Gardner and Shaffer 2004).

This chapter complements the analytic hierarchy process (AHP) offered by Johnson (Chapter 13) and the community-business matching model (CBM) outlined by Cox et al. (Chapter 14) by providing a foundations for using TRED analysis as a mechanism to meet multiple community development goals, which include not only identifying regional clusters through technical analysis, but also creating sustainable and effective strategies to build both a stronger economy and a stronger sense of community and social capital. We first develop the foundation for this mechanism, and then outline one possible structure for using TRED analysis as a foundation for broader community economic development efforts. Beyond these introductory comments, the chapter has three additional sections. In the second section, we outline strategic planning within a community economic development setting. Next, we discuss the essential conditions communities need before undertaking effective and sustainable TRED-based economic development efforts. In the fourth section, we propose one possible strategic planning and educational programme that can be built around TRED analysis. We close the chapter with a review of the key concepts offered.

Community strategic planning and practitioner roles

With phrases such as "New Public Management", "Reinventing Government", and "New Governance" entering the public dialogue, policy-makers, businesses, non-profits, and citizens are looking for new ways to undertake economic development. In the spirit of Bryson (1990), effective communities are embracing strategic planning and visioning to structure discussions and form action plans (Ayres 1996). In practice, communities have adopted three general forms of strategic planning efforts: comprehensive planning, strategic visioning, and strategic planning. Although there is certainly overlap across the three forms, there are important differences as well. Comprehensive planning tends to be holistic in nature and addresses a range of issues from land use planning to housing development to environmental protection planning; economic development is but one component of a much larger effort. Strategic visioning is often aimed at identifying a desirable future or a broad set of goals that the community is striving to achieve. It is not projecting trends, but conceptualizing what might be possible in light of anticipated opportunities and known constraints. Strategic planning presumes that such a vision is in place and aims to identify specific actions that can be taken to achieve the vision (Carlson 1990).

In the strictest sense, Carlson (1990: 11) maintains that "strategic plans are, for the most part, a dissection and extension of today's problems rather than an evaluation of tomorrow's opportunities". If a community is undertaking a targeted regional economic development (TRED) effort with the goal of identifying appropriate regional industrial clusters, it is presumed that the community's vision, or tomorrow's opportunity, is already well defined and achievable. As we argue below, the community's vision is vital in determining the filtering processes that are required to identify appropriate clusters. We suggest that packaging a TRED effort within a strategic planning process can help the community move forward on several fronts. First, the strategic planning process provides a structured framework for conducting the TRED analysis and identifying appropriate strategies. Second, the TRED analysis can reinforce or refine the community vision. Third, the process we suggest below can add to the community's social capital, an achievement that can have a much broader community impact than narrower economic development efforts (e.g., Debertin and Goetz 2005).

As in the business world, there are numerous models of strategic planning within a community economic development setting (Walzer 1996). The Community Economic Analysis programme developed by Glen Pulver and Ron Shaffer at the University of Wisconsin-Extension in the early 1980s asked four basic questions: where have we been, where are we now, where are we going, and how do we get there? These questions set the stage for a strategic planning programme that helps communities craft a vision for themselves and identify specific economic development strategies to achieve that vision. Although economic growth and development is often the issue that brings the community to the table, the strategic planning process may uncover underlying issues that the community was unaware of or did not realize needed to be addressed before undertaking formal economic development efforts. For example, a community may discover that it lacks local institutions or organizations that are required to pursue economic development such as a business association, chamber of commerce, or a specialized government agency or committee. In the end, nearly all community strategic planning processes have common themes. Strategic planning is "a disciplined effort to produce fundamental decisions and actions that shape and guide what an organization is, what it does, and why it does it" (Bryson 1995: x).

Through strategic planning, organizations or, in our case, communities can:

- examine the environment in which they exist and operate;
- explore factors and trends that affect the way they do business and carry out their mission;
- frame the strategic issues they must address; and
- find ways to address these issues by reexamining and reworking organizational mandates and missions, costs and financing, management, and organizational structures.

The benefits of strategic planning include increased effectiveness and efficiencies, improved understanding and better learning, better decision-making, enhanced organizational capabilities, improved communications and public relations, and increased political support (Bryson and Alston 1996: 3).

A strategic plan should include an examination and/or development of organization-wide:

- mission, vision, and values;
- formal and informal mandates;
- internal and external environmental scans;
- identification of strategic issues;
- strategy formulation and selection;
- implementation plans; and
- evaluation of the change process and implementation.

As Walzer (1996) and Ayres (1996) note, how these basic elements play out within community strategic planning and/or visioning programmes is as varied as the communities which undertake such efforts. This is both a strength and a weakness. It is a strength in that each community entering into such a process is unique and requires flexibility in how it approaches the planning process. The weakness is that structure of a Bryson-type strategic planning process can be lost and the sustainability of the outcomes questioned.

As we suggest later in this chapter, TRED can serve as a focal point for building an effective community strategic planning process that achieves multiple goals. First and foremost is that the process can identify specific economic development strategies that are suggested from the TRED analysis. The second, and most relevant to university-based TRED efforts, are the educational opportunities created through the strategic planning process. Each step of the strategic planning process creates a "teachable moment" to help local decision-makers and citizens learn about the local economy and the principles of economic development and growth.

We build our framework on how community economic development practitioners interact with communities. As Shaffer et al. (2004) note, practitioners can undertake several approaches when working in a community. These include technical assistance, self-help, conflict, asset-based, and self-development (Christenson 1989). Practitioners are not tied lock-step to any of these in their pure form as described here; rather, they are more typically blended in accordance with the specific situation at hand.

The technical assistance approach is prevalent in most applications of TRED and Porter's method for identifying clusters. Here, a consultant prepares a report and delivers it to the interested parties, presuming that the community is prepared to act upon the recommendations. This approach assumes that the community is well organized, has identified economic development through cluster development as the goal, and is moving toward a plan of action (Christenson 1989). The practitioner supports task-oriented actions. For the practitioner, approaches to technical assistance vary with whether one is doing policy *development* or *implementation*. In policy development, the practitioner uses the analytical tools as outlined in several chapters in this volume to identify potential clusters. These analyses are then used to help formulate policy. Policy implementation assistance is the next stage, in which practitioners translate the insights and recommendations of the TRED analysis to into formal initiatives.

The self-help approach is based on the premise that community residents can, should, and will solve their own problems (Christenson 1989). Here the practitioner facilitates the process where consultants conduct the targeted cluster analysis, and then help the community identify strategies based on the results. The self-help approach requires that the community has in place the requisite institutional structure and problem-solving skills. This observation is developed in more detail in the next section of the chapter.

Some advantages of the self-help approach are that it often builds a stronger sense of community, it often evolves into a holistic approach, it builds a self-sustaining ability to deal with new problems, and it allows for community-specific strategies to build clusters. Yet there are some disadvantages. It works best in smaller communities, but change is often slow. Special interests may cloud issues and cause the true community self-interest to take a longer time to appear. Since the practitioner is concerned about the community learning to "do it itself", accomplishing specific tasks may be secondary. Finally, in the absence of a well-crafted TRED analysis, decisions may be based on presumptions rather than fact.

Community scale is particularly relevant to the discussion. One of the powers of Porter's cluster approach is that it moves the notion of space beyond municipal or political boundaries to a functional economic region, which can comprise anywhere from a handful of communities to a large geographic area literally composed of hundreds of communities. But broadening the reach has its potential downside. Our experience suggests that as the size of the region or number of communities undertaking the TRED-based strategic planning effort increases, the sense of process ownership and the resulting strategic effort declines. People relate best to their own community – which may be as small as a neighbourhood – and within the self-help approach this level of effort is most effective. As the geographic scale of the effort increases, people's commitment may decline. The challenge is motivating people to think regionally rather than locally. While Porter's cluster framework motivates such thinking, the sustainability of action on such a level is yet to be fully documented.

Conflict is the third approach and is based on the premise that the community is fragmented or gridlocked (Christenson 1989). The practitioner works to break the gridlock, thereby thrusting the community forward into a new state of being. Here, the practitioner works either as an advocate or mediator. Given our interest in using TRED analysis as a catalyst for sustainable strategic planning and educational programming, the conflict approach does not help us.

Recently, asset-based community development (ABCD) has emerged as a fourth practitioner approach that is particularly relevant to our purposes (Green 2008). According to Kretzmann and McKnight (1993), there are essentially two different ways to do economic analysis. The first way is the needs/deficiency model, and the second is the asset-based model. The needs/deficiency model focuses on what is absent or problematic or what a community needs. Once a TRED analysis has been completed and potential cluster industries identified, this approach focuses on the barriers that will hinder or prevent the community from moving forward.

ABCD also sees a community as home to a variety of assets: what is present, the capacities of its residents, and its organizational and institutional base. In short, assets are capacities, gifts, and abilities and the crucial step is identifying and linking them. ABCD is internally focused in terms of agenda building, and relies on the problem solving abilities of local residents, local associations, and local institutions. ABCD is relationship-driven, and emphasizes building and rebuilding local networks among individuals, associations, and institutions. In a TRED setting, this approach focuses on those community's assets that can be used to build clusters identified in the targeted cluster analysis.

One can almost think of this approach within the context of force field analysis (Hustedde and Score 1995). Force field analysis is often used within strategic planning processes to identify factors that will both hinder and aid in the implementation of the action plan. For each strategy, participants are asked to identify potentially hindering and aiding factors, and then consider a course of action to overcome hindrances and build on aiding factors. Force field analysis can often help prioritize strategies that have few hindrances and many factors working in their favour while at the same time identifying strategies that are not viable. In a way, the use of force field analysis can be viewed as a means to solve strategy implementation problems before they arise.

The final approach we examine is self-development, which departs from the deterministic model that local economic development is predestined by location, initial resource endowment, or economic/social structure. Self-development challenges the perception that communities are at the mercy of larger economic forces, instead encouraging them to act proactively. From this perspective, local human capital is crucial for creating opportunity, which implies self-reliance. Self-development is counter to the laissez-faire, neo-classic view of the economy. With the latter, a community is forced to accept the forces of the larger economy.

Strategic planning and/or visioning can be a powerful process for helping communities think through the information TRED analysis provides in their attempts to build clusters and target economic development. Practitioners can play numerous roles in this process, ranging from a technical analyst to a facilitator of strategic thinking. Unfortunately, not all communities are in a position to undertake such efforts. They may be plagued by apathy at best, and resignation at worst. For these places, practitioners must first establish an environment that facilitates optimism. If not, any targeted cluster-based economic development is likely doomed.

Necessary conditions

Effectively applying TRED analysis in promoting targeted economic development presumes that certain community-level elements are in place; not all communities are ready to effectively pursue economic development and growth activities (Cavaye 2001; Shaffer et al. 2004). As Woods (1996) notes, no single planning process or set of preconditions can ensure success, but there are some common elements that must be in place. In essence, these preconditions may be viewed as necessary but not sufficient to ensure the effective use of TRED analysis as a basis for economic development, and have much to do with what the community development literature sometimes calls "social infrastructure" or "social capital". Another layer of this discussion centres on the notion of civic engagement at the local level derived through activities such as community organizing, citizen participation, and community-based decision-making (Lovan et al. 2004; Turner 1999).

According to some, differences in civic engagement among communities are largely due to differences in social capital (Coleman 1988; Putnam 1995; Turner 1999). Social capital refers to features of social organizations that facilitate coordination and cooperation for mutual benefit, such as norms, social trust, networks, and reciprocity (Flora 1998; Flora et al. 1996). To say that a person is trustworthy means that there is a high probability that she will perform an action that is beneficial, or at least not detrimental to us, a critical condition for individuals to consider engaging in some form of cooperation with them (Hansen 1992). Reciprocity is a mutual expectation or understanding that a given action will be returned in kind. Networks facilitate coordination and communication, and thus allow dilemmas of collective action to be resolved (Putnam 1995). At the same time, networks of civic engagement embody past successes and collaboration that can serve as a cultural template for future collaboration. Although social capital is inherent to the relationships and interactions between people in a community, there is recognizable difficulty in effectively addressing social capital due to its inherently abstract nature, and the fact that it is a public good.

Swanson (1996) talks about social infrastructure, a form of social capital, as the capacity and will of individuals and communities to provide or take advantage of opportunities that enhance their economic and social well-being. There are several community characteristics associated with social infrastructure. The first is the role of individual and community decision-making, and the capacity to make choices. To a large extent, this depends on the quality of information available and the ability to decipher that information, specifically the capacity to learn. This characteristic emphasizes the skills for making informed decisions when faced with a potentially confusing menu of choices. A keen ability to process information is particularly crucial with TRED analysis, where the analytical sophistication and volumes of data provided can overwhelm decision-makers and citizens.

The second characteristic is the nature of the community's negotiation process in determining the collective good, including its capacity to work together. What is the distribution of political and economic power? Is it widely distributed or narrowly held? What is the quality and focus of inter-action among participants in the economic development decision-making? To instill a capacity for innovative behaviour, the community almost needs an atmosphere of "immunity" or "indifference" that permits individuals to experiment with different ways of doing things. Without this atmosphere, tradition becomes the standard and change remains virtually non-existent.

Flora and Flora (1993) discuss entrepreneurial infrastructure, rather than social capital, and its relationship to community economic development. Essentially, they forward several dimensions that define entrepreneurial infra-structure. The first is symbolic diversity, or a community-level orientation toward inclusiveness rather than exclusiveness. An important aspect is that the community engages in constructive controversy, as opposed to raucous conflict or superficial harmony, to arrive at workable community solutions by focusing on community processes, depersonalizing politics and broadening of community boundaries. Controversy is accepted in the community so that disagreements are dealt with in a positive fashion rather than perceived as conflicts. One way of looking at this is to think in terms of win-win outcomes versus win-lose outcomes. This is a comprehensive means of thinking of civic engagement.

By depersonalizing politics, disagreements are seen as honest differences to competing solutions and those offering alternatives are not seen as inherently evil (Lovan et al. 2004). Here, the process, rather than winning, is the focus. This is particularly true in the public setting, where political rivals may not only dismiss any idea of compromise and cooperation, but may actively undermine their rivals' efforts. This can be particularly true at the national or state level, where one administration's initiatives and programmes imple-mented are ignored or actively overturned by the next (Gardner and Shaffer 2004; Shaffer 2001).

Some maintain that at the local level, the motivation for involvement centres on a broader concern for community betterment rather than political gain. Unfortunately, local politicians often base their behaviour on what they observe at the national and state level. An analogy of the type of conduct we envision might be of parenting. What one tries to do as a parent is not necessarily a win-lose type of outcome but to get the child to gain some understanding and perspective. The community also thinks in terms of a broad definition of who should be involved in the decision and that there are permeable boundaries as to who should be involved. In other words, one draws the boundaries as inclusively as possible and reduces the perception of "us versus them".

Network quality is the final dimension of Flora and Flora's entrepreneurial infrastructure. This considers things such as network diversity, including but not limited to, ethnic, class, and gender diversity. We think about what the Floras call "horizontal networks" because we learn best from people like ourselves. At the same time vertical networks are also essential because regions need to be linked to the world outside. For example, a community may learn from the experiences of similar nearby communities (horizontal), but at the same time is willing to draw on the experiences of larger and distant places (vertical). Resource mobilization, an essential element of entrepreneurial infrastructure, is when the community learns to rely on its own resources first, rather than looking elsewhere, such as toward more senior levels of government, non-local businesses, or foundations. But, again, sustainability of local policies almost mandates that those policies be determined by local dialogue and decisions.

Drawing on social capital's essential premises, Woods (1996) and Wall and Luther (1989) disclose the seven "secrets" to effective community economic development:

1   Positive attitude.
2   Entrepreneurial spirit.
3   Bias for action.
4   Focus on controllables.
5   Plan for development.
6   Strategic outlook.
7   Vision for the future.

The most successful communities not only possess a desire to build an action plan but are also willing to seek new opportunities. Further, they think creatively in building a vision and identifying actionable strategies. This includes seeking out new solutions to old problems, looking within the community for new leaders who bring fresh perspectives and ideas, and looking outside the community for innovative ideas.

Most of our writing so far is admittedly academic or conceptual, outlining only general ideas. Accordingly, we have not provided practitioners with a specific checklist of items that need to be in place to enhance a community's probability of success in its economic development endeavors. We address this now by outlining a set of tools practitioners can use to help determine the sufficiency of a community's social capital and entrepreneurial social infrastructure. These tools have been developed and implemented by a number of community development scholars, notably Woods (1996), Woods and Slogget (1998), Shaffer et al. 2004, and Lewis (2004). These checklists range from simple yes/no questions, to statements that use a Likert-type response scaling, to simple discussion points for the practitioner and community to consider. A complete listing of all the possible questions/statements that have been offered is beyond the scope of this chapter, but a sampling is helpful.

- There exists a local organization responsible for promoting economic development.
- There is widespread community participation in community economic development efforts.
- Volunteerism is high within the community.
- Adequate resources exist to support some level of local activity.
- There is a willingness to invest local resources in local projects.
- There are working relationships with state and federal agencies.
- The local media is supportive and involved.
- Voter turnout for local elections is high.
- People listen to one another for understanding.
- Key business leaders are actively involved in economic development efforts.
- Local government is usually responsive to the problems of existing businesses.
- There exists a viable and active local business association or chamber of commerce.
- The community maintains an up-to-date economic profile.
- The community has a fully funded infrastructure capital improvement plan.
- Local financial institutions effectively support community economic development.
- There is the capability to provide labour force training and skills when needed.

Social capital's adherents suggest that as the degree of positive responses to these statements increases, successful economic development efforts are more likely. Conversely, if the community responds negatively to a majority of such statements, it is reasonable to think that many of the preconditions for effective economic development have not been met. In the latter case, the community might consider focusing more energy on building local capacity. This would include identifying new leaders, promoting volunteerism, creating local institutions, and building a stronger sense of community.

A community's willingness to think beyond its immediate spatial boundaries is a key element in effectively pursuing targeted industry clusters. Because local governments, especially rural ones, play a vital role in economic development, people often think of development efforts only within the boundaries of governmental units. But county boundaries were defined decades ago, with a primary criterion that all county residents could travel by horse from their home to the county seat, conduct their business, and return home in the same day. Obviously, transportation modes have changed, and municipal and county boundaries must accordingly be recognized as simply an artifact of old political processes. Instead, clusters should be based on economic regions, which are delineated by the flows of goods, services, and labour, reflected in shopping and commuting patterns.

If defining boundaries by horse and buggy makes little sense today, we must ask if the spatial boundaries of counties and local governments make sense in a modern economy. Unfortunately, there is no clear-cut answer. From a Jeffersonian democracy perspective, smallness is preferred because it provides the greatest opportunity for broad-based citizen involvement. Indeed, within the public finance literature there is strong evidence, both theoretical and empirical, that as the size of the community grows the preferences of the citizenry becomes increasingly diverse (Shaffer et al. 2004). The result within larger communities is that any compromise is likely to be unsatisfactory to a majority of the citizens. At the same time, economic clusters function at the scale of what regional economists call a functional economic area. Depending on the particular cluster, this region may consist of a geographic area ranging from a handful to many counties.

The fact that economic and political boundaries seldom overlap presents a significant challenge to communities as they pursue targeted cluster development. If the economic region is the basis of a targeted economic development effort, then communities need to think beyond their own borders and be willing to collaborate with other jurisdictions. This adds a new layer of complexity, as local decision-makers and citizens must now work effectively both within their community and across communities. The obstacles are formidable. In reality, local elected officials are beholden only to their electorate. Although the region might benefit from a collaborative effort, policy-makers must be convinced that their constituents will benefit from a regional project, or at least not be adversely affected. When such decisions involve choosing what to invest in, where to invest, and how to pay for it, then parochialism can swamp any effort, no matter how well intentioned.

While citizens can quickly determine the costs of a regional effort, they have a harder time understanding the benefits, especially if they do not directly occur in their municipality. From an educational perspective, the benefits of regionalism are subtle, yet they can be taught to lay audiences. For example, it is easily recognized that people commonly live in one community, work in another, and shop in a third. Thus, with a little prompting, people grasp that "economic shocks" in one place quickly spread across municipal borders. An important benefit of a regional approach, then, is that it internalizes economic spillover effects.

A second benefit is what is often referred to as "economies of scale". The concept is that expensive – but highly desirable – projects may be cost-prohibitive if undertaken by a single government, but become affordable if the costs are spread out over a larger population. Applied to TRED, this means that it may be more cost effective (and useful) to work on a few coordinated large-scale initiatives than a multitude of smaller ones.

As states and communities explore cluster development in the spirit of Porter, policy-makers and the citizenry are starting to think regionally (e.g., Federal Reserve Bank of Kansas City 2004). This is a very positive development and something to be further encouraged. Within our discussion of social capital, the idea is whether or not communities are willing to think creatively and act regionally within a cooperative framework.

Outline of a TRED educational programme

To help practitioners work with communities in implementing a TRED analysis and craft appropriate strategies and action plans, we turn to the Take Charge programme developed by Janet Ayres and others and published by the North Central Regional Center for Rural Development at Iowa State University.[2] The Take Charge programme combines the analytical tools outlined in Hustedde et al. (1993) and elements of strategic planning to form both an educational programme and an effective process for working with communities in economic development. Variations of the Take Charge programme include Wisconsin's Community Economic Analysis programme developed by Ron Shaffer and Glen Pulver and the Illinois Institute for Rural Affairs' Mapping the Future of Your Community programme developed by Norm Walzer.[3]

The objectives of the approach are threefold. The first centres on identifying appropriate clusters to target and promote, and strategies to build a companion programme initiative. The majority of the chapters in this volume focus on this objective. The second objective builds on the TRED effort as an opportunity to help participants increase their awareness of regional economic strengths, weaknesses, opportunities, and threats (SWOT). While a formal SWOT analysis is not necessarily proposed, the main outcome is significantly enhanced economic awareness and knowledge. As we mentioned above, a primary benefit to states and communities that explore Porter-type clusters is the realization that the functional economic area extends beyond any political boundaries. Comprehending that a regional approach is required is a major step forward for many communities. The third objective centres on the notion of community or social capital development discussed in the previous section. In effect, engaging a community to think and act regionally is community development because it broadens its thinking about itself and how it fits into the larger economy. In addition, by spending time and energy on the TRED process through the strategic planning exercise reinforces the community's entrepreneurial social infrastructure.

The proposed process suggests assembling two overlapping teams composed of the practitioner(s) and community (region) members. The first team, the research team, helps craft the economic analysis underlying the TRED effort. Here, the practitioner reviews the various analytical methods and assesses the resources and capacity needed to conduct the analysis, and the team then selects the research method. A research schedule is outlined and timelines established where the various screening processes described in other chapters are applied to determine the industries that will serve as the basis of the clusters. Here, the research team can craft filters and threshold levels that best fit the community's vision and values. The end result is a selection of potential cluster industries, including an analysis of the strengths and weaknesses of each cluster, and an assessment of the regional assets that make the cluster a suitable target.

The second team, which overlaps with membership from the research team, enters into a structured strategic planning process. Here, a Take Charge-type process is employed. The process can be composed of three to four workshops. The first workshop outlines the results of the TRED analysis, identifies strengths and weaknesses within each cluster, and offers the suitability assessment performed by the research team. The task of presenting the analysis to the second team should not fall on the shoulders of the practitioner alone – rather, it should be shared among members of the research team. Having community members present the group's findings reinforces the sense of ownership not only in the analysis but in the process as well. This meeting's primary purpose is educating the second team about the community's economic structure and the identified potential clusters. One important outcome from this first meeting is prioritizing the set of clusters on which the community wishes to focus.

In most instances, it is probably sufficient to select three clusters, ranked from highest to lowest priority. But how to choose? One popular cluster selection criterion centres on the idea of long-run regional economic diversification. This argument is based on standard portfolio analysis, where the risk of loss is minimized by diversifying assets or industrial structure. Applied to Porter's notion of comparative advantage, such thinking may lead regions to incorrectly conclude that they should only consider industries that enjoy agglomeration advantages *across* industries. Work by Wagner and Deller (1998) suggests that regions that have stronger internal industrial ties, specifically agglomeration *within* industries, tend to have higher growth rates and more stability. While seemingly countering broad-based diversification arguments, the logic makes intuitive and practical sense as a long-term strategy. In the short run, individual cluster development projects should focus on comparative advantage and specialization, but in the long run, diversification efforts should envelop short-term efforts. Over time, clusters would be unique as regions diversify.

The second workshop focuses on a discussion of economic development strategies specifically aimed at the promoting the selected clusters. Strategies can range from working with existing cluster businesses to build institutional capacity and firm networking, to business retention and expansion-type programming, to firm recruitment strategies. The goal here is to broaden how the team thinks about the range of possibilities, with traditional recruitment efforts as just one of many potential strategies. The challenge is to refine and focus the strategies to the specific priority clusters. Although academic research has laid the theoretical and empirical foundations of TRED analysis and cluster development, additional work to create unique cluster development strategies is still needed.

The third (and potentially fourth) workshop focuses on identifying specific action steps that the community can pursue, including deciding which strategies will be implemented, deciding who will take responsibility for implementation, deciding how any necessary funding will be secured, and developing a detailed follow-up and evaluation plan. Based on our experiences, it is vital that these tasks do not fall to the practitioner. Members of the second team must be willing and able to step up and be actively involved in implementing the strategies, evaluating progress, and reporting back to the full team. Here, tools such as force field analysis (outlined above) are useful in refining strategies and action plans as well as motivating team members to assume greater leadership roles. The practitioner's role is to serve as a resource to the action team in providing additional materials as needed, defining organizational roles, and, perhaps, serving as a cheerleader for the team's efforts.

This stage's final task is establishing specific timetables for the action plan and benchmarks for assessing performance. The timetable establishes guidelines for subcommittees to work and report back to the larger team and imposes a form of accountability and discipline on the team. The process of thinking through benchmarks helps in refining both strategies and the team's thinking about economic development. The practitioner's role at this point is to act as a facilitator, reminding the team, subcommittees, and team leaders what they agreed to; monitoring benchmarks; and encouraging the effort.

Although the approach we outline is straightforward, implementation is not easy. Fundamental challenges include defining the region, determining team membership, identifying feasible strategies, and garnering buy-in to a regional approach across communities. As we discussed at length above, it is generally the case that the relevant community seldom coincides with the boundaries of a single municipality. One benefit of communities thinking in terms of Porter-type clusters is an appreciation of thinking regionally. This raises a question about team membership: should a regional approach be taken from the beginning, or should the TRED analysis and strategic planning effort outlined here be used as the first step in moving to a regional approach?

Although there is no clear or simple answer, we offer a couple of observations that may shed some light. A sound organizational infrastructure underlies the most successful community economic development programmes. By this we mean that economic development programmes are most effectively implemented by entities focusing on a certain geographic scale. While varying across communities, one such collection of organizations might consist of neighbourhood or downtown business associations, a municipal chamber of commerce, a county economic development corporation, and a regional collaborative of communities, such as a council of governments. Most local leaders have long recognized the benefits of marketing tourism assets on a regional basis. Today, we recognize collaborative regional organizations might be the best approach to facilitating cluster-based economic development. Indeed, as we suggested earlier, it is not unusual for the practitioner to defer requests for assistance with an economic development initiative to first focus on building a region's institutional capacity or organizational infrastructure. In fact, a TRED-type analysis focusing on cluster development can catalyse the formation of such organizations and spur shared regional strategies.

Still, we recognize the reality that parochial interests and attitudes can often trump collective efforts. We are, after all, working in the real world, where individual human interest prevails. We have two responses. First, virtually every one of the modelling techniques and community processes outlined in this volume has equal if not sometimes greater utility in its application in a single community. TRED is not a cluster development strategy alone. Indeed, many of these techniques have been used successfully for decades in advance of Porter-type cluster analysis. The beauty of the TRED approach is its widespread applicability, wealth of educational utility, and potential to enhance a wide variety of economic development initiatives.

Our second response to the "us first" perspective that prevails among many local leaders is that even if they choose to go it alone, they would be well served by recognizing and marketing their *regional* asset base. As indicated earlier, economic flows respect no political boundary absent artificial barriers. People are willing and sometimes quite content travelling great distances for employment, goods and services, and other amenities. Thus, local economic development programmes will be stronger by recognizing and promoting the regional labour market, trading relationships, and transportation and communication linkages on which people and businesses depend.

We suggest that from a community perspective, a grassroots approach could be undertaken with the long-term goal of building regional perspectives and partnerships. Local communities can initiate smaller scale TRED analysis and planning efforts that grow into regional efforts. Because of the time commitment needed to build regional partnerships and instill local willingness to accept a regional approach, this necessarily requires a long-range outlook. The potential risk is that as the region grows in physical size, the sense of ownership of the analysis and process becomes weaker, hindering efforts. Clearly, no standard answer exists because of the uniqueness of individual communities. Some communities already think and act regionally, and these communities are best positioned to build on TRED and cluster development. Other communities may have high levels of social capital or entrepreneurial social infrastructure but are not yet thinking in a regional manner.

Conclusions

In this chapter, we have outlined one potential educational initiative built on TRED analysis and cluster development. Drawing on the tools of community visioning and strategic planning, we suggest a process by which communities identify potential industry clusters and build social capital through ownership of the analysis. Unfortunately, not all communities are ready to undertake or benefit from TRED analysis. We describe what we term the necessary, but not sufficient conditions that should be in place prior to a community undertaking a TRED analysis. Regions possessing threshold levels of social capital or entrepreneurial social infrastructure will have a much better chance for success in cluster-based economic development efforts. The challenge facing the community development practitioner is that there are no clear quantitative preparedness indices, nor are there well-defined measures of the relevant spatial community or region that should define the analysis. As more communities express interest in TRED analysis and cluster development, the experience gained will provide a more solid basis for future prescription.

Notes

1   This chapter builds on three previous papers by the authors, including Deller and Shields (1998), Leatherman and Deller (2001), and Shields and Deller (2003).
2   The programme is available at http://www.ncrcrd.iastate.edu/pubs/contents/153.htm.
3   For a detailed discussion of a family of programmes such as Take Charge, Community Economic Analysis, and Mapping, see Walzer (1996).

References

Ayres, J. (1996) "Essential elements of strategic visioning", in N. Walzer (ed.), *Community Strategic Visioning Programs*, pp. 21–36, Westport, CT: Praeger.

Bryson, J.M. (1995) *Strategic Planning for Public and Nonprofit Organizations*. San Francisco: Jossey-Bass.

Bryson, J., and Alston, F. (1996) *Creating and Implementing Your Strategic Plan: A Workbook for Public and Nonprofit Organizations*. San Francisco: Jossey-Bass.

Cavaye, J. (2001) "Rural community development: new challenges and enduring dilemmas", *Journal of Regional Analysis and Policy*, 31(2): 109–24.

Coleman, J.S. (1988) "Social capital in the creation of human capital", *American Journal of Sociology*, 94(Supplement): S95–S120.

Debertin, D.L., and Goetz, S.J. (2005) "Rural poverty, amenities and social capital", *Southern Business and Economics Journal*, 28(4):

Deller, S.C., and Shields, M. (1998) "Economic impact modeling as a tool for community economic development", *Journal of Regional Analysis and Policy*, 28(2): 76–95.

Federal Reserve Bank of Kansas City. (2004) *New Governance for a New Rural America: Reinventing Public & Private Institutions*, Kansas City, MO: Federal Reserve Bank of Kansas City, Center for the Study of Rural America.

Flora, C.B., and Flora, J.L. (1993) "Entrepreneurial social infrastructure: a necessary ingredient", *Annals, American Association of Political and Social Sciences*, 529(September): 48–58.

Flora, J.L. (1998) "Social capital and communities of place", *Rural Sociology*, 63(4): 481–506.

Flora, J.L., Flora, C.B., and Wade, K. (1996) "Measuring success and empowerment", in N. Walzer (ed.), *Community Strategic Visioning Programs*, pp. 57–74, Westport, CT: Praeger.

Gardner, R., and Shaffer, R. (2004) "The national rural development partnership in the United States: a case study in collaboration", in W.R. Lovan, M. Murray, and R. Shaffer (eds), *Participatory Governance: Planning, Conflict Mediation and Public Decision-Making in Civil Society*, pp. 61–84, Burlington, VT: Ashgate.

Green, G.P. (2008) "Asset based development in rural communities", In G.A. Goreham (ed.), *Encyclopedia of Rural America, 2nd edn*, Millerton, NY: Grey House Publishing.

Hansen, N. (1992) "Competition, trust and reciprocity in the development of innovative regional milieux", *Papers in Regional Science*, 71(2): 95–105.

Hustedde, R., and Score, M. (1995), "Force-field analysis: incorporating critical thinking in goal setting", in *CD Practice: Promoting Principles of Good Practice*, Milwaukee, WI: Community Development Society.

Hustedde, R., Shaffer, R., and Pulver, G. (1993) *Community Economic Analysis: A How To Manua.* (RRD141), Ames, IA: North Central Regional Center for Rural Development. Online. Available HTTP: <http://www.ncrcrd.iastate.edu/pubs/contents/rrd186-readonly.pdf>.

Leatherman, J.C., and Deller, S.C. (2001) "Building local government capacity: the toolbox for outreach educators", *Journal of Regional Analysis and Policy*, 31(1): 91–110.

Lewis, A. (2004) *Community Economic Development Index*, Madison, WI: Center for Community Economic Development, University of Wisconsin-Extension. Online. Available HTTP: <http://www.uwex.edu/ces/cced/economies/preparednessindex_final_02_06.pdf>.

Lovan, W.R., Murray, M., and Shaffer, R. (2004), "Participatory governance in a changing world", in W.R. Lovan, M. Murray, and R. Shaffer (eds), *Participatory Governance: Planning, Conflict Mediation and Public Decision-Making in Civil Society*, pp. 1–22, Burlington, VT: Ashgate.

Putnam, R.D. (1995) "Bowling alone: America's declining social capital", *Journal of Democracy*, 6(1): 65–78.

Shaffer, R. (2001) *"Building a national rural policy and the National Rural Development Partnership"*, *Journal of Regional Analysis and Policy*, 31(2): 77–91.

Shields, M., and Deller, S.C. (2003) "Using economic impact models as an educational tool in community economic development programming: lessons from Pennsylvania and Wisconsin", *Journal of Extension*, 41(3). Online. Available HTTP: <http://www.joe.org/joe/2003june/a4.shtml>.

Swanson, L. (1996) "Social infrastructure and rural economic development", in T.D. Rowley, D.W. Sears, G.L Nelson, J.N. Reid, and M.J. Yetley (eds), *Rural Development Research: A Foundation for Policy*, pp. 103–21. Westport, CT: Greenwood.

Turner, R. (1999) "Entrepreneurial neighborhood initiatives: political capital in community development", *Economic Development Quarterly*, 13(1): 15–22.

Wagner, J.E., and Deller, S.C. (1998) "Measuring the effects of economic diversity on growth and stability", *Land Economics*, 74(4): 541–56.

Walzer, N. (ed.) (1996) *Community Strategic Visioning Programs.* Westport, CT: Praeger.

Woods, M.D. (1996) "Precondition for successful program implementation", in N. Walzer (ed.), *Community Strategic Visioning Programs*, Pp. 75–92. Westport, CT: Praeger.

Woods, M.D., and Sloggett, G. (1988) "Strategic planning for economic development in rural areas and small towns of Oklahoma", Extension Factsheets, Number 859, Stillwater: Oklahoma Cooperative Extension Service, Oklahoma State University. Online. Available HTTP: <http://pods.dasnr.okstate.edu/docushare/dsweb/Get/Document-441/AGEC-859pod.pdf>.

18 Industry targeting
Theoretical underpinning and practical application

David W. Hughes

Introduction

Many communities in Appalachia continue to experience stagnant growth, high levels of poverty, unemployment, out-migration, and a resulting loss of population. The Central Appalachia Empowerment Zone (CAEZ) was established to foster economic opportunity in Braxton, Clay, Fayette, Nicholas, and Roane counties in West Virginia. These counties are among the poorest in the state, and fostering economic growth is a major challenge for local policy-makers. Clay County is the only county that lies entirely within the CAEZ. Economic development indicators reveal a picture of a county with a stagnant economy.

As indicated in other chapters, many counties have only a small budget to support economic development (Homm et al. 2000). Hence, development efforts need to be refined to ensure maximum payoff from limited resources. Target industry analysis is a tool that can be used to refine such efforts. The analysis is a systematic method for identifying suitable industries for a given area or community. The future prospects of such industries are also evaluated and the attributes of the industries are then matched with local economic development goals. Local policy-makers and business leaders can use the resulting information in business recruitment, retention, and expansion efforts.

As discussed in other chapters, results from input-output models, particular the IMPLAN model building system, often play a key role in industry targeting studies. For example, the approaches used by Deller (Chapter 19) and Barkley and Henry (Chapter 10) rely heavily on input-output models. Results of a target industry analysis for Clay County provide a case study for examining how the accuracy of an input-output model can influence target industry recommendations. Although they are most relevant for IMPLAN users, we present data check methods that can be used in evaluating other types of input-output models. This chapter also emphasizes for all types of models, the need to develop a greater sensitivity to how changes in model assumptions and data can influence changes in policy recommendations.

This chapter briefly discusses overarching and more specific concepts in using input-output models to make industry targeting recommendations. The discussion then turns to the concepts of synthetic and hybrid input-output models and model accuracy. I place an emphasis on tying these concepts to industry targeting efforts. I then review the socioeconomic situation of Clay County to provide context. This discussion is followed by our application of an input-output model in a Clay County industry targeting study. Emphasis is placed in the discussion on how changes to the model were made to enhance accuracy. The major concerns are how these changes influenced the overall picture of the Clay County economy and possible changes in industry targeting recommendations.

Industry targeting and IO models

Industry targeting studies identify the set of industries that a community or region can attract or develop (what is feasible) and a set of industries that a community or region should attract or develop (what is desirable). Because lack of growth is the major concern in Clay County, I centre the analysis on the former. Other chapters in this volume consider the question of what is desirable from a community's perspective.

Industry targeting studies are based on an amalgamation of concepts and theories including export base theory, import substitution, industry location theory, and industry clusters. Much of the current popularity of industry targeting probably stems from the concept of industry clusters (see, however, Chapter 5, by Woodward and Guimarães). Shields et al. lay out the relationship between industry targeting and economic clusters in rural areas in Chapter 3. Similarly, Woodward and Guimarães (Chapter 5) discuss the Porter model, which is the impetus behind much of the current cluster policy efforts. The relationship between industry targeting and industry location theory is discussed in Deller, Chapter 4, and in Leatherman and Kastens, Chapter 7.

Researchers and economic practitioners have used input-output (IO) models to indicate possible industry targets in several ways based on major theoretical concepts. For example, consistent with Barkley and Henry (Chapter 10), export base theory (Richardson 1972), with its emphasis on export enhancement – expanding what a region sells to the outside world – has been a part of an industry targeting effort. The presumption is that the region already has an emphasis on and a comparative advantage in the production of exported commodities. In the Barkley and Henry approach, industries with increases in location quotients over time or industries with an location quotient of greater than 1 are both possible industry targets (and a large or growing location quotient can be indicative of an enhanced exports approach). Likewise, IO models have been used to show industries that sell large levels of output outside the local economy (i.e., regional exports) (this work, Holland et al. 1997, and Sorte et al. 2000 among others). Such industries may be targeted for growth as a way to further enhance exports. In their study of a regional economy in Oklahoma, Homm et al. (2000) also emphasized the importance of these concepts by targeting industries on the basis of their levels of exports.

Another logical consequence is an emphasis on so-called value-added products. For example, Lamie et al. (1997) identified high-impact and high-potential wood products industries in South Carolina through a screening process based on input-output determined input requirements, income and employment effects, export markets, and linkages to input suppliers (as estimated by an IO model). Wright et al. (1998), in another study with a natural resource orientation, targeted food, fiber, and forestry industries for development of rural areas in South Carolina. They provided a comprehensive look at the competitive position of 150 food, fibre, and forestry processing industries at the two- and three-digit level. The focus of the study was on industries that have favoured rural areas in South Carolina for new or expanded plants compared to Georgia and North Carolina.

In Clay County, coal is the primary export, so a reasonable strategy could be attracting industries that use coal as a major input. For such a rural area, natural resource endowments play an important role in determining why primary manufacturers would locate there, as such firms must minimize the transportation cost of bulky and/or perishable inputs (Kohls and Uhl 1998; Deller, Chapter 19). Accordingly, earlier industry targeting studies that have focused on developing more rural regions have tended to emphasize natural resource based industries.[1]

Import substitution (Richardson 1972; Deller, Chapter 19; Barkley and Henry, Chapter 10) is also based on export base theory and multiplier analysis. IO models have been used to identify local industries that do not buy locally. Key input suppliers for such industries may be targeted as a result of IO model output (Holland et al. 1997; Sorte et al. 2000; and Homm et al. 2000). For target industry analysis, import substitution is based on the concept that external suppliers are satisfying a local market and perhaps local producers can more readily meet this market.

IO models also generate economic multipliers, which are a major feature of economic clusters. For example, Leatherman and Kastens (Chapter 7) use multipliers generated by regional input-output models as a measurement of the degree of cluster development. Because relatively large multipliers mean relatively well-developed backward linkages, larger than average multipliers imply the presence of ready access to either local input suppliers or local output markets (depending on the side of the transaction), which is an attribute of well developed clusters. Hence, IO models can be used to identify clusters and key sectors in clusters. Because of these uses, model accuracy is key in making appropriate industry targeting recommendations. As will be discussed next, accuracy is a particular concern because of the way in which regional IO models are generally constructed.

Accurate input-output models for industry targeting

General considerations

Users need to account for input-output model strengths and weaknesses in making their industry targeting recommendations. Model strengths include the large amount of data generated concerning the general nature of a local economy. For example, our model of a rural economy in West Virginia generated detailed information in terms of employment, returns to factors of production, and industry sales for 70 local industry sectors and demand data for 528 commodities. Linkages within the local economy and with the outside world are also well described. These linkages provide valuable information for industry targeting studies concerning import substitution, export enhancement, and multipliers.

Input-output models also have well-known limitations that curtail how such models can inform industry targeting studies. Without outside information, capacity constraints are not imposed in such models in terms of inputs or outputs. For example, if an industry is at full capacity and faces constraints to further growth (such as limited wood supplies for wood products), the sector is not a good target regardless of what input-output model results may indicate. Further, constant returns to scale are assumed, as are fixed relative input use and market allocation of output. These model assumptions also give pause in making industry targeting recommendations. For example, because IO models are insensitive to prices, rapid input price increases for a sector could mean a sector is not a good target despite model results. Standard models also do not speak to future growth paths of industrial sectors or to a host of non-market considerations such as environmental or quality of life impacts, or types of labour skills needed. Accounts contained in input-output models can be used to provide estimates of "current" industry profitability. For example, such accounts provide explicit estimates of returns to owner-operators (proprietors' income) and other capital (which includes depreciation charges, interest payments, and corporate profits). However, returns to capital can be "low" or even negative, and multipliers for the sector in question can still be relatively large based on strong backward linkages. Hence, model results such as multipliers do not account for the lack of profits.

Synthetic (ready made) and hybrid models

A different set of issues relate to the use of input-output models built with systems such as IMPLAN. IMPLAN is one of several ready-made modelling systems (others include the RIMS models developed by US Department of Commerce, Bureau of Economic Analysis, and REMI for price-flexible models), where secondary regional data are combined with the economic linkages found in the US input-output tables to generate regional input-output models in one computer package.[2] In such models, firm production technology in the region is assumed to be the same as for the US economy: for example, food crop farmers in Idaho are assumed have the same input mix as food crop farmers across the US; or, if the US farmers spends 30 per cent of revenues on pesticides, their Idaho counterparts will do the same. Such models must also accurately reflect where inputs are purchased (either in or outside the region). If inputs purchases primarily occur outside the region, the impacts will be negligible and multipliers will be small. Accordingly, IMPLAN and other ready-made models provide reasonably accurate estimates if first, the region of interest has similar production (input-output) relationships as the national economy, and second, model coefficient accurately reflect inter-regional trade relationships (in IMPLAN, the latter are reflected by regional purchase coefficients). However, regional economies can differ from the national economy in economic structure and model coefficients may over- or underestimate actual purchases within the regional economy as opposed to regional imports (Lahr 1998). Accordingly, as for other ready-made or synthetic model, results of any IMPLAN-based model should be validated for accuracy with changes to the basic model when warranted.

Hybrid IO models are ready-made models, modified by including primary or secondary data to more closely reflect the economy being studied (Lahr 1998). For industry targeting studies, the implication is that including such primary or secondary data would enhance the accuracy of industry targeting study recommendations. Using the previous hypothetical example, an industry targeting study based on a ready-made input-output model might recommend a chemical fertilizer plant as an industry target because of the perceived high demand by local farmers. However, assume that the actual use of pesticides by local farmers was only 2 per cent on the dollar (that is, the ready-made model grossly overestimated the level of local demand). At that level of actual local demand, pursuing such a plant would not be a viable industry targeting recommendation. A hybrid model that properly reflected local economic linkages would not produce such a recommendation (based on erroneous data in this case). The model reflected in this chapter is a hybrid model, with an emphasis on how changes to the model influence possible industry targeting results.

A body of literature has been generated based on the concepts first introduced by Jensen (1980) of holistic versus partitative accuracy. Holistic accuracy refers to the degree to which an input-output model, especially a non-survey or ready-made model, provides a generally accurate picture of a given economy. Partitative accuracy refers to the accuracy of individual cells in the input-output matrix. Only holistic accuracy is obtainable; for us the question is whether the Clay County input-output model provides holistic accuracy for industry targeting purposes. That is, is the model sufficiently accurate in providing industry targeting recommendations that are "grounded in the truth"?

In two studies that used an approach similar to that used here (Holland et al. 1997; Sorte et al. 2000), an input-output model was first generated with IMPLAN-based databases and software (Minnesota IMPLAN Group, Inc, 2000). Regional data generated by the US Department of Commerce was then used to improve model accuracy. Sortie et al. (2000) then ground-truthed the model with several local businesses. These two studies were also based on the policy concepts of export enhancement, import substitution, and cluster development.

Clay County study

Clay County socioeconomic structure

Clay County provides a good case study for industry targeting because of the economic challenges (lack of growth, higher than average rates of out-migration and poverty) that the region faces. Our goal was to provide informed decisions to local leaders concerning feasible targets that could help meet this outstanding need. Given that many places, especially rural places, face similar challenges and have similar resource-based economies, a study of industry targeting in Clay County is informative for industry targeting efforts.

Clay County is located in central West Virginia, 42 miles northeast of Charleston, the state capital. Much like other non-metropolitan (rural) areas in West Virginia, it has not experienced significant economic growth in recent years. According to Goetz and Lego (2000), per capita income in Clay County ranked 146 out of 148 non-metropolitan counties in a region stretching from Maine to West Virginia in 1998. Unemployment in Clay County in 2003 was 10.0 per cent, exceeding the state unemployment rate of 6.1 per cent (W. V. Programs of Employment Security 2005).

Most growth in the county has occurred in both its western end and along Interstate 79, which is more accessible to Charleston. Currently, one coal mine, several sawmills, a wooden roofing truss manufacturer, and an electrical motor repair facility are the chief non-service sector employers. As in many other rural West Virginia counties, the Board of Public education is the single largest employer at 14.3 per cent of all jobs (County Profiles W. V. Programs of Employment Security 2005), which is not uncommon for many rural regions.

The county's need to develop a sustainable economy is underscored by the high levels of out-commuting and poverty. Like many communities in West Virginia and other parts of Appalachia, declines in the local supply of coal or substitution of capital for labour in the production of coal and wood products, and in some cases, foreign competition, have led to substantial economic dislocation. These events have interplayed with the fact that certain people have always experienced limited economic opportunity because of social isolation. In 2000, 1,653 out of 3,128 local non-farm workers were employed outside of the county. In 2004, the number of people of all ages in poverty in Clay County was estimated at 2,311 (22.4 per cent of the county population versus 12.7 per cent nationally and 16.2 per cent for West

Virginia), and an estimated 31.2 per cent of all children lived below the poverty line (versus 17.8 per cent nationally and 22.6 per cent in West Virginia) (US Census 2007).

The county is 342 square miles in size, but a combination of steep terrain and flood plain designation in flatter areas limits development. The county has a population that has hovered around 10,000 over the past several decades, with few minority members. In recent years, county government and the government of the town of Clay have both experienced financial uncertainty due to fluctuations in coal severance tax revenues, a primary source of local government funding.

Educational attainment levels are low in Clay County. According to the 2000 census, 63.7 per cent of the age 25 and older population had at least a high school diploma (versus 80.4 per cent for the US and 75.2 per cent for West Virginia), but only 7.3 per cent had a bachelor's degree (versus 24.5 per cent nationally and 14.8 per cent for the State) (US Census Quickfacts 2000). Over the last decade and a half, school dropout rates have decreased significantly, but better education is leading to higher rates of out-migration (a general tendency in rural West Virginia).

The low per capita income, high unemployment rate, and concentration of poverty mean that Clay County is eligible for United States Department of Agriculture Empowerment Zone/Enterprise Community status. Consequently, the entire county is located within the Central Appalachia Empowerment Zone, an enterprise community. Further, Clay County has been consistently designated as a distressed county by the Appalachian Regional Commission (2007). Although some would argue that the county is not ready for an industry targeting effort, local leaders still sought ways to enable economic growth. Such efforts would also be greatly enhanced, however, if coupled with local leadership development and strategic planning efforts. Finally, targeting efforts may be enhanced if conducted at the regional level. However, physical and social isolation both may form barriers to regional efforts.

A general lack of development points to a need for a major restructuring of the local economy. However, like in rural areas in general, funding for economic development efforts is limited. Further, lack of a highly educated workforce and ready access to a large population of consumers means certain types of businesses (such as so-called high-tech sectors) are not feasible candidates for development in or for attraction to Clay County. Still, industry targeting does allow policy-makers to concentrate efforts on determining what industry to develop from a feasible set; hence, it is an especially appealing development tool.

Clay County input-output model

We targeted our research efforts toward verifying and, when appropriate, changing the original Clay County input-output model (1997 data). We feel that such efforts are important, because a misspecified model could yield inaccurate results and hence, erroneous conclusions and recommendations. The result was a so-called hybrid input-output model, where a non-survey input-output model, such as the one produced by IMPLAN, is changed to improve accuracy that is based on knowledge of the local economy and superior data (Miller and Blair 1985).

The original IMPLAN model was verified and, when appropriate, changed based on four data sets: the ES202 data set for Clay County from 1997–1999 at the four-digit Standard Industrial Classification (SIC) Code level; the Regional Economic Information System (REIS) data set for 1997–1998 at the two-digit SIC Code level produced by the US Department of Commerce; information concerning the level of self-employment in industries based on the North American Classification System (NAICS) also produced by the US Department of Commerce; and the ReferenceUSA Business Database (formerly the American Business Disk).[3]

Undisclosed ES202 data at the four-digit level were obtained from the West Virginia Bureau of Employment Programs for 1997–1999. The data set covers approximately 90 per cent of all employees in the state (WV Bureau of Employment Programs 1995). Wage data reported in the data set included compensation in the form of pay (wages, salaries, tips, and gratuities), and reimbursements for work-related travel spending on meals and hotels. However, ES202 data do not include the self-employed; it also excludes certain forms of labour income that are included in the definition of earnings used by the US Department of Commerce and in IMPLAN.[4] Accordingly, the REIS data set was also employed in calibrating the IMPLAN model for Clay County.

The calibration of the IMPLAN model is similar in many respects to that found in the *IMPLAN User's Guide* (Minnesota IMPLAN Group 2000). However, our version of the model has the added advantage of being based on a completely disclosed ES202 data set for Clay County (IMPLAN relies on county business patterns to account for data not disclosed in their ES202 data set). Further, their data set for a county involves the RAS matrix bioproportional adjustment procedure based on a state data set, which we found to produce inaccurate results for some industries.[5] For example, the supply estimate of local Doctors and Dentists (490) in the original IMPLAN model was much too high, because jobs and income in a Nursing and Protective Care (491) facility had been inappropriately credited there.[6] As in the IMPLAN model itself, adjustments excluded agriculture, construction, railroads, and certain government sectors because of non-coverage problems.

The IMPLAN sectoring scheme provided in Appendix A of the *IMPLAN User's Guide* (2000) was used as the basis for summing our Clay County ES202 data set for number of establishments, number of jobs, and total covered wages. The ratio between earnings (from REIS) and ES202 wages at the two-digit level (for West Virginia) was used to bridge ES202 wage data for each IMPLAN sector in the Clay County model into earnings estimates. The ratio between these earnings-based estimates were in turn used to provide estimates of industry output and of all elements of value added in the modified Clay County IMPLAN model. Employment estimates were obtained in a similar fashion, except that more recent data concerning self-employment at the state level (US Bureau of the Census 2001) were used to provide the bridging ratios. Our estimates were then compared to those found in the ReferenceUSA Business Database. We made some minor adjustments to our estimates in certain service sectors based on sectors that our estimates seemed to miss.

Finally, we evaluated the estimates of Regional Purchase Coefficients (RPCs) used in IMPLAN. Supply Demand Pool (SDP) values and RPCs are important in estimating regional imports and exports in any IMPLAN-based input-output model. The SDP is the maximum amount of regional supply that is available to meet regional demand. It is the ratio of regionally produced net commodity supply to gross regional commodity demand. A SDP of less than 1 means that the commodity in question will be imported, even if none of that regional supply is a domestic export (Alward et al. 1989).

The RPC is a measure of the actual amount of local demand that is satisfied by local production. For a given commodity, it represents the ratio between regional purchases of regional (county) output and the total net regional (county) supply of the commodity. RPCs for all non-service commodities in IMPLAN (Commodities 1 to 438) are estimated econometrically. RPC estimates for IMPLAN service commodities (Commodities 438 to 514) are calculated on the basis of observed 1977 values for state supply, exports, and imports. Because the SDP is the maximum amount of regional supply available to meet regional demand, it is the upper bound on the RPC values used in IMPLAN models (Alward et al. 1989). RPCs are used to account for crosshauling (the simultaneous exporting and importing of the same commodity).[7] Of course, allowing for crosshauling increases the amount of both commodity exports and imports. For example, for a given commodity, the county produced $10 million in net supply while local demand for that commodity was $8 million. In this case, if a strict SDP approach was used, regional (county) level imports would be zero and regional (county) level exports would be $2 million. However, if the commodity in question had an RPC of 0.8, then 80 per cent of local demand would be been met by local supply and regional imports would be $1.6 million while regional exports would increase to $3.6 million (i.e., the level of crosshauling would be $1.6 million).

RPCs were modified for a number of commodities based on discussions with local policy-makers and on our judgement and knowledge of the local economy. For example, the RPC for selected trade oriented commodities were reduced from 1 to 0.9, to reflect the fact that an interstate runs through the western end of the County and a certain level of such goods would be sold to travellers. Thus, the changes indicated that a certain level of the commodities were exported (while imports also increased). We also examine the impact of following a strict SDP procedure (i.e., for each commodity net regional supply is assumed to meet all local demand before being shipped elsewhere).

Model results

Model results are analysed in several different ways. First, the effect of RPCs on regional trade estimates in the Clay County model is examined. Next, we review the impact of our modifications to the model based on estimates of commodity imports and exports. This review is important, because these estimates play an important role in our ultimate policy recommendations. We then review the sectors with the largest levels of imports and exports in the model. Our concerns and satisfaction with these model results are emphasized. We then make some suggestions about targeting industries for local recruitment or development. Finally, we discuss how our changes to the model influenced and did not influence industry targeting recommendations.

Influence of Regional Purchase Coefficients (RPCs)

The examination of RPCs is especially important for an industry targeting study because estimates of imports and exports drive many of our recommendations. Furthermore, the process by which RPCs are currently generated and used in IMPLAN is not a strength of the model. The estimation is based on old (1977) data, and for services it is based on values observed at the state level. These values may or may not be appropriate for rural areas and many years later. In fact, researchers at IMPLAN are currently in the process of updating their RPC estimates based on a gravity model procedure (Olson and Alward 2000). Because our emphasis was on trade relationships, we decided to test the influence of RPCs on trade estimates (the RPC scenario) as opposed to using only SDP coefficients (the strict SDP scenario).

The use of our modified RPCs in the input-output model of the Clay County economy had only a minor effect on the results of this study. Changes in our estimate of trade due to the use of a set of different RPCs was quite small (a $4.680 million increase) in the modified model. Only 4.0 per cent of estimated total exports and 2.4 per cent of estimated total regional imports were due to the use of the IMPLAN RPC procedure. That is, there were small relative decreases in total regional (county) exports and total regional (county) imports because the strict SDP procedure was followed, or cross-hauling was disallowed. The increase in trade estimates due to the use of RPCs was concentrated in three commodities, Industry Machinery NEC (354) at $1.376 million, Forestry Products (24) at $0.915 million, and Used and Second Hand Goods (518) at $0.801 million.

Commodity estimates were also ranked in terms of relative levels of imports and exports. All else equal, higher levels of imports would support the idea that the commodity was a candidate for import substitution and hence, targeting, for example. A larger than average level of exports would, all else equal, mean that the commodity in question was a candidate for export enhancement or value added processing (and hence, targeting efforts).

The rankings of commodities in terms of imports and exports were also examined under the strict SDP (where the SPD was used as the RPC for all commodities) and the RPC scenarios. In terms of exports, using RPCs versus the use of a strict SDP approach resulted in moderate changes in the rank of export between various commodities. Among the top 20 exported commodities, only Forestry Products (24) had a marked change in rank, moving from 34th in exports under the SDP-only scenario to 18th under the RPC scenario. Although the level of exports changed for 11 commodities out of the top 20, the changes were small. Among the top 10 exports, seven commodities retained the same rank with a very slight change in the order of the other three commodities. The Spearman's correlation coefficient (Hogg and Tanis 1983) was 0.9006 for the 79 commodities with meaningful (at least $1,000) levels of exports in either scenario. This result also indicated little change in the estimate of exports whether or not RPCs were used.

Imports showed an even smaller change under the strict SDP versus RPC scenarios. Among the top 20 imported commodities, 18 retained the same rank under either scenario. Among the top 50 commodities in terms of estimated imports, only Industrial Machinery NEC (354) had a marked change, with an increase in rank from 436 under the strict SDP scenario to 28 when RPCs were employed. Forestry Products (24) and Used and Second Hand Goods (518) had marked changes in rank going from the strict SDP scenario to the RPC scenario. The Spearman's correlation coefficient was 0.9423 for the 453 commodities with meaningful (at least $1,000) levels of imports in either scenario. This result also indicated little change in the estimate of imports when RPCs were used or not used. Based on these results, the use of RPCs by themselves would have little influence on any IMPLAN-based recommendations concerning industries to target for Clay County.

The original, ready-made IMPLAN model for Clay County was also analysed in terms of how much RPCs influenced trade estimates. As compared to a model in which the strict SDP scenario was used, trade increases by $6.287 million due to use of RPCs. Out of $131.958 million in domestic exports, 4.8 per cent was due to the use of RPCs. Out of $204.075 million in total imports, 3.1 per cent was due to the use of RPCs. In terms of ranking commodities based on relative levels of imports and exports, the original model of the Clay County economy showed less sensitivity to the use of RPCs than did the modified version. The Spearman's correlation coefficient was 0.9254 for the ranking of commodities based on their export levels (as opposed to 0.9006 for the modified model) and 0.9778 based on their import levels (as opposed to 0.9423 for the modified model).

Trade estimates in the original versus the modified model

Because of the relationship between the RPC and the SDP coefficients, changes that we made to the model influenced our estimates of trade. That is, by changing gross supply estimates in the model, the SDP coefficient could alter the RPC for a given commodity, which would, in turn, affect trade estimates.

The most important comparison was between the estimates of exports and imports in the original model versus those same estimates from the modified version in terms of the relative levels of commodity trade. As previously indicated, changes in the relative rank of a commodity could alter industry targeting recommendations. For this analysis, a comparison was only made of RPC-based estimates between the original and modified versions of the model.

The relative level of exports between the original and modified versions of the Clay County economic model showed both similarities and differences. As shown in Table 18.1, the top three commodities were the same in terms of

Table 18.1 Comparison of domestic regional exports for selected commodities from the Clay County model, 1997

Commodity		New Version Estimated Exports		Original Version Estimated Exports	
		Level (Millions $)	Rank	Level (Millions $)	Rank
37	Coal Mining	67.085	1	66.060	1
38	Natural Gas & Crude Petroleum	5.444	2	15.586	2
482	Miscellaneous Repair Shops	4.314	3	6.739	3
522	State & Local Government – Education	3.406	4	0.000	47
354	Industrial Machines N.E.C.	3.262	5	2.700	10
505	Religious Organizations	3.169	6	3.552	7
54	New Government Facilities	1.736	7	1.736	12
480	Electrical Repair Service	1.621	8	0.000	47
140	Structural Wood Members- N.E.C	1.580	9	3.860	5
518	Used and Secondhand Goods	1.496	10	1.173	13
500	Social Services- N.E.C.	1.460	11	4.001	4
133	Logging Camps and Logging Contractors	1.416	12	0.682	19
56	Maintenance and Repair Other Facilities	1.363	13	1.032	15
435	Motor Freight Transport and Warehousing	1.228	14	3.780	6
51	New Highways and Streets	1.166	15	1.166	14
498	Job Trainings & Related Services	1.021	16	0.162	23
524	Rest Of The World Industry	0.971	17	0.000	47
24	Forestry Products	0.915	18	0.915	16
55	Maintenance and Repair- Residential	0.764	19	0.830	17

513	U.S. Postal Service	0.743	20	0.724	18
39	Natural Gas Liquids	0.709	21	2.086	11
517	Scrap	0.280	22	0.083	28
12	Feed Grains	0.182	23	0.222	22
463	Hotels and Lodging Places	0.160	24	0.000	47
3	Ranch Fed Cattle	0.159	25	0.000	46
445	Water Supply and Sewerage Systems	0.140	26	0.000	47
134	Sawmills and Planing Mills-General	0.108	27	3.285	8
454	Eating & Drinking	0.073	28	0.000	45
13	Hay and Pasture	0.060	29	0.104	25
144	Prefabricated Wood Buildings	0.041	30	0.093	26
7	Hogs- Pigs and Swine	0.020	31	0.000	47
284	Fabricated Plate Work (Boiler Shops)	0.018	32	0.015	30
285	Sheet Metal Work	0.016	33	0.013	31
9	Miscellaneous Livestock	0.015	34	0.012	32
40	Dimension Stone	0.007	35	0.007	34
295	Plating and Polishing	0.005	36	0.004	38
391	Aircraft and Missile Equipment-	0.005	37	0.004	36
460	Insurance Agents and Brokers	0.004	38	0.293	20
174	Newspapers	0.004	39	0.092	27
446	Sanitary Services and Steam Supply	0.003	40	0.143	24
220	Miscellaneous Plastics Products	0.003	41	0.004	37
296	Metal Coating and Allied Services	0.002	42	0.002	42
332	Pumps and Compressors	0.002	43	0.002	39
271	Metal Heat Treating	0.002	44	0.002	41
282	Fabricated Structural Metal	0.002	45	0.002	40
142	Wood Pallets and Skids	0.002	46	0.016	29
190	Cyclic Crudes- Interm. & Indus. Organic Chem.	0.002	47	0.007	33
336	Power Transmission Equipment	0.002	48	0.002	44
147	Wood Products- N.E.C	0.001	49	0.002	43
141	Wood Containers	0.001	50	0.005	35
490	Doctors and Dentists	0.000	51	0.292	21
502	Other Nonprofit Organizations	0.000	52	3.188	9

exports (Coal, Petroleum, and Miscellaneous Repair Shops). However, other commodities, such as Electrical Repair Services (480), with $1.621 million in exports and ranked seventh in among all commodities, had marked differences in estimates (Figure 18.1). The Spearman's correlation coefficient between exports from both model versions with meaningful levels was a relatively low 0.2568, indicating marked differences in export rankings between the two sets of results.

The estimates of imports in the original versus modified version of the Clay County input-output model were also compared and contrasted. An especially large increase was noted in imports for certain medical services (Table 18.2, Figure 18.2). For example, imports of Doctors and Dentists (490) increased

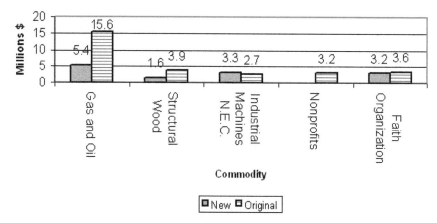

Figure 18.1 Selected new and original commodity domestic export estimates, Clay county, 1997.

Table 18.2 Comparison of regional imports for selected commodities from the Clay County model, 1997

Commodity	New Version Estimated Imports		Original Version Estimated Imports	
	Level (Millions $)	Rank	Level (Millions $)	Rank
462 Real Estate	12.507	1	16.642	1
492 Hospitals	12.036	2	10.352	4
461 Owner-occupied Dwellings	11.777	3	11.777	2
447 Wholesale Trade	9.787	4	11.297	3
311 Construction Machinery and Equipment	6.841	5	6.546	5
454 Eating & Drinking	6.276	6	6.106	6
490 Doctors and Dentists	6.228	7	0.415	46
456 Banking	4.615	8	4.252	10
443 Electric Services	4.561	9	2.908	14
459 Insurance Carriers	4.402	10	4.589	9
210 Petroleum Refining	4.374	11	3.814	11
441 Communications- Except Radio and TV	3.631	12	5.365	7
455 Miscellaneous Retail	3.275	13	2.768	15
496 Colleges- Universities- Schools	3.146	14	2.020	23
384 Motor Vehicles	3.067	15	3.077	12
491 Nursing and Protective Care	3.009	16	4.787	8
493 Other Medical and Health Services	2.822	17	2.622	17
433 Railroads and Related Services	2.653	18	2.630	16
124 Apparel Made From Purchased Materials	2.521	19	2.528	18
494 Legal Services	2.426	20	2.935	13

451	Automotive Dealers & Service Stations	2.407	21	1.911	25
195	Drugs	2.347	22	2.370	19
506	Engineering- Architectural Services	2.304	23	1.810	27
449	General Merchandise Stores	2.295	24	2.257	20
463	Hotels and Lodging Places	1.986	25	1.763	28
458	Security and Commodity Brokers	1.849	26	2.248	21
437	Air Transportation	1.759	27	1.888	26
354	Industrial Machines N.E.C.	1.376	28	1.359	30
516	Noncomparable Imports	1.375	29	1.444	29
452	Apparel & Accessory Stores	1.355	30	1.273	32
488	Amusement and Recreation Services- N.E.C.	1.347	31	1.262	34
519	Federal Government – Military	1.312	32	0.000	50
475	Computer and Data Processing Services	1.234	33	2.042	22
58	Meat Packing Plants	1.197	34	0.401	47
24	Forestry Products	1.175	35	1.925	24
453	Furniture & Home Furnishings Stores	1.156	36	1.044	37
450	Food Stores	1.094	37	0.249	48
508	Management and Consulting Services	1.093	38	1.065	36
479	Automobile Repair and Services	1.062	39	0.197	49
477	Automobile Rental and Leasing	0.977	40	1.318	31
474	Personnel Supply Services	0.939	41	1.272	33
104	Cigarettes	0.931	42	0.931	39
448	Building Materials & Gardening	0.926	43	0.937	38
312	Mining Machinery- Except Oil Field	0.916	44	0.877	41
470	Other Business Services	0.883	45	1.115	35
95	Bottled and Canned Soft Drinks & Water	0.882	46	0.884	40
434	Local- Interurban Passenger Transit	0.847	47	0.671	45
518	Used and Secondhand Goods	0.801	48	0.844	42
213	Lubricating Oils and Greases	0.792	49	0.779	44
436	Water Transportation	0.774	50	0.792	43

from $0.415 million in the original IMPLAN model to $6.228 million in the modified version. The lower import estimate in the original model was due to an erroneous allocation of a Nursing and Protective Care (491) facility to the Doctors and Dentists sector. Other notable changes included an increase in the level of imported Electric Services (443) and Education Services (496) and a decrease in imports for Communications other than Radio or Television (441). However, the Spearman's correlation coefficient between imports from both model versions was a relatively high 0.9118, indicating a good deal of similarity in rankings between the two sets of results. This result is expected, since the demand for many commodities is largely, if not completely, met

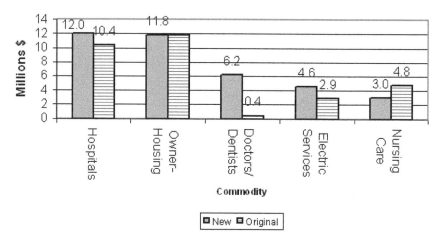

Figure 18.2 Selected new and original commodity import estimates, Clay county, 1997.

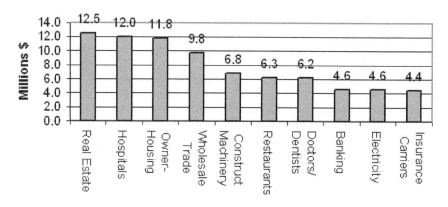

Figure 18.3 Top 10 imported commodities in Clay county, 1997.

outside the county. Hence, our modifications to the model, which are exclusively on the supply side at this point, would not alter the estimates of imports for most of these commodities in any major way.

Model estimates of imports and exports

Model estimates of important imports tended to meet our expectations (Figure 18.3). Large imports were concentrated in finance-related services such as Real Estate (462) ($12.507 million), Banking (456) ($4.615 million), and Insurance Carriers (459) ($4.402 million). Imports were also concentrated in medical services. For example, Hospital Services (492) had imports at $12.036 million, Doctors and Dentists Offices (490) at $6.229 million, and imports of Nursing and Protective Care Facilities (491) were estimated at

$3.009 million. The concentration of imports in financial and health services was expected, as it was consistent with the makeup of urban to rural trade observed elsewhere (Hughes and Litz 1996; Hughes and Holland 1994). Our expectation, confirmed by discussions with local individuals and consistent with central place theory (Christaller 1966), is that these services are provided by the Charleston-area economy.

Estimates of other important imports in the regional economy also met our expectations. The large level of imports for Restaurants (454) ($6.276 million) is probably due to out-commuting to work by many local residents and limited local choice (Figure 18.3). The coal industry is responsible for the importation of Construction Machinery and Equipment (311) at $6.481 million. Virtually all (more than 99 per cent) of the demand for Construction Machinery and Equipment was held by Coal Mining (37) in the Clay County model.

The only anomaly in the results presented in Figure 13.3 was for Owner-Housing (461) with imports of $11.777 million. The US Department of Commerce created this sector in the national input-output table to account for the imputed value of home ownership (which is a part of national income and product accounts). That is, this sector is an estimate of what homeowners would pay if they were renters instead of owners. This sector accounts for various expenses of owning a home, such as closing costs for home mortgages. Likewise, IMPLAN also contains the sector for consistency with national income accounting (Minnesota IMPLAN Group, Inc. 2000). Hence, by definition, this sector is an imputed valuation to ownership. Although it may be conceivable to have trade in the commodity (such as vacation home ownership by non-residents), it is unlikely that such a high level would be occurring in Clay County. Based on data from the 2000 Census, the county is not a major vacation home destination area. Thus, this result is probably a model artifact where estimates of supply and demand do not reflect reality.

Model estimates of major exports only partly met our expectations. Coal (37) was by far the largest export, at $77.052 million, and well over 10 times larger than Gas and Oil (38) at $5.556 million (Figure 18.4). This result was expected, given the dominance of coal production in the local economy. The importance of wood products (Logging Camps and Logging Contractors (133)), at $1.712 million in exports, and Structural Wood (140), at $1.673 million in exports, was also expected. Wood products are also an important part of the local economy, although not nearly important as coal.

However, large levels of exports in other commodities were a surprise. For example, Local Government was projected to export $3.406 million in K-12 Education (522) to the outside world (Figure 18.4). It is very doubtful that the local public education system has provided such a large level of educational services to non-residents. The large export for Faith Organizations (505), at $3.169 million, was also a surprise. It is doubtful that many people travel into Clay County regularly to attend religious services. Miscellaneous Repair

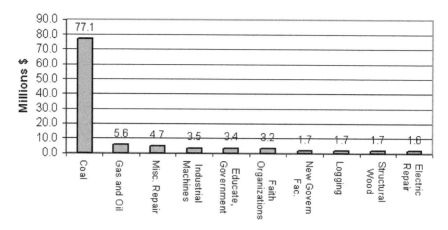

Figure 18.4 Top 10 exported commodities in Clay county, 1997.

Services and Electric Repair Services are other commodities that we did not expect to be major exporters.

Model results indicate industries that could be targeted for local development. In particular, consistent with a value-added processing strategy, where further local processing of local natural resources is encouraged, one area that should be investigated for targeting is the forest products sector. Although certain parts of the sector have been under increasing pressure from international competition, other forest products industries have experienced growth. Certain value-added forest products sectors may consider Clay County as a region for further development. This result is consistent with both the findings of Lamie et al. (1997) in their industry targeting study for upstate South Carolina and with a value-added processing approach.

One also at least wonders if a degree of import substitution could occur in certain sectors. For example, a firm that is headquartered in Charleston dominates the local real estate market. Would it be possible for local competition to arise so that they could at least gain a share of this local market? The city of Charleston is located in Kanawha County, but local leaders complain that the northern part of the county is in general underserved by the metropolitan economy. A company with a market strategy that concentrates on northern Kanawha County, Clay County, and some of the surrounding counties might be feasible to develop. Another area worth considering for import substitution could be certain carefully selected medical services. Research indicates that development of the local medical sector is an important element in attracting new industries and retaining local residents (St Clair 2000). A carefully constructed import substitution strategy is consistent with the recent emphasis in the economic development literature on local entrepreneurship and small business development.

Model results prompt the question whether the changes made to the

IMPLAN model led to major changes in industry targeting recommendations. Based on a value-added export enhancement strategy, changes in model estimates did not influence recommendations. That is, pursing certain types of wood product-based sectors with potential for growth is seen as a feasible industry targeting strategy under both set of results. On the other hand, import substitution-based recommendations do differ between the two sets of results. In particular, estimates of imports of Doctor and Dentists Offices rose from $0.4 million in the original estimates to $6.2 million in the new estimates. The recommendation concerning an import substitution-based policy of targeting medical services would not have been made without this change. Interestingly, these findings are inconsistent with the Spearman's correlation results. As previously discussed, the Spearman's correlation between the original export and new export estimates was 0.2568, implying a marked change in export rank between the two estimates. The same measure between original and new import estimates was 0.9118, indicating a good deal of similarity in rankings between the two sets of results.

Summary and conclusions

Industry targeting is a useful tool for areas wishing to grow but with limited industry recruitment and development budgets. The concept has its theoretical roots in many areas including cluster analysis, export base theory, value-added processing strategy, and import substitution policy. Clay County is a location in central West Virginia that is in desperate need of economic growth. Hence, industry targeting efforts should be useful to local policy-makers.

To reiterate, our approach is justified because based on theory, estimates of exports, imports, economic linkages, and multipliers from regional IO models have been used to support industry targeting recommendations in a variety of settings. Industry targeting recommendations have relied on the accuracy of IO models in a holistic way (i.e., to make policy recommendations). This chapter is a case study of how making adjustments to an IMPLAN-based model of a county economy in turn changed model results and ultimately industry targeting recommendations. Although the case study is especially relevant for IMPLAN users, it presents data check methods that can be used in evaluating models built using other approaches. Also, for all types of models, it highlights the need for developing a greater sensitivity to how changes in model assumptions and data can influence changes in policy recommendations.

Results indicate that the use of RPCs in the IMPLAN model of Clay County would not significantly change our policy recommendations. However, changes that were made to the basic input data to enhance accuracy would alter certain recommendations. Hence, researchers should carefully evaluate underlying economic models when making industry targeting recommendations. However, in general, the IMPLAN-based IO model building procedure provided information that was generally useful and accurate in many respects.

Model results also suggest a policy of enhanced value-added processing of local natural resources for Clay County policy-makers. The careful development of certain services may also serve as an effective import substitution policy. In particular, real estate and certain medical services could be evaluated as possible candidates for development by local or outside entrepreneurs.

Notes

1 As pointed out by one of the editors of this volume, more recent literature has emphasized the role of natural resource-based amenities in attracting residents to rural areas. However, these studies have generally not taken an industry targeting tack.
2 Although this study centres on IMPLAN, one goal is to demonstrate a method for examining how model accuracy can influence industry targeting recommendations for all types of ready-made regional models.
3 ReferenceUSA is an Internet-based library reference service provided by the Library Division of infoUSA (ReferenceUSA 2000). The database contains detailed information on nearly 12 million US businesses. This information is amassed from Yellow Page and Business White Page telephone directories; annual reports, 10-Ks and other SEC information; federal, state and municipal government data; Chamber of Commerce information; leading business magazines, trade publications, newsletters, and major newspapers; and postal service information, including National Change of Address updates. Business information is verified each year by telephone, and information for businesses with at least 100 employees is verified twice a year.
4 The vast majority (98 per cent) of this income is payments by employees to privately administrated employee benefit plans. The remainder is payments to corporate directors and other miscellaneous fees.
5 In an RAS procedure, known or new matrix control total are used to update or change the unknown individual cells of the matrix (Miller 1998). For more details, see Miller (1998) or Miller and Blair (1985). In IMPLAN, a vector RAS is used to provide data for non-disclosed sectors. For more detail, see Minnesota IMPLAN Group (2000).
6 The industry sectoring scheme is for the version of IMPLAN in use when the study was conducted.
7 Research has indicated that crosshauling is very prevalent for many reasons (Beggs 1986) and that estimates of regional trade flows may be the largest source of error in non-survey models such as IMPLAN (Stevens and Travors 1980). Hence, the use of RPCs is designed to reduce such errors by allowing the crosshauling phenomena to occur (Minnesota IMPLAN Group, 2000).

References

Alward, G., Siverts, E., Olson, O., Wagner, J., Senf, O., and Lindall, S. (1989) *Micro Implan Users Manual*, St Paul: University of Minnesota, Dept. of Agricultural and Applied Economics.
Appalachian Regional Commission. (2007) *Program and Policy Review of Distressed Counties in Appalachia*, Washington, DC: Author. Online. Available HTTP: <www.arc.gov/index.do?nodeId=3102> (accessed April 5 2007).
Beggs, R. (1986) "Non-Survey Interregional Input-Output Modeling", Unpublished Ph.D. dissertation, Department of Geography, University of Iowa, Iowa City.

Bryson, John M. (1990) Strategic Planning for Public and Nonprofit Organizations: A Guide to Strengthening and Sustaining Organizations. San Francisco: Jossey-Bass.

Carlson, Chris. (1990) "Leadership in the 1990's: Creating a Strategic Vision." Western City. (May): 10–13.

Christaller, W. (1966) *Central Places in Southern Germany*, translated by C.W. Baskin, Englewood Cliffs, NJ: Prentice Hall.

Christenson, James A. (1989) "Theories of Community Development." In Community Development in Perspective. James A. Christenson and Jerry W. Robinson, Jr. (eds.). Ames, Iowa: Iowa State University Press.

Goetz, S.J., and Lego, B. (2000) "County economic development index for the rural northeast US, 2000", University Park, PA: The Northeast Regional Center for Rural Development.

Hogg, R.V., and Tanis, E.A. (1983) *Probability and Statistical Inference*, New York: Macmillan.

Holland, D.W., Geier, H.T., and Schuster E.G. (1997, May) "Using IMPLAN to identify rural development opportunities", General Technical Report INT-GTR-350, Ogden, UT: United States Department of Agriculture, Forest Service, Intermountain Research Station.

Homm, L., Woods, M., and Doeksen, G. (2000, January) "Target industry analysis and local economic Development", Stillwater: Oklahoma State University Department of Agricultural Economics.

Hughes, D.W., and Litz, V. (1996) "Rural-urban economic linkages for agriculture and food processing in the Monroe, Louisiana Functional Economic Area", *Journal of Agricultural and Applied Economics*, 28: 337–55.

Hughes, D.W., and Holland, D. (1994) "Core-periphery economic linkage: a measure of spread and possible backwash effects for the Washington economy", *Land Economics*, 70: 364–79.

Kohls, R., and Uhl, J. (1998) *Marketing of Agricultural Products* (8th edn), Englewood Cliffs, NJ: Prentice Hall.

Kretzmann, John P. and John L. McKnight (1983) Building Communities from the Inside Out: A Path Toward Finding and Mobilizing a Community's Assets. Chicago: ACTA Publications.

Jensen, R. (1980) "The concept of accuracy in regional input-output models", *International Regional Science Review*, 5: 139–54.

Lahr, M. (1998) "A strategy for producing hybrid input-output Tables", Paper Presented at the 12th International Conference on Input-Output Techniques, New York, May 21.

Lamie, R., Barkley, D., Henry, M., and Syme, J. (1997, January) "Targeting secondary wood products manufacturing: identifying 'high impact,' 'high potential' industries", Research Report, Issue 97-1, Clemson, SC: Clemson University Department of Agricultural and Applied Economics.

Miller, R.E. (1998) "Regional and interregional input-output analysis", in W. Isard, I.J. Azis, M.P. Drennam, R.E. Miller, S. Saltzman, and E. Thorbecke (eds), *Methods of Interregional and Regional Analysis*, Brooksfield, VT: Ashgate.

Miller, R.E., and Blair, P.D. (1985) *Input-Output Analysis: Foundations and Extensions*, Englewood Cliffs, NJ: Prentice Hall.

Minnesota IMPLAN Group, Inc. (2000) *IMPLAN Professional Version 2.0 User's Guide, Analysis Guide and Data Guide*, Stillwater, MN: Author.

Olson, D., and Alward, G. (2000) "Updating IMPLAN RPCs", Paper Presented at the 2000 National IMPLAN Users Conference, Fort Collins, Co, Oct. 12–13.

Reference USA. (2000) Reference USA Website, West Virginia University Library. Online. Available HTTP: <http://reference.infousa.com/index2.asp> (accessed June 5, 2001).

Richardson, H.W. (1972) *Input-Output Analysis and Regional Economics*, New York: John Wiley and Sons.

Sorte, B., Weber B., Youmans R., and Holland, D. (2000) "Benton County input/output model: evaluation and implication", Paper Presented at the 2000 National IMPLAN Users Conference, Fort Collins, Co, Oct. 12–13.

Stevens, B., and Trainor, G. (1980) "Error generation on regional input-output analysis and its implications for non-survey models", in S. Pleeter (Ed.), *Economic Impact Analysis: Methodology and Applications*, Amsterdam: Marinus Nijhoff.

St Clair, C.F., Doeksen, G.A., Fyre, J., Schott, V., and House, J.R. (2000, March) "The impact of the health sector on the economy of Atoka County, Oklahoma", Stillwater: Oklahoma Cooperative Extension Service, Oklahoma State University.

US Bureau of the Census. (2001) "County Quickfacts". Online. Available HTTP: <http://quickfacts.census.gov/qfd/states/54/54015.html> (accessed August 10, 2001).

US Bureau of the Census, Bureau of Economic Analysis. (2000) Regional Economic Information System CD-ROM, 1969–1998.

——. (2001) "Economic census nonemployers statistics for West Virginia". Online. Available HTTP: <http://www.census.gov/epcd/nonemployer/1997/us/> (accessed August 15, 2001).

WV Bureau of Employment Programs. (2001) Unpublished Employment Statistics, 1997–99. Charleston: Author.

——. (2005a) County Profiles. Online. Available HTTP: <http://www.wvbep.org/bep/LMI/CNTYPROF/DEFAULT.HTM> (accessed November 20, 2006).

——. (2005b) Employment Statistics. Online. Available HTTP: <http://www.wvbep.org/bep/LMI/> (accessed November 20, 2006).

Wall, Milan, and Vicki Luther. (1989) Clues to Rural Community Survival. Lincoln, NE: Heartland Center for Leadership Development.

Wright S., Henry, M., and Barkley, D. (1998) "Targeting food, fiber and forestry industries for development of rural South Carolina", Research Report Issue 98-2, Clemson, SC: Clemson University Department of Agricultural and Applied Economics.

19 Import substitution and the analysis of gaps and disconnects

Steven C. Deller

Introduction

As argued in some of the other chapters of this volume, community and regional organizations vested with the promotion of economic growth and development are constantly searching for effective tools and methods to advance their efforts. The interest in cluster developments that has been spurred by the work of Michael Porter (1990, 1996, 1998, 2003) has renewed interest in targeted economic development efforts. There has been a concerted movement away from the old philosophy of "shoot anything that flies and claim anything that lands", to more strategic behaviour in identifying the specific types of industry to promote at the local and regional levels.

Policy-makers and economic development practitioners are now asking the more focused question: in what types of industry does our region have a competitive advantage? As communities have been exploring this question within the spirit of clusters, many have begun to look within themselves for opportunities rather than outside the community. As noted by Deller and Goetz (Chapter 2), there has been a series of "new waves" of approaching economic development at the local and regional levels. But students of local and regional economic development often conclude that these "new waves" are not really new in and of themselves, but are simply new ways of thinking about old ideas.

Within the US, the first wave focused on recruitment of firms, usually manufacturing plants, away from neighbouring regions by offering low taxes, cheap labour, few regulations, and inexpensive land. Communities that were successful often found their new economic base (i.e., newly arrived firms) to resist the recruitment of any firm that may place upward pressure on wages and to be unwilling to support higher taxes resulting from higher demand for public services or support any attempts at comprehensive planning that may result in future restrictions on land use. But out of these efforts, questions were raised about the types of industry that should be recruited. For example, in the Midwest much attention was, and still is, focused on the automobile industry or agricultural value-added processing, such as biofuels. The notion of regional comparative advantage began to mature, and analytical tools aimed at identifying those comparative advantages began to emerge. Studies seeking to better understand the notion of firm location decisions formed the academic backbone for most of these tools (Deller, Chapter 4).

These studies tended to use traditional and more advanced statistical modelling approaches. Examples include Goode and Hastings' (1989) work in the northeast region of the US, Goetz's (1997) work on food manufacturing industry locations at the state and county levels, Leatherman et al.'s (2002) industrial targeting analysis of the Great Plains (see also Cader et al., Chapter 8), Goetz and Rupasingha's (2002) study of high-tech industry clustering, as well as Reum and Harris's (2006) modelling of the Mountain West and Deller et al.'s (2006) analysis of retail and service businesses in Wisconsin. Here, limited dependent variable methods such as logit, probit, and double hurdle procedures for count data were used to derive probability estimates of the presence of specific business types. Higher probability estates are then compared to existing businesses to help identify industries to target for promotion. In practice, the results of the earliest types of these studies fueled the focus of industry recruitment in the spirit of first-wave thinking.

The landmark work of Birch (1979) suggested that small enterprises are particularly important in generating job growth, and this has renewed interest in the idea of Schumpeter's (1942, 1961) innovative entrepreneur in the economic growth process. Coupled with the observation that there has been an extraordinary escalation in the number of small and medium-size establishments nationwide, there has been a renewed interest in the promotion of small firms as an economic development strategy (Aquilina et al. 2006). Although Birch's work has been widely challenged (e.g., Brown et al. 1990; Dunne et al. 1989), it has served as the foundation for the second wave of economic development policy (Acs 1999; Shaffer et al. 2006). This policy approach is aimed at creating new small businesses, as well as retaining and expanding existing small firms. Eisinger (1988) championed this shift in thinking, labelling it the "Rise of the Entrepreneurial State", and argued that this long-term thinking about economic growth and development would result in more sustainable growth and development patterns that would be self-reinforcing. In a follow-up study, Eisinger (1995) lamented that the "Entrepreneurial State" was dead and states had returned to industry recruitment and the first wave of thinking. His hypothesis for the return to the old thinking centred on the political pressures of the re-election calendar. In a nutshell, working with small businesses and entrepreneurs does not draw the media attention that politicians receive from successful recruitment efforts.

The resulting conflict between the first and second wave of development efforts, as Eisinger notes, flows directly from conflicting desires of the politicians and practitioners. Politicians seek to be re-elected and need the name recognition that comes with media coverage of successful recruitment efforts, and they need to be able to point to tangible outcomes. Practitioners, however, desire to have a meaningful impact on the local and/or regional economy and see the fruits of their labour grow over time. One can also think in terms of the discount rate of the key players in the promotion of local and regional economic development policies. Politicians are looking at the next election cycle, which favours the first-wave approach, whereas practitioners generally understand the long-term perspective that is required.

The tension between politicians, particularly at the state level, and practitioners demanded that a new way of thinking about economic growth and development policy be brought to the table. Porter's introduction of clusters into the policy debate has created a unique "teachable moment" to help policy-makers and economic development practitioners think about their local economy in different ways. A central theme of the present volume is that within the framework of clusters many of the older analyses and tools that supported the first and second waves of development need to be revisited. While there are important criticisms of the way in which Porter identifies clusters (Woodward and Guimarães, Chapter 5), it is clear that the basic idea of clustering and focused or targeted economic development has gained widespread interest and acceptance. This raises the question: are systematic and reliable tools available for community decision-makers to "pick" appropriate industries or sectors to be favoured?

One of the overriding intents of this edited volume is to revisit many of the older, more traditional tools used in targeted regional economic development (TRED) such as the firm location models observed above. The central question is, can the set of traditional industry targeting tools prove to be useful in the spirit of Porter's clusters? I believe that the answer to both of these questions is an overwhelming yes; there are systematic and reliable tools and they can help communities think through what are appropriate clusters. Although many have argued that Porter's clusters are nothing new and are simply a repackaging of the traditional notion of agglomeration economies, the widespread embrace of Porter's clusters by state and local politicians as well as many economic development practitioners has opened the door to revisiting older tools in a new light. In other words, it has created a "teachable moment" to think more broadly about first-, second-, and third-wave development policies at the same time.

Several of the approaches for thinking about cluster analysis within the spirit of TRED that are outlined in this volume use the notion of interindustry linkages. Barkley and Henry (Chapter 10), for example, developed the Regional Economic Development Research Laboratory (REDRL) approach and use three screens to sift among promising industry prospects. Certain screens use a number of different criteria or benchmarks that an industry must meet in order to pass. This increases the rigour of the analytical and empirical approaches. The three screens with component measures listed where applicable are as follows.

Screen 1. The industry must have experienced recent growth in employment, must have a minimum number of firms (e.g., three) and total workers (e.g., 200), and must satisfy two specialization and competitiveness criteria as measured by the location quotient and shift-share analysis.

Screen 2. The industries surviving screen 1 are ranked according to the strength of their local purchases (inputs) and sales (outputs), using the input-output (IO) modelling system IMPLAN. As Barkley and Henry note, the firms on the other side of these transactions (input sellers and output purchasers) are excellent candidates for a second phase of industry targeting.

Screen 3. In this last step, candidate industries are evaluated according to national employment growth, firm size, wages paid, fixed assets, income multipliers, and import substitution possibilities.

Out of the above sifting, the REDRL method can isolate a subset of industries that is particularly worthy of attention in industry targeting efforts.

A key to the REDRL approach is the use of the IO modelling system IMPLAN. As discussed in more detail in Hughes (Chapter 11), IO analysis is an accounting method to describe a specific regional economy. One can think of IO as a "spreadsheet" of the economy in which the columns are the buyers (demand) and the rows capture the sellers (supply). Any particular cell where a column and row cross is the dollar flow between the buyer and the seller of a particular good or service. The sum of any particular row is the total supply (or output or total sales) of that particular industry, and the sum of any particular column is total demand of the industry. Given the laws of supply and demand within competitive markets, total demand must equal total supply.

Traditionally, IO models, and IMPLAN in particular, are used as a mechanism to generate economic multipliers that can be used for impact assessment or a scalar measure of interindustry linkages that can be used for other analysis (e.g., Cader et al., Chapter 8). Only recently have IMPLAN-derived IO models been used to have a broader discussion of regional economic structure and the identification of potential industries to target for further analysis in the spirit of industry targeting and cluster analysis.

Hughes (Chapter 11), however, suggests that the use of IO modelling, particularly top-down models such as IMPLAN, must be undertaken with great care because of the manner in which the models are constructed. For smaller and particularly rural areas, the assumptions that must be acted on in order to construct the actual IO model can result in erroneous conclusions. Although Hughes concludes in his case study that "in general, the IMPLAN-based IO model building procedure provided information that was generally useful and accurate in many respects", his arguments about the inherent weaknesses of top-down IO models must be taken seriously. Because the methods outlined in Barkley and Henry (Chapter 10), as well as the "Wisconsin Approach" outlined in this chapter, rely on the detailed descriptive data contained in IO analysis and specifically IMPLAN-derived IOs, the methods of model construction must be understood and appreciated.

As outlined below, the level of detailed information provided by IMPLAN can give the illusion of accuracy. Alluded to by Hughes (Chapter 11) and argued effectively by Buss (1999), this level of detail can be misinterpreted not only by policy-makers and community development practitioners but also by the analyst conducting the targeting investigation. This can easily result in the "overselling" of the results and the investment of time and resources on specific elements of a potential cluster that may be misplaced. Not only will this result in wasted resources, but it can also discredit new approaches to economic growth and development efforts.

This chapter comprises three additional sections. The next section provides an overview of the logic of import substitution within a regional construct. Then, a specific example of the "gap and disconnect" approach to import substitution using IO and IMPLAN in particular is provided for a sample of regions in Wisconsin. Each of these examples has been used in an economic development strategic planning process with local economic development organizations. The chapter closes with a review of how the approach has been used as in outreach education and the limitations to the approach.

Import substitution as a cluster strategy

As noted in Deller and Goetz (Chapter 2), the strategy of import substitution became popular with developing countries shortly after World War II. Burton (1998) writes that there was tremendous pressure to "do something" to rebuild after the Great Depression and WWII, and developing countries were seeking new ideas. Because of the experiences of the Great Depression coupled with the perceived success of the Soviet economy and misreading of Keynesian theory, market solutions were rejected. The economies of many developing countries were dependent on agriculture and other extractive industries (e.g., mining), and hence governments focused on how to improve the productivity of agriculture and move to higher stages of development. The commonly held belief was that agriculture needed to become more mechanized, thus improving labour productivity and income and creating demands for manufactured inputs. Given this internal look, the notion of promoting manufacturing to provide needed inputs into existing industries (e.g., agriculture and mining) was advanced. In other words, rather than promote agricultural productivity by importing the necessary manufactured goods, policies would be created to promote the internal growth of these manufactured goods. The policy of import substitution was born.

Because these discussions were taking place at the national level, particularly in India as well as South and Central American countries, these import substitution policies focused on foreign trade policy. The idea was to limit the import of key manufactured goods through tariffs, attempts to influence exchange rates, and simple import bans. This policy had both an internal and an external focus: internally supplying local demand for manufactured goods by agriculture and promoting the export of agricultural goods externally.

As outlined in detail by Burton (1998), there was some initial evidence of success, but lack of quality data and conflicting results and evidence led to the policies being questioned by 1970. In addition to the lack of clear evidence of success, other factors came into play. First, the theoretical foundation was being challenged, with more attention paid to the importance of economic agents being able to respond to proper market signals. Because the policies were being implemented through trade barriers, true market prices and hence market signals were distorted. Burton's (1998) basic conclusion, which is consistent with Krueger (1993), is that the engine of economic growth is learning and innovation, and protecting certain industries eliminated market incentives for such learning and innovation. This is also consistent with Porter's notion of clusters, where innovation plays a key role. As Deller and Goetz (Chapter 2) note, the laying of the theoretical foundation of the "Washington Consensus" on free trade and open markets was beginning by 1970. Second, it was becoming clear that the command economy of the Soviet Union was not as successful as once believed, again reinforcing the movement to the Washington Consensus. Third, there was growing evidence that the export-focused policies adopted by Asian countries such as Japan, Taiwan, and Korea were more successful than import substitution strategies. Finally, lack of institutional capacity to implement the policies, coupled with at times ramped corruption, further discredited import substitution as an economic development strategy. By the mid-1970s, import substitution as an economic development strategy was discarded.

It is vitally important to keep in mind, however, that nearly all of the academic and policy discussion of import substitution as an economic development policy has been as a national policy with a focus on international trade. Even discussions of import substitution within the context of Porter's clusters, such as Rodriguez-Clare (2007), or endogenous agglomeration models, such as Puga and Venables (1999), tend to focus on national economies and trade policies. At the subnational level, such as a state or province, policy options such as setting trade quotas or tariffs are not available. At the subnational level, the notion of import substitution, however, takes on a very different and useful meaning. As Burton (1998) noted, the problems with import substitution at the national level were not necessarily with its theoretical shortcomings, but rather with its implementation. State, provincial, or local governments can not pass laws or policies that restrict trade in any meaningful way. Thus a central argument against import substitution does not exist.

I suggest that thinking in terms of identifying and promoting regional clusters within the framework of import substitution becomes more meaningful. If we think of targeted regional economic development (TRED) as not just a technical analysis that provides policy-makers and practitioners with specifically named industries but rather part of a larger educational programme, import substitution takes on a new and interesting meaning. As outlined in Deller et al. (Chapter 17) as well as Nelson et al. (Chapter 16), the process through which TRED analysis takes place is equally as if not more important than the results. By thinking in terms of import substitution as outlined below, policy-makers and practitioners can merge first- and second-wave development policies, see the value of a larger regional approach, and learn the value of public-private partnerships in fostering clusters.

TRED analysis is not just a tool to support first-wave development opportunities; within an import substitution framework, TRED opens the door to thinking about existing industries, how these existing industries are interconnected, and levels of imports and exports. By examining existing industry interconnectedness the notion of "gaps" and "disconnects" can be used to help identify industries upon which attention should be focused. Using input-output modelling, specifically IMPLAN, the transactions table can be used to look not only at industry scale, but also at input and export levels and specific inter-industry connections. As described by Hughes (Chapter 11), IMPLAN can provide detailed trade flows tracking regional purchases as well as regional imports and exports.

When making input purchase decisions firms can buy locally or import into the region. By examining industry import data we can identify industries that are importing particularly large dollar values. Firms that comprise this particular industry may decide to import rather than buy regionally for two reasons. First, there is no regional industry that is able to supply the required inputs. Here there is a "gap" in the regional economy, and that industry *may be* targeted for further consideration. If such a local industry does exist, that could supply the imported input, we have the case of a "disconnect" within the regional economy. Again, the industries that appear to be "disconnected" *may be* targeted sets of industries to focus attention on for further action. The idea here is that the region is looking to build stronger relationships within regional clusters by strengthen inter-industry linkages. This is accomplished through the strategy of import substitution.

There could be several reasons for a "disconnect". The first is a lack of knowledge between the purchasing and selling firms. Here public policy is clear: implement strategies to build bridges across firms within the respective industries, for example, through networking. The second is that the region of analysis is too small in a spatial sense, and from the importing industries' perspective, they are purchasing locally. For example, an industry in Milwaukee, Wisconsin may be importing large levels of a particular input from the Chicago region. From a Milwaukee and/or Wisconsin perspective, this level of importing may not appear to be "optimal", but from the industrial perspective the relevant region does not stop or start at the Wisconsin-Illinois state line. By further exploring and thinking about where inputs, as well as exports, are flowing from and to, the idea of a larger regional approach may become apparent to local policy-makers and practitioners. Third, it may be that there is a viable business explanation as to why a disconnect exists. These may range from the custom nature of required inputs to the inability to come to contractual terms. For example, in a study of St Croix County, Wisconsin, Janke and Deller (2004) discovered that local hospitals were importing a large volume of business management consulting services despite the presence of a viable local management consulting industry. On further examination by a team of local economic development practitioners (amounting to one phone call to the administrator of the largest hospital in the county), it was determined that the consulting services were highly specialized and there was a national firm located in the Twin Cities of Minnesota that provided nearly all the hospitals in Wisconsin with this particular service.

There are also several viable reasons why there may be a significant "gap" in the local supply chain. For example, the size of the gap may not be sufficiently large to attempt to attract one or more firms, encourage a local firm to expand, or encourage entrepreneurial activity to fill the gap. Or it may the case that the supplying industry is one that the regional community does not desire. In early stages of the St Croix study mentioned above, the investigators uncovered a large and vibrant plastics manufacturing industry, which was composed of numerous smaller firms (in the spirit of Porter, a viable cluster). This industry was importing a significant volume of plastic resins, the basic input into their production processes. A member of the research team familiar with the industry clearly stated that the plastic resins industry was tightly linked to the petroleum refining industry in the southern states and, in his words, "it could stay there".

The key to the approach outlined here and in other chapters of this volume is that the TRED approach, in this case import substitution, opens the door to providing not only rigorous economic analysis, but also a mechanism to expand the thinking of local policy-makers and practitioners. By using input-output analysis, potential clusters can be identified and means to strengthen those clusters considered. By thinking in terms of import substitution, local policy-makers and practitioners can move beyond simple recruitment as in the first wave of economic development and move to include second-wave strategies that focus on existing businesses and entrepreneurship. By exploring import and export flows, the concept of the relevant regional structure and the need to think regionally and act in cooperative arrangements can be better understood. But, as eloquently argued by Buss (1999) from a broader perspective and by Hughes (Chapter 11) from an IO- and IMPLAN-specific perspective, there are inherent problems with the approach outline here. When it is used as an educational tool to help policy-makers and practitioners to think more broadly and deeply about economic development, however, significant changes can be effected through this kind of analysis.

The "Wisconsin Approach"

In the same vein as the REDRL approach (Barkley and Henry Chapter 10) and the process described by Buss (1999), the "Wisconsin Approach" to TRED through import substitution proceeds in a multistep fashion. It is important to keep in mind that the Wisconsin Approach is designed to be a university-based outreach educational programme as much as it is a technical analysis programme. The logic of the educational approach is outlined in Deller et al. (Chapter 17) and will not be repeated in detail here. Two points are important to review, however. First, the study is treated as a team effort between members of the community and university faculty and staff. In Wisconsin, the community resource development educator from the University of Wisconsin-Extension is a key player. Thus key research decisions, such as which industries to focus on, are made not by the university faculty and staff but rather by the research team. This creates greater understanding and ownership by the community members. The premise of a research team is often presented as a problem of "too much data" and that part of the project is sifting through the volume of data. If the community is unwilling or not in a position to participate fully in the TRED analysis, then we suggest that they are not ready to undertake a TRED-type study. Second, the key criteria on which to evaluate industries, such as absolute size of the industry by metric, output per employee or labour income per employee, or fastest growing sectors based on the trend analysis, are determined by the research team. By allowing the research team to determine the selection criteria, community values are more closely reflected.

The Wisconsin Approach has been applied in several settings across the state (e.g., Janke and Deller 2004; Muench and Deller 2001) and was the backbone of the Northeast Wisconsin Economic Opportunity Study completed in 2004 (http://www.neweconomyproject.org/), which resulted in the multicounty public-private partnership organization The New North (http://www.thenewnorth.com/), which has served as the model for five other multicounty public-private partnership organizations. But in each case, the specific steps undertaken and the key criteria applied were a joint decision of the research study group. Thus, if one were to compare and contrast different applications of the Wisconsin Approach, each would appear different and unique. Given the overriding educational mission of the programme, this is to be expected.

The Wisconsin Approach uses two primary sources of data. The first is the county-level Bureau of Economic Analysis' Regional Economic Information System (BEA-REIS) and more specifically the Woods and Poole, Inc. enhanced BEA-REIS dataset. The Woods and Poole, Inc. dataset has four advantages over the publicly available BEA-REIS data. The first is that Woods and Poole, Inc. bridges the SIC and NAICS break that occurred in 2000–2001. Second, they have developed reasonably successful routines for filling data cells that are not reported by BEA because of disclosure rules. This is particularly helpful when working with small rural counties or groupings of counties that include small rural counties. Third, in addition to the BEA employment and income data Woods and Poole, Inc. provide certain demographic data, retail sales estimates, and detailed income distribution data. The one aspect that Woods and Poole, Inc markets heavily is their

30-year forecasts for each of the variables in the dataset. While one can challenge the viability of 30-year forecasts for every US county across several socioeconomic variables, as a teaching tool they are more than adequate. The second dataset is IMPLAN, which is described in detail by Hughes (Chapter 11). The key pieces of information are the base year and commodity trade reports and the industry import matrix.

The analysis is composed of three parts. The first part of the analysis focuses on trends using traditional growth indices, and the county of analysis is compared to the state and the US. Trends in population, income, and employment and earnings by industry at the one-digit SIC level are shared with the research team. Discussions about relative growth levels of the study area provide an informal "first screen" in terms of the targeting exercise. In essence, drawing attention to and discussing relative growth rates and notions of stability opens the door to a better understanding of which sectors, although broadly defined at the one-digit SIC, are growth sectors from a larger macroeconomic perspective. This analysis is particularly relevant when discussing the transition of the macroeconomy away from a goods- to a services-producing base. This is the first opportunity to have the research team think more broadly than manufacturing as the engine of economic growth. This discussion also allows for an initial discussion about the overall performance of the regional economy to see if the data support or refute local perceptions.

While local knowledge is vital to the Wisconsin Approach, at times the local perceptions are at odds with reality. For example, in the study of St Croix County (Janke and Deller 2004), there was a general perception that the county was experiencing rapid economic growth due to its close proximity to the expanding Twin Cities of Minneapolis and St Paul. The trend data, while revealing strong growth across several metrics, was not as robust as generally believed. The subsequent discussions lead to an in-depth dialogue about the significant spatial variation in economic growth across the county. The western part of the county, the closest to the Twin Cities and separated from Minnesota by the St Croix River, can best be described as rolling countryside with a mix of forests and pasture land, while the eastern part of the county is composed of flat cropland. The discussions led to a clear decision that the economic growth and prosperity of the western part of the county must be replicated in the eastern part. All subsequent analysis and policy deliberations returned to a central theme about how the poorer eastern part of the county would benefit from the action.

The second part of the analysis conducted within the Wisconsin Approach uses the detailed IMPLAN data to focus attention on which industries, as defined by IMPLAN, dominate the local economy. The idea here is not only to identify the largest industries but also to introduce and discuss the various ways in which the economy can be measured. From IMPLAN four metrics of economic activity are used: total industrial output, employment, wage and salary (labour) income, and total income. For the research team, rankings of all sectors from largest to smallest are provided for discussion purposes. Based on the decision of the research team, this list of metrics can be narrowed and the "threshold" for reporting to the larger community determined.

Consider, for example, the case of the "I-43 Corridor" used in the Northeast Wisconsin Economic Opportunity Study (2004), which comprises three counties: Brown, Manitowoc, and Sheboygan. This region includes the city of Green Bay to the north and runs south along interstate I-43 and Lake Michigan. The top 25 industries across the four metrics are reported in Tables 19.1–19.4. The research team was not surprised to see the importance of paper as well as cheese production in terms of industrial output (Table 19.1), but was somewhat astonished by the size of the wholesale trade sector. When considering employment (Table 19.2), eating and drinking establishments along with state and local public education (K–12, technical schools, and the universities) become much more important. The great importance of wholesale trade and motor freight transportation and warehousing was particularly critical to further discussions. The lower importance of paper mills in terms of employment was surprising to the research team and led to a lengthy

Table 19.1 Largest sector: I-43 corridor

Industry Sector	Industry Output (Million Dollars)	Share of Total (%)
Paper Mills, Except Building Paper	1,696.775	5.4
Cheese, Natural and Processed	1,573.415	5.0
Wholesale Trade	1,303.215	4.2
Motor Freight Transport and Warehousing	1,051.473	3.4
Miscellaneous Plastics Products	994.247	3.2
Electric Services	905.842	2.9
Metal Sanitary Ware	884.848	2.8
Meat Packing Plants	776.136	2.5
New Residential Structures	673.290	2.2
Doctors and Dentists	668.980	2.1
Banking	618.902	2.0
Insurance Carriers	587.053	1.9
State & Local Government – Education	547.698	1.8
Hospitals	547.542	1.8
General Merchandise Stores	522.331	1.7
Real Estate	517.880	1.7
Metal Stampings, N.E.C.	512.262	1.6
Eating & Drinking	465.819	1.5
Public Building Furniture	453.051	1.4
Plastics Materials and Resins	406.237	1.3
Maintenance and Repair Other Facilities	393.414	1.3
New Industrial and Commercial Buildings	350.945	1.1
Paper Industries Machinery	347.001	1.1
State & Local Government – Non-Education	346.262	1.1
Engineering, Architectural Services	340.264	1.1

Source: IMPLAN base data and author calculations.

Table 19.2 Largest sector: I-43 corridor

Sector	Employment	Share of Total (%)
Eating & Drinking	14,946	5.1
State & Local Government – Education	13,084	4.4
Wholesale Trade	12,495	4.2
General Merchandise Stores	9,336	3.2
Motor Freight Transport and Warehousing	8,691	2.9
Hospitals	8,606	2.9
Metal Sanitary Ware	8,534	2.9
Miscellaneous Retail	7,976	2.7
State & Local Government – Non-Education	7,746	2.6
Amusement and Recreation Services, N.E.C.	7,076	2.4
Doctors and Dentists	6,774	2.3
Food Stores	6,084	2.1
Maintenance and Repair Other Facilities	5,755	1.9
Paper Mills, Except Building Paper	5,666	1.9
Miscellaneous Plastics Products	5,608	1.9
Automotive Dealers & Service Stations	5,316	1.8
Insurance Carriers	5,082	1.7
Insurance Agents and Brokers	4,650	1.6
Labor and Civic Organizations	4,345	1.5
New Residential Structures	4,182	1.4
Real Estate	4,141	1.4
Personnel Supply Services	3,737	1.3
Engineering, Architectural Services	3,626	1.2
Banking	3,510	1.2
Cheese, Natural and Processed	3,467	1.2

Source: IMPLAN base data and author calculations.

Table 19.3 Largest sector: I-43 corridor

Sector	Wage and Salary Income $ (Millions)	Share of Total (%)
State & Local Government – Education	547.698	6.0
Wholesale Trade	515.250	5.6
Metal Sanitary Ware	387.511	4.2
Doctors and Dentists	370.745	4.0
Paper Mills, Except Building Paper	335.427	3.7
Hospitals	296.755	3.2
Motor Freight Transport and Warehousing	294.278	3.2
State & Local Government – Non-Education	268.422	2.9
General Merchandise Stores	247.360	2.7
Miscellaneous Plastics Products	208.289	2.3
Maintenance and Repair Other Facilities	198.492	2.2
Insurance Carriers	192.249	2.1
Electric Services	181.761	2.0
Cheese, Natural and Processed	157.919	1.7
Eating & Drinking	145.900	1.6
Automotive Dealers & Service Stations	141.664	1.5

Metal Stampings, N.E.C.	130.616	1.4
Engineering, Architectural Services	125.052	1.4
Paper Industries Machinery	124.396	1.4
Commercial Sports Except Racing	118.595	1.3
Aluminium Foundries	117.998	1.3
Food Stores	117.861	1.3
Banking	116.960	1.3
Miscellaneous Retail	106.477	1.2
New Residential Structures	98.894	1.1

Source: IMPLAN base data and author calculations.

Table 19.4 Largest sector: I-43 corridor

Sector	Total Income $ (Millions)	Share of Total (%)
Wholesale Trade	897.549	6.0
Electric Services	763.821	5.1
Metal Sanitary Ware	652.748	4.3
Paper Mills, Except Building Paper	561.754	3.7
State & Local Government – Education	547.698	3.6
Motor Freight Transport and Warehousing	493.834	3.3
Doctors and Dentists	453.882	3.0
General Merchandise Stores	411.816	2.7
Banking	409.847	2.7
Real Estate	368.384	2.4
State & Local Government – Non-Education	346.262	2.3
Hospitals	335.798	2.2
Insurance Carriers	334.383	2.2
Miscellaneous Plastics Products	299.606	2.0
Cheese, Natural and Processed	298.375	2.0
Maintenance and Repair Other Facilities	275.256	1.8
Automotive Dealers & Service Stations	250.412	1.7
Eating & Drinking	224.820	1.5
Metal Stampings, N.E.C.	213.640	1.4
Miscellaneous Retail	201.380	1.3
Food Stores	194.535	1.3
Insurance Agents and Brokers	168.070	1.1
Engineering, Architectural Services	154.083	1.0
New Residential Structures	148.530	1.0
Commercial Sports Except Racing	146.095	1.0

Source: IMPLAN base data and author calculations.

discussion of the mechanization of the paper industry and other manufacturing processes and how this mechanization has altered the demand for labour. While the notion of "King Paper" was reaffirmed to a certain extent, the simple descriptive analysis not only reinforced the conclusions from the trend analysis that the regional economy has moved to a service base, but the sectorial detail also helped to reinforce the idea.

The next step was the introduction of location quotients into the discussion.

For the Wisconsin Approach, I take an average of the shares across all four metrics as opposed to using one metric such as employment. The top 25 location quotients for the I-43 region are provided in Table 19.5. The sanitary wares industry in the region is reflective of one company that is a major producer of table silverware. Local knowledge of the company spurred useful discussion of the notion of how a small handful of companies in the region can be national and indeed international leaders within the particular industry. Unfortunately, shortly after the study was released, the silverware company announced that it was relocating its production facilities overseas.

The final step of this part of the analysis placed the three monetary metrics on a per jobs basis. This allows for cross regional comparisons, such as how the region of interest compares to the US or the state, for example, and provides a basis for thinking about productivity (output per worker) as well as job quality (wages per job). These data for the I-43 region are provided in Tables 19.6–19.8. The research team naturally was drawn to the rankings of wage and salary income per job thinking that this would be a top priority screen (Table 19.7). The very high wage and salary income for the I-43 corridor region for commercial sports is attributed to the Green Bay Packers

Table 19.5 Location quotient I-43 corridor

Sector	LQ
Metal Sanitary Ware	315.656
Paper Industries Machinery	75.525
Malt	75.069
Laboratory Apparatus & Furniture	68.049
Creamery Butter	52.002
Cheese, Natural and Processed	46.251
Leather Gloves and Mittens	24.946
Public Building Furniture	24.055
Aluminium Foundries	24.034
Paper Mills, Except Building Paper	22.278
Metal Stampings, N.E.C.	19.165
Printing Trades Machinery	19.140
Manifold Business Forms	19.114
Carburetors, Pistons, Rings, Valves	15.829
Converted Paper Products, N.E.C	15.580
Packaging Machinery	15.127
Boat Building and Repairing	12.832
Leather Tanning and Finishing	12.481
Blended and Prepared Flour	11.548
Industrial Patterns	10.867
Lime	10.737
Canned Fruits and Vegetables	10.282
Fasteners, Buttons, Needles, Pins	9.665
Woodworking Machinery	9.132
Dental Equipment and Supplies	8.784

Source: IMPLAN base data and author calculations.

Table 19.6 Industry output per job

Industry	US ($)	Wisconsin ($)	I-43 Corridor ($)
Petroleum Refining	2,706,850	2,631,539	2,440,768
Gas Production and Distribution	1,022,254	878,843	908,770
Creamery Butter	642,312	643,963	668,583
Cyclic Crudes, Interm. & Indus. Organic Chem.	762,287	647,507	667,118
Roasted Coffee	668,618	539,015	591,688
Plastics Materials and Resins	663,844	585,967	588,065
Condensed and Evaporated Milk	596,114	535,441	576,528
State and Local Electric Utilities	605,680	528,187	539,956
Paperboard Mills	508,824	490,959	487,739
Cheese, Natural and Processed	456,885	439,735	453,861
Malt	414,926	418,889	421,260
Commercial Sports Except Racing	137,862	183,873	403,614
Dog, Cat, and Other Pet Food	440,992	425,574	397,901
Special Industry Machinery N.E.C.	425,772	391,741	394,223
Meat Packing Plants	385,163	385,433	385,292
Fluid Milk	378,274	368,369	377,521
Prepared Feeds, N.E.C	393,609	389,289	371,693
Pickles, Sauces, and Salad Dressings	369,016	370,375	369,711
Sanitary Paper Products	424,519	390,400	365,881
Electric Services	461,603	347,741	360,525
Secondary Non-ferrous Metals	379,947	374,548	357,471
Paints and Allied Products	374,337	343,195	333,008
Mineral Wool	191,009	194,082	328,839
Internal Combustion Engines, N.E.C.	361,358	355,188	315,467
Bottled and Canned Soft Drinks & Water	345,166	340,413	302,890
Totals	102,061	94,994	105,723

Source: IMPLAN base data and author calculations.

football team. A short discussion of professional sports teams as an economic development strategy was quickly dismissed when local knowledge of the team and its players, along with the Milwaukee Brewers baseball team, suggested that few of the players lived in Wisconsin year-round and the vast majority of these wages and salaries leaked out of the area.

Consider, for example, creamery butter, which has the third highest output per worker in the three county region and compares favourably to both the US and Wisconsin. When compared to the location quotient (Table 19.5), this may be one sector for further consideration. Creamery butter is not in the top 25 for wage and salary income per job, but is within the top 25 for total income per job at $97,000, which is much higher than either the US or Wisconsin averages. Using traditional screening criteria such as those used in the REDRL approach, the dairy industry and creamery butter in particular may be an area for further consideration in terms of a potential cluster. Given

Table 19.7 Wage and salary income per job

Industry	US ($)	Wisconsin ($)	I-43 Corridor ($)
Commercial Sports Except Racing	74,644	111,336	264,294
Mineral Wool	56,852	57,882	118,808
Railroads and Related Services	78,902	71,780	78,990
Electric Services	76,729	69,544	72,341
Gas Production and Distribution	85,598	61,167	71,234
Flavoring Extracts and Syrups, N.E.C.	106,049	53,430	67,802
Iron and Steel Forgings	48,584	51,484	66,528
Security and Commodity Brokers	141,646	87,385	66,412
Machine Tools, Metal Cutting Types	53,063	55,062	65,851
Surgical Appliances and Supplies	53,253	36,380	64,948
Pulp Mills	69,418	62,037	64,732
Malt	58,114	60,249	61,467
Industrial Furnaces and Ovens	48,268	51,532	61,329
Bags, Plastic	39,349	44,167	60,690
State and Local Electric Utilities	72,015	58,118	60,224
U.S. Postal Service	63,291	60,375	59,808
Synthetic Rubber	64,469	60,324	59,315
Paper Mills, Except Building Paper	67,395	64,186	59,196
Glass and Glass Products, Exc Containers	51,376	37,610	59,011
Cyclic Crudes, Interm. & Indus. Organic Chem.	81,413	49,335	57,572
Paperboard Mills	65,016	58,599	57,238
Power Transmission Equipment	46,965	54,514	57,006
Special Industry Machinery N.E.C.	77,869	54,719	56,529
Animal and Marine Fats and Oils	43,574	39,264	56,303
Paper Industries Machinery	54,075	56,129	55,128
Totals	34,000	30,274	31,058

Source: IMPLAN base data and author calculations.

that Wisconsin prides itself as being the "Dairy State" and agricultural processing and dairy in particular have been identified as a cluster at the state level, it seems reasonable for the I-43 region to also consider dairy as a cluster. The research team, however, elected to focus its energies in other directions based primarily on prior discussions about the rising role of services.

The strength of the Wisconsin Approach and the use of the research team is that by walking through the analysis step-by-step and engaging in a broader discussion, the team not only can come to a more informed decision, but because it is the team's decision, not the university faculty and staff's or a private consultant's, the results of the study is "owned" by the community. By owning both the process and the results of the analysis, the likelihood of sustainable outcomes are maximized. Rather than allowing the analysis to determine the industries to focus on, the discussion results in a fuller and more in-depth analysis with local knowledge being an integral part of the final recommendations.

Table 19.8 Total income per job

Industry	US ($)	Wisconsin ($)	I-43 Corridor ($)
Commercial Sports Except Racing	102,960	139,521	325,579
Electric Services	389,231	293,221	304,001
State and Local Electric Utilities	270,165	218,034	225,932
Mineral Wool	99,224	101,611	206,010
Flavouring Extracts and Syrups, N.E.C.	303,802	152,294	193,356
Gas Production and Distribution	279,157	162,913	188,693
Condensed and Evaporated Milk	180,113	132,315	166,287
Pickles, Sauces, and Salad Dressings	152,966	153,913	153,448
Malt Beverages	275,011	339,899	134,404
Sanitary Paper Products	175,028	150,848	132,984
Communications, Except Radio and TV	184,983	135,946	126,688
Roasted Coffee	181,073	76,916	124,179
Cyclic Crudes, Interm. & Indus. Organic Chem.	199,478	102,471	120,477
Paperboard Mills	136,307	120,946	118,134
Banking	166,494	121,443	116,771
Iron and Steel Forgings	79,878	83,959	108,740
Paints and Allied Products	140,484	116,382	108,038
Railroads and Related Services	107,411	97,715	107,531
Pulp Mills	116,522	102,523	106,981
Bags, Plastic	68,402	75,499	103,780
Burial Caskets and Vaults	100,434	79,857	102,642
Paper Mills, Except Building Paper	114,604	107,499	99,138
Malt	92,209	95,846	98,015
Animal and Marine Fats and Oils	75,682	68,092	97,543
Creamery Butter	72,340	73,905	97,224
Totals	58,309	48,791	50,940

Source: IMPLAN base data and author calculations.

The analysis up to this point has been purely descriptive, without references to import substitution. At this step of the discussion, the notion of imports as well as exports is introduced to the research team by simply reporting out the exports by industry ranked from highest to lowest (Table 19.9). In this table, intermediate imports are also reported to provide insights into the degree to which that industry's product is being imported into the region. Consider miscellaneous plastics products, which has about 5,600 jobs in the I-43 region with an average wage/salary income of $37,000. According to the IMPLAN transactions table miscellaneous plastics products export approximately $980 million worth of product and at the same time other industries import almost $400 million worth of miscellaneous plastic products. Indeed, if we rank industries on the level of intermediate imports (Table 19.10), we can see that plastic products is the third largest product imported for intermediate use. From an import substitution perspective, the

Table 19.9 Top 25 industry on exports, I-43 corridor

Industry	Total Exports $ (Millions)	Intermediate Imports $ (Millions)	Employment	Wage/Salary Income per Job ($)
Cheese, Natural and Processed	1,155.5	18.3	3,467	45,553
Paper Mills, Except Building Paper	1,152.4	233.0	5,666	59,196
Miscellaneous Plastics Products	983.3	397.2	5,608	37,141
Metal Sanitary Ware	768.1	3.5	8,534	45,409
Electric Services	654.0	53.7	2,513	72,341
Paperboard Mills	615.6	109.2	327	57,238
Meat Packing Plants	612.1	7.1	2,014	32,469
Metal Stampings, N.E.C.	403.0	11.5	2,864	45,611
General Merchandise Stores	350.8	0.5	9,336	26,494
Aluminum Foundries	315.3	46.9	2,648	44,566
Insurance Carriers	309.6	14.7	5,082	37,830
Motor Freight Transport and Warehousing	285.6	–	8,691	33,859
Canned Fruits and Vegetables	256.9	10.9	1,210	40,595
Construction Machinery and Equipment	216.3	3.0	1,021	54,211
Manifold Business Forms	213.5	4.0	1,436	45,073
Public Building Furniture	204.0	0.0	2,395	39,305
Doctors and Dentists	193.7	–	3,255	22,066
Boat Building and Repairing	179.7	4.7	1,677	31,375
Engineering, Architectural Services	171.0	66.9	2,357	20,935
Sausages and Other Prepared Meats	170.2	0.1	908	50,031
Fluid Milk	155.1	6.4	446	49,149
Converted Paper Products, N.E.C	151.3	10.5	785	40,981
Commercial Printing	147.0	57.4	2,169	36,262
Amusement and Recreation Services, N.E.C.	146.3	0.6	1,089	10,852
Pickles, Sauces, and Salad Dressings	144.7	1.9	282	39,806

Source: IMPLAN base data and author calculations.

Table 19.10 Top 25 industry on imports, I-43 corridor

Industry	Total Exports $ (Millions)	Intermediate Imports $ (Millions)	Employment	Wage/Salary Income per Job ($)
Wholesale Trade	111.2	580.1	12,495	41,237
Dairy Farm Products	0.3	409.9	997	19,641
Miscellaneous Plastics Products	983.3	397.2	5,608	37,141
Computer and Data Processing Services	1.5	346.5	514	19,051
Cyclic Crudes, Interm. & Indus. Organic Chem.	1.3	285.6	8	57,572
Blast Furnaces and Steel Mills	19.7	251.4	–	–
Paper Mills, Except Building Paper	1,152.4	233.0	5,666	59,196
Petroleum Refining	0.4	232.0	5	19,429
Cattle Feedlots	0.0	227.3	20	18,464
Real Estate	26.7	225.0	2,584	13,639
Communications, Except Radio and TV	2.5	222.7	675	46,381
Management and Consulting Services	1.2	180.2	997	21,672
Banking	132.1	173.0	3,510	33,324
Security and Commodity Brokers	1.9	139.7	442	66,412
Sawmills and Planing Mills, General	2.1	138.6	110	29,048
Personnel Supply Services	0.2	133.5	1,057	41,959
Advertising	64.6	130.1	2,166	16,330
Hogs, Pigs and Swine	0.0	129.5	11	6,986
Industrial Machines, N.E.C.	127.3	122.8	1,146	44,146
Pulp Mills	76.2	118.3	57	64,732
Ranch Fed Cattle	0.3	116.4	531	5,434
Paperboard Mills	615.6	109.2	327	57,238
Feed Grains	74.1	95.0	318	2,927
Other Business Services	0.1	94.6	163	22,010
Gas Production and Distribution	0.7	94.1	93	71,234

Source: IMPLAN base data and author calculations.

question is why is there such a relatively high level of imports while so much local production is being exported?

Another example that the research team considered is within dairy farm production and dairy processing. Cheese is the largest product exported from the region, slightly more than paper products, with nearly $1 billion worth of exports (Table 19.9). Over $400 million worth of dairy farm products, specifically milk, are also imported into the region. Because so little raw milk appears to be exported out of the area and such a large amount is imported presumably for cheese production, there appears to be the potential for dairy farm expansion in the area. The Wisconsin Approach takes the analysis one step further and uses the industry import matrix to detail which industries are importing dairy farm products, predominantly milk, and to what extent (Table 19.11). Here we can see that the cheese industry is the major importer of dairy farm products, with about $350 million worth of milk being imported, followed by $49 million for fluid milk (i.e., bottled milk) production, with the remainder being imported for the production of butter, condensed and evaporated milk, and ice cream. Based on this analysis, plus the

Table 19.11 Top five imported commodities and importing industries

Imported Commodity	Industries Importing Commodity	$ (Millions)
Wholesale Trade	Cheese, Natural and Processed	59.0
	Paper Mills, Except Building Paper	53.1
	Miscellaneous Plastics Products	25.2
	New Residential Structures	25.0
	Public Building Furniture	19.2
Dairy Farm Products	Cheese, Natural and Processed	349.2
	Fluid Milk	47.8
	Creamery Butter	7.1
	Condensed and Evaporated Milk	4.7
	Ice Cream and Frozen Desserts	1.0
Miscellaneous Plastics Products	Miscellaneous Plastics Products	72.0
	Paper Mills, Except Building Paper	37.3
	Public Building Furniture	33.9
	Plastics Materials and Resins	26.4
	New Residential Structures	17.7
Computer and Data Processing Services	Wholesale Trade	32.9
	Banking	26.4
	Paper Mills, Except Building Paper	23.9
	Doctors and Dentists	22.9
	Engineering, Architectural Services	12.8
Cyclic Crudes, Interm. & Indus. Organic Chem.	Plastics Materials and Resins	105.3
	Paper Mills, Except Building Paper	78.5
	Miscellaneous Plastics Products	32.3
	Paints and Allied Products	14.7
	Paperboard Mills	8.3

Source: IMPLAN base data and author calculations.

analysis of the creamery butter industry above, dairy could be a targeted industry "cluster", consisting of cheese, fluid milk, and miscellaneous other dairy products such as butter manufacturing. As I mentioned above, on consideration of the typical wage and salary income per job of about $19,600, the research team elected to remove dairy farms from the list of potential targeted industries and elected not to focus energy on dairy as a potential cluster. It is of interest to note that subsequent to the study's release, a subcommittee was formed to examine how dairy farming within the region could be made more profitable and raise incomes per job.

One sector that the research team wished to focus on more was that of computer and data processing services. Based on the rankings of intermediate imports, about $350 million of these services were imported into the region. Although wages/salary per job were relatively low, there was sufficient interest to explore the sector in more detail. A subset of the research team was of the opinion that this sector could offer the foundation for a cluster. Local knowledge of one data processing company in the area suggested that although the wages may not be high, the company allows workers to operate out of home offices with flexible hours. This subgroup of the research team thought that such flexible employment opportunities should be further explored because of the diversity of the potential labour pool in the region. Using the information about which industries in the I-43 area are importing the services shown in Table 19.11, a subteam agreed to contact some of the banks, doctors' and dentists' offices, and engineering and architectural firms to explore their needs for computer and data processing services in more detail. Based on the experience in St Croix County, it could be that the existing computer service businesses are not offering the required services (i.e., gap), but further research, such as conducted by the subteam, may reveal this to be a case of disconnect.

Given the cautions of Hughes (Chapter 11) about the accuracy of the IMPLAN data when conducting this type of detailed descriptive analysis, a word is warranted about data accuracy experiences with the Wisconsin Approach. Hughes concludes that in the end, improving the accuracy of the base data did not fundamentally alter the policy recommendation. Our experience with the Wisconsin Approach has found only very few cases where local knowledge uncovered serious problems with the IMPLAN data. Indeed, the research teams are generally impressed with the accuracy of the data. As an educational tool and a mechanism to facilitate focused discussion, the descriptive data from IMPLAN can be very powerful.

Conclusions

Michael Porter and the notion of clusters have rejuvenated many regional economic development efforts and have helped move local economic development policy along on several fronts. First, the discussion of clusters and regional comparative advantage has broadened local policy to move beyond traditional recruitment strategies that form the first wave of economic development strategies. Indeed, by looking within the region to identify clusters, interest in building on existing businesses, or second-wave thinking, has been renewed by local policy-makers. Although economic development practitioners have long embraced a blending of first- and second-wave development strategies, it has been a tougher sell for politicians to see the value. Second, a focus on clusters makes it clear that individual communities do not exist in isolation and that regional perspectives are required. This has resulted in a number of regional public-private partnerships, which some have argued represent the third wave of development strategies.

The Wisconsin Approach outlined in this chapter refocuses the notion of targeted regional economic development (TRED) toward the idea of import substitution. Using input-output analysis, specifically IMPLAN, detailed descriptive analysis of not only industrial size but also interindustry linkage can be studied. Using an educational approach as outlined in Deller et al. (Chapter 17), the Wisconsin Approach uses TRED within the framework of import substitution to structure a broader discussion about regional economic structure. The research team, which comprises not only university researchers and extension educators, but more importantly, also members of the community of interest, is an integral part of the study. Key decisions about which industries to focus on and how are made by the community members of the research team. This process not only elevates the team's awareness of the regional economy but also empowers them to make more informed decisions about economic development strategies.

The Wisconsin Approach does presume that there are certain levels of social and institutional capital within the region of interest. In other words, the region must be ready to undertake such an effort. Key players within the region must be ready, willing, and able to be part of the research team. If these players remove themselves from the process, then one could reasonably argue that the region is not ready to undertake such a study. Regions that have active chambers of commerce, economic development corporations, and local units of government that are active in community efforts may benefit from undertaking a TRED analysis. If, on the other hand, the leaders of local institutions expect "the answer" to be handed to them in a consulting report, then they are not ready to undertake a TRED or cluster analysis. Our experience with the Wisconsin Approach is that the data analysis ends up taking a backseat to in-depth and focused discussions about the regional economy.

References

Acs, Z.J. (1999) *Are Small Firms Important: Their Role and Impact*, Boston: Kluwer Academic.
Aquilina, M., Klump, R., and Pietrobelli, C. (2006) "Factor substitution, average firm size and economic growth", *Small Business Economics*, 26: 203–14.
Birch, D.L. (1979) *The Job Generation Process: Final Report to Economic Development*

Administration, Cambridge, MA: MIT Program on Neighborhood and Regional Change.

Brown, C., Medoff, J., and Hamilton, J. (1990) *Employers: Large and Small*, Cambridge, MA: Harvard University Press.

Burton, H.J. (1998) "A reconsideration of import substitution", *Journal of Economic Literature*, 36(2): 903–36.

Buss, T. (1999) "The case against targeted industry studies", *Economic Development Quarterly*, 13(4): 339–56.

Deller, S.C., Kures, M., and Ryan, W. (2006) "An analysis of retail and service sector count data: identification of market potential for Wisconsin counties", Department of Agricultural and Applied Economics Staff Paper No. 492, University of Wisconsin-Madison/Extension. (January). Online. Available HTTP: <http://www.aae.wisc.edu/pubs/sps/pdf/stpap492.pdf>.

Dunne, T., Roberts, M.J., and Samuelson, L. (1989) "Growth and failure of U.S. manufacturing plants", *Quarterly Journal of Economics*, 104: 671–98.

Eisinger, P. (1988) *The Role of the Entrepreneurial State*, Madison: University of Wisconsin Press.

——. (1995) "State economic development in the 1990s: politics and policy learning", *Economic Development Quarterly*, 9: 146–58.

Goetz, S.J. (1997) "State and county-level determinants of food manufacturing establishment growth: 1987–1993", *American Journal of Agricultural Economics*, 79: 838–50.

Goetz, S., Deller, S.C., and Harris, T. (2007) "Targeting regional economic development: an outline of a national extension educational program", NERCRD Rural Development Paper No. 38, University Park, PA: NERCRD.

Goetz, S.J., and Rupasingha, A. (2002) "High-tech industry clustering: implications for rural areas", *American Journal of Agricultural Economics*, 84(5): 1229–36.

Goode, F.M., and Hastings, S.E. (1989), "The effect of transportation service on the location of manufacturing plants in non-metropolitan and small metropolitan communities", in W.R. Gillis (ed), *Profitability and Mobility in Rural America*, University Park and London: Penn State University Press.

Janke, J., and Deller, S.C. (2004, November) "The structure of St Croix County economy: a study for economic opportunity", Department of Agricultural and Applied Economics Miscellaneous Staff Paper, University of Wisconsin-Madison/Extension. Online. Available HTTP: <http://www.aae.wisc.edu/pubs/misc/docs/deller.St%20Croix%20Report.2004.pdf>.

Krueger, A. (1993) "Virtuous and vicious circles in economic development", *American Economic Review*, 83(2): 351–55.

Leatherman, J., Howard, D., and Kastens, T. (2002) "Improved prospects for rural development: an industrial targeting system for the Great Plains", *Review of Agricultural Economics*, 24(1): 59–77.

Muench, D., and Deller, S.C. (2001, September) "The economic structure of the Fox Valley: a study of economic opportunity", Department of Agricultural and Applied Economics Staff Paper No. 444, University of Wisconsin-Madison/Extension. Online. Available HTTP: <http://www.aae.wisc.edu/pubs/sps/pdf/stpap444.pdf>.

Porter, M. E. (1990) *The Competitive Advantage of Nations*, New York: The Free Press.

——. (1996) "Competitive advantage, agglomeration economies, and regional policy", *International Regional Science Review*, 19(1–2): 85–90.

——. (1998) *On Competition*, Cambridge, MA: Harvard Business School Press.

——. (2003) "The economic performance of regions", *Regional Studies*, 37(6&7): 549–78.

Puga, D., and Venables, A.J. (1999) "Agglomeration and economic development: import substitution vs. trade liberalization", *The Economic Journal*, 109(April): 292–311.

Reum, A., and Harris, T. (2006) "Exploring firm location beyond simple growth models: a double hurdle application", *Journal of Regional Analysis and Policy*, 36: 45–67.

Rodriguez-Clare, A. (2007) "Cluster and comparative advantage: implications for industrial policy", *Journal of Development Economics*, 82: 43–57

Schumpeter, J.A. (1942) *Capitalism, Socialism & Democracy*, New York: Harper & Row.

——. (1961) *The Theory of Economic Development*, Cambridge, MA: Harvard University Press.

Shaffer, R., Deller, S.C., and Marcouiller, D. (2006) "Rethinking community economic development", *Economic Development Quarterly*, 20(1): 59–74.

Conclusion

20 TRED

Conclusion and the future

Steven C. Deller, Stephan J. Goetz,
Thomas R. Harris, and Alison F. Davis

> It's a lot easier to go out and attract a new company, or even build a new stadium, than it is to alter the psychological makeup of a region. Regional leaders must become more aware of how their region's collective personality shapes the kinds of economic activities that it can do and the kinds of people it can attract, satisfy and retain.
>
> R. Florida (2008: 213) in *Who's Your City?*

In his latest book, *Who's Your City?* Richard Florida (2008) discusses how powerful, productivity-enhancing agglomeration benefits are driving the growth of mega-cities both in the US and worldwide. Such cities include New York, London, Tokyo, and the San Francisco Bay area. Referring to Zipf's power law, he argues that the population, productivity, and income advantages enjoyed by these mega-cities today will only increase in the future – along with congestion and pollution cost disadvantages. If mega-cities are on an inexorable trajectory toward growth and rising productivity, then the role for economic development policy in these cities is small and possibly limited to removing obstacles to further growth. The mega-city areas are basically in good shape, and at best require policy intervention to take the edge off the disadvantages and costs associated with population congestion, as well as anticipating future institutional and infrastructure needs of these huge cities. At the same time, Florida paints a bleak and even ominous future for those regions – the valleys in his world – that are not mega-cities. This includes cities that are second- and third-tiered, places like St. Louis, Louisville, and Milwaukee, and, of course, rural areas.

As noted in Deller (Chapter 4), one could argue that Florida's conclusions fall more within the field of urban economics and that they have limited relevance to industrial targeting and clusters. But his arguments, along with the conclusions of the "new economic geography", point to the need for all but the mega-cities to be proactive in fostering economic development and growth. As noted in Chapters 1 and 2 of this volume, under the broad position reflected in the Washington Consensus, the notion of proactive targeting of specific industries is viewed by many (e.g., Buss 1999a, 1999b) not only as a misuse of limited resources but also as an impediment to future robustness of the regional economy (Bartik 1985).

Throughout this edited volume, the authors have argued that if "done correctly", where one worries not only about the content of the analysis but also the process through which the community is engaged in the analysis and subsequent economic development planning efforts, targeted regional economic development (TRED) can have a very positive impact on the community of interest. Deller, Leatherman, and Shields (Chapter 17) along with Nelson, Woods, Homm, and Doekson (Chapter 16) as well as Johnson (Chapter 13) argue that TRED should be used as the foundation of a combined educational and strategic planning process. Along similar lines the Community Business Matching (CBM) model of Cox, Alevy, Harris, Andreozzi, Wright and Borden (Chapter 14) provides a framework for communities to examine their goals and identify desirable tradeoffs that are consistent with a TRED analysis. Johnson (Chapter 13) shows how industrial targeting studies can better reflect local community preferences, by employing the Analytical Hierarchy Process (AHP).

At the same time, we concur with certain arguments advanced by opponents of TRED and caution that care must be taken when undertaking a TRED analysis. In particular, the idea of hired consultants handing a list of potential targeted industries to community and regional leaders can be dangerous and can do more harm than good. But we strongly disagree with the conclusion that all TRED analysis should be abandoned. As Wiewel (1999) noted, this is akin to throwing the baby out with the bath water.

The intent of this edited volume has been first, to review the current thinking in industry targeting policy; second, to discuss the socioeconomic theoretical foundations of industry targeting; third, to present alternative methods of identifying industries for targeting in different community settings; and fourth, to provide a procedural framework for using TRED as a means to educate and move the community forward. What we have not offered in this volume is "the" answer to how to undertake a targeted regional economic development analysis. There is no single answer because each community and region of interest is different. Economic structures, levels of social capital or entrepreneurial spirit, and institutional capacity vary significantly across the economic landscape. What works effectively in one region may not work in another. The ability of the economic development practitioner to customize the TRED to the needs of the region is vital to the success of the effort.

The impact of Porter's clusters

Porter's theory of clusters suggests that while some regions might have a comparative advantage because of factor endowment levels, this is not enough to be globally competitive. Regions must also have an investment-driven economy that makes factor endowments more productive. Investments could be made in education to develop a more skilled worker or for technology to become more innovative. There is no argument that investments in education, infrastructure, and innovation are essential to remain globally competitive. What is missing from Porter's analysis is a strategy to assist regions that do not receive the same level of investments or that do not respond as well to investments. These are the areas that typically do not have visible clusters, particularly compared to their neighbouring areas. As a result, the region is unable to identify the types of clusters they should be able to create. To develop a sustainable economic development strategy for those regions that are starting at the beginning, we need to extend Porter's cluster theory because we are trying to develop an economic development strategy at a relatively small regional level.

Porter (2000: 27) suggests that cluster theory is a replacement for the traditional industry attraction model. He writes that "[a]*ll* clusters can be desirable" (emphasis in original) and that "all offer the potential to contribute to prosperity". Porter continues, "[i]nstead of targeting, therefore, all existing and emerging clusters deserve attention". However, Woodward and Guimarães in Chapter 5 of this volume remind us that in essence cluster development requires a targeted development strategy. Regions that are in the infancy of development efforts need something tangible to pursue, and should not pursue everything. This suggests that Porter's cluster theory will not succeed in and of itself, but that it must be paired with a targeted regional economic development model. Once a potential cluster has been identified, then the sectors that are part of the cluster would likely be recruited, as in the first wave of development thinking, or promoted from within, as in the second wave of development thinking. Porter's cluster theory needs to be combined with targeted economic development methods to provide the community with the necessary tools to improve their current economic situation.

As we have seen in this volume (e.g., Shields, Barkley, and Emery in Chapter 3, Deller in Chapter 4, and Woodward and Guimarães in Chapter 5), the notion of clusters is not new and may indeed be a simple repackaging of old ideas around agglomeration economies and growth pole/centre theory. Even so, from a community and regional economic development perspective, the notion of Porter's clusters has rejuvenated the thinking about development and growth not only in many parts of the US but also around the world. Porter has created a "teachable moment" for community and regional leaders as well as economic development practitioners to think beyond traditional economic development strategies.

What we have learned

We can walk away from this volume with several observations:

1   Economic development outside of mega-cities is a great challenge. Large urban areas, or mega-cities, have significant economic development advantages through population size and agglomeration effects, including

innovation spillovers. Smaller urban and rural areas are likely to have limited numbers of input suppliers as well as buyers. If thin markets become even thinner, a breakdown in and subsequent loss of economic activity occurs.

2   Input-output models are silent on spatial linkages. National linkages can provide focus, but analysts need to further drill down into local data and may even have to collect primary data for proper understanding of small urban and rural economic development targets. Still, IO models, such as those based on IMPLAN, can provide a wealth of information and stimulate new ways of thinking about economic development.

3   Targeting successful regional economic development may require the use of several techniques. Porter's clustering approaches are good but primarily limited to one empirical estimation method, specifically location quotients. Successful regional economic development targeting may mean use of several tools such as location quotients, shift-share analysis, occupational targeting, probability-of-location analysis, and community input using analytical hierarchy approaches.

4   Education and especially outreach education are essential, as discussed by Deller, Leatherman, and Shields in Chapter 17. Most small urban and rural areas do not have economic development or planning offices, and when they do exist they are understaffed. Knowledge of what is meant by regional economic development targeting is essential for community and regional decision-makers who are often overwhelmed by targeting results because they lack basic background knowledge and understanding of the subject.

5   As mentioned in Nelson, Woods, Homm, and Doeksen (Chapter 16), fiscal impacts of targeting need to be examined. Porter's clustering procedures are silent on county and local government fiscal impacts from targeting. By not incorporating fiscal analysis, or indeed social, cultural, and environmental impacts, with economic targeting, unintended consequences may arise. Through proper alignment of local fiscal, social, cultural, and environmental structure and community infrastructure, economic development targeting can be more successful at the local level.

6   Targeted economic development is not just done in a regional or spatial vacuum. As Hughes (Chapter 11) shows, important linkages may arise between urban and rural areas. Input or value-added opportunities created in an urban area may spill over into and benefit nearby rural areas. It may be advantageous for a rural area to supply an urban sector or further refine an urban sector's output. Therefore, a regional approach should be considered because it broadens the potential scope of economic development opportunities geographically. This speaks to a difficult question that has been raised in this volume but not answered: What is the relevant spatial definition of the region to be analysed?

7   Many individuals ranging from academics to economic developers to practitioners to elected officials have been exposed to Porter's clustering

approaches. Many in state and local government have learned about this approach without gaining a full understanding of it, much like students who can draw supply and demand curves but can not explain why they are drawn the way they are. As Deller (Chapter 4) and Woodward and Guimarães (Chapter 5) note, the previous lack of a coherent theoretical foundation makes it difficult for even academic economists to provide a coherent explanation as to why some clusters work and others do not.

8　Regional targeted economic development must consider normative as well as positive approaches. Positive analysis tells us what is, for example using the outcome from a probability analysis as well as results from other econometric and input-output procedures. Normative analysis tells us what should be. This is where process is as important as content. The use of the Analytical Hierarchy Process and the Community Business Matching model provides information about the community's goals for economic development. The Community Business Matching model measures a community's desirability for certain industries by determining how businesses match up with preferences for development by the local community. Through this analysis, economic development professionals can better target business for location and can develop strategies to improve their local economy for economic sectors they would like to target.

9　This volume provides to university outreach education and extension personnel several programmes that can be implemented in any state. The Clemson REDRL (Chapter 10) approach provides procedural information to complete a targeting study for a given community or area. Feser, Renski, and Koo (Chapter 12) and Goetz, Shields, and Wang (Chapter 15) provide information for identifying specific industries to target, including the use of bubble charts for examining location quotients. Nelson, Woods, Homm, and Doeksen (Chapter 16) provide procedures to conduct an industrial targeting programme with county and local government fiscal and feasibility analysis. Finally, Deller's (Chapter 19) input substitution approach using gaps and disconnects provides a venue to help local economic decision-makers understand their local economy.

What we have also learned is that much work remains to be done to develop and implement effective targeted regional economic development analysis and outreach educational programmes. In addition to the methodological issues and details of the processes of working with communities, more theory needs to be developed to improve our understanding of clusters. We are again reminded of Krugman's physicist who claimed that "firms agglomerate (or cluster) because of agglomeration (or cluster) effects". We must move from an inductive theory to a deductive approach that can serve as a more solid foundation for analysis and policy formulation. We agree with Buss (1999) that there is much that we do not yet know about TRED, and that more formal research is urgently needed to evaluate and to improve targeting projects that have been and are being implemented across the country. New institutional designs could be considered under which those consultants and rent-seekers who propose that particular industries be targeted for development also bear a portion of the financial risk, and reward, associated with such targeting efforts.

Future directions

While economists have yet to reach a consensus about "the" optimal economic development strategy, many would agree that indiscriminate smokestack chasing is becoming, or needs to become, a strategy of the past. Economic development specialists and practitioners have a responsibility to provide local policy-makers and concerned citizens with additional decision-making tools to assist them with creating innovative new strategies to combat low income levels, stem outmigration of the highly educated population (especially youth), and provide clarity on how to thrive in the emerging global economy. At present, the void in terms of economic development research tools for practitioners in local communities is large. Acs et al. (2008) conclude that local governments and their staff usually lack the expert knowledge needed to make good decisions about specific industries or firms that ought to be targeted for promotion. As we have seen throughout this volume, such promotion can be in terms of traditional recruitment, internal entrepreneurship, and/or expansion of existing businesses. Yet the political reality remains that local government is expected "to do something" for its constituency, and it is with this fact foremost in mind that we have compiled this volume.

The volume brings together a broad suite of tools and methods for improving the industry targeting process in an educational setting. These tools focus not only on what is possible but also what is desirable from the community's perspective. Importantly, we emphasize the word *process* because a major benefit of TRED is the human and social entrepreneurial capital that can be built within the community through a properly implemented programme. The process starts and ends with the community. In the future, we will develop additional materials from this book that practitioners can use in economic development planning based on the TRED theme. These materials will fill the gap between innovative research methods developed in universities and the practical implementation of these methods at the community level.

More specifically, the TRED outreach programme that we have in mind is needed for several reasons. Community and regional organizations vested with the promotion of economic growth and development are constantly searching for effective tools and methods to advance their efforts. The purpose of economic development research is to find a mechanism that will not only enhance growth in stagnating and declining areas but also help steer the nature of development in growing areas. If the academically promising methods that scientists create never find their way to the community level, we are just producing literature for other academics to read. If we accept the challenge of the "engaged university" as outlined by the Kellogg Commission on the Future of State and Land Grant Universities (1999), we must work to bridge the gap between academically interesting research and the needs of the community, however the community is defined. This outreach tool takes many innovative economic development strategies straight from the university into the community.

In the past, few educational resources have been available for practitioners to use in a community that describe the many facets of holistic economic analysis. Hustedde et al.'s (2005) *Community Economic Analysis: A How to Manual* was written for individuals interested in the analysis of a community's economy. The authors detail the mechanics of important tools such as economic multipliers, trade area analysis, and location quotients, among others. Unfortunately, the manual's usefulness does not extend to users within the community as a whole because it lacks a description of how community members can use the economic analysis. The Hustedde et al. manual has been used as the analytical technique component of Janet Ayres et al.'s *Take Charge* programme (1990), which builds a community strategic planning process around economic development. The final product is not only an educational programme but also an effective process for working with communities in economic development. The success, and limits, of *Take Charge*-type programmes is discussed in detail in Walzer (2006).

The intention of the TRED educational programme will be to provide an analytical toolbox that describes the basics of clustering and the value of targeting industries for the purpose of economic development. This set of resources developed in the next stage will be written for the practitioner who can choose to proceed as a facilitator, a self-help leader, or a technical assistant for a community that is ready to explore economic development planning. Thus, the final product will follow the *Take Charge* theme in that it will comprise a how-to manual for the analytical tools described in the TRED book, in addition to including the essential step-by-step process of creating a strategic plan as a community.

References

Acs, Z., Glaeser, E., Litan, R., Fleming, L., Goetz, S.J., Kerr, W., Klepper, S., Rosenthal, S., Sorenson, O., and Strange, W. (2008) *Entrepreneurship and Urban Success: Toward a Policy Consensus*, Kansas City, MO: Ewing Marion Kauffman Foundation.

Ayres, J., Cole, R., Hein, C., Huntington, S., Kobberdahl, W., Leonard, W., and Zetocha, D. (1990) *Take Charge: Economic Development in Small Communities. Empowering Rural Communities for the 1990's*, Ames: NorthCentral Regional Center for Rural Development, Iowa State University.

Bartik, T. (1985) "Business location decisions in the United States: estimates of the effects of unionization, taxes and other characteristics of states", *Journal of Business and Economic Statistics*, 3(1): 14–22.

Buss, T.F. (1999a) "The case against targeted industry strategies", (Forum), *Economic Development Quarterly*, 13(4): 339–56.

—— . (1999b) "To target or not to target, that's the question: a Response to Wiewel and Finkel", *Economic Development Quarterly*, 13(4): 365–70.

Florida, R. (2008) *Who's Your City? How the Creative Economy Is Making Where to Live the Most Important Decision of Your Life*, New York: Basic Books.

Hustedde, R., Shaffer, R., and Pulver, G. (2005) *Community Economic Analysis: A How To Manual*, Ames: North Central Regional Center for Rural Development, Iowa State University (May).

Kellogg Commission on the Future of Land-Grant Universities. (1999) *Returning to our Roots: The Engaged Institution*, Third Report, Battle Creek, MI: Author.

Porter, M. (2000) "Location, competition, and economic development: local clusters in a global economy", *Economic Development Quarterly*, 14(1): 15–34

Walzer, N. (ed) (2006) *Community Visioning Programs: Practices and Experiences*, New York: Praeger.

Wiewel, W. (1999) "Policy research in an imperfect world: response to Terry F. Buss, 'The case against targeted industry strategies,' " *Economic Development Quarterly*, 13(4): 357–60.

Index

Pennsylvania 18, 38; food industry
clusters 291–3, 295, 296–7, 299–308;
identification of clusters 43
periphery markets 206–7; *see also* core-
periphery models
Perrat, J. 60
Perroux, F. 59
pharmaceuticals 192; value chain in
Maine 229, 232
Phillips, P.D. 257
"picking winners" 6; difficulty of 38,
185–6
Pitelis, C.R. 61
Plains Economic Targeting System
(PETS) 8, 44, 103–25; aggregate
business sectors 108–9, 110; building
networks of economic activity 119–20,
120–1; conceptual model of business
growth 105–8; methods used to create
109–16; outlook for Smith County
116–18
plan exchange 272
planning process 314–16
plastic products 113, 381–4
Poisson regression model 90, 154, 156–7,
167–70
policy development assistance 329
policy implementation assistance 329
politicians 366–7
pooled labour force 84, 86–7, 89, 96
population: double hurdle firm location
model 154, 158, 159, 160, 162; impact
of agglomerations on the economy 91,
92–4
population density: location choices 136,
139, 140–3, 146; midrange and rural-
urban linkages 207
population growth 149; AHP 247–51
Porter, M.E. 2, 4, 6–7, 35, 36, 38, 49, 59,
60, 91, 119, 183, 216–17, 218, 283, 288,
365, 367; impact of Porter's clusters
392–3; Porter's cluster strategy and
industrial targeting 8, 68–83
Porter diamond model 44, 73–4
Portland, Oregon, trade area 202–5
positive analysis 395
poverty 153
Powell County 164, 165
Power, D. 60, 61, 62
practitioners 325, 336; and politicians
366–7; roles 326–31, 338
preferences, community *see* community
preferences
primary manufacturing trade 202

printing and publishing 112
privatization 24
productivity 59, 305–7, 378, 379
profit maximization 90; firm location and
47, 49–54
property rights 24
property values 153; AHP 247–51
public expenditures 24; local
governments 90, 92
public housing 25
public-private collaboration 70, 73–4
public-private partnerships 29–30, 31–2
Public Works and Commerce
Development Act 1965 26
public works programmes 19
Pulver, G. 327, 336

quality of life 263, 264
"queen contiguity" 287

railroads 18
random utility maximization models 129
ranking industry clusters 186, 191–5
ready made input-output models 346–8
real estate sector 360, 362
recession 135–6
reciprocity 331
recruitment 2, 365–6
Reeder, R. 28
regional comparative advantage 48–9, 54
Regional Economic Development
Research Laboratory (REDRL)
approach 9, 183–97, 395; criteria for
selecting industry clusters 186–95,
367–8; ranking industry clusters 186,
191–5; selection of screening criteria
186, 187–9; value chains for clusters
186, 189–91
regional governance 198
regional production systems 35
regional purchase coefficients (RPCs)
351–2, 352–4
regional thinking and acting 334–6, 338,
339
relative importance, scale of 245
relocation 270–1
representativeness 274
research parks 49, 128
research team 336–7, 373
retail sector 208
retention 316
Reum, A. 105, 366
revealed choice 270
Richardson, H.W. 199

For Product Safety Concerns and Information please contact
our EU representative GPSR@taylorandfrancis.com
Taylor & Francis Verlag GmbH, Kaufingerstraße 24, 80331 München, Germany

T - #0051 - 230425 - C0 - 234/156/23 - PB - 9780415743549 - Gloss Lamination